Mathilde Wesendonck
Isolde's Dream

Mathilde Wesendonck

Isolde's Dream

JUDITH CABAUD

AMADEUS PRESS
AN IMPRINT OF HAL LEONARD LLC

Published in 2017 by Amadeus Press
An Imprint of Hal Leonard LLC
7777 West Bluemound Road
Milwaukee, WI 53213

Trade Book Division Editorial Offices
33 Plymouth St., Montclair, NJ 07042

The poems of Mathilde Wesendonck were translated from French by the author.

All of the correspondence quoted throughout the book is in the public domain.

Permissions can be found on page 281, which constitutes an extension of this copyright page.

Printed in the United States of America

Originally published as *Mathilde Wesendonck ou le rêve d'Isolde*
© Actes Sud, 1990

Book design by Michael Kellner

Library of Congress Cataloging-in-Publication Data

Names: Cabaud, Judith, 1941- author.
Title: Mathilde Wesendonck, Isolde's dream / Judith Cabaud.
Other titles: Mathilde Wesendonck. English
Description: Montclair, NJ : Amadeus Press, 2017. | Translated from the
    French. | Includes bibliographical references and index.
Identifiers: LCCN 2017009761 | ISBN 9781574674910 (hardcover)
Subjects: LCSH: Wagner, Richard, 1813-1883--Relations with women. |
    Wesendonck, Mathilde, 1828-1902.
Classification: LCC ML410.W1 C11513 2017 | DDC 782.1092 [B] --dc23
LC record available at https://lccn.loc.gov/2017009761

ISBN: 978-1-57467-491-0

www.amadeuspress.com

In fond memory of my husband, Jean Cabaud

CONTENTS

PART IV: *Return to Germany*

Many things in a lifetime are bound to be forgotten;
Very few remain unforgettable;
And yet, those are the memories that determine the meaning
And value of human existence.

—MATHILDE WESENDONCK

PREFACE

A biography is not a novel. However, during my years of research on Mathilde Wesendonck, I discovered many pieces to an unknown puzzle that had to be patiently reconstructed in order to understand all the elements of a life experience that seemed to have been invented by some romantic author.

A faithful description of this woman, revealed through numerous unedited documents and manuscripts, led me to place her in a social and historic context; the "novel" is therefore a true story.

I thank Jürg Wille and Werner Zimmermann for allowing me access to the archives of the Zurich National Library, and Manfred Eger for access to those of Wahnfried in Bayreuth.

My gratitude goes to Franz Wesendonck for his help in reading and translating the unedited manuscripts of Mathilde and to Myrrha von Aretin and Olivier von Beaulieu for the correspondence in their possession. I also thank Jacques and Rosemarie Cabaud, Jean-François Ricornet, Henri Perrier, and Jean Carles for their collaboration, and especially my husband, Jean, whose Wagner collection was the starting point for all my work.

I have used three principal abbreviations for the main characters' documents: M. W. for Mathilde Wesendonck, O. W. for Otto Wesendonck, and R. W. for Richard Wagner.

Mathilde Wesendonck
Isolde's Dream

Prologue: Berlin, 1902

In the last years of the nineteenth century, the German empire was governed with forceful persuasion by Kaiser Wilhelm II. Grandeur and modernism were his ambitions; on land and on sea, rearmament was a reality. Even the conservative wing of the old German culture would not be able to stop him.

That day, at the beginning of summer, after a refreshing rainfall, the scent of the trees in bloom on Unter den Linden and the mild drowsiness of late afternoon hanging over the city had cast an irresistible torpor on its inhabitants.

Two gentlemen, obviously foreigners, were standing on the corner of Linden and Friedrich-strasse, one of the busiest of the capital, contemplating the city dwellers rushing to and fro in the *neu Berlin*, a grand metropolis with high hopes for the new century.

In an hour these two Frenchmen were going to meet a famous woman. They had carefully prepared their interview even before arriving in the Prussian capital. The older man, Louis de Fourcaud, a professor at the École des Beaux-Arts in Paris, happened to be working on a book about Richard Wagner, which would appear only after World War I. At present, after visiting the city and its monuments, swathed in the arrogance of its new opulence, and before traveling south to attend the Bayreuth Festival at the end of July, these "true Wagnerites," as George Bernard Shaw would have called them, intended to accomplish an essential rite of their pilgrimage, something only a few of the privileged had managed to do before them: pay homage to the living muse of Wagner's *Tristan and Isolde*, Mathilde Wesendonck.

At the turn of the century, the rise of the kaiser's power coincided with the coronation of his British cousin Edward VII. But Berlin could boast of having become a true cultural and intellectual rival to Vienna. All over Europe art was changing with the times; here with the young Thomas Mann, author of *Buddenbrooks*; in Paris with the première of Claude Debussy's *Pelléas et Mélisande*; in Austria with Gustav Mahler's *Kindertotenlieder* added onto the concert programs; and in Russia with Maxim Gorky's realistic descriptions of social outcasts.

The world was in transformation. Romanticism had vanished. A new post-Symbolist aesthetic trend deriving from Freud's psychoanalytic discoveries and associating art with love, love and death, eros and thanatos, had appeared in literature. It all seemed to have arisen out of a sort of materialistic frenzy created by the industrial era.

The two Frenchmen were now walking down the avenue, which was "bordered by four rows of beautiful trees, bright luxurious hotels, and rich mansions." In the fresh-scented air, the swishing sound of silk and taffeta mingled with laughter and shouts and was accompanied by the rhythmic metallic strains in the distance played by a military street band.

At the Brandenburg gate, they contemplated the equestrian statue in bronze crowning the Doric columns inspired by the Parthenon of ancient Greece. There, on the Pariserplatz, Four-caud told his companion the story of how the imposing monument had been removed from Berlin by Napoleon Bonaparte after one of his military campaigns, and returned in 1814, after Waterloo, to the Prussian capital.

"Its final destiny, I suppose."

"Destiny is fickle, but one never knows . . . "

Then they turned right into the Friedensallee and continued as far as the Königsplatz. The greenery was denser as they approached the Tiergarten, the oldest English-style park in the city. Faded flowers, cream and pink, adorned the branches of the horse-chestnut trees; some of their tiny petals were scattered over the dark cobblestones still shining here and there after the late spring rain. They finally crossed the square in front of the Reichstag.

"Imitation Renaissance?"

"*Grundesjahr*, of course . . . "

"A bit heavy, *n'est-ce pas?*"

"Quite!"

The Tiergarten faced the stone mansion on the corner of In den Zelten, no. 21. From the street, lined with restaurants and beer gardens, they could still get a glimpse of the Reichstag through the boughs of the majestic green trees bordering the park, and, in the middle of the square, the Victory Column.

Frau Wesendonck received guests in the blue room on the second floor only in the afternoon. They rang, and the butler opened the door to the two visitors. The vestibule was decorated with marble statues, green plants, and rich oriental rugs. Before climbing the stairs, they glanced at the sumptuous rooms *en enfilade* on the ground floor where the Wesendoncks had some of their paintings and books on fine arts. The wide staircase led to the second floor. In the purple room reserved for receptions, near the window, they admired at length a painting by Arnold Böcklin: *The Silence of the Forest*, one of its owner's favorites.

Then came the blue room, its walls lined with shelves of volumes by the great authors. This was her personal library. A little farther on stood a white marble bust of Wagner, and on the table was set a crystal vase filled with exotic flowers.

Here they were at last! Indeed, sitting in a big armchair, dressed all in black, was Mathilde Wesendonck in person. With the curtains drawn, the only light in the semi-darkness was shed by two candles on a dresser behind her, so that she appeared as a sort of ageless silhouette coming out of a dream. Despite the nearly stifling atmosphere of the room, "Mathilde, slightly shivering, was all wrapped up in a shawl, the elegance of which only an eye experienced in luxury could guess the worth. Her fine-featured face was framed in black lace and on her still beautiful, though faded hands she wore sapphires that matched the blue of her surroundings."[1]

The mistress of the house was in frail health and needed care and attention, and since her husband Otto's death in 1896, she hardly went out anymore. For months on end, she would stay at home; or, when she did venture into a carriage that would wait for her at the doorstep, it was to visit her grandchildren Fritz, Otto-Gunther, and Inga. This was her only distraction in the life of delicate luxury she was used to. "Mathilde has always had a taste for perfection, which is a rare trait in wealthy German ladies," wrote her friend, the journalist Marie von Bunsen.[2] Besides this, and the fact that she had lived in several other countries, her attachment to Germany was quite manifest. She had no complex about being patriotic, and her grandson, Baron Friedrich Wilhelm (Fritz) von Bissing, described in his recollections about his grandmother how from her windows she liked to look down on General Helmuth von Moltke, the army chief of staff, and his troops parading down the avenue.

However, for the past ten years she had kept herself away from public life and the social obligations of high society. At first it was to look after Otto, who had grown ill and impotent; then, after his death, her own health began to fail. Now the old lady received few visits, most of them from her grandchildren, for whom she wrote fairy tales and plays for their puppet shows. As the children grew up, Mathilde observed the next generation with great interest: Siegfried, the son of Richard and Cosima Wagner; and Ulrich, the grandson of François and Eliza Wille. Her circle of friends was limited, but occasionally she would deign, with charm and grace, to meet foreigners.

As she sat in the shadow of the library, the two visitors spoke with her about the modern world. Mathilde was quite fluent in French, having attended a French school in her youth. Now her thoughts were turned toward the past. She no longer took part in intellectual movements such as the pan-Germanism of the 1870s—or any other trend, for that matter.

Except for a few biographies, the most "modern" book she was interested in concerned the new translation of Aeschylus recently edited by Ulrich von Wilamowitz-Moellendorf. Nevertheless, shortly beforehand she told Marie von Bunsen about the Wagner biography that had just been published by Houston Stewart Chamberlain. Later, in the *Deutsche Revue*, Marie wrote: "I explained to Frau Wesendonck that some people who had known her family in Zurich felt offended by the author's ignorance in his brief and rather nasty account concerning the episodes which had occurred there. I heard her say in her deep, metallic voice that she accepted all these representations, even if they were unfair. ''You must absolutely read this book,' she told me. 'It is magnificent; a splendid biography. A few mistakes here and there are not very important.'"

In his young years, Fourcaud had known Richard Wagner personally and had become one of his most fervent advocates. It was now precisely about Wagner that Frau Wesendonck recalled her memories of the time that had formed the highlight of her existence. Her role in the life of the great musician and the influence she had exerted on him have indeed remained to this day unknown to biographers, even regarded with suspicion, triviality, and injustice. Of course the love she inspired in the Master of Bayreuth may have undergone a total eclipse, but in fact the memory of Mathilde haunted his dreams till the end of his life.

The summer evening was darkening. In the street below, by the glow of gaslight, crowds were strolling along the banks of the Spree. In the reflection of the glistening pavement, wet from the rain, the city lights sparkled like a myriad of stars.

In the blue room, which had grown quite dark, on the table, "in a box like a repository for sacred relics, Mathilde kept and jealously watched over the letters written to her by the composer of *Tristan*, and sometimes, rereading them, she would comment on him and on herself."

"Never will we forget that painful outburst of unspeakable pride," wrote Fourcaud in later years. For in fact, that evening, with her hand poised gracefully on the box of missives, Mathilde declared in a sudden passion: "Wagner put me rapidly aside; I have been to Bayreuth only on visits, hardly recognized by anyone, practically unknown, and yet *I* am Isolde!"

PART I

Before

PART I

Before

I

Roots

In February 1848, on a street in Paris not far from the Madeleine, a banquet held by the partisans of a political opposition movement had just been prohibited by the royalist government of Louis-Philippe I, Duke of Orléans. All night long a contingent of the National Guard had patrolled throughout the area around the boulevard des Capucines. The weather was bitterly cold. In the early morning the fog had thickened in the narrow back streets of the quarter, where everything seemed to be very calm. Only the resounding echo of cavalry horses' hooves, their uniformed riders, with their shakos and ready weapons, silhouetted against the mist as they moved swiftly across the scene. As soon as they passed, a man with his horse and wagon standing in front of his workshop unharnessed the animal. At this silent signal a group of young men rushed out of the darkness and pushed the wagon over onto one side, barring the way. At the same time windows were opened and carriage entrances were set ajar to let men in arms, women, and even children out, carrying all sorts of objects and pieces of furniture, piling them on to the newly formed barricade. Chairs and mattresses were thrown down from the windows. With hammers and other tools they ripped the cobblestones from the pavement and prepared mounds of them to be used as ammunition. Then, all of a sudden, a partisan opened fire, and shooting began. After several days of fighting and rebellion, the Orléanist monarchy finally abdicated in favor of the Second Republic.

The spirit of revolution had extended all over Europe—to Hungary, Italy, Poland, and Germany. In this vast country across the Rhine, with its little kingdoms, dukedoms, and principalities, the ideas of the French Revolution of 1789 were slow to penetrate. But the philosophy of the eighteenth–century Enlightenment, with its principles of rationalism and the illusion of "liberty, equality, and fraternity" introduced by the Napoleonic invasions, had found a favorable environment among these Germans, who were still somewhat innocent dreamers. At a time when the people of the Germanic provinces were more interested in beer and music than in ideology, Bonaparte taught them what they had ignored until then: patriotism, nationalism, and Jacobinism.

Following the example of the Paris insurrections of 1848, each of the great German cities in turn also caught fire. In Berlin the king of Prussia, Frederick Wilhelm IV, tried to calm the situation by stating that he was a friend of freedom and proposing the establishment of a constitution. But this show of goodwill came too late; students and workers set up barricades in the streets, and the army assailed them with cannon fire. In the end, to appease the population, the king exiled his brother, the future Kaiser Wilhelm I, who was considered to be responsible for the repression.

In Italy Giuseppe Mazzini became the leader of a group resisting the authorities. His ideological and political movement, the Risorgimento, extolled the virtues of freedom in Italian unification. In Turin his assembled acolytes called for the national liberalism inspired by France. In Hungary, in Poland, in Bohemia, peasants and workers rebelled against the sovereigns of the Triple Alliance, whose reactions had been too slow to solve the problems arising out of modernization.

At the time Europe was like a stormy sea: for the past two years an economic crisis has paradoxically resulted from the benefits of the new trend in industrialization. Growing prosperity had only widened the gap between the rich and the poor. It was also in February 1848 that Karl Marx, former editor-in-chief of the *Rheinische Zeitung* of Cologne, had published in London his *Manifesto of the Communist Party* in collaboration with Friedrich Engels, the son of a rich industrialist of Barmen. The pamphlet had gone completely unnoticed.

The king of Prussia thought the time was ripe for holding a constituent assembly of all the states of the German confederation. This was to take place in the church of Saint Paul in Frankfurt-am-Main that same year in May. In preparation for the event, a preliminary session would be held in March.

In Frankfurt that year, the Römerbergplatz and the adjoining streets of the old city were full of excitement. For several weeks all the hotels and inns were filled with delegates from all over the country, each one representing a region and a political opinion. Here was a group of Austrian reactionaries; on the other side of the street left-wing reformers had booked rooms. All were gathered together according to their social order—Saxons, Bavarians, Rhinelanders, and even, from neighboring provinces, Slavs and Danish—landed gentry, conservative Catholics, and liberal bourgeois. The majority of these people were clearly in favor of a united Germany, but most were still for a constitutional monarchy. The main question on the agenda was one of authority: should a great unified Germany be governed by Austria, or should a smaller entity of the land remain under the protection of Prussia?

Into this feverish atmosphere arrived a couple of young travelers from Düsseldorf. A man accompanied by a very young woman had accommodations reserved for them in a hotel occupied by the Rhinelander liberals: Otto Wesendonck and his ravishing young wife, Mathilde. They stood in the doorway, looking through the noisy, tobacco-smoky lobby for Otto's brother Hugo, newly appointed representative for the city of Düsseldorf at the Parliament of Frankfurt.

Otto at thirty-three was tall and handsome. A rich merchant in Elberfeld, he had spent almost half of his life in the United States. His attitude toward political events was a bit detached.

Mathilde, his wife, was twenty years old, very pretty, and utterly ignorant of what was happening. Scarcely out of adolescence, newly free from her parents' hearth, this was the first time she had been confronted with such an animated crowd. She looked around with an innocent air and almond-shaped blue eyes. Her features resembled a Raphael painting, refined and underlined by a charming small round chin. She wore her dark blond hair in romantic style, and her dress, although modest, revealed her exquisite taste.

According to contemporary witnesses, the raging atmosphere of the Parliament of Frankfurt, with its stormy interventions and vehement declarations, lacked seriousness. It appeared to be something like Ulysses' boat while the captain was asleep, with the sailors fighting over the rudder and the winds of discord having been released from the goatskin pouch offered to them by Aeolus. For want of experience and perspective, the adventurers of this new industrial society could not imagine how high they would have to climb to see what was to come. And the protagonists of this drama did not know that after that fateful year they would scatter across the world—some going to the United States, others to Great Britain, and the more fortunate ones to Switzerland. This was precisely what happened to young Mathilde, who, in that beautiful land of lakes and mountains, would go on to live for posterity an exceptional love story.

~

Mathilde Wesendonck was born Agnes Luckemeyer on December 23, 1828, in Elberfeld, a township in the ancient province of Berg now integrated into the urban complex of Wuppertal. Her birthplace, the house at Kipdorf 27, was destroyed in the bombings of 1943. Agnes arrived one year after Beethoven's death and two years after Weber's; they were the two musicians she admired the most throughout her youth. When she turned four and was just learning how to read, Goethe died in Weimar.

Her roots went throughout an entire culture. Situated near what was considered the "cradle of German civilization" where, in fact, some of the first prehistoric remains were discovered in Europe, this region of Germanic myths and legends was destined to be a sort of "melting pot." Even for Wagner in *Der Ring des Nibelungen*, the Rhine, which flowed through Mathilde's native land, symbolized the birth and the origin of all life. Years later, Wagner himself made an association between that mysterious Rhineland and the traits of the woman he loved: "On the Rhine, a few children slender and blond, embarked and, further down the river, disembarked. They were just like your children; one of them was the image of Myrrha! I knew then I was traveling in your native country!"

Two days before Christmas of 1828, toward nightfall on a Tuesday afternoon, Karl Luckemeyer, accompanied by two witnesses—his associate Friedrich Winkelmann, and his friend the chief of police, Karl Theodore Augustus, the count of Seyssel d'Aix—made his official declaration at the registry office that his wife, Johanna *née* Stein, had given birth to a female child at 3:15 a.m. Trappert, the officer in charge at the town hall, noted the information and methodically affixed his signature to the birth certificate.

Agnès was the second child of Karl and Johanna. An older brother, Karl Rudolph, had come into the world in 1825, and two other children were to follow: Edward in 1830 and Marie in 1836. Agnes was baptized in their neighborhood Lutheran church. In regard to such a peaceful and conventional family, no one could guess the exceptional destiny of this little girl.

The Luckemeyers had originated from majority-Protestant Bergisches Land. The province lay along the east bank of the Rhine. Hills and slopes alternated with green-hedged farmlands, and down the river, townships with medieval walls overlooked the countryside.

In 1815, at the end of the Napoleonic era, the Congress of Vienna had returned the Rhineland and the dukedom of Cleve to the king of Prussia. However, the inhabitants continued with the industrial development the French emperor had encouraged. In 1806 the Napoleonic Code inaugurated the Confederation of the Rhine, and the region played an important role later on in the belated transformation of the feudal system.

Friedrich Wilhelm III knew the Rhineland to be influenced by the ideas of the French Revolution and, despite his own aristocratic conservatism, wished to reconcile with the region's bourgeoisie. To avoid conflict with these entrepreneurs, who were creating the wealth of the land, he invented a *Zollverein* (customs union) that eventually became a principle of free trade and circulation among the states and regions of northern Germany.

The ambitious merchants and craftsmen of Bergisches Land came in great numbers to the cities of the Rhine valley and the Wupper river. By the end of the eighteenth century, the ancestors of the Luckemeyers and other families such as the von der Heydts, the Winckelmanns (from eastern Prussia), and the Wesendoncks had settled in the region of Elberfeld and Krefeld, whose textile mills had been producing silk since 1770. There the raw materials—cotton, hemp, wool, and silk—were transported by river and then spun into thread, dyed, and woven. At the beginning of the nineteenth century the Luckemeyer family were cotton dyers, having developed a procedure for extracting a dye called Turkey red from the root of the rubia plant.

By 1828 Karl Luckemeyer had extended his interests and investments to all phases of cotton and silk production; as time went by, he abandoned the manufacturing aspect of his enterprise and devoted himself to commercialization. He needed efficient financing as well as rapid and modern transportation. In 1828 the Luckemeyers settled in Düsseldorf, where Karl founded a bank and shipping company in the Hohestrasse. He and his partners then turned their attention to the problem of transportation. The Wupper and the Rhine were about to become transport links to a new and growing prosperity: Luckemeyer's firm was the first to use the newly invented commercial English steamboats on the Rhine.

From then on boats carrying goods could come into any port on the Rhine without paying duties and taxes. The first steamboat navigation company in the area, the Dampfschiffahrtsge-sellschaft für des Mittel und Niederrhein, was thus founded by Luckemeyer and his associates. Despite his lack of technical knowledge and experience, Luckemeyer realized that the future would prove him right. A man of action and audacity, his clairvoyance was remarkable. And as the German shipyards could not keep up with his ambitious project, he ordered his first modern merchant freighters from Rotterdam, along with the motors and machines manufactured in England. By 1838 there were regular steamboat routes from Cologne to Mainz.

A little later on he brought new plans to London and had his first ship built with a steel hull. The construction of the *Victoria* cost him ten thousand pounds. He and his crew sailed the vessel, with its double masts and a black-and-white chimney, across the English Channel. On August 13, 1839, as he was approaching the port of Düsseldorf, Johanna, his wife, and their four children—Karl, Agnes, Edward, and the little Marie—cheered him from the riverbank. Luckemeyer was awarded distinctions from the municipality and the royal government of Prussia. The king conferred on him several honorific titles, and decorations, among them being named consul and *Kommerzenrat* (Royal Advisor for Trade). Later, in 1849, after the stormiest moments of the revolutions were over, Agnes's father was appointed vice mayor of Düsseldorf, giving him a voice in his city's political affairs.

As a little girl Agnes lived in the luxurious style of the wealthy German bourgeoisie. Her parents had furnished their home with dark, heavy wood furniture that shone from repeated polishing. At the family table she would raise her eyes only to admire the queen, her mother, or contemplate at length the paintings hanging on the opposite wall—pictures of sailors and of the Flemish countryside, as well as stiff, formal portraits of her ancestors. Simple decoration on old earthenware, shiny silver spoons and forks on the lacy tablecloth, her mother's singing voice, and song and laughter were part of the poetic enchantment of these young years. And when the god, her father, spoke of his business and the navigation company, Agnes could see in imagination the handsome steamboats that Luckemeyer had launched on the river, as if the Rhine were his to play with, dotting it with little vessels and their crews.

With Karl Rudolph, her brother, little Agnes would watch from afar the members of Düsseldorf's high society during the lavish receptions and splendid dinners given by her parents; Luckemeyer, at the peak of success was admired and envied. On her father's face with its narrow lips and obstinate jaw, she could read more than what was said about his severe principles of duty and his taste for perfection.

It was probably her mother who gave her the capacity to dream. Born in 1801 like her husband, Johanna came from a wealthy family in Cologne, where her father, Johann Heinrich, was a banker. Thanks to the alliances of her numerous sisters, she was related to all of the Rhineland's high society.

In this environment occasions for family banquets and reunions were numerous. However, Agnes seemed to have been a rather introverted child, creating in her imagination a world of her own. When in later years she wrote fairy tales for her grandchildren, her own mother appeared frequently under the name of *die Waldfrau*, the lady of the forest, who had "a warm and loving heart"; or else she became Frau Perchta, who "spreads her blessing like a golden ray of sunshine." Gentle, kind, and maternal, this mother figure took up a permanent place in Agnes's soul.

Recently in a dream, I saw
My mother standing at my bedside
As she often did in the evening
When she came to see her children.

She pulled the sheets up with her pretty hands
And did it so nicely;
Then took the quilted covers
And enveloped me with care.

Her lips poised on my eyelids for a kiss;
She also kissed me on the mouth;
Plunged in pure delight,
I imagined her to be quite well again.[1]

Her mother's love and the warmth of the family hearth played a dominant role in Mathilde's life. As a grown woman, she remembered and imitated her mother, becoming a tender maternal figure to her own children.

A contemporary witness, the poet Wolfgang Müller von Königswinter—a nephew of Johanna by marriage—was struck by her gaiety when he visited the family: "Frau Luckemeyer was a simple woman with good common sense, but mischievous and teasing; her husband was refined, with the most graceful attitudes for a man of the world; he had the sharpest of minds in conversation." He went on to describe Karl Luckemeyer as a most "distinguished, sensitive, and cultivated" person.[2]

Johanna instilled a taste for the arts in her children, while Karl insisted on the importance of duty. In Mathilde's mind the two notions formed a whole: the idea of duty was forever linked to her view of aesthetics. Along with her brothers, she would recite the poems of Goethe and Schiller, and she devoured the romantic writings of Novalis and Hoffmann. She and her brothers played music together, and they loved to stage dialogues of the dramatic authors then in vogue.

At the time Agnes was born, women were educated at home. Young ladies of the bourgeoisie had private tutoring, if possible by a Frenchwoman; but their education, outside of domestic duties, consisted of art, music, and dance, along with a smattering of geography, history, and literature. "A young lady who wanted to study," wrote Eliza Wille in her memoirs, "had only the books that were not taken away from her and the conversation of educated men."

In a letter to Wagner in 1861, Mathilde gave some details on the outdated education of young noblewomen: "Our German princesses are in general brought up too strictly at home, and only for homemaking; they learn how to keep house, that is, to economize with respect to their pocket money, and they are touching in the simplicity of their attire and appearance."

Girls also learned singing, painting in watercolors, and needlework, especially embroidery and tapestry. Young ladies from wealthy bourgeois families would gather at the home of one of them to discuss art, literature, philosophy, and morals. During her voyage in Germany, Madame de Staël wrote back to her father, Necker, that she found these social gatherings excruciatingly boring; she described the women as very conventional—*à la prussienne*, lined up like Prussian soldiers.[3] And Agnes was brought up in just this Prussian manner, her environment maintaining a fragile balance between liberalism and conservatism.

Baron von Bissing, Mathilde's grandson, wrote in his memoirs how his grandmother maintained that as a tiny child, she learned how to walk holding the hand of a Prussian army officer. "In that way," he wrote without irony, "she remained straightforward all her life."[4]

Nonetheless, in Düsseldorf education was evolving toward modernism. Children of good families were beginning to be sent into fine schools. Agnes went to a *Töchterschule*, the school for young ladies run by Frau Lieth. The rich bourgeoisie and minor nobility sent their girls there to learn how to read, write, and speak with elegance and facility. The girls were also thoroughly instructed in dance and deportment. Agnes got along quite well with the young sisters Bertha and Alwina von der Heydt. Already endowed with great beauty, she stood out among her classmates and led an easy and happy girlhood.

The cultural life in Düsseldorf offered many occasions to meet the famous men who would visit her parents. In 1833 Felix Mendelssohn was appointed musical director of the city. He organized a Rhine Festival at which the finest musicians of the day were invited to interpret classical and contemporary composers such as Schumann, Spontini, Spohr, Salieri, Mozart, and Boieldieu. The singspiel (opera with spoken recitative) was very fashionable then and would eventually evolve into a modern lyrical form by joining the arias of Italian opera to the German lied, as is seen in *Der Freischütz*, Carl Maria von Weber's most popular work.

The Luckemeyers received many guests: musicians, composers, and painters from the Fine Arts Academy, such as Peter von Cornelius and the brothers Achenbach, leaders in the arts of the school of Düsseldorf. Agnes would listen to their discussions with great attention. Besides, she was very musically inclined. She studied the piano with diligence and with her teacher played Weber overtures in piano four-hand arrangements. And after the concerts and recitals, when the singers and musicians were invited to their home, she would hide in some corner of the room, unseen by the guests, to listen to the arias of Agatha and Max from *Der Freischütz*. Bathed in the colors and harmony of Weber's music, the world seemed to take on another aspect. Lost in her dreams, in her mind's eye her parents' salon became the forest in moonlight, with thick mists moving down the slopes of the hills. In his music, Richard Wagner would also remember this romantic atmosphere pervaded by the sound of horns and the pretty arabesques of the flutes and clarinets. Agatha, the heroine, dreams she has been changed into a white dove that her fiancé, Max, tricked by the devil, will shoot down. In turn, Agnes dreamed of the pure, ideal love exalted in Weber's music. "Hast du nie gehört, daß Träume in Erfüllung gingen?" (Have you never heard that dreams do come true?), sings Agatha.

In 1843 Agnes was fifteen. In order to improve her knowledge of foreign languages, her parents decided to send her to France. They should have chosen a school or an institution for young ladies in Paris, but since 1840 a conflict had risen between Germany and France: the "Rhine crisis" was one of the consequences of the Orléanist monarchy, isolated from the great powers in Europe—England, Russia, Prussia, and Austria—and their expansionist policy in North Africa and in Turkey. The dissension came about as the result of a misunderstanding. On January 11, 1840, in the National Assembly, the deputy Alphonse de Lamartine made a speech in which, in moderate terms, he exhorted the French government to concentrate its development efforts on the European continent, rather than being concerned about what was happening in the Near East, and to focus principally on the problem of the border on the Rhine. A German journalist translated the word "development" as "expansion," and the subject became explosive. In answer to Lamartine, a lawyer named Niklaus Becker published a poem called *The German Rhine*. These mediocre lines of poetry provoked a roar of protest all over Germany. The French hastened to redefine the Rhine as a "natural border"; they claimed that the majority of the population living on the left bank of the river up to the border with the Netherlands were in favor of France, and that, last but not least, French civilization was naturally superior to that of their German neighbors.

After his trip to Germany, Victor Hugo wrote in a short text called *Le Rhin*: "All this side of the Rhine loves us; I almost mean is waiting for us." And a little further: "Let's be friends and give us back the left bank of the Rhine—since it is ours—before we start to get really angry."[5]

The Germans were expecting an invasion of French troops any day, but finally the disagreement was mooted by a change of government in France. By 1843 the incident had been temporarily forgotten, although it left in its wake an air of mistrust and resentment.

Given these circumstances, then, Karl Luckemeyer chose not to send his daughter to Paris. Instead, he enrolled her at a boarding school in Dunkirk, a port on the North Sea near the Belgian border, so that it would be easy to leave the country in case of danger.

They sailed down the Rhine to Rotterdam on one of her father's steamboats. From there, packet boats took off in the direction of Calais or Dunkirk before crossing the English Channel, and Luckemeyer accompanied Agnes to her final destination since he also planned to call on some of his shipping and textile business contacts while there. Agnes stayed at the school for three years, till 1846, but she did not enjoy her sojourn. She told her grandson that she spent more time explaining the principles of the German confederation to her classmates than learning French. Life on the other side of the Rhine seemed to her dark, sad, and chaotic. This first contact with the northernmost region of a Mediterranean country, its inhabitants imbued with Jansenism, was for her an ordeal that reinforced her love for her native Rhineland.

Besides, she cruelly missed her musical activities, which had been such an important part of her social life in Düsseldorf, a city Napoleon had first considered suitable for turning into a *petit Paris*. In Dunkirk she was deprived of theater and concerts, not to mention those long evenings at home during which her parents and friends got together to play piano, sing airs from the latest opera, or sight-read a string quartet.

She thought nostalgically of the lovely promenades with her mother along the Rhine, in the bright colors of autumn or in the mists of winter. She longed to see again the wooden houses in the country with flowers at each window, the hills covered with vineyards, and the endless dark forests.

Finally, at eighteen Agnes returned to Düsseldorf, now equipped with all the refinements that education had to offer a young lady. She was then as charming as a porcelain doll and as beautiful as a madonna in a painting. She was going to lead a very brilliant social life in the two years she had left before marrying Otto Wesendonck.

2

Long Live Mathilde!

———◆———

A ll the eligible young men in Düsseldorf were attracted to Agnes. Wrapped in her dark velvet cape, her face framed by a beribboned bonnet, she rushed across the Marktplatz accompanied by her mother and little sister Marie. The three women passed the Flemish-style Rathaus, where a very excited group of people was discussing politics.

It was the beginning of 1848. That Sunday morning, while men were sitting in cafés, reading newspapers, and drinking dark beer, Johanna threaded her way across the crowded street to take her two daughters to church. During the service Agnes, conscious of her charm, could not prevent herself from letting her eyes wander to gaze at some of the more elegant young men who were attracted to her beauty. She liked to please, and seeing one or two of them flustered would have given her a childish feeling of satisfaction. She might have even resembled the Eva of Wagner's *Meistersinger* in the circumstances, but the young man who was distracting her the most was not Walther von Stolzing. He was a serious-faced widower, thirteen years older than she, named Otto Wesendonck.

Otto's family had originally been called Van der Wesendonck, the name of all those who lived as tenant farmers in the hamlet called Wesendonck, not far from the border between Germany and the Netherlands. Most of them had lived for generations in an area of the lower Rhine at Xanten, designated a *civitas ad sanctos* (city of saints) in homage to the fourth-century Christian martyrs led by Saint Victor, a captain in the Roman army. He and his men, refusing to worship the Roman gods, converted to Christianity and were martyred together and buried in Xanten. Later on, the legend of the *Nibelungenlied* used some of these events, and Victor, whose name translates as "Siegfried" in German, was described as a dragon killer. Roman domination had often been represented in this manner. During the fourth and fifth centuries the legions carried banners with them over which they displayed the head of a dragon in bronze and the body in cloth, a kind of balloon that floated in the air, designed to frighten their adversaries and feed their imagination. Thus was born the legend of Victor assailing his enemies—or Siegfried killing the dragon. Between 1213 and 1226, during the construction of the cathedral in Xanten, the name Wesendonck was often found to be that of a mason, a builder, or a stonecutter.

By the seventeenth century the Wesendoncks who had settled in Moers, on the border with the Netherlands, had risen to become such town notables as post-office directors, lawyers, and mayors. One descendant, August Jakob Wesendonck, settled later on farther south, in Elberfeld, on the right bank of the Rhine. At that time the river was considered the border between France and Germany, a territory occupied by the troops of the French general Adam Philippe, comte de Custine, and that by annexation was part of France from 1789 to 1797. The soldiers of Napoleon had invaded the streets of Cologne, Mainz, and Düsseldorf. They would parade with gilt and feathers before pillaging the farms and the fields. But the opposite bank of the Rhine escaped French occupation and benefited from the orderly influence of the Prussians.

Like Karl Luckemeyer, August took over the local textile industry, and in 1802 he founded a silk factory, Wesendonck und Klier. He also had a hand in the manufacturing of a dye called Turkey red. Also like Karl Luckemeyer, he went on to commercialize silk, dyes, and cotton. All of these people belonged to an elite group of Lutherans, Reformed Protestants and Calvinists living side by side all along the Rhine valley and united by the king of Prussia in a sort of spiritual coalition known as a *Zollverein*. These forms of Protestantism were embraced in particular by the bourgeoisie affiliated with big business, as well as merchants, industrialists, bankers, and shipowners, probably for pragmatic reasons. In reaction to the Catholic monarchies of the time, Reform Christianity provided a moral justification for their activities and at the same time favored the principle of democracy. These families thus represented an engine for the economic, social, and political development of Prussian Rhineland. Moreover, their repeated material successes were the symbol and tangible proof of God's divine blessing.

In the minds of these men a new way of thinking appeared that would take advantage of the political stagnation of conservative reaction and at the same time be the impetus for the creation of a new ruling class: the liberal bourgeoisie.

In 1811 August Wesendonck married Sophie Scholten from Moers. They had five children, four sons and one daughter. Their second child, Otto Friedrich Ludwig, was born in Elberfeld on March 16, 1815, a few months before the final signing of the Congress of Vienna. He was raised in the same growing prosperity as young Agnes. His education must have been as rigorous and serious as that of other young men whose brilliant futures were all cut out for them. If the first concern of his training was to succeed before anything else, we can imagine that young Otto, whose features reflected a fine degree of sensitivity, was also interested in the arts. That was part and parcel of German cultural life in those days: the great romantic authors, musicians, and composers were treated with respect by all the members of society.

August Wesendonck knew how to decide for his sons. In 1833, as Luckemeyer was going into business in the Hohestrasse, he sent the eighteen-year-old Otto to New York to learn the textile trade in the company Loeschigt und Wesendonck, founded by his family. One year later Otto's brother Hugo, who was to play an important role in the Parliament of Frankfurt in 1848, began his studies in the law. The third son, August Jr., also went to the United States but wound up settling in Virginia; Moritz Reinhard, the youngest boy, eventually left for Russia.

While living in the United States Otto ignored the growing political unrest in Europe. He was busy learning the complexity of business, and he lived like an American. He became as fluent in English as in his native tongue.

On one of his frequent visits to his family, in Krefeld, he met Mathilde Eckhardt. They married in October 1844. During their honeymoon in Florence, Mathilde caught typhoid fever; she died just two months later, on December 8. Deep in mourning, Otto left alone for America. During the crossing he spent long hours in meditation to revive his spirits after this cruel event. In 1847 he returned once more, surviving a stormy sea crossing, and visited his family again. His own sister, another Mathilde, had died at the age of twenty-four, and his mother, Sophie, had preceded her to the grave. Women seemed to him like ephemeral creatures, butterflies on summer nights who fleetingly appeared in and disappeared from his life.

In November 1847 Agnes Luckemeyer came to Cologne for her cousin Emilie Schnitzler's wedding to Wolfgang Müller von Königswinter. For the occasion Otto Wesendonck, with his broad brow, his eyes deep with sadness, and his wild and romantic look—like a young flying Dutchman—met Agnes for the first time at the home of the Steins, her grandparents.

∿

All during 1848, in spite of the excitement of the revolution, Agnes continued to live a sheltered life. She was something of a real-life Scarlett O'Hara, heroine of *Gone with the Wind*, who, up until the very moment the Civil War broke out, never ceased to receive her suitors, shining like the sun in their presence.

In Düsseldorf, receptions, recitals, concerts, and theater evenings, were the main social activities. In gilded drawing rooms upholstered in silk, surrounded by her suitors, Agnes was attracted to the only man who remained aloof from her. He spoke little and smiled rarely. Compared to the generation of flighty (by comparison) young men her own age, she preferred this gentleman, mellowed by experience and ordeal. She would say, "A man who has crossed the ocean so often cannot have a narrow mind."

The families were satisfied. Marriage would only make their ties in business and their converging political convictions better.

Agnes had mixed feelings of fascination and compassion for Otto. They now saw each other quite often, both preferring the calm atmosphere of private discussions on the many subjects about which both were passionate. Agnes had found in him the peace and strength she would celebrate in one of her poems:

> *I would like your heart to be my last resting place;*
> *At your side I would recline with all my being.*
> *I would fall asleep in the calm.*
> *I would rest there as if*
> *I were on my father's hearth.*[1]

Promises were exchanged, and the wedding was set for May 19, 1848.

While the seamstresses were preparing her gown for the ceremony and the ladies of the house were still occupied with the trousseau, the members of the liberal democratic party of Karl

Luckemeyer and Hugo Wesendonck were busy writing the draft of their speech at the preliminary session, which would be held in Frankfurt on March 31. Hugo, a young attorney and the passionate brother of Otto, was to represent the city of Düsseldorf. He had drawn up a program of reforms in favor of the poor and had formed an opposition to the royalist government of Friedrich Wilhelm IV. Endowed with a keen sense of justice, Hugo had carefully studied the problems caused by the rapid industrialization of Germany's cities. The rural population had swarmed in great numbers toward urban centers, creating a new social category: the proletariat. At the same time, the country's relative wealth had led to a population boom, even in rural areas. Young people were going to town to find work faster than work could be offered to them.

In March, at the *Vorparlement* (preliminary session), where the notables were assembled, Hugo Wesendonck attacked the heavy Prussian bureaucracy that made it difficult and even impossible to take action in these important matters. An assembly of representatives from all the German states was called on May 18 at Saint Paul's Church in Frankfurt.

In early April the women of the Luckemeyer household were sewing and fitting Agnes's wedding gown and trousseau. Lace and ribbons were attached to the sleeves and the bodice, a ruffle was sewn onto the hem of the skirt. As for the young bride, she was thinking more about her books of poetry and her paintings than the revolutionary ideals discussed by her brothers and father. They offended her. She spent hours playing the piano, embroidering, or reading Goethe and Schiller. She had always had a tendency to dream, as can be seen in the Ferdinand Sohn portrait: her clear gaze drifts off somewhere toward the horizon, and her face has an angelic expression but, at the same time, expresses a somewhat ambiguous mixture of seriousness and superficiality.

The couple took walks in the Königsallee under the beautiful budding chestnut trees. She had been to all the boutiques, choosing curtains and furniture for their future home in the Schwanenmarket. At times Otto seemed somber and absent to her. Long moments of silence let unanswered questions float between them, like owls suspended in the air in mute immobility. Unexpressed feelings, unfinished sentences made Agnes realize what her fiancé had actually suffered in the past. After such a long interval of solitude, he could hardly believe in the happiness of marriage once again. His soul was inclined to a memory of which Agnes wanted to relieve him. She wanted his full happiness, not in forgetting his first wife, Mathilde, but in being herself like the sun that would dissipate his sadness and light the depths of his soul. Yet, shortly after their engagement Otto wrote to his former mother-in-law, Sophie Eckhardt, that the features of his future spouse resembled "the beloved face" of his first wife.[2]

On May 19, 1848, the day after the stormy opening of the Frankfurt Parliament, Otto married Agnes in Düsseldorf. She brought him everything a husband could legitimately expect from a wife: her body, her mind, her dowry. And what is more, in a movement of pure compassion for his earlier ordeal, she sacrificed her given name in order to take that of his deceased mate. She thus offered him the ambiguous joy of being able to murmur at intimate moments the first name so dear to him: Mathilde. Defying destiny and death that day, Agnes Luckemeyer, like a romantic heroine, became Mathilde Wesendonck.

3

Meeting in Switzerland

———◆———

In May 1848, despite the fine spring weather, the violent winds of revolution were blowing over Germany. In the turmoil, they blew everyone away, like blind men swept by the gusts to wherever the storm would take them.

The young newlyweds, Otto and Mathilde, postponed their honeymoon to stay in Frankfurt in the midst of these serious events. It was not the moment to dream before the landscapes of the Mediterranean; moreover, in such circumstances, Otto wanted to refrain for a while from the sad memories of his earlier experience.

In Frankfurt, the old free city of the Holy Roman Empire, in order to avoid the crowd gathering in excitement on the Römerberg, they would stroll along the Zeil, the main avenue of the city, or walk around on the narrow streets of houses with pointed roofs. Representatives from all over the country were assembled in the Gothic-inspired Saint Paul's Church. Each delegate wanted to turn things to his own advantage, and Hugo debated endlessly, negotiating possible solutions or compromises. Given all the disorder, Hugo could not manage to convince the confederates that a unified agreement would be profitable to all.

A lithograph of Hugo Wesendonck in 1848 reveals his striking resemblance to his older brother, Otto. Both had a broad brow, but Hugo's gaze was much more determined. Otto, on the other hand, was more pragmatic than ideological. Hugo's expression, though half hidden by his beard, was severe. With a pencil raised in his right hand and a sheet of paper in his left, he stood in the attitude of a pedagogue.

Attorney at the bar of Düsseldorf, he argued with the liberal democrats, led by Franz Raveaux. When his party elected Hugo representative to the Prussian Landstag, the minister of justice of the royal government used this as a pretext to refuse him access to the bar in Berlin. When he returned to the Rhineland to participate in the *Vormärz*,[1] he was also appointed to represent his city. As the official deputy at the main session on May 18, he was given parliamentary immunity, as was the custom.

However, Hugo went beyond the limits of what the other delegates were expecting to hear: he recommended the idea of creating a unified Germany that would be under the auspices of a "democratic emperor," not simply an executive body submitted to a constitution. He wanted a sort of pan-Germanist republic with a king-president at its head, the United States of America transposed on the Continent into the United States of Germany. Nevertheless, Hugo was no dreamer. To implement his political ideas, "From the very first days at Frankfurt, he demands that the Union army of the Bund be sworn into the Parliament and that the supreme commandment of this army be designated by the Parliament. This motion was rejected at a great majority. The *Kölnische Zeitung* of Karl Marx considered this measure as 'infantile.'" But Hugo was convinced that without an army and a navy, the German constituent assembly had no chance of winning over the conservative forces.[2]

After this failure, Hugo abstained from most of the debates. In fact, most Germans wished to keep their prince and their regional identity. The majority would have been content with a strong program of reforms. In the events that followed, government repression became a pretext for legitimizing the extreme leftist revolutionary minority.

Otto and Mathilde, although present, observed all this from afar. For the young bride, life continued with incessant receptions and dinners at which, according to her grandson Fritz von Bissing, she was the center of attention. Like Scarlett again, involved in the Civil War against her will, Mathilde was living through a critical period of her country's history. The couple's preoccupations were focused on their own family's needs, especially bringing support to Wilhelmine, Hugo's wife, and their two children. For his part, Otto provided financial aid to his wild brother while forging his own professional future.

In February 1848 all of Germany began celebrating the "peoples' return of spring," which remained an illusion. It lasted until June, when the reaction in Paris repressed all revolutionary activity. The German poet Georg Herwegh, known for his *Gedichte eines Lebendigen* (Poetry of a Living Being, 1841), exiled voluntarily in Paris and an important member of the Young Germany movement, joined Gottfried Kinkel in the ranks of the revolutionary insurgents in Bade. As soon as they left France, Heinrich Heine, who was left behind in his Parisian exile because of his poor health, began writing, probably under the influence of Marx, his "activist" poetry, entitled *Zeitgedichte* (Poems of the Times).

François Wille, a journalist from Hamburg, and his wife, Eliza, a strong and courageous woman who would later play an important role in the relationship between Richard Wagner and Mathilde Wesendonck, were also present among the members of the *Vorparlement*. In Eliza's own words: "Wille had been appointed delegate by a group of deputies from the coastal regions of Hannover. His action had now become overwhelming. Volunteers were flocking to his house in answer to his call to fight for Schleswig-Holstein. As a member of Parliament, he possessed clear and lucid judgment on the burning questions that brought to a climax the exaltation of many others."[3]

However, after the riots and the fiasco that would ensue in 1849, the province of Schleswig-Holstein was "handed over to the Prussian diplomacy and reintegrated into its old dependency on the state of Denmark; it was no longer possible for those who had taken part in this struggle to remain in Hamburg." François and Eliza Wille chose Zurich as their future home.

In Leipzig, a citizens' assembly was demonstrating in favor of a constitution that would end censorship and reform the electoral vote. Friedrich August II, king of Saxony, who flattered himself as "beloved" by his subjects, was taking half-measures for what he considered to be a half-revolution.

In Dresden the *Kapellmeister* Richard Wagner, born in 1813 in Leipzig and already renowned throughout Germany for his first three great works, *Rienzi*, *Der fliegende Holländer*, and *Tannhäuser*, was in the throes of his new artistic creation, and at the moment of the *Vormärz* he was deaf to the clamor of the throng. But once the score of *Lohengrin* was finished on April 28 and the sound of cannons replaced the magical chords of its Prelude, he became involved. On May 11 he presented a "Plan for the Organization of a National German Theater in the Kingdom of Saxony" in which he demanded an increase in salary for the musicians, as well as better working conditions and a greater concentration of power for the *Kapellmeister*.

After many disappointments Wagner was to play a political role, sometimes revolutionary, sometimes in conciliation with the monarchy. He had friends on both sides: one was Edward Devrient, who favored a constitutional monarchy; another was August Röckel, an advocate of the republic. Wagner tried to reconcile the two, but in playing the part of Molière's Master Jacques, servant of Harpagon, both parties renounced him as a friend.

In February 1849, after a short pause, Wagner's life was filled once more with artistic frustration; for example, the theater director of Dresden refused to present *Lohengrin* on Wagner's own stage. In revenge, the musician joined the rebellious insurgents and outlined his project of reforms before the theater's entire administration. In March, having met with the revolutionary extremist Mikhail Bakunin, he found himself in jeopardy, threatened by the royal authority.

One month later, on March 27, the Parliament assembled again and voted, by a small majority, in favor of a liberal democratic constitution for the entire German confederation. The direction of this new unified structure of northern Germany was entrusted to the Prussian king Friedrich Wilhelm IV, who in response humiliated them with a clear refusal. The confederates were astonished and indignant. From his point of view, the king was probably thinking mostly about his foreign policy; he feared the general disapproval of the other members of the Holy Alliance, Austria and Russia, who would reproach him for receiving his crown from the commoners of the Parliament's deputies rather than from hereditary princes. Furthermore, he would be considered a friend to the French Republic. Official repression from the royal authority in Prussia thus put an end to the Frankfurt Parliament.

So as not to lose all their fortune, or simply to avoid rotting away in prison, many moderates were ready to make amends and even accept positions in the royal government. Mathilde's father became the vice mayor of Düsseldorf; one of his friends, August von der Heydt, was appointed a minister to Prussia. As for Hugo Wesendonck, he had voted for the principle of electing an emperor by the people and for a constitution approved by the king. He and his friends were disappointed, and all would have to assume that their final destinies lay in exile, forced labor, or death.

During this year, 1849, Otto and Mathilde Wesendonck lived in Düsseldorf in great uncertainty and trouble. Hugo had taken part in the Frankfurt riots, where Princes Lichnowsky and Auerbach, partisans of the far right, were lynched by a mob on the Pfingsweide. In spite of his exhortations, Hugo was helpless to prevent the murders. In his opinion, no man should be punished for his ideas. But then, when he was writing his memories of 1848, Hugo had been living in the United States of America for fifty years: "After the doors of the Frankfurt Parliament closed, some deputies, equipped with their parliamentary immunity, thought they could start over again in Stuttgart. They were counting on a good welcome from the people. But barricades had been set up all around the official buildings of the city, and the insurgents had to flee in all directions." For him, the Frankfurt Parliament was "a festival for the German bourgeoisie that gave Germany a serious lesson in democracy."[4]

However, an arrest warrant was issued for Hugo Wesendonck, and on September 28, 1850, he was sentenced to death in absentia. Otto proposed going to America with him to help manage his affairs. He was thinking of settling there with Mathilde, but his young wife was expecting a child, and the voyage was impossible for her.

Throughout the year, everywhere, rebellions started again: in Dresden, secret meetings took place at night in Wagner's garden with August Röckel, Bakunin, and Gottfried Semper. This newcomer, who would become the most famous architect of his era, was involved in the insurrection of 1849 in a singular way: During the riot "he [Semper] watched some young men building a barricade and he stopped to see how they were managing. He soon realized that the young rebels were more than incompetent in the art of construction, and he could not prevent himself from remarking, as Jürg Wille tells it: 'Hey, friends, that will never hold!' One of them looked up and admitted it. 'But if the famous Semper wanted to give us a bit of advice . . . ,' he said."I'll willingly help you," he answered, removing his coat and pulling up his shirtsleeves. After that, he went his way down the street, thinking of something else, and never knew that his barricade had been the last to fall."[5]

At Wagner's, the conspirators wanted to arm the people and challenge the authorities. The Saxon minister Friedrich Ferdinand von Beust called on the Prussian troops to help. Blood was shed and a fire was set in the old theater, then in the town hall. On seeing the blaze, Wagner was horrified; his ambition was to "unite the people on the principles of the law, patriotism, and the imperial constitution, rather than to give the country over to revolutionary disorder, the issue of which was uncertain." He joined in with his companions to chant: "All united to push away the Prussian invader!"[6]

A temporary government was proclaimed. On May 6, from the summit of the tower on Holy Cross Church, Wagner was posted to watch the movements of the troops, which were slowly closing in on the city. After meeting with his friends one last time, he fled Saxony for Zurich with his wife, Minna, his dog, and his parrot. They went first to his sister's in Chemnitz, then to the home of Liszt in Weimar.

Toward the end of the year, with Prussia victorious, the storm seemed to subside. Röckel was in prison, Marx in London. The "shipwrecked" men reached land again, by boat, by raft, or by swimming the distance. Hugo Wesendonck had to leave via Schaffhausen, then Cherbourg, whence he embarked for the New World. The United States profited the most from the exile of these brilliant offspring of the 1848 Revolution. When Hugo saw the American coastline looming on the horizon, Wagner, also sentenced to death, was crossing the Bodensee, Lake Constance, to enter Switzerland with a false passport supplied by his friend Liszt. His revolutionary companions in exile, Hermann Marschall von Bieberstein, Gottfried Semper, Hermann Köchly, Ludwig Eckhardt, Gottfried Kinkel, Julius Haimberger, and Georg Herwegh—some of them future admirers of Mathilde—reappeared one after the other in Switzerland.

Back in Düsseldorf, on November 27, Mathilde gave birth to a son, whom the couple christened Paul. A pleasant moment to be with one's family in one's native land! But she also was living the last days of her carefree youth.

When Wagner set foot on the shore, his only baggage consisted of his future projects in his head. To put them down on paper, he needed only the ideal conditions and life experience. Alone in the land of Helvetia, the storm over and the danger removed, Wagner, like his hero Siegfried, was perhaps thinking of his mother, whom he had lost the year before. His marriage with Minna Planer had been shaky for several years and still was. The only emotion he had never yet fully realized in his life was true love.

As for Otto and Mathilde Wesendonck, they were still to live some dramatic hours before arriving in this port of tranquility—Otto as a successful businessman and Mathilde as a blank page.

4

In the Land of George Washington

In Düsseldorf, March 21, 1850—the first day of spring—was cold and dreary. Winter still lay over the countryside, and the beautiful trees of the Königsallee were bare.

On a small, quiet street, the sounds of footsteps and swishing dresses, below with tired faces covered by mourning veils, drifted by in the silence of a morning dirge. The toll bell of the Protestant church accompanied a few people dressed in black who were following the funeral procession behind a tiny coffin. It was that of Paul Wesendonck, who only briefly crossed the life of his young parents. Otto was stoic, but for Mathilde, with her great sensitivity and delicate temperament, the death of her little one came as a blow, a short but painful awakening. Life could bring things other than pleasure.

Later, she learned to sublimate her sorrow in writing poetry:

When I was still young and lighthearted
I had no worries
No trouble was ever so great
That it prevented me from hoping: "Tomorrow will be better!"

Now that I know what life has in store for us,
My hopes have shrunk.
But one thing has grown in me without measure: it is my pain,
And to that, there will be no end.[1]

During this time Mathilde would gaze out the window without seeing the roofs of the city and the leafless trees. Her sadness in the wake of this beloved little child's death was difficult to overcome. The empty cradle uncovered an abyss. Otto, who had already lived through great tribulation, wanted to pull Mathilde out of her melancholy. As a man of pragmatism and action, he thought immediately of a voyage to the United States. His brother had settled in Philadelphia with his family, and Otto's own financial affairs were in New York. He decided to take Mathilde to America. His business had prospered in his absence, and a new life was awaiting them.

Eighteen-fifty was also the year California entered into the union. After a war with the

Mexicans, the Americans annexed the land bordering the Pacific Ocean in 1848. Shortly afterward gold was discovered in open mines, in rivers, and in the rocks of sunny valleys. In a wave of excitement, the Gold Rush began. Go west, young man! A new saga of adventure had started in which everyone who traveled across the American continent, in body or in soul, was now moving west to unthought-of horizons in a seemingly boundless land. Daring men arrived on the spot, and businessmen in New York, Boston, or Philadelphia invested in new properties west of the Mississippi. And artists dreamed. From his room in his Zurich exile, Wagner composed the poetic outline of *Das Rheingold*, in which Alberich dug for gold, Wotan commanded, and Loge held the reins of finance.

In May 1850 Otto and Mathilde set sail for New York. During this period, which saw a tremendous wave of immigration to the United States, "nearly two million people crossed the Atlantic in the direction of America, that is, one million more than in the seventy years since the War of Independence."[2]

Businessmen like Otto Wesendonck, voyagers looking for adventure or seeking all kinds of opportunities, or simple adventurers and gold miners looking for wealth, were less numerous than the poor immigrants who had fled Europe's wars, persecutions, and famine. The Wesendoncks, like other people of means, must have taken a modern vessel that functioned on steam and sails, one equipped with the first metallic hulls, manufactured in England. In fine weather the crossing lasted between fourteen and fifteen days.

Otto and Mathilde bade their parents goodbye in the port of Düsseldorf and took a steamboat to Rotterdam before reaching the British coast. In the luxurious cabin reserved for them, Mathilde had trunks full of sumptuous dresses and her still brand-new trousseau. The excitement of preparing for the voyage had given her courage. Soon the anxiety of the embarkment was far behind, and the gusts of sea breezes blew away her fears. After the crowds at departure, they began to relax and feel the enthusiasm of those who travel far and wide. Settled in first class, "Luxury is everywhere. The drawing room reserved for the ladies is extremely elegant. No salon or boudoir on terra firma can compare with its interior decoration and furnishings. The apartment is in the style of Louis XIV or Louis XV with gilt edges on furniture, delicate white trimmings, sculptures, and wooden paneling executed to perfection."[3]

Substantial meals were served frequently and took up quite a bit of time in the daily schedule. At nine o'clock the Wesendoncks would have breakfast. Mathilde found it amusing to read the menu out loud: "Choice of tea, coffee, biscuits, rolls, fish, poultry, ham, cold mutton, and eggs." At lunchtime in the main dining room she could order cold cuts, and after four in the afternoon an interminable dinner was served. An amazing variety of choice was theirs—"soups, mutton, beef, pork, calf, poultry and bacon; plum-pudding, jams, and cakes." All the food was accompanied by fine wines from Bordeaux, Porto, and Madeira.

During the voyage Otto told her anecdotes about his youth spent in America, funny stories, his first reactions to Anglo-Saxon manners and many a slang expression used in this country of "barbarians." She laughed, widened her eyes, and let herself go in the atmosphere of gaiety around her.

On these luxurious transatlantic liners, orchestras played in the evening and gave concerts or accompanied balls. Some passengers played checkers, whist, or poker all day long. Bets were made on the distance they traveled each day and the probable duration of the crossing. There were also dangers, especially in winter. The navigation companies would follow the shortest route, which did not exclude the risk of icebergs, but they had to do better than their competitors. However, in the present season of their voyage, the sea had the reputation of being "moderate and favorable."

> *And the gusts swell the sails,*
> *And the sun shines in burning enticement;*
> *The clouds sail by, the ship lays away . . .*
> *At the hull play the waves and the winds.*[4]

Soon the American coastline loomed in the distance like a long, bluish ribbon. As the ship neared the port of New York, Otto and Mathilde stood on the top deck watching the tugboats meet them at Sandy Hook in order to guide the crew in the shallow waters of the harbor.

Mathilde must have been surprised to see vast flat marshlands on the continent; she was used to the more "civilized" beauties of old Europe. As for the island of Manhattan, she did not find downtown New York particularly inspiring. On side streets, identical brownstone houses stood in horizontal rows, and wooden houses with flat roofs alternated with high-rise buildings. The architecture seemed more or less rudimentary. To the north of the island stood wooded hills and, on the other side of the Hudson River, the outline of the continent seemed to disappear in a persistent fog, even in fine weather.

The Wesendoncks' first contact with America took place at customs. After many business trips, Otto was used to the unpolished manners of these Anglo-Saxon officials and their prying questions. Mathilde's trunks were roughly opened. Seeing her magnificent wardrobe, a suspicious customs officer demanded an explanation. What did she count on doing with so much brand-new stuff? The lady answered with impertinent condescension, "Did you think that in the country of George Washington I was going to wear old clothes?"

They settled for a while in a hotel at 40 Broad Street, near Otto's office at Loeschigk, Wesendonck and Co. At that time the population of New York City was 555,000, and it was one of the most important commercial ports in the world. The principal avenue of the city, Broadway, was a large street lined with all types of shops. It extended diagonally across Manhattan, four miles long, from Battery Park in the south to the north of the island, where it waned into a country road. The Wesendoncks, as was to be expected, had taken their rooms in the most fashionable part of Broadway. At that time the Carlton House was one of the city's best hotels. Otto could easily go to his office near Wall Street, where the stock exchange was already the theater in which men's fortunes were made and unmade in the blink of an eye.

The young couple would walk down the avenue, where droves of people were strolling along on sunny days. Fiacres, coaches, tilburies, cabriolets, and hansoms crowded the streets. The population was cosmopolitan, uprooted, down-to-earth, sometimes rude and even coarse. People were always rushing, but always helpful if you stopped to ask them something. Women wore bright-colored dresses in silk or satin, trimmed with ribbons, pompoms, or fringe. Men folded their shirt collars down so as to accentuate their fashionable sideburns, their fine mustaches, and their opulent beards.

At the corner of Broadway and the Bowery stands were set up on market days with beautiful fruit from the southern states—oranges, lemons, huge watermelons. In shops, signs announced the arrival of fresh shellfish. On one window was written "Oysters of all kinds." Mathilde noticed a few Irishmen with Gaelic accents, black people, and sailors of all nations. In pubs and taverns Otto pointed at the color reproductions of George Washington and Queen Victoria, and to the emblem of the American eagle. At ease in the American idiom, he could talk to anyone he met, but Mathilde remained reluctant to engage in conversation with people she did not know. So young and barely out in the world from her family environment, she was bored in this New World, where everything seemed rough, uncouth, and unsophisticated. Otto wanted her to be happy in New York, but concerts were rare, and the theaters, such as the Park and the Bowery, had very small repertories; at the Olympic only vaudeville was played. She could not see that the true dramatic arts in New York were being enacted in the streets, in real life.

In the beginning all the members of the German colony, which consisted mainly of those who had fled the events of 1848, such as Karl Schurz and Friedrich Hecker, greeted them most warmly. But the real elite of the town was composed especially of sharp businessmen interested in economic potential and political issues in a country that was only at the beginning of its immense growth.

The Wesendoncks were graciously admitted into New York's high society. The couple discovered these people to be very hospitable and refined in their own way. Receptions in their town houses were very elegant, with a spirit of ostentation that could shock only those who were not themselves nouveau riche. These wealthy ladies would gather together in the afternoon to drink tea, gossip, or do charitable work. In the evenings they attended balls or formal dinners, where it was unthinkable to talk about music and poetry, and still less to broach the subject of politics and idealism, as Mathilde understood them. It was a mercantile society with just a smattering of British civilization.

Summers in New York were suffocating. Residents would flee the city for the shores of Long Island Sound or the grassy hills of Staten Island. The Wesendoncks went to visit Hugo, who had settled in Philadelphia from the very beginning of his stay in the United States.

Otto's business affairs were prospering. To please his young wife, whose gaiety was waning day by day, he proposed to his firm that he assume the full representation of their company in Europe. The couple could thus return to Germany at the beginning of the fall and then settle either in Lyon or in Zurich.

Their return voyage took place in September, before the bad weather. They bade adieu to America and took off full sails and steam to their native land.

And the gusts swell the sails . . .
At the hull play the waves and the winds.[5]

The transatlantic crossing left them in Rotterdam, whence they traveled to Düsseldorf. Mathilde was happy to see her family again, even though it was only a short interval before Otto's obligations took them finally in their turn, to Switzerland.

PART II

Isolde's Dream

5

The Overture to Tannhäuser

———◆———

Overlooking an English garden arrayed in autumn colors, Mathilde could contemplate the deep mirror of Lake Zurich from the hotel. At dawn the first pink rays of sun lit up the vineyards on the west bank and highlighted the reddish glow of the leafy vine stocks after the grape harvest. To the south, little villages with gray walls and purple roofs were spread out on the shore, blurred by the mist rising from the lake.

A steamboat with a high yellow-and-black chimney was crossing the lake; at the stern flew the Swiss flag, a white cross on a red background. The rhythm of the paddleboat wheel accompanied the church bells ringing in the distance. Far-off, a few sailboats stood immobile. And on the horizon, beyond the green slopes, towered the snow-capped mountains of the Glarus Alps, dominated by the Tödi.

The Wesendoncks had arrived in Zurich on October 21 and rented a suite of rooms on the first floor of the Baur au Lac, the city's most elegant hotel. They thought they would stay no longer than a month in these accommodations while they sought to purchase an estate suitable to their needs.

Otto had become the official representative in Europe for his American silk firm. Returning from America, compromised by his famous revolutionary brother, his arrangements in Germany had become uncertain. And rather than settling in Lyon, another center of textile business, the couple preferred German-speaking Zurich, a geographic center between Italy, France, and northern Germany. In reality, the thirty-five-year-old Otto's fortune was considerable; he needed only to manage and reinforce what he possessed. As a shareholder in a multinational business, he could live on his private income and devote himself to his wife's happiness.

At the end of 1850 Mathilde turned twenty-two. The large reception rooms of the Baur au Lac were silent and empty, and she passed her days in pleasant monotony. Unlike what she experienced in New York, her boredom unfolded in the calm and luxury to which she was accustomed. In American society one could choose one's company from people of many origins. On the contrary, in Zurich, Mathilde fell passively back under the influence of her European culture and traditions. To her delight, she had only to glance at the announcements—on November 8 Mozart's *Don Giovanni* was being performed, and on November 29, *The Magic Flute*!

This first winter in Switzerland was also a happy one for Mathilde because she was expecting a child. After her adventurous trip to the land of George Washington, she went out very little, led a quiet life, and rested most of the time. The following summer, on August 7, 1851, in her apartment in the Baur au Lac, she gave birth to a girl, Myrrha—a true joy in a pleasant life. Looking back, she wrote about this period of her life as a "self-satisfying paradise." She had a reasonable affection for her husband. With good humor and compassion for one another, tenderness created an agreeable atmosphere between them. Could love be anything else?

There was a series of concerts being given from January to April at the old Tonhalle and in the Grand Casino. The overture to Weber's *Euryanthe* was played, followed by Beethoven's Third, Fifth, and Seventh Symphonies, and after that a performance of *Fidelio*. Everything Mathilde loved! She began to notice here and there the name of a German orchestra conductor on the programs, well-known for his former revolutionary activities and for his original compositions.

"You know, my dear, that former *Kapellmeister* from Dresden, we haven't had the opportunity to listen to his music yet. He's a short fellow from Saxony with a big head. They say he's a genius. I'm sure you have already heard his name—a certain Richard Wagner."

While the Wesendoncks were getting used to their new surroundings and doing their best to occupy their hours, Wagner did not find time hanging heavy on his hands after his flight from Dresden. At first he lived in a little house on the left bank of the lake in the Sternengasse in the suburb of Enge, about fifteen minutes from the city center. The lodging, which no longer exists, was called Zum Abendstern ("the evening star"). But Wagner's friends in Zurich did not wait long before giving it another name, Villa Rienzi, despite its modest size and appearance. The musician could live there in relative tranquility. From his doorstep he had a view of the city, the lake, and the Glaris Alps. His garden bordered the shore, where he could take out a little boat or go swimming without being noticed.

Since the summer of 1850 he had occupied the first floor with his "family." They included of course his wife, Minna, and also Nathalie—her daughter, born out of wedlock, who had been raised to believe she was Minna's sister—as well as two less conventional but equally important members, his spaniel, Peps, and his very famous parrot, Papo.

But Wagner's situation was not as comfortable as it may have seemed. The marriage had been on the point of collapsing for several years. The couple were never able to have children, and their frequent quarreling turned the artist's attention toward other horizons. His search for ideal love, which he had never experienced, had left him unsatisfied.

As for Minna, she had become old and bitter. Furthermore, Nathalie did not want to accept her "sister's" authority and created uproars that more than once had chased the master from his house.

Minna Planer, a former actress from the theater in Magdeburg, had married Richard when he was only twenty-three, at a moment in his life when, as a young and not particularly precocious musician, he was far from showing his true talent. As he rose in his career, she managed to follow his genius up to the composition of *Rienzi*, which had proved to be a great popular success. But after that, her comprehension could not keep up. She had thus held on nostalgically to his first success, which was a sort of imitation of the Meyerbeerian model of grand opera, thanks to which he had been appointed *Kapellmeister* to the royal court of Dresden. This was a considerable social and economic advancement in her eyes. Since then she had reproached him continually for his revolutionary activity, which had cost him his position and shattered their existence.

In his autobiography, Wagner described Nathalie as "heavy in body and mind," and also "clumsy and stupid." Peps, immortalized in the portrait by Clementine Stockar-Escher, in which the dog is seated on the lap of its mistress, had, if we are to believe Richard, the nerves of its master and was thus nicknamed "Peps the fidget." As for Papo, it should have been its master's consolation, because it knew how to whistle several motifs from Beethoven's symphonies, but the women of the house had taught it otherwise to say, among other things, "Wagner is a bad husband!"

Among the frequent visitors to the house, two young men distinguished themselves by their regular attendance. One was Karl Ritter, whose mother had offered Wagner an annual pension of five hundred thalers; the other, Hans von Bülow, was known as Franz Liszt's best student. Ritter moved into an attic room just over his idol's apartment, thus adding his presence to Wagner's entourage.

The Revolution of 1848 had put a temporary end to the soaring of Wagner's musical inspiration. After he finished the score of *Lohengrin* in April 1848, he dawdled with outlines of scenarios for his future works and tried to formulate his aesthetic theories. Shortly after his failure, he was disappointed in politics and frustrated by the revolutionary actions he had himself undertaken. He revealed his disillusion in "A Message to My Friends": "The turn political events took made me see the truth: reaction and revolution were clearly opposed and it became evident that either we had to come back completely to the past or break off entirely with it. . . . The lies and hypocrisy of the political parties filled me with a feeling of disgust that put me back into my most complete solitude."[1]

In December 1851, the coup d'état of Napoleon III in Paris put an end to all Wagner's hopes in revolutionary France. The result was the despondency with which he expressed his bitter feelings in a letter to his friend Ernst Benedikt Kietz: "Politics is nothing but the bloodiest hatred I feel about our civilization, contempt for everything it has produced and nostalgia for nature."[2]

In short, when Wagner was not productive, he was depressed. By October 1848 he had finished an outline for a poem entitled "Siegfried's Death." But he felt deep down that it was only a starting point. By tracing back to the origin of things, to fundamental causes, and with pure logic, he planned to conceive a work that would embrace the entire history of mankind. His four-opera cycle *Der Ring des Nibelungen* would become an artistic transcription of his thoughts. In this year, 1851, Wagner realized that the composition of such an epic work would not be possible without redefining beforehand his own conception of art and his relationship to the world. Consumed with his idea of *true* revolution, he was convinced that a radical change would also be necessary in matter of lyric opera. He spent five years writing didactic pages, the synthesis of which was published in his five-hundred-page book *Opera and Drama*. The follow-ing year he would rush up the stairs of the Baur du Lac in order to read his work, page by page, to an admirer and lady of quality: Mathilde Wesendonck. She was going to hand over to this adventurer of the arts her mind and soul, like a blank page.

But shortly before that, for twelve evenings at the end of January and the beginning of Feb-ruary 1851, the Villa Rienzi was effervescent. In the little house on the shore of Lake Zurich, Wagner read out loud his writing on the ideal relationship between literature and music. His Zurich friends who came to listen to him were more and more numerous, and Minna in her role of hostess did her best to greet the guests, preparing pastries and punch for them.

One of the listeners whom Wagner held in high esteem was Jacob Sulzer, first secretary of state in Zurich, who had met the musician on the official occasion of looking over his passport and papers. In the years to follow Sulzer and Otto Wesendonck would offer their time and patience in managing Wagner's financial affairs, which were always complicated. Sulzer later became the presiding judge of the Swiss Confederation. At this time, however, he was attracted to the artist and often came to visit him to engage in interminable discussions of art. In his autobiography, *My Life*, Wagner described him as "a man of character and real integrity." It seems it was Sulzer who gave Wagner the idea of writing about his theory on opera. Sulzer had shown Wagner a newspaper article, thinking it corresponded to his conceptions. Wagner reacted as though it were a provocation and began writing *Opera and Drama*.

On that winter evening, Sulzer brought along a colleague, Franz Hagenbuch, a Swiss offi-cial and a "quite capable and worthy" amateur flutist, noted Wagner. Several other listeners also arrived, including Ludwig Ettmüller, professor of Germanic literature and specialist in legends and sagas, as well as a future admirer of Mathilde. He was a picturesque fellow whom Wagner later consulted many times about his works. His interest in Scandinavian eddas and his high-strung personality encouraged Wagner to joke about him in nicknaming him "Eddamüller." He appeared to be like Tintin's friend the absent-minded Professor Calculus, who always spoke in passionate terms about the things that interested him. In her inimitable descriptions, Eliza Wille told an anecdote about the solemn Ettmüller during his young years: "He made a sensa-tion when he crossed the town wearing medieval attire with a large lace collar, carrying a guitar with blue ribbons in order to sing a serenade to a young lady of Zurich who later became his wife." Then, "In the last years of his life, Ettmüller had a long, stiff, white beard, which made him look like Santa Claus."

Another original character in this group of friends was Bernhard Spyri, a young attorney and editor-in-chief of Zurich's conservative newspaper the *Eidgenössiche Zeitung*, which curi-ously was favorable to Wagner in spite of his revolutionary past. Opposed to this tendency was the radical daily, the *Neue Zürcher Zeitung*, which kept its distance from the musician, taking on a paradoxically liberal position. Bernhard's wife, Johanna Spyri, became the well-known author of several children's books, including the classic *Heidi*.

Among other guests was Alexander Müller, who had first given lodgings to Wagner in the Rennweg. He was an old classmate from Würzburg who had settled in Switzerland and was now a music teacher. One of his colleagues, Wilhelm Baumgartner, helped to create a contrast with the very serious Sulzer. Wagner mentioned him as "a cheery fellow, with no inclination to concentrate on anything."

During the preceding weeks Wagner had met Adolf Kolatschek, another refugee from Dresden who had first emigrated to Stuttgart and a reporter on the staff of a monthly German review. Wagner described him as a "man of some manners, but rather boring." However, it was at Kolatschek's in Zurich that Wagner for the first time met Georg Herwegh, the exiled revolutionary poet who was to have a fervent friendship with the composer. Wagner described him in *My Life*: "With his aristocratic style and manners of a man accustomed to well-being and elegance, he seemed to be a true product of his time." During the preceding reunions, when Wagner was reading passages from his texts, Minna had remarked that "Kolatschek fell asleep and Herwegh cared only for the punch."

That evening, for the first "official" reading of *Opera and Drama*, everyone was present except Herwegh. As for Wagner, he was in a state of nerves. He proceeded by metaphors that he developed more or less in the way he led the musical motifs of his operas. It was already obvious that he was carrying within his soul the major work of the *Ring*, like a pregnant woman. All his musical and literary theories were like a gestation that would result twenty-three years later in the completion of *Götterdämmerung*. During the reading Wagner's voice rang and his eyes shone. His ideas were constantly illustrated by metaphors and comparisons:

"Music is the woman. The nature of woman is love, but this love is that which conceives and, in doing so, gives itself with no afterthoughts. Woman achieves her full individuality in a moment of abandon. She is the spirit of the water, which flows in murmurs across the wavelets of the element, with no proper soul until the love of a man gives her one. The innocent gaze of the woman is the mirror to infinity in which man recognizes love by her generating his own reflection. As soon as he has recognized himself, the universal aptitude of woman is to love him with complete abandon."[3]

Wagner then qualified Italian opera as *fille de joie* and French music as *coquette*. "But," continued Wagner, "another type of unnatural woman also exists and reviles us, that is, the *prude*, whom we find in the so-called music of German opera."[4]

"What kind of man must he be for a woman to love him without reserve?" At the end of this long demonstration, Wagner finally answered: it is the poet! Man is the poet, the idea, action. The woman, who is music, is feeling and intuition. From their union comes the fruit of true musical drama.

Opera and Drama appears in the history of lyric music as something of a *summa*, in the style of Thomas Aquinas. Wagner wanted to define the essence of poetic and musical drama. He made comparisons with all the great masterpieces of humanity since antiquity. Describing the state of decadence in which he esteemed opera to have fallen in his time, with his own vision he set out to be a reformer of musical drama for the art of the future.

∾

In Zurich, the Wesendoncks were still staying at the Baur du Lac, as they had not yet found a house big and beautiful enough to suit their elegant lifestyle. Otto was searching for a piece of property on which to build a villa not too far from the city center, with all its social and cultural attractions. It was finally in 1853, with the help of Herr Baur, that they acquired a vast estate just outside the city limits at Enge, on top of a green hill. In 1857, after four years of construction, they finally moved into their new home. They had been living in the Baur du Lac for seven years.

Little by little the Wagners became acquainted with high society. "Zurich is developing quickly," wrote Wagner to his friend Uhlig. "Hundreds of elegant mansions have been built this year due to the arrival of an ever increasing number of foreigners with the finest backgrounds and professions who have come here to escape the conflict going on all over Europe."

In September the Wagner family moved out of Zum Abendstern into a ground-floor apartment in the Zeltweg, number eleven. The building was one of the "Escher houses," so called because of the owner's name. Minna arranged and decorated their interior according to the taste of her famous husband. The new location brought Wagner closer to the theater and concert halls of downtown Zurich; it would take him only minutes on foot to get to his rehearsals. Besides, he was glad to be in the city again among his old—and new—acquaintances.

That winter the local Allgemeine Musikgesellschaft (Music Society) wanted to engage Wagner once more to conduct a series of concerts for its subscribers. The master was not keen on the idea, since orchestra conducting was for him a nerve-racking affair. They tried to entrust the young Karl Ritter with the task, but he turned out to be quite incapable. When it came to his old profession of *Kapellmeister*, Wagner graciously gave in to his friends' solicitations and undertook another season of performances.

The orchestra comprised twenty-four permanent members, Occasionally they would be joined by a few amateurs. For the concert on January 20, 1852, Wagner programmed the Overture to *Egmont* and Beethoven's Eighth Symphony. He wrote: "As I always required three rehearsals for each symphony, and since many of the musicians had to come from a great distance, our work acquired quite an imposing and solemn character. . . . My facility in interpreting music at that time attained a degree of perfection I had not hitherto reached, and I recognized this by the unexpected effect my conducting produced."[5]

Wagner's exceptional gift for interpretation undoubtedly gave special depth to these extraordinary scores and made an immense impression on the Wesendoncks. Otto and Mathilde also attended the concert on February 17 during which the master conducted the Overture to *Coriolanus* and Beethoven's Fifth. Then and there, at that very moment, new enthusiasm seemed to seize him. Wagner suddenly felt himself not only applauded but admired. He had noticed in the audience a special presence that he described as a "magnetic field," which lent him great fervor.

After the concert the Wesendoncks were invited to meet Wagner at the home of one of the musician's old friends, Hermann Marshall von Bieberstein. The two had been classmates together in Leipzig, then accomplices in Dresden during the insurrections of 1848 and 1849. As an attorney Marshall had taken part in the provisional government and along with Wagner had had to flee the capital of Saxony during the uprisings. By chance, they had shared a postal carriage, become separated before reaching the Swiss border, and then run into each other two weeks later in Zurich. Marshall had worked as a journalist on the *Tagblatt*, as an insurance agent, and finally as a professor of economics at the university. Wagner sublet him the small flat in the back courtyard of the Escher houses, near the Zeltweg, which he had occupied at the beginning of his stay. That was precisely where the Wesendoncks went that night.

After this exhilarating musical evening, Marshall's wife had supper ready for the guests. When the master came bursting into the room, the air was full of excitement as everyone rushed toward him. Laughing boisterously, he shook the frost off his cloak and greeted his friends, gesticulating in his inimitable way. He always found something original and witty to say to each one, especially when they were attractive ladies. Obviously, with his great insight, he could tell at first glance what kind of women they were.

He stopped in front of the Wesendonck couple. "They both had the blond imprint of their native land," Wagner wrote later. There, in the eyes of young Mathilde, Wagner felt again that exceptional feminine presence, that "magnetic effect" that he had experienced from his conductor's stand during the last two concerts.

The portraits of Richard Wagner and Mathilde Wesendonck dating from this period reveal that they bore a striking resemblance to each other. Richard's enigmatic gaze seems to be contemplating the same secret, far-off land as Mathilde's.

Finally, when the master himself described that fateful evening at Marshall's in his autobiography, he mentioned also a violent quarrel with a Professor Osenbruck, whom he described as full of "obstinate and inflamed paradox." We can imagine that this may have been a deliberate attempt to mask the emotion he dared not reveal. At any rate, he spoke of this dispute in later years as a mere joke.

As calm was restored at the reception and the hour grew late, a toast was proposed.

"Let us drink to Herr Wagner's success!"

"To his future concerts where he will let us hear his own compositions!"

Wineglasses were raised at arm's length. Richard and Mathilde could not help exchanging glances. She usually appreciated the admiring looks of the opposite sex, but this time she was forced to lower her eyes before the artist's eloquent gaze. This act of drinking brought a strain of music to Wagner's mind, like Siegmund when Sieglinde restores him after his wild flight through the forest, or like Siegfried when he drinks the cup of oblivion in *Götterdämmerung*; or like Tristan when his lips receive the offering of the love philter from Isolde. Water, liquid, and fluidity were the continual obsessions of the composer of the *Ring*: the Rhine and its association with the beginning of life in the womb, the flow of vitality, water, wine, and women. At this moment Richard and Mathilde were completely isolated from the world, as if total obscurity surrounded them and at the same time enveloped their glowing faces in a glare of blinding light. Forgetfulness in an infinity of silence surrounds those who drink in the unknown rapture of a starry night. The philters of love and forgetfulness are one and the same.

When the hubbub of the room returned to their ears, the spark of love had struck them both. Friendly voices tried to seat Wagner into an armchair, but he refused to sit still. Despite his recent cure, he was still a nervous wreck.

"Master, when shall we hear some of your works in Zurich?"

"The orchestra of the Association will have to take on extras!"

Herwegh insisted: "You must at least give us a performance of the Overture to *Tannhäuser.*"

A few days prior before March 16, Mathilde attended the last rehearsals for this concert and noted in her memoirs the care with which Wagner tried to explain the meaning of his music to the fifty-two musicians assembled for the occasion, as well as the galvanizing effect he exerted over them.

"There is no need to worry," he wrote to Uhlig at the end of February. "I will have eighteen or twenty violins, six violas and five cellos. . . . Besides, our little orchestra has made remarkable progress: the winds—clarinets, oboes and horns—are all first-class." That evening, March 16, 1852, the Zurich orchestra conducted by Richard Wagner performed Beethoven's Sixth Symphony, "an excellent contrast," noted Wagner, to the Overture to *Tannhäuser*. Mathilde wrote later: "Never shall I forget my first impressions of *Tannhäuser* under his direction in the darkened concert hall of Zurich's Kunsthaus. My heart was filled with joy and happiness. It was like a revelation. We were all galvanized by the master's charm."

These discreet reflections reveal only to a certain degree the internal confusion expressed later in Mathilde's own poems, a distant echo of the thunderclap that had just resounded in her life. Submerged then in an unexpected maelstrom, she described this period in later years to her friend Eliza Wille as one of *Sturm und Drang*.[6]

Another famous writer described it with more precision. Eight years later Charles Baudelaire wrote a vibrant letter to Richard Wagner on the subject of his concerts given in Paris in 1860, during which he had heard the Overture to *Tannhäuser* and the Prelude to *Lohengrin*: "What I felt is indescribable, and if I may be allowed to do so, I will try then to make myself understood. First, it was as though I already knew this music, and with some reflection, I understood where this illusion came from; it was as though this music were mine, and I recognized it like any man recognizes the things he is meant to love." This thought of the famous French poet was no doubt the very idea making its way into the mind and soul of Mathilde Wesendonck. "Then, what particularly struck me," continued Baudelaire, "was its greatness. It represents what is great and leads to what is great. Everywhere in your works I found the solemnity of great sounds, the grand aspects of Nature and the solemnity of the great passions of man. One is immediately enraptured and enthralled. . . . I felt . . . the joy of understanding, to feel myself penetrated, imbued by a true sensual voluptuousness, like flying in the air or sailing on the sea."[7]

In 1862, one year after the disastrous Parisian performances of *Tannhäuser*, Baudelaire wrote an essay in the *Revue européenne* under the title "Richard Wagner" in which he tried to describe the effect of Wagner's music on his soul: "I remember that on hearing the first few measures, I experienced one of those amazing impressions that almost all men with an imagination have known in dreams. It was as though I could defy the laws of gravity."[8] Baudelaire spoke of an "immense horizon and an expanse of light: a vastness . . . a vivid clarity, an intensity of light increasing so rapidly that no words and meanings in the dictionary would suffice to express this ever growing fervor and whiteness."[9]

In her inner thoughts, Mathilde also heard the song of the sirens that had fascinated Ulysses. She was being carried over one of those summits where a luminous beam of light allowed her to perceive the abyss under her feet. And there she saw her own heart opened to the light of love. It would throb forevermore at the sound of Richard Wagner's name.

Baudelaire might have been able to explain why: "There, we find the sensation of spiritual and physical bliss; solitude, contemplation of something infinitely great and beautiful, an intense light that rejoices the eyes of the soul . . . finally, the sensation of space, endless to the last limits of what is conceivable."

~

At the end of the Overture to *Tannhäuser,* thundering applause rang through the hall. Even the music critic of the local paper, the *Eidegenössische Zeitung*, stated that everyone was convinced of Herr Wagner's being not only a great conductor, but an eminent composer as well.

Four days later, on March 20, Wagner declared once more to Uhlig: "The performance of the *Tannhäuser* Overture was given; it went admirably well, far beyond any of my expectations. You can judge especially by its *terrifying* effect. I don't mean the applause that broke out in the immediate aftermath, but the symptoms of this effect. . . . The women were particularly overwhelmed; it made such a strong impression on them that crying and sobbing could be heard. This result absolutely astonished me. One woman has solved the riddle: people regard me as a preacher condemning *hypocrisy*."

Notwithstanding the plurals "women" and "tears," Wagner was undoubtedly referring to a single person. Besides, at the end of the letter Wagner made an indirect confession: "As usual, it is the eternal feminine that fills me with tender illusions and makes me feel the delightful charm of existence. The moist and gleaming eyes of a woman often fill me with new hope."

The lady who solved the "riddle" was none other than the one he had met at Marshall's a month ago. She was the source of that unwritten melody, so transparent and fluid, making his soul swell with inspiration, the one whose eyes were contemplating the same distant glow as he, the one who resembled him like a sister:

Siegmund: *You are the image*
I was hiding within myself.[10]

6

"It Is with Myself That I Speak When I Speak with You"

Hope is like a little boat
That nostalgia moves away from the shore.
It rocks in the midst of wild storms,
Never to see land again.

—Mathilde Wesendonck,
in *Gedichte, Volksweisen, Lieder, Sagen* (1874)

Between the environment of the commercial bourgeoisie in which Mathilde had been brought up and the intellectual and artistic world to which she had been recently introduced, there existed a gentlemen's agreement in which a certain degree of contempt was implicit. Artists' performances produced moments of communion, but at the end of the evening all were expected to retreat to their own worlds. For most of the nineteenth century such barriers were often responsible for creating social classes. On the divide stood social conformity. However, after the tumult of the Revolution of 1848, men and women from several countries had sought refuge in Zurich. There they found themselves thrown together regardless of social status, intermingling as the shipwrecked do after the storm. Thus Wagner and his wife, from modest origins; Hans von Bülow, a Prussian aristocrat; the rich bourgeoisie, such as the Wesendoncks and the Willes; and others situated on various levels of the social ladder all established their lives in the Swiss Confederation.

In her homeland Mathilde's pleasures and distractions had always been reasonable; they would never go beyond the limits of convention. How could she now bear the tidal wave engulfing her soul when she had heard the Overture to *Tannhäuser*?

Her husband had always been preoccupied by business and politics and, to a lesser degree than his wife, by music and literature. He was full of goodwill and was somewhat interested in everything, trying to fill in the gaps in his lack of culture. He had a natural inclination for music and painting, but for distinguishing the better from the mediocre, he counted on his wife's tastes. His open-mindedness, which gave him the allure of an aristocrat, came in fact from his familiarity with the different people he had met during his voyages and the languages he spoke.

His generosity toward his wife was limitless, and the nobility of his character was well-known. He was a man of fine education. In musical matters however, he saw things through

Mathilde's eyes, and right now they reflected the gaze of Richard Wagner. Otto was therefore naturally inclined to become one of the composer's staunchest supporters. He was attracted to the artist, and it is clear that his own finesse and sensitivity were growing from his contact with the new Wagnerian aesthetics in his household. After the March 16 concert he wrote with great enthusiasm on April 1 to a German friend, Robert Franz:

> An orchestra conductor of the highest quality, a complete artist in the very fiber of his being and in each one of his impulses, an agreeable and witty person, [Wagner] made the local orchestra improve in a very short time, conducting concerts—Beethoven symphonies, overtures, etc.— and recently the wonderful and moving Overture to *Tannhäuser*. The musicians consider him with great esteem and they love him. . . . They took part in it with so much pleasure that, truly, what could be reached was attained. Even as a poet, you can judge of him from his poetry: *Der fliegende Holländer*, *Tannhäuser*, and *Lohengrin*, which was published very recently in Leipzig with an introduction entitled "Three Operatic Poems," all grandiose, as well as those that are still unfinished, like "The Young Siegfried" and "Siegfried's Death," allow us to expect something perfect.

To Otto's mind, Wagner was ready to sacrifice everything for his artistic ideal, in which he "considers to be the highest achievement possible for him." Very few people at that time understood Wagner's genius so well. At the end of his letter Wesendonck, always pragmatic, proposed a fund-raising effort from among the musician's friends. He explained to Franz that "he is opposed to taking a regular job." And he mentioned with a rare perceptiveness Richard's peculiar destiny: "Placed in a situation in which he would be free to create according to his genius, he could become a man of durable and decisive influence on art. One day or other, his creations will have for sure the greatest of impacts."

As for Wagner, to whom the king of Saxony refused amnesty, and who was being spied on by the Prussian authorities even in Switzerland, he suffered cruelly from being so far away from the places where his operas were going to be played. He wanted to be able to supervise the preparations, the stage directing, and the scenery—for example, for the production of *Lohengrin* that Liszt had presented in Weimar in 1850. Moreover, Wagner had never heard a single note of his creation played by an orchestra. And now he was receiving proposals concerning *Tannhäuser*: the theaters in Prague, Berlin, Breslau, Schwerin, and Wiesbaden were asking for permission to represent these works. Wagner dreamed of these performances, which he could not possibly attend. He wrote short texts containing instructions for the representations of his operas. Like a mother talking to her young, he made all kinds of recommendations for interpreting them; the tone of his letters to his friend Uhlig, in Dresden, was like that of a father inquiring about his children while they were abroad. With no children of his own at the time, his works alone served him as posterity.

Still worse were his money problems, which pursued and harassed him wherever he went. Surrounded by his creditors, impelled by his genius, he would have to face many other crises of despair before being able to dedicate himself to the immense work waiting for him: *Der Ring des Nibelungen.*

At this time of life his physiognomy was highlighted by the intensity of his eyes, which witnesses described as deep blue in color. With thin lips and a small mouth, his face had an expressive mobility that surprised more than one of those who called on him. His head was large compared to the rest of his body, but his short legs were sturdy and gave him a kind of saunter. He had almost the look of a goblin, with a silhouette that appeared somewhat deformed. He was afflicted with a facial tic, skin conditions, and psychosomatic problems of digestion; he was prone to periods of depression and emotional fatigue that affected him in his musical composition.

However, the meeting with the young and beautiful Mathilde lightened this physical burden, which weighted down his creativity. Charmed by the sound of her voice, he at once found and lost himself again. Indeed, he forgot himself and concentrated rather on everything she said. Beyond the superficial effect, she confronted him with practical considerations: "We are waiting for you to produce one of your operas here in Zurich. After this Overture to *Tannhäuser*, everybody wants to see what will follow onstage."

Wagner was hesitant. Since Dresden he had been writing only outlines, poems, or explanatory texts.

"And with your talent for training the musicians here," chimed in Otto, "I'm quite sure that with some reinforcements from other Swiss cities, you will obtain from them exactly what you wish."

Supported by the clear gaze of Mathilde's eyes, Wagner at last agreed to a performance of *Der fliegende Holländer* in Zurich. The director of the opera, one Herr Löwe, started looking for a set decorator in Germany, but the only one available was a certain Ludwig Caesmann from Hamburg whom Wagner knew to be a "vagabond scene painter."

"My *Holländer* will be ready to take off by the twentieth. Right now the sea is being painted, vessels are in construction; everything is topsy-turvy. Once again I will be importuned on all sides!"

A considerable increase in the number of orchestra musicians was necessary, and it was up to Wagner to pay for their accommodations and salary as well as offer some of them compensation for the number of lessons they would miss giving during the ten-day performance schedule. He hired a musical director from Aarau as first violinist, another one from Burgdorf, then a cellist from Donaueschingen. In addition, he had to offer indemnities to the Zurich theater for the number of days it would have to be closed for rehearsals.

Finally, on April 25, 28 and 30 and May 2, 1852, the performances were given. A Frau Rauch-Werner sang Senta; a Herr Pichon, the Dutchman; and a Herr Benno-Fischer, Daland. Every evening the house was packed, even though the price of seats had gone up considerably for the occasion—the first row cost five francs.

"The performances were excellent," wrote Wagner to his friend Uhlig,

but naturally I mean only from the point of view of *opera*. On the first evening, I realized that

I would have to abandon all my illusions concerning *drama*, and be satisfied to have underlined at its best whatever was still left of what I call *opera* in *Der fliegende Holländer*. But the fact that it had a success as an *opera*, I understand it now and I willingly recognize that the impression made on the public was unexpected, profound and serious. The women were of course the first to react. After the third performance, they gave me a crown of laurels and nearly buried me under their flowers.

Of course, we know whom he meant by "women."

The next day the press in Zurich opened meaningful discussions on Wagner's work. As for him, he was exhausted: "The effort I had to spend in the realm of rehearsals that I was not used to anymore contributed to irritating my nerves. Suffering a great deal, I set aside my radical principles about doctors and, on the advice of Wesendonck, I consulted Doctor Rahn-Escher. This man, with his very reassuring manner, managed, with his moderate and soothing treatment, to put me back on my feet in such a way that I could bear it."[1]

Here was a Wagner pacified not only thanks to his medical treatment, but also by the attentive presence of one who had already taken first place in his heart. The vision of Mathilde-who-heals, the one who took care of the wounded Tristan, was in embryonic form before they had even met. Mathilde, however, was watching herself and refrained from saying with her lips what her eyes revealed in spite of everything. This was obviously how the exchange of looks between lovers became a theme common to scenes in *Die Walküre* and *Tristan*.

Later Mathilde added, with great modesty, a description of how Wagner had defined her at this time: "That is how I arrived at Wagner's house, without knowing anything about his art. He told me I was like a blank page . . . that he would willingly write upon."

"The master," she told us in her memoirs,[2]

began to lead me to penetrate the secret of his artistic intentions, after which he read to me his *Three Operatic Poems*—which absolutely delighted me—then the introduction that he had written for his volume; and then, little by little, he read me, one after the other, all his writings in prose. At the same time, on discovering my taste for Beethoven's music, he sat down and played the sonatas of this master. If he was preparing to conduct a concert or a symphony by Beethoven, before and during rehearsals he would play excerpts until the smallest detail would become familiar to me. He would rejoice when I was able to follow and ignite my enthusiasm by his flame.

After that Wagner often went by the Baur au Lac from his lodgings in the Zeltweg. With his typically rapid pace, it would not take more than ten minutes. He crossed the bridge over the Limmat, where the lake comes to an end, and sometimes stopped there to contemplate the snow-capped Alps, planning to go on long excursions in the summer. Not having written a single note of music since 1848, yet having been in the process of developing his aesthetic theories in his prose writing, his need for musical creation suddenly surged back into his soul once his search for the eternal feminine led to the discovery of a new muse. In *Opera and Drama* he had identified music with woman and described love as the faithful image that she would reflect of the man. It all came to a head in the presence of Mathilde. In a flash she had opened up the horizon of a new land, the country toward whose direction they had both been looking since the beginning.

In the grand hotel full of complicit silence, Mathilde received Wagner's visits. The high French windows with heavy drapery filtered the declining light of the late afternoon. Playing his role as host at teatime, Otto would offer Wagner a good cigar in a cloud of compliments; the performances of *Der fliegende Holländer* had met with unanimous enthusiasm from his admirers.

At twenty-three, Mathilde was more beautiful than ever. Her maternity had enhanced her radiance; her voice had matured, and her gestures were of the utmost elegance. Sitting in front of large sheets of music, she devoted herself to studying composition and harmony taught by the master. Notions of musical technique would no longer have any secrets for her, wrote Wagner to Otto with a touch of humor, the next summer from his vacation on the shores of Lake Maggiore: "How are the studies in counterpoint going for *Donna* Mathilde? I hope that by the time I come back, she will have finished her fugue. I could teach her how to compose operas *à la Wagner*, to get some profit out of it. You should sing in it—a role for you could be translated into English, as you sing only in that language."

But this study of musical technique was only the first step in what Wagner called the "total artwork"; he intended to explain it to Mathilde, and even to Otto. The year before he had published a brochure containing some of the ideas in *Opera and Drama*. Titled *A Message to My Friends*, he finished it in August 1851 and then utilized it as a preface to the text of *Three Opera Poems*: *Der fliegende Holländer*, *Tannhäuser*, and *Lohengrin*. The discussions between Richard Wagner and Mathilde Wesendonck were meant to initiate the woman into Wagnerian principles—mythology, leitmotif, and a synthesis of the arts—and to address the question of their practical execution within the framework of a scenic festival.

She listened with all her heart and mind to the brilliant remarks of this utopian revolutionary, this idealist discouraged from politics, this fugitive under surveillance by the secret police of a mistrustful bourgeoisie. Our political outcast resembled his character Siegmund, the brother in the first act of *Die Walküre*, when the runaway standing on his enemy's hearth tells the beautiful Sieglinde, who understands everything, about his origins, his ideals, his deception, and his flight.

"Therefore," said Wagner, "the first principle of my art must be the utilization of myth. It's the ideal material for a poet. Myth is a primitive and anonymous poem, issued from the people which was changed or modified by the great poets of ancient civilizations. Indeed, in myth, human relations strip this formulation of conventions which are comprehensible only to abstract reasoning. Only a myth can describe what life may consider as forever young and really human. Besides, conventional historical drama neglects reality for appearances, like judging a man for the clothes he wears, rather than man himself, *true* man."

"But how can you define this true being?"

"It is a man who is free, strong and beautiful."

Otto turned around on his seat and took a puff of his cigar: "Pure utopia, *mein Herr.*"

"Man redeemed by love!" answered Wagner.

Mathilde recalled these conversations on the idea of myth when she started to write her own tales and dramas, but of course she lacked the soaring genius of Wagner to attain the summits he contemplated.

Sitting at the piano, Richard played some sonatas of Beethoven, which she loved. Listening attentively, she might have heard in the bass notes the sound of her own heartbeat. During these conversations he would develop his idea of "continuous melody" until he reached his own idea of leitmotif, without giving it a name (the term was invented by his successors).[3]

"I had already understood the use of musical themes," continued Wagner,

> in order to make my poetic intentions clear through feeling long before I even thought of composing my *Holländer*. For this opera, I first had the idea to write Senta's Ballad in the second act, and I composed the text and the melody at the same time. I unintentionally put into that piece the thematic germ for the music of the whole opera; it was the image of the complete drama as it unfolded in my mind. . . . When I set out to write the music, that thematic image spread spontaneously like a coherent framework for the whole work; I only had to develop the different elements present in the Ballad by following their own inclinations to the end. This is how the main tonality of the poem took on its precise thematic forms.[4]

The evenings with Mathilde lasted for hours, and Wagner talked constantly, illustrating his ideas on the piano. The sudden emergence of reality into this magic circle would be a practical remark from the husband or a nursemaid bringing little Myrrha in to see her mother. Seeing the young woman as a loving mother, Wagner would find himself lost in thought in his utopia, where the woman, the mother, and the goddess were one and the same. He told her about his poem of the *Nibelungen*, the prose outline of which he had just finished. The only way for an epic poem comparable to Homer's to come to life would have to be a scenic festival. Here the artist revealed his revolutionary character: for the ideal performance of his work, he felt, it would be necessary "to abandon to the flames bourgeois civilization with all its theaters utilized only for material gain."[5]

"He wants to build a theater on the Rhine or in Switzerland or anywhere, to attract the best singers and musicians, create a complete set just for the occasion so that the performance would be perfect. . . . He would give it three times a week—free, of course. Then the theater would be destroyed and the whole thing finished."[6]

Such a project was less extravagant than it seemed. In his letter to Uhlig, Wagner wrote: "At the end of a year of preparation, my complete work will have been performed over a four-day period. At that moment I will also have enabled revolutionary man to recognize the *meaning* of that revolution, in the best sense of the term. *That* audience will understand me; the one at the present time cannot."

After these exalted ideas were expressed with the utmost emphasis, the artist having been swept away by his own enthusiasm, there was a moment of silence in the Wesendoncks' drawing room. Mathilde and Richard found themselves alone.

At the piano, Wagner calmed himself by playing the ethereal chords of the Prelude to *Lohengrin*. It was getting dark outside, and the streetlights were illuminating the lakefront. Their reflection danced on the ripples of the water.

The prelude over, Wagner explained: "Lohengrin was searching for the woman who would believe in him, who would be capable of not asking him any questions—his name, his origin—but who would love him for what he was, as he appeared to her, wholeheartedly. What he desired most was to be understood through love."

Late that night Wagner walked home through the streets of Zurich; the inner vision of his monumental *Ring* obsessed him. He decided to go over his outline and rewrite it in verse. The beautiful and motherly woman who was listening to him had taken up residence in his mind and soul. Wagner-Wotan-Siegmund-Siegfried, all and one at the same time, had just discovered the eternal feminine he needed to motivate his creativity. As he walked, he carried away with him the image of the one he had just left behind. He continued on to converse with her in his inner self, and, as Wotan says to Brünnhilde, his favorite child, in *Die Walküre*:

It is with myself that I speak when I speak with you.

7

A Sonata for Mathilde

As soon as they arrived in Switzerland, François and Eliza Wille bought their beautiful estate, Mariafeld. The Wille family came originally from Neuchâtel, but in the course of events and because of their ties with the German language, they settled in the area close to the Wesendoncks and the Wagners. Their mansion and its occupants were to play an important role in the love story between Richard and Mathilde.

Eliza Wille, a gifted writer, described their new residence:

> Mariafeld is located about four kilometers from the city. . . . From the terrace, overlooking the countryside with its meadows and vineyards on gentle slopes, the house rises up in the midst of the garden, which is quite simple, though the design of its contours and alleys has maintained something of its patrician and noble origin. Two ancient walnut trees and a tall sycamore cast their shadows on the courtyard, from which a flight of steps leads to the door. A well with spring water, as pure as it is refreshing, standing under two willows, is also among Mariafeld's numerous advantages. From the garden and the house, the view extends beyond the lake to the opposite shore, where hamlets and villages alternate with beautifully cultivated green fields. To the south, the imposing Glaris Alps appear on the horizon.

At a time when Eliza was Mathilde's only friend and confidante, she always acted with discretion toward the Wesendoncks and Wagner. Eliza Wille, *née* Sloman, was the daughter of a wealthy shipowner in Hamburg. François, her husband, had been active in journalism and politics. His "pugnacious disposition had involved him in several duels and his head and face bore the traces of scars of more than one sort," and his physiognomy has been described as "an album in which the enemies of his youth had signed their names with their swords."[1]

On a fine Sunday in May 1852, Wagner, accompanied by Georg Herwegh, came for the first time to pay a visit to the Willes at Mariafeld. On other occasions he brought Minna with him. Eliza described all these characters indulgently but also cuttingly. For example, she spoke of Herwegh as "a man of the world, a bit blasé . . . but who would have been more at home among the companions of the Regency than with the partisans of anarchy. . . . The mental passion that makes a fanatic . . . had caused his virility to degenerate into laziness."

Eliza usually preferred to stay behind the scenes when the men exchanged views. She would be at work on some embroidery, tapestry, or knitting, listening to everything that was said, yet saying nothing herself. These occupations led Mathilde later on to give her the nickname of "dear spinner" when she autographed one of her books to her friend.

Eliza met Wagner in 1843 in Dresden, the day after a performance of *Der fliegende Holländer* in which the era's great soprano Wilhelmine Schröder-Devrient had sung Senta. Eliza was there also for the premiere of *Rienzi*, in which the title role was sung by the famous tenor Josef Tichatschek. She noted years later in her memoirs that in the performances "everything was rich, passionate, and stirring."

Wagner, Wille, and Herwegh walked around in the garden, where the tender green of budding trees lightened up the somber groves of pines. Their animated discussions centered on the arts, politics, and philosophy. Here in Mariafeld Wagner was considered an equal, not as a genius and great artist, as he was at the Wesendoncks'. "In our house, Wagner did not find admirers . . . , but friendship and plain hospitality; he was satisfied with this, and we would almost forget that he could desire more than that."[2]

"Herwegh was not a musician, but Wagner liked his company," continued Eliza. "It was the same for Wille." It was Herwegh who one day brought the works of Schopenhauer to Mariafeld. The name was still unknown to the two other men. They began an endless discussion of some of his ideas, although they did not know anything about them, and Wille seemed enthusiastic. Later on the master of Mariafeld would go every year to Frankfurt to pay a visit to the old philosopher. Wagner in turn began to be interested in his doctrine, which he assimilated immediately into his own thoughts. And when he reread his prose text of *Der Ring des Nibelungen*, he was amazed to discover that, like Molière's *bourgeois gentilhomme*, he had been already thinking for the past five years in terms of Schopenhauerian ideas without knowing it!

Mariafeld would be the theater both for tender scenes between Richard and Mathilde and for foreboding moments with Hans von Bülow and his wife, Cosima. The stage was also set there for a dramatic scene when the lovers broke off their affair and another one when a despondent Wagner was being pursued by his creditors before his rescue by King Ludwig II of Bavaria.

That same year in Mariafeld, 1852, Wagner honored his hosts by giving them a "world premiere" in the presence of Herwegh and Henrietta von Bissing, Eliza's sister, of the complete text in its first draft of *Der Ring des Nibelungen*.

As he tells us in his autobiography, *My Life*, on the evening of December 18, as soon as he arrived at Mariafeld, Wagner began reading *Das Rheingold*. Then, as the night was still young, he started on *Die Walküre*, which he had finished only around midnight. In the blue room, seated around the big table on sofas and in comfortable armchairs, they listened to the captivating sound of his voice. The words expressed something of the music, thanks to the fascinating alliterations, on themes yet unknown. His hosts were impressed . . . and tired! The next day, December 19, Wagner read to them "The Young Siegfried," which was to become *Siegfried*, and, in the evening, *Götterdämmerung*, originally titled "Siegfried's Death."

Eliza Wille wrote that during this last reading she had to leave the room to take care of her child, who was sick with a fever. Wagner was upset by this interruption and the next day reproached her for being another "Fricka"!

∾

Six months before this memorable evening, on a rainy day in June 1852, Otto and Mathilde were spending a few days in Fluntern, halfway up the Zürichberg, a half an hour from the city. Wagner was staying with his Minna at the Pension Rinderknecht in order to take a rest after the exhaustion he suffered in the wake of the *Holländer* performances. Mathilde related their brief sojourn in her memoirs.

During the whole month of June, on the pretext of resting, Wagner worked like mad. He went over his prose outlines and began the versification for *Die Walküre*. Despite his need for full concentration, he could not resist inviting friends to keep him company. From Germany came Julie Ritter Kummer, with her Dresden *Konzertmeister* husband and their child; Cäcilie Avenarius, Richard's beloved sister, who knew how to calm her brother down and create a good work atmosphere for him; and a friend from Austria, the poet Hermann Rollet.

During a picnic that Wagner described as punctuated by rain showers, Mathilde noticed that Minna was an accomplished hostess. She had prepared the most refined dishes and an English specialty of roast veal on a spit, done to a turn. "All her guests were satisfied," remarked Mathilde, "and she was skilled in the art of doing a lot with very little."

The conversations also were pleasant. Minna could not resist talking about the time of Richard's great success with *Rienzi* in Dresden. Mathilde, a little bored, did not want to annoy her and remained silent. At first Minna took this for arrogance, but she cruelly felt how far the beautiful young Frau Wesendonck was above her in social rank and still more her power of seduction. Strangely enough, she noticed in the young woman's eyes the same kind of far-off gaze she had seen on the face of her "mad husband," who had just written this impossible poem called "Die Walküre." Indeed, in the first act, Hunding saw it too:

> *How like my wife he is;*
> *That same shiftiness*
> *Gleams out of his eyes as well.*

In the early mornings Wagner and his friends went for walks in the surrounding woods. The wonderful scents of the forest after the rain floated in the air. From the top of the Zürichberg could be seen a panorama of the lake, the city, and the snow-capped Alps. Everywhere on nature, spring was at work.

> *On balmy breezes soft and lovely*
> *Wonder-working wafts the Spring.*
> *Through woods and meadows its breath blows,*

Its eyes, wide-open, are smiling.
Lovely birdsong sweetly proclaims it.
Blissful scents exhale its presence.
From its warm blood sprout glorious flowers,
Buds and shoots grow from its strength.
With an armory of delicate charm
It conquers the world.[3]

After reading the first act Rollet asked Wagner as they walked through the woods: what music could he possibly compose on "Winterstürme wichen dem Wonnemond" (wintry storms have given way to the moon's delight)? With a twinkle in his eyes, Wagner started spontaneously to sing the Spring Song and wrote down the theme right away in a little notebook. He would give it a definitive form just three months later. Indeed, during this time he wrote to Liszt: "My *Walküre* is splendid! . . . I will compose the music with great ease and very quickly, for it will be only the *accomplishment* of a work already finished."[4]

On rainy evenings, sitting in front of the fire at the inn, the Wesendoncks listened to the master read his verse and speak about his projects. He explained the evolution of his cycle from "Siegfried's Death" (*Götterdämmerung*) by going back to *Die Walküre*. He finished this fabulous epic poem where it began: with the music of the Prelude to *Das Rheingold*.

"When you write and compose, Master, is it the idea of the poem that imposes the music on you, or the contrary?" asked Rollet.

"A subject can attract me," answered Wagner, "only if it contains a poetic and musical meaning. Before writing the first line, outlining the smallest scene, I am already exhilarated by the musical scent of my work, I have all the notes in my head, the characteristic themes, so that once the verse is completed, the scenes put together, the opera is in itself practically finished. The musical details can be worked out over time with the reflection that follows the actual creation of the work."[5]

When the rain was over, the clouds dispersed and a moonbeam floated through the trees outside the inn. Cäcilie noticed the strange light coming through the window, and the poet came out with the solution: "Der Lenz lacht in den Saal!" (Spring smiles into the room!), Everyone had to laugh, and good humor enveloped the group. Only Mathilde, sitting silent on her chair, dared not raise her eyes. Sieglinde's lines echoed through her mind: "You are the spring for which I longed in the frosty wintertime."

To break the spell, Minna began to serve her guests. She did so gracefully, but whenever Wagner spoke too long about his *Nibelungen*, she threw in sour, ironic little remarks. Approaching Mathilde, she described Richard's triumphs in Dresden. "And in *Tannhäuser*, Frau Schröder-Devrient made an unforgettable Venus, Tichatschek was a fantastic Rienzi! Ah, if only Richard wanted to start again to work on a subject like that!"

Mathilde looked at her in surprise. After what she had heard of *Die Walküre* this very evening and the other poems the master had given them to discover in the preceding weeks, not to mention how often Richard's gaze fell upon her, such remarks seemed to be off topic. She retorted to Minna that she would not compare *Rienzi* to any of Wagner's later works.

In a postscript to an undated note sent by Wagner to Mathilde, his "very faithful protector of the Arts!," he noted: "I have all sorts of trouble in my household because yesterday you spoke disrespectfully about *Rienzi*!"

In February 1853 Otto Wesendonck convinced the management of the Baur au Lac to lend its grand ballroom to Richard Wagner for a public lecture on the poem "Der Ring des Nibelungen," which he had just finished. In January the composer had fifty copies of it printed at his own expense for his close friends. On four consecutive evenings, February 16–19, he read his text in front of the Wesendoncks, the Willes, and an increasing number of listeners—professors from the university, local celebrities, members of the government, journalists, and writers. The German biographer Martin Gregor-Dellin described the scene: "The people of Zurich hung on every word that fell from his lips. . . . He read everything, including the stage directions. With his arm outstretched, he outlined the gestures of the actor . . . , showed the height of the mountains; sometimes he raised his small hand over his head like a burning torch that he followed with his eyes, then murmured again in a low voice, like the saddened god talking to Brünnhilde at his feet: 'Als junger Liebe Lust mir verblich . . .' [when young love's delights waned in me . . .]."[6]

The superb inflections of his voice in this recitation fascinated some and charmed others, but many of the most thoughtful listeners wondered how such a text could be set to music. That is probably why Wagner noted that it was generally the women, as usual, who understood him the best—because of their intuition, which allowed them to guess the very fabric of the work in the music of the words. Men take apart and analyze, but women get the full impact of the text, and by some kind of natural instinct they know what the author means. Not all of them, of course, but one in particular more than the others.

In 1853 Otto Wesendonck bought the land on the Green Hill situated at Enge. No doubt he would have preferred to entrust the plans of his villa to the famous Gottfried Semper, but the rebellious young architect had been living in London ever since his flight from Dresden in 1848; it was only in 1856 that he came to Zurich, where he had accepted a professorship at the Polytechnic Institute. Meanwhile, Otto contacted Leonhard Zeugheer, a Swiss architect, who came up with several projects. The Wesendoncks' choice fell on an outline inspired by the Villa Bartholoni, built by Felix-Emmanuel Callet in Geneva and based on the masterpieces of Andrea Palladio, the great architect of the Renaissance.

The construction of this pseudo-Italian *palazzo* took four years. Situated on top of the hill, with its Doric and Ionic columns, it ostensibly overlooked, somewhat anachronistically, the surrounding houses, with their pointed roofs, beige façades, and windows framed by painted shutters. In the distance, the city slept in the shadow of the Zürichberg, and the silhouettes of its slender church spires stood above its reflections on the lake.

Otto would take Mathilde and little Myrrha to visit the site, where measurements were being made, the ground examined, and digging begun. The manager of the construction project was Johann Jakob Locher. The Wesendoncks walked up the Gablerstrasse on the Green Hill, where Mathilde imagined the plantations to be made for the future park. Here they could put a fountain, there a row of trees and at the end of the alley, a terrace from which they would be able to enjoy the beautiful view over Lake Zürich.

Mathilde was delighted. The gaiety the young bride had experienced in Düsseldorf returned, and she found here in Zurich, at Otto's side, everything she could possibly want. She was to soon become the envied mistress of the social and cultural life of the time. And since she was already the muse of a genius as important as Wagner, she would be living out the childish dream of reigning over the heart of her beloved from her enchanted palace.

A few years later Mathilde wrote a fairy tale in which the heroine was a little girl fascinated by the song of an exotic bird. The young maiden, although risen to heaven in her dream, would have to renounce this happiness, which was nevertheless so close to coming true. Richard Wagner, to whom Mathilde sent this story, which was imbued with autobiographical references, praised her unreservedly.

In February the Friends of Music Society opened a subscription to collect funds for financing a Wagner festival in Zurich. Otto Wesendonck was the major donor. Wagner estimated that hiring musicians from several cities in Switzerland and Germany for a week of rehearsals and performances would cost about nine thousand francs, and that was the sum Otto gave him.

On the program Wagner listed some extracts from works of his little-known to the public. He conducted, from *Rienzi*, the March of Peace; from *Der fliegende Holländer*, the overture, Senta's Ballad, and Sailors' Chorus; from *Tannhäuser*, the Overture, the Entrance of the Guests at the Wartburg in the second act, and the Pilgrims' Chorus; and finally, from *Lohengrin*, Elsa's Procession to the Cathedral, the Wedding March, and the Bridal Chorus.

The musicians were all first-rate. The only soloist was Emilie Heim, the wife of Ignaz Heim, a local orchestra conductor. They also lived in the Escher houses of the Zeltweg, near Wagner's lodgings, and we know that the lady had eyes for Richard, another subject of disagreement with Minna. In *My Life* the composer noted that "she sang with a beautiful natural voice that needed training, but her zeal was beyond reproach."

As for this first Wagner festival, we might wonder whether the city of Zurich could somehow have done what Bayreuth was to accomplish twenty years later. Did the blame lie with the fact that the necessary reforms in favor of the artists had not been enacted? Or was the will to properly finance the event lacking, as Wagner later said accusingly to the Wesendoncks? Outside of the monetary considerations, the element that did seem the most decisive was no doubt a political one: Wagner was an outlaw supported by the German community in a neutral country that shunned the idea of provoking its neighbors, whether Prussian or French, to invade its territory. It was therefore quite understandable that the Swiss authorities prudently kept their distance from any potentially controversial artistic occasion.

A few days before the first concert, as an introduction, Wagner gave public lectures consisting of extracts of his texts to *Der fliegende Holländer*, *Tannhäuser*, and *Lohengrin*, as well as the preface to his publication *Three Opera Poems*. The concerts took place on May 18, 20, and 22. On the last evening, to celebrate Wagner's fortieth birthday, Mathilde had the concert hall decorated with flowers and, following the performance, hosted a magnificent banquet. In the words of Emilie Heim, "Herr Wesendonck went from stall to stall, accompanied by a servant carrying an enormous basket of flowers and laurel wreaths." After the applause died down, bouquets rained onto the stage, further exciting the composer-conductor's intense emotional state. One member of the chorus came forward and recited a poem of praise written by an "unknown person"; that was believed to have been Mathilde, but Max Fehr's research reveals that the author was Johanna Spyri, an ardent admirer of Wagner and the wife of the journalist Bernhard Spyri. According to witnesses, the "most beautiful of women" presented him at the end with a crown of laurel, which, according to the Zurich press, Wagner refused to have placed on his head. Finally, a lady in the chorus brought forward a gift of a silver cup.

The newspapers that reported this triumph declared unanimously that the quality of Wagner's music was truly "miraculous."

To Liszt, who was unable to attend, Wagner wrote the "bottom line" of this event: "For the success of this celebration, I pay tribute to a very beautiful woman."

Wagner had not composed a single score for the last five years and he had just finished the gigantic poem of the *Ring*, in whose margins he had scribbled a few notes here and there. Already able to imagine and even sing passages of his future cycle, he was about to break the silence. But he hesitated to swim in the ocean of that E-flat major chord that permeates *Das Rheingold*. In his procrastination, however, he found an ideal sort of recreation: writing a short piece, a "humoresque in polka form," for his beautiful pupil Mathilde Wesendonck. The sheet music he sent her was accompanied by a note dated May 29, 1853: "Here some sweet warmth for the ice of yesterday." Apparently Wagner was repenting for some strong words, thus this little piece. Then, three days later, Otto and Mathilde were invited to his home:

Most Honorable Lady,   June 1, 1853

     With your permission, may I ask if you can join us this evening? If so, I would like to suggest that we spend a few quiet hours in our house, until ten o'clock. I will invite no one else so as not to ruin this holy evening. I am hoping for a friendly "yes."

Yours,

Richard Wagner

These were the first steps in their loving friendship, which was intended to be beyond the sensual, a friendship that was sometimes epistolary, sometimes also literary, in which Wagner could pour out, in elaborate terms, his great need for affection.

A few days later the Wesendoncks went to Germany to visit their families. Myrrha, who was two years old, finally met her Rhineland grandparents. While Otto was in Düsseldorf, Wagner asked him for an advance: 2,000 thalers, to be deducted from the receipts he was counting on for the next performance of *Tannhäuser*, which he had planned to perform in Berlin for the past two years. He needed money to ensure the peace of mind he needed to work on his composition: "At this time, what I require is to be completely invigorated so that I may regain the youthful fervor I need after five years without composing, and to start working joyfully and cheerfully again on my great project."[7]

After receiving an acknowledgment from his friend, Wagner, feeling thus "invigorated," composed a little sonata in one movement with the inscription "For the Album of Frau Mathilde Wesendonck." He sent it to Bad Ems in Germany, the spa where Otto and Mathilde were staying, accompanied by a letter addressed to Otto: "To inaugurate with dignity my new debt and be worthy of your trust, I am going to pay off a former one. Give the enclosed sonata to your wife, my first composition since *Lohengrin* (six years ago). I will soon give you news again. Beforehand, give me the joy of sending me yours."

Like his hero Siegfried, Wagner would later forget the woman he loved: twenty years later he sent the same sonata to Judith Gautier, saying, "I promised it to a young woman who was very kind to me, in exchange for a lovely cushion that she gave me as a gift."

Mathilde reacted in her own way on receiving this sonata, and she thanked the composer by return post. Wagner had sent it to Otto for her, and Mathilde thanked Richard through Minna, putting things back into balance. But the tragedy was on the horizon for these two couples.

Mathilde also told Minna that she did not understand the meaning of his autograph inscription on top of the page, an extract from the first scene of the Norns in *Götterdämmerung*: "Wisst Ihr, wie das wird?" (Do you know what will happen?). How could she? It was too early to anticipate what this handful of notes could express—an absolute love that was impossible in this world but rather, according to the composer, could be fulfilled only in death.

Poor little sonata! It contained a little gold dust from *Tristan* and also the germinal theme of the death warning in Act II of *Die Walküre*. The music of the Norn scene is extremely vast. From where they stood on the top of the world, these prophetesses could not hear the clamors of the men and women who loved each other so fervently on earth. They could not see Mathilde sight-reading her little sonata, trying to decipher the meaning of the inscription. While she was reading it aloud, Wagner, the good Oedipus, was for his part interrogating the oracle of Delphi. At the crack of dawn one of the Norns tosses the threads of the mysterious rope of destiny to her sister, singing the same theme: "Wisst Ihr, wie das wird?"

8

G.s.M.

———◆———

The events of 1848 had paradoxically reinforced the conservative monarchies of Germany and Europe. During the first years of the Second Empire, France was entrusted with an enormous sum of capital to invest. After the coup d'état of Napoleon III, nephew of Napoleon I, Paris was in full transformation. The new prosperity would grow, thanks to a strong, stable centralized government. Its cultural influence was attracting visitors from all over Europe.

In the autumn of 1853 the Wesendoncks spent two weeks in the French capital. At the beginning of the year, great excitement had taken hold of the city on the occasion of the wedding of the emperor and Eugénie de Montijo, a beautiful Spanish aristocrat. Everyone knew that this Napoleon was full of good intentions. He believed in the doctrine of Claude Henri de Saint-Simon concerning the progress of science and industrial development. According to him, moral good follows necessarily in the footsteps of material progress. With the nomination of Georges-Eugène Haussmann in June 1853 as prefect of the Seine department, vast projects for urbanism and growth commenced. Housing and living conditions for the common people were to be improved. Open-air parks were established, and huge numbers of trees were planted. With Haussmann's urbanization plan the hovels and miserable lodgings of the old quarters disappeared, and large boulevards lined with sycamores and horse-chestnut trees opened new vistas across the entire city.

Otto and Mathilde Wesendonck booked their rooms at the Hôtel du Louvre, two minutes away from the large road works implemented by imperial decree. The rue de Rivoli, begun by Napoleon I, was being extended to the Hôtel de Ville. At the Louvre Palace itself, scaffoldings had been put up for the enlargement of the two west wings. The Wesendoncks took walks on the new boulevards, mingling with strollers who stopped to sit on the terrace at fashionable cafés; watching other people go by was a national pastime, and passers-by in turn would eye those who sat at the small round tables. In those days Parisians were eager to show off their wealth, and the fashionable set would make a show of driving down the Champs-Elysées in horse-drawn carriages. The Bois de Boulogne, a vast park southwest of the city, the plans for which the emperor was said to have drawn up himself, had been opened to the public, and people could drive their carriages up and down a brand-new avenue named for the empress.

Arm in arm with her husband, Mathilde attended concerts and went to the *opéra-comique* on the rue Le Peletier, where Meyerbeer and Rossini practically had a monopoly on the performances. Otto took her to the Hall of Paintings in 1853, a typical Parisian event where high society and the bourgeoisie mixed with the artists and their models. They also visited the Louvre. Over the years Otto, who considered himself an "enlightened art lover," bought some of these paintings and by the end of the century had assembled them in his personal collection.

During one of their promenades one day, they met Wagner. The musician had just left Zurich to join Liszt in Basel; from there the two companions traveled together to Paris. Since October 10, set up in the Hôtel des Princes on the rue de Richelieu, Wagner had led a busy life: visits, the filling out of administrative application forms, and social gatherings were very frequent and occasioned so much expense that he wondered where all the money he had borrowed had gone, for none of this helped his work become known.

Sometimes Liszt would take him for a walk in the late evening along the deserted boulevards, and sometimes he would invite him to have dinner with his family—his young children, Blandine, Cosima, and Daniel, were very shy. Then he introduced him to the woman he wanted to marry, Princess Caroline zu Sayn-Wittgenstein, whose own daughter, Marie, a beauty of fifteen, received from Richard the title of "Child."

Wagner also met Berlioz, and heard Meyerbeer's *Robert le diable* at the Opéra while sitting next to Liszt and suffering from nervous headaches. His last trip to Italy in September—all expenses paid by Wesendonck—had exhausted him. It was at that moment, in the town of La Spezia, weak and sick with dysentery, that, lying on a sofa and having fallen into a restless sleep, he heard within his being a note, a tonality—E-flat major—and felt a kind of torrent rising within himself. He had the impression of being half-drowned on the rapids of a tumultuous river; on regaining consciousness, he recognized in this experience the initial impulse to write the prelude of *Das Rheingold*. On returning to Zurich "to compose or to die," as he said, he did neither, returning instead to his everyday routine. Then he hesitated, dithered, and found himself unable to immerse himself in his composition; beset by worries, as restless as a caged lion, he could not manage to create.

Since his arrival in Paris on October 9, he needed money—"an enormous amount of money," he wrote to Minna on the sixteenth. "If not, nothing is possible here." And when he announced the imminent departure of "Liszt and his *madame*," he pleaded with his wife to come and join him: "The Wesendoncks are here, you can always stay with them, in case I would have some amorous adventure that you would not like to see or attend. . . . Today Liszt is coming with me to visit the Wesendoncks, but all our evenings are so busy that we could not even spend one with them. . . . Frau Wesendonck was delighted to hear that you are coming too."

That afternoon Otto and Mathilde agreed to go with Wagner the next day to the Louvre to see the Flemish and Italian paintings. By special favor, they were allowed to visit Eugène Delacroix's studio, set up in a wing of the museum. But the musician left his friends beforehand and postponed their meeting for another day.

Absorbed by the people he met, diminished in his physical form, he waited for Minna to come on October 20. She was expected to give him once more that secure feeling of the motherly hearth he needed so badly. Wagner told us that his sojourn in Paris was "important and unforgettable" principally because of the recital he attended by the Maurin-Chevillard Quartet of Beethoven's String Quartets in E-flat major and C-sharp minor. Wagner marveled at the "intelligent zeal with which the French musicians have mastered a treasure that is still treated brutally in Germany. Only in Paris did I discover the Quartet in C-sharp minor, and for the first time I clearly understood the melody."

In the weeks to come, these musical impressions were to trigger the composition of *Das Rheingold*, as formerly, also in Paris, hearing Beethoven's Ninth Symphony had sparked in Wagner the inspiration he needed to create *Der fliegende Holländer*.

As for Otto and Mathilde, outside of their acquaintances, their promenades, and their visits to different museums, their artistic and intellectual environment was relatively limited; the circle of associates and rounds of business related to Otto's American firm, Loeschigk and Wesendonck, took up most of their time. Otto had recently made another trip to New York. In July 1853 Mathilde mentioned it with some familiarity in a letter to Minna, saying that she would not go this time to America: "As difficult as it was to make the decision, I was so strongly advised not to take this trip for the sake of our little girl that I did not have the courage to leave. I don't yet know what I'm going to do during this long separation from my husband: in any case, I will stay with my parents. My mother keeps me company in Schwalbach, and then I would follow her wherever she might go. I do not want to see Zurich again without my lord and master."

Later that autumn the Wesendoncks returned to Paris. Business contacts and more refined visits started again. Mathilde observed the way of life in the capital with admiration and some degree of irony, for the Parisians could be frivolous and serious or impertinent and polite, all at the same time. She noted the interior decoration in the fashionable houses they were invited to, no doubt taking inspiration for her villa in Zurich. In the drawing rooms of these ladies, with their billowing crinolines, ruffles, lace, and ribbons, the atmosphere was that of a "museum of decorative arts made comfortable by an upholsterer who has multiplied draperies, seats, fantasy furniture . . . a modern pastiche of old style, or a new empress *à la Pompadour*! This eclecticism aimed more at effect than authenticity."[1] The style was heavy; the tone was light.

They returned to Zurich amused by the tumult of Parisian life and yet a little disgusted by so much brilliance. For Mathilde, the artificial brightness of imperial Paris was but a wan glow compared to the blaze of daylight rising in her heart.

Wagner was also back in Zurich, having returned October 28. He felt he could no longer put off his work. In the space of nine weeks he jotted down the whole outline of his composition and orchestration for *Das Rheingold*, and from February to May 1854 he finished the complete score, including the orchestration, while leading the busy and exhausting life of an orchestra conductor. Indeed, that winter he conducted symphonies by Beethoven, Haydn, and Mozart, overtures by Weber and Gluck, and extracts from *Rienzi* and *Tannhäuser*.

Mathilde thought of Richard constantly. He visited her in her drawing room of the Baur au Lac, as she said later: "In the afternoon he would play on my piano and try out what he had composed in the morning. It was between five and six o'clock. . . . He gave himself the nickname 'the twilight man.' He brought liveliness wherever he went. When he would come in sometimes looking tired and downhearted, it was wonderful to see that after a short moment of rest, his face would light up again, and when he went to the piano, fire blazed in his eyes."[2]

This was no doubt the best moment of the day, when the high windows of Mathilde's apartment, the lake, and the sky were all adorned by the pink and purple hues of sunset. The young woman took in these moments of tranquility as if they were coming from another world, in a serenity that she thought would be eternal. "To him only I owed the best of what I had."

One day, during this fervent period of composing *Das Rheingold*, she saw Wagner arrive with a perplexed look on his face. Without a word he sat down at the piano and played the Valhalla leitmotif. It did not satisfy him, and he started over again. The majesty of the chords describing the Olympian abode of the gods was expanding.

"Master, it's wonderful!" Mathilde cried enthusiastically.

"No, no, it could be better."

Wagner got up suddenly from the piano bench. As Mathilde wrote: "He paced up and back with impatience for a few minutes in the room; then he ran out. The next afternoon he did not come back, nor the day after, nor the day after that. Then he reappeared, silently slipping through the doors so as not to be seen, and sat down again at the piano to play the magnificent passage exactly as it was before."

"And now?" she asked.

"Yes, yes, you are right," replied Wagner. "It couldn't be better."

The winter passed, and in the spring, Mathilde received a visit from her younger sister, Marie, from Düsseldorf. She was eighteen years old and was just coming out.

In March Mathilde's illustrious friend sent this note to Otto:

> Homer slipped discreetly out of my library. Where are you going? I asked him.
>
> He said: To Otto Wesendonck to congratulate him on his birthday.
>
> I answered: Congratulate him also for me.
>
> > March 16, 1854
> >
> > Richard W.

On May 11 the Wesendoncks, Willes, and Herweghs assembled to listen to Wagner read and play extracts from his *Rheingold*. He was relaxed, charming and affable with the ladies. To entertain the young Marie Luckemeyer, who liked to dance, the gallant and courteous musician, always indebted to the Wesendoncks, dedicated a waltz to her on May 31: the *Zürcher Vielliebchen*, "waltz, polka, or a touch of something else." It was a little recreation for the composer between *Das Rheingold* and *Die Walküre*. Although the main theme is in the style of a Chopin waltz, but treated derisively, we can hear what was already running through his head. When played slowly, bits of musical phrases can be heard that were actually developed in the first act of *Die Walküre*.

Mathilde was attentive not only to the master's mind, but also to his physical condition. She found him tired, his facial features a bit too drawn. He was ill from the effort he had expended in writing his score. In March 1854 Wagner complained to Liszt about the exhausting labor of revising his *Rheingold*: "I am working flat-out. Could you find me someone capable of recopying my illegible outlines in pencil onto a score that would be a little neater? . . . This rewriting is killing me!"

It was at that time that Mathilde gave Wagner a new, state-of-the-art pen that Otto had brought back from the United States. In June Wagner wrote again to Liszt:

> You don't have to look for a copyist anymore for me: Frau Wesendonck gave me a present—a pen with a permanent gold nib that turns my handwriting into calligraphy! No one can flee one's destiny! . . . You will not see *Rheingold* before it takes on a form worthy of it, the form I dream of giving it; but this work can only progress during my hours of leisure and long winter evenings, for now I cannot stop, I have to start the composition of *Die Walküre*, whose delightful strains make all my limbs tremble.

In the last days of June, under Mathilde's dazzled eyes, Wagner jotted down on paper the first draft of Act I of *Die Walküre*. He interrupted this work to take Minna to Seelisberg on Lake Lucerne, where she undertook a thermal cure for her heart disease. Their household was doing poorly, but Richard maintained an almost filial tenderness for the wife who had lived through so many difficult years with him. It was again Otto Wesendonck who paid for the trip, the cure, and the accommodations for Minna. She was to return after that to Germany to rest at home and to try—in vain—to obtain amnesty for her husband from the king of Saxony. From a financial point of view, the composer was meeting with nothing but disappointment. In Berlin there were a great many difficulties with producing his works, and his publishers refused to give him an advance. Yet this did not prevent him from filling his heart and mind with Mathilde. He put off his money problems to a later date; now it was the time to compose his *Walküre*. During August he worked continuously on the music of the first act. The annotations in the margins of the manuscript reveal the source of the artist's musical inspiration: on June 28 he had begun the outline for the Prelude by writing at the top of the page the letters *G.s.M.*—"Gesegnet sei Mathilde" (blessed be Mathilde).

The first act of this second work of the cycle begins with the reunion of the Wälsung children—Siegmund and Sieglinde, sired by Wotan on a mortal woman. Through them the god was trying to redeem the sin committed by the theft of the gold. Siegmund was supposed to be the "free hero" who would restore the accursed ring to its origins, but these twins were predestined to be slaves—Siegmund wandered aimlessly through the world, while Sieglinde was forced to marry a brute named Hunding. At the beginning of the first act Siegmund, pursued by his enemies, seeks refuge on Sieglinde's hearth. The brother and sister have not seen each other since they were young children. For Wagner this was the encounter with the one who was his destiny, the one whom he resembled, the "sister of his soul" in the strongest sense of the word. As he was composing the first act, Wagner jotted down at least sixteen times on the draft of the score the mysterious signs that specialists have tried to fathom ever since. They were in reality a declaration of love for Mathilde Wesendonck.[3]

On the margin next to the following scenic directions "Siegmund looks at Sieglinde in the eyes, begins with gravity, and says . . . Friedmund darf ich nicht heissen [you can't call me Peace]," we read on the manuscript in Wagner's hand *W.d.n.w.G.!!*, which has been deciphered as "Wenn du nicht wärst, Geliebte!!" (if it were not for you, my beloved!!).

After Siegmund cries to Sieglinde, "Die Sonne lacht mir nun neu" (the sun is shining for me again), the confession is clear: *I.l.d.gr.*—"Ich liebe dich grenzenlos" (I love you infinitely).

At the direction "Siegmund and Sieglinde look at each other with emotion," he scribbled, *L.d.m.M.??*—"Liebst du mich, Mathilde??" (do you love me, Mathilde??).

When Sieglinde leaves the room at the insistence of Hunding, Siegmund remains alone on the hearth, and Wagner noted again, *G.w.h.d.m.verl.??*—"Geliebte, warum hast du mich verlassen??" (my love, why have you forsaken me??).

By the end of that summer of 1854, Richard Wagner would have expressed in Act I, Scene 1 of *Die Walküre* the most passionate love of his life. After transposing the rest of his story with Mathilde in *Tristan und Isolde*, he sang out his rapture to the entire world in the explosion of his musician's soul, like the spring that burst into the life of the two Wälsung children. Several years later he declared his gratitude to Mathilde for having served as the muse who had carried him to such heights of inspiration. The intensity of his love can be measured by the elevation of his music. But apart from the letters to Mathilde, which were published only after her death, Wagner kept silent about the source of his artistic creation. After 1865, when he dictated his autobiography, *My Life*, to his future wife, Cosima Liszt, expressly for King Ludwig II of Bavaria, he tried to minimize his relationship with Mathilde, either from a sense of modesty regarding Mathilde, or because he needed to show some tact with respect to his new wife. However, the determining influence of Mathilde in the composition of *Die Walküre* is an unalterable fact.

This impossible love plunged Richard into an even greater state of depression that only added to all his other problems. That autumn he worked without interruption in order to finish his composition of *Die Walküre*. He was now perfectly ready, in this melancholy mood, to assimilate the pessimistic philosophy of Schopenhauer.

The second of the four protagonists in this domestic drama was Wagner's wife, Minna, who was suffering from heart problems—in both senses of the term. This woman had founded the cohesion of their fruitless marriage on her motherly love, to which Wagner was very sensitive. She had created from scratch their domestic happiness, as a stage director sets up the props and scenery of a drama, but without having the capacity to play the role herself. She had always acted like a mother to Wagner, a mother who was always waiting for him next to the fireplace, knowing that he needed her. That is why he always came back and never abandoned her for long. He would send her sums of money far beyond his means, write her letters filled with endearments and loving nicknames, and give her a detailed report of all his aches and pains, as a child would to his mother. They spoke to each other in Saxon dialect with the familiarity appropriate to what is called a mother tongue.

It was no wonder, then, during these years of disappointment, that this mother also became bitter and cruel. She was possessive and jealous and often made scenes. They separated, they came back together again, they did each other good, they did each other evil. Their relationship was passionate, but not amorous. Minna would suffer and make her husband suffer until the very end.

Then, of course, there was Mathilde's husband. Otto Wesendonck was not Hunding. This character was conceived by Wagner in 1850, after his amorous adventure with Jessie Laussot, whose husband had far more in common with the brute described in the first act of *Die Walküre*. An analogy with Otto is unthinkable. He was a man of distinction and generosity, thoughtful and capable of judging the situation. Otto knew that Mathilde was young and inexperienced, but he was also aware of her goodness and her moral strength. He trusted her completely. As for himself, he seemed to have an endless reserve of courage and selflessness that commands admiration. So many inner battles, however, would leave scars on his soul. For many years he suffered from psychosomatic illnesses, including episodes of rheumatism. Finally, he was repaid for his pain and greatness of soul when Wagner modeled *Tristan*'s good King Marke on him. That was really his portrait. Meanwhile, out of love for his wife, Otto continued to provide Richard considerable financial assistance. As for Mathilde, he arranged to have her travel a good deal.

Mathilde was the muse, sometimes clearly, sometimes unconsciously, who discovered that it was possible to love two men at the same time, one with passion, the other with compassion. And at times she would fuse them into one. The part to play had its charm: balance was everything. Standing over the abyss with a balancing pole in her hands, she walked unsteadily but never fell. The dilemma was temporarily resolved by her two pregnancies in three years and a long stay in Paris that would remove her from the danger for a while. In her heart, however, Mathilde savored this wonderful love and, like Siegfried, bathed in the heat of its flames without getting burned:

Can one cup contain all the golden light of the sun?
And you, my love, you so small, you want to have all the world's delight!
The immensity of love, enclosed in limits
And all the joy of heaven in the dream of life.[4]

9

Tristan

O n September 4, 1854, Wagner began the preliminary draft for the second act of *Die Walküre*. On top of the first page of the text, he briefly described the scene between Wotan and Brünnhilde: "In the distance, a gorge stretches up from below to a high ridge of rocks, and from there the ground slopes downward again toward the front of the stage. Wotan, dressed for battle and carrying his spear; Brünnhilde, dressed as a warrior maiden, also in full military attire."

Remembering this feverish period of creation, Wagner wrote eleven years later in *My Life* this insignificant sentence: "I continued the composition of *Die Walküre* and was living the same secluded life, using my hours of leisure only for long walks in the area."

Minna had gone back to Dresden, leaving Nathalie with Wagner to take care of domestic chores. On September 7 Richard, accompanied by his "sister-in-law, Nette," was invited to dinner at the Wesendoncks' at the Baur au Lac. Mathilde, to whom Wagner had often spoken of his mountain excursions, observed that since they had come to Switzerland three years before, she had never seen close-up the snow-capped peaks she saw from her balcony. Otto wasted no time in persuading Wagner to be their guide. "It's the least I can do," said Richard, but he did not finish his sentence—he did not want to broach the difficult question of his money problems. The mountains attracted him, in fact, because he sensed they might inspire in him the spirited musical themes he needed for the first scene of Act II. Besides, Minna was absent, and the domestic row between Wotan and Fricka was still far-off.

On September 8 Wagner and the Wesendoncks left for Glaris, a small, picturesque town at the foot of Vorder Glärnisch. The next day, farther south, they followed the Linth valley by Bad Stachelberg, and in Linthal they began their ascension of the Sandalp. Up there, opposite the Tödi, the highest peak in the Glaris Alps, you have only to bend over to pick a bouquet of edelweiss. The site is magnificent. Wagner breathed in deeply this atmosphere for his scene between Wotan and his valkyrie. The chief god would send Brünnhilde down there into our sad existence, under the mists and beyond our Olympian dreams in order to protect his son Siegmund, fleeing with the fragile Sieglinde.

On September 10 they returned to Glaris and turned west toward Schwyz and the pyramidal summits of the Mythen. They went along the beautiful Klöntalersee, then across the Pragel pass to arrive in the Muota valley. The countryside was green and fresh. From the tops of the cliffs waterfalls descended down through the forests, covered in pines and larches, and over the steep slopes, into the bottom of the gorge. Mathilde would transpose all this into her poetry in later years:

THE CATARACT

In a roar, the streams from staggering heights descend the precipice
And the foaming tide spills all the blood of its heart.
And yet, it escapes from suffering death, reborn in a myriad of raindrops
In which the rays of sun are reflected.
The blue of heaven, the celestial troop of brilliant stars,
The dreamy moon; all of these are present in the tiniest drop.
Nature is so: the smallest is always for you
A mirror of greatness and of all.
And in the ephemeral image, you see yourself until infinity.
Humanity, how you resemble this wild waterfall![n]

After crossing the village of Muotathal, the travelers went that evening to Brunnen, on Lake Lucerne. They had accommodations at the Hotel of the Golden Eagle, whose proprietor, a Colonel Auf-der-Maur, had become a good friend of Wagner's on his frequent excursions. In her memoirs Mathilde noted that, as soon as they arrived, Wagner "played at the hour of twilight on the mediocre-sounding piano of the dining room extracts from Beethoven's 'Eroica' Symphony and his Symphony in C minor." At night, everyone fell fast asleep, as is usual at high altitudes. "But," wrote Mathilde, "in the morning, at breakfast, I was greeted by the luminous chords of *Lohengrin*."

On the eleventh they took a boat at Brunnen to cross the lake. They were off to Beckenried, then went on foot to Emmeten and Seelisberg, at an altitude of 800 meters (2600 feet), on a road bordered by beautiful fields and prairies. They spent the night at the Hotel Sonnenberg, well-known to Wagner, who had stayed there with Minna. "It was the best discovery I had made in Switzerland," he wrote in *My Life*. "It's such a delightful and beautiful sojourn, that I dream of returning there to die." From Seelisberg the three of them together wrote a letter to Minna in Saxony—one that, it was said, made her rage with jealousy toward Mathilde.

Finally, on the twelfth, very early in the morning, they left in the direction of Mount Rigi. Halfway there, however, in Goldau, Wagner left his friends in a rush; he suddenly felt the need to compose and resume his work where he had left off in Zurich. The Wesendoncks continued their journey, crossing mountain pastures and forests, up to the summit of the Rigi, at 1800 meters (5900 feet). They spent the night there to wait for the magnificent dawn of a new day. At sunrise an immense panorama of the Alps opened up before their eyes: the Jungfrau, the Eiger, and the Mönsch were a dazzling sight. From up there "a sound soft and primitive, the alphorn, a wooden horn three meters long, can be heard."[2] In preceding years, during his mountain-climbing excursions, Wagner had heard this instrument, so typical of the Alps; he would remember its sound later on in the orchestration of *Götterdämmerung*.

Otto and Mathilde took advantage of the beautiful sightseeing as far as fifty kilometers (thirty-one miles) in all directions in half of Switzerland and part of Germany. But with Richard gone, Mathilde felt nothing but emptiness under her feet. Ever since he had left for Zurich she thought of him constantly, that little man down there on the plains, no bigger than a pinpoint, who was creating a work that would go beyond all these summits. She contemplated the view without really seeing it; she had the impression that Wagner had carried the mountains off with him to put them in his music.

For several months, as was his habit, Wagner lived far above his means. His friends in Zurich were somewhat alarmed to see him going through money like water, money he had borrowed—especially from Otto Wesendonck. At the beginning of the summer, Jakob Sulzer, who had often lent him small sums, found himself unable to come to his aid once more when Wagner was confronted with two unpaid bills of fifteen hundred francs each. In June 1854 Sulzer wrote to Wesendonck in Germany. As she did each year, Mathilde had gone to visit her family in the Rhineland. Otto, on vacation with her in Bad Schwalbach, received Sulzer's letter and answered him in these terms: "The sum of Wagner's debts is much greater than what you say. He mentions a thousand francs owed to his tailor, another unknown sum owed to a certain Kölliker. . . . We should know," he added, "the exact amount of his whole debt if we really want to help him. One thing that is certain: the money should not be handed over directly to him. . . . At first I thought of giving the funds to Frau Wagner, but that seemed too humiliating to me." Wesendonck was clearheaded, even though his kindness and thoughtfulness outweighed his severity. "The best intentions in the world have limits. If I may utter a word of blame, he has too little regard for his friends. Otherwise he would not put himself in such a difficult situation for everyone."

It had all begun in 1853, when Wagner felt the need to do up his lodging in a luxury disproportionate to his means. Comparable to a pregnant woman near her term preparing the cradle and clothing for her child, sometimes with an excess of refinement, Wagner, big with his cycle, felt the pressing desire to be surrounded by precious silks and costly furniture to decorate his interior. His lifestyle, his trips, and his inability to think in practical terms obliged him to borrow money several times, from Sulzer and especially from Wesendonck. Ever since his exceptional concerts in Zurich, which had themselves been financed by Wesendonck, Wagner incessantly begged his muse's husband to advance him sums of money in expectation of fees for theater performances that never materialized.

By Easter 1854 Wagner was obliged to admit to Wesendonck that he was incapable of paying him back. Otto behaved in his usual noble fashion, completely forgiving the musician his debt, but with a little man-to-man conversation on the necessity of not making elaborate plans for money he did not yet have.

In autumn of 1854 Wagner was working feverishly, composing the second act of his

Walküre, which he completed on November 18. Meanwhile, he finished the definitive clean copy of *Das Rheingold* on September 26. He managed all this work in his house, which had fallen silent with Minna's visit to Saxony. But the shadow of his debts haunted his conscience again. Not daring to face Wesendonck directly, he wrote to Sulzer on September 14 to set before him all his financial misery. He needed 10,000 Swiss francs—7,000 for local debts and 3,000 to reimburse his friend Karl Ritter, whose mother had already bestowed on the composer a pension of three thousand francs annually. Wagner's idea was to fill the gap by digging another hole. He asked Sulzer to persuade Wesendonck that he would soon be capable of paying back these 10,000 francs after he received the theater fees, notably from Berlin, for the performances of *Tannhäuser* and *Lohengrin*. He estimated his future income at 21,000 francs, which could be sent directly to Wesendonck, who in turn would pay his debts and give him an annual pension. For this he would need 2,000 francs a year for current expenses. Another bill of 500 francs needed to be paid right away. As soon as Sulzer received this letter, he went to see Wesendonck. On September 29, Otto sent 7,000 francs to liquidate the debts of this intrusive "colonizing" friend, and he laid out the conditions in no uncertain terms: "to mortgage on the sums to be paid on the future performances of his operas." Wagner then received 500 francs in quarterly payments for his domestic needs.

Two days later Wagner wrote again to Sulzer explaining that he had unfortunately made a mistake in estimating his debts at the sum of 10,000 francs. He had forgotten a few smaller sums, which amounted to 342 francs, and he needed also 350 francs to pay his rent. He promised, however, never again to spend beyond his income. Sulzer notified Wesendonck, who, surprised by this new request and the promise that accompanied it, authorized him to pay the 342 francs and the rest on his account, enjoining him to find out if everything had really been confessed this time. Moreover, Sulzer was to make Wagner understand that under no circumstances would he lend a favorable ear to any other requests, and that he was firmly counting on the income promised from the theaters. Otto wrote: "I believe that Wagner has the intention of strictly standing by his income and not contracting any other debts. But I also think it will do no harm to make him realize that I will not be responsible for any future debt, and that I hope we will be spared any new discussions of this kind."

Otto therefore paid the extra 342 francs and the 350 for his rent. On sending the money to Sulzer, he warned him: "We have had, you and me, enough trouble, and in the end, you have to know how to be firm."

Despite this humiliation, Wagner would start over again, and Wesendonck would still come to his aid, especially when Breitkopf und Härtel refused to give him an advance for the publication of *Das Rheingold* and *Die Walküre*: the publishers doubted the practical possibilities of fully staging these operas. Otto Wesendonck's words may seem a little harsh, but this was simply his usual way of doing business. And Otto would be generous again, far beyond the limits of friendship—for example, in 1857, when he granted his impenitent debtor a house on his property for a fictive rent. The lodging, it must be pointed out, almost adjoined the one he shared with Mathilde, his beloved spouse.

Despite the extent of his fortune, Otto Wesendonck was not going to open up a bottomless cash register in favor of a capricious genius, no matter how great. His unfailing generosity deserved better than the harshness or even the injustice with which Wagner described their relationship in his autobiography. It seems that the musician had concentrated on his benefactor the ungrateful and symbolic role of his entire problem of chronic indebtedness before his providential encounter with King Ludwig II. Besides, in *My Life*, written for the monarch, he needed to accentuate the contrast between his previous conditions, described as miserable, and the privileged situation created for him by the Bavarian king.

But Wagner-the-artist nevertheless recognized for posterity in *Tristan* the true, disinterested role of Otto Wesendonck and gave a title no less than "king" to Isolde's husband, the magnanimous Marke.

Pygmalion loathed the vices given by nature
To women's hearts; he lived a lonely life,
Shunning the thought of marriage and a wife.
Meanwhile he carved the snow-white ivory
With happy skill; he gave it beauty greater
Than any woman's: then grew enamored of it.[3]

During the autumn of 1854, while continuing his composition draft of *Die Walküre*, thanks to Herwegh Wagner acquainted himself with a book that had been forgotten in Germany for thirty years and had just been rediscovered: *The World as Will and Representation* (*Die Welt als Wille und Vorstellung*), by Arthur Schopenhauer. It was no doubt his pessimistic analysis of the human condition that attracted Wagner. From the bottom of his solitary retreat, temporarily rid of his pecuniary worries, the musician could measure the extent of his disillusion with regard to politics, society, love, and marriage. The only true love he had ever known was deep in his heart, on a starry night in the land of dreams with an unattainable woman. Schopenhauer came just in time to justify his personal experience philosophically.

The world is its representation; we cannot conceive of it in any other way than by our intelligence. Will is the real world, the "thing-in-itself." The world as representation is the world of appearances. Schopenhauer believed that humans were motivated only by their basic desires, or "will to live," that is, the drive to oppose and dominate the forces of destruction that threaten them. But the intelligence is subordinated to the will-to-live. Because evil and suffering accompany all life and human effort, to renounce the Will is to renounce all forms of suffering. So here it was the solution to all of Wagner's problems! And as the artist so well illustrated in his opera heroes, each person has two beings in one, the carnal and the spiritual. The consequences of this intellectual approach that Wagner would adopt for himself would be different according to its application—to the man himself, or to the artist.

This distinction was not perceptible to Galatea (Mathilde) in her present state. Although she had become more than a "blank page," she had not yet quite become fully autonomous, and the last gesture that the unconscious Pygmalion (Richard) would give with his sculptor's chisel to the beautiful statue, before it breathed, was to help her mind come to the light of this Schopenhauerian thought, which would leave its mark on her.

As far as the artist was concerned, Wagner, in love, would sublimate his passion by composing *Tristan und Isolde*. As for Mathilde, she never managed to heal the scars of the lessons she had learned too well from her master of music.

> *The sculptor marveled and loved his beautiful pretense.*
> *Often he touched the body, wondering*
> *If it were ivory or flesh—he would not*
> *Affirm it ivory. He gave it kisses,*
> *Thinking they were returned, and he embraced it.*[4]

Schopenhauer's influence on Wagner is more apparent in *Die Walküre* than in *Tristan*, although the composer did not know the philosopher when he was writing the poem of the cycle. Nevertheless, the character of Wotan embodies a vision of the world that is none other than Schopenhauer's. In Act II, when the god realizes that his fault was to have renounced love to obtain power, he sees in his own hypocrisy the root of all evil in the world. What he has left, he tells Brünnhilde (the incarnation of his will, free from all constraint), is that he aspires to the conclusion of all things: "Das Ende, das Ende."

> *Away then with lordly splendor,*
> *Divine pomp and shameful boasting.*
> *Let fall to pieces all that I built!*
> *Only one thing I want now:*
> *The end, the end!*[5]

And when love compelled his favorite daughter to disobey him and save Siegmund, the son he loved in spite of everything, he would banish Brünnhilde, his own will, by putting her to sleep on a rock surrounded by flames.

With *Tristan* it would be different. In *My Life*, Wagner wrote: "The serious state of mind into which the reading of Schopenhauer had brought me was no doubt the reason I was searching for an ecstatic expression for my feelings, and this is how I conceived of my poem." This "state of mind" would lead him to outline the libretto for a theme he had long known. In 1844 a version of the Tristan story by the twelfth-century Gottfried von Strassburg was published in modern German, translated by Hermann Kurz. Wagner had a copy of this edition in his library in Dresden. At that time he had studied it carefully, and he also read translations by Karl Immermann and Friedrich von der Hagen, as well as the Middle English version of the poem, *Sir Tristrem*, by Thomas of Erceldoune. Ten years later it was reading Schopenhauer that brought him back to this legend. However, the atmosphere underlying a work is not the work, and such a philosophical enlightenment could only have skimmed the surface; the essential part was missing. The ideas of Schopenhauer and his principle of denouncing the will-to-live touch only the appearances. The glorification of night as opposed to day, the subject of the lovers' second-act conversation, shows that the individual will, represented by the day, gives way to the night, which denies it. That's all for Schopenhauer! It is the same for the idea that death is the ultimate solution to unrequited love; but this is only an illusion, for death sublimated through love in Wagner opens the door to a new life. "See him smiling calmly. How he gently opens his eyes. Friends! Look!"[6] sings Isolde over Tristan's dead body. "Can't you feel it, can't you see it?" Isolde sees him alive because she has entered with him into another life of transfiguration.

What would Schopenhauer have said? For the philosopher, renouncing the will-to-live constituted nirvana in this world and nothingness in the world to come. Wagner, on the other hand, went beyond death into a new life, in a sort of mystical communion in which you have only to replace the human lover with the divine. We know that in the first outline for *Tristan*, Wagner was thinking of introducing the character of Parsifal at the bedside of the dying hero so as to bring him some supernatural consolation. But the composer's the dramatic sense led him to put off this kind of intervention for another operatic subject.

Thomas Mann claimed that *Tristan* was heavily influenced by the fundamentally erotic character of Schopenhauer's metaphysics. But with Wagner it is impossible to separate the carnal from the spiritual, and the composer went beyond a purely physiological conception of the philosopher, who, from this point of view, was a precursor of Freud. According to Schopenhauer, the will-to-live is associated with the sex drive, the very "heart of the will-to-live," and it occurs in all our expressions of desire—which strangely resembles the conception Freud would have of the libido. However, Wagner's *Tristan* contains a new dimension, one that is almost biblical, of the fusion between eros and agape,[7] in the ecstatic sense of the Song of Solomon, in which divine love is compared to human love.

Let him kiss me with the kisses of his mouth,
For thy love is better than wine.

Wagner actually reversed the metaphysics of love according to Schopenhauer. *Tristan* was also a sort of mystical allegory, like the Song of Solomon: "Love is as strong as death; the coals thereof are coals of fire. . . . Many waters cannot quench love, neither can the floods drown it."

Pygmalion offered up a sacrifice and prayed,
"If the gods can give whatever they may wish,
grant me a wife (without daring to mention an ivory statue) like her."
. . . The maiden felt his kiss—She blushed and trembled:
When she raised her eyes, she saw her lover and heaven's light together.[8]

In 1854 it was too soon to evoke Pygmalion's kiss to Galatea in the story of Richard and Mathilde. It would occur three years later on September 18, 1857, when Wagner brought her the finished poem of *Tristan und Isolde*. That day, she said, "Now I have nothing more to desire!" The statue took life and Wagner with it, as he reminded her the following year in a letter he sent to her from Venice: "That day, at that moment, I was really born. . . . An affectionate woman who was shy and hesitating threw herself with sublime courage into the ocean of suffering and pain in order to obtain for me this splendid instant, saying *I love you!* . . . In this way, you were destined to die in order to give me life; I received your life so as to leave this world with you, suffer with you, die with you. Then the magic of unappeased desire was annihilated!"

This breath of life given to Galatea-Mathilde awakened in her an awareness of her own intellectual life. In 1857 she revealed herself as a poet, and her works, enriched by the genius of Wagner, would take on the indelible tone of Schopenhauer. Wagner recognized in her writings something of himself and put them into music under the title *Wesendonck Lieder*.

One of them, "Stehe still!" (Be Still), illustrated particularly well the philosophy lessons Mathilde had learned:

> *Rushing, roaring wheel of time,*
> *You measure of eternity;*
> *Shining spheres in the vast firmament,*
> *You that encircle our earthly globe:*
> *Eternal creation, stop!*
> *Enough of becoming; let me be!*

As a good student of Schopenhauer, Mathilde celebrated the celestial movements, the stars, and all that derives from the will, as opposed to the Hegelian concept of evolution.

> *Ye powers of generation, cease,*
> *Primal thought, that endlessly creates,*
> *Stop every breath, still every urge,*
> *Give but one moment of silence!*
> *Swelling pulses, restrain your beating:*
> *End, eternal day of the will!*

These "powers of generation," in the words of Schopenhauer, signify the will. The Frankfurt philosopher taught the suppression of the will, the end of thought, and the repression of instincts. "Desire, be still!" wrote Mathilde, who knew all too well the "swelling pulses" of her passion. She would have sung in unison with Wotan, "End, eternal day of the Will!"

> *So that in sweet forgetfulness*
> *I may take the full measure of all my joy,*

When eye blissfully gazes into eye,
When soul drowns in soul:
When being finds itself in being
And the goal of all hopes is near,
Then lips are mute in silent amazement.
The heart can have no further wish:
Man knows the imprint of eternity
And solves your riddle, blessed Nature!

Here again Mathilde called on the principles of the philosopher. It is necessary to dissipate the illusion of the self, to expel one's love for oneself. This can happen through compassion, which implies our recognition of the other's identity. Through his intelligence, man is called on to see his own being globally, as an inner force hidden in the secret laws of nature. But for Mathilde, nature can only be holy because it is innocent, knowing neither life nor death.

Mathilde Wesendonck was therefore more romantic than Wagner, who criticized the end of this poem: "I felt greatly like changing the expression "blessed nature." The thought is correct, but not the expression. Nature is not blessed except where it can rise to serenity. But out of love for you, I did not modify anything."

∾

At the end of 1854 Wagner was still working on his cycle, reading Schopenhauer, and visiting the Wesendoncks. He conceived of a *Tristan* to express his inner torment, for the story of Tristan and Isolde (in the second and third acts) is his and Mathilde's story. The ideas of Schopenhauer were only an intellectualization of a fact: Tristan loves Isolde, who has to marry King Marke. Their impossible love can only come to life after a transfiguration in death. Richard loved Mathilde, who was married to Otto. For Richard, this love would be sublimated into the music of a unique opera, the finished composition of which would plunge Mathilde into a kind of purgatory for the rest of her life.

Shortly before Christmas in 1854, Wagner wrote to Liszt: "I still have to finish the dramas of the *Nibelung* cycle for the love of Siegfried, who is the most beautiful dream of my life. *Die Walküre* has exhausted me so much as to make me refuse this recreation; I am up to the second half of the last act. . . . But because I never in my life experienced the true happiness that love gives, I want to raise this dream, the most beautiful of all dreams, to the height of a monument in which this love will be satisfied from beginning to end. I have outlined *Tristan und Isolde* in my head. Its musical conception is very simple, but very strong and lively: when I finish this work, I will cover myself with the black sail that floats at the end . . . to die."[9]

10

The Calm before the Storm

I can't help thinking that if we had a real life, we wouldn't need art," wrote Wagner in 1852. "Art begins precisely where life leaves off, when there is nothing else ahead. So we cry out to art: 'I desire, I wish,' . . . I cannot imagine that a man who is really happy should ever think of art. To live truly is to possess fulfillment. Is art anything but a confession of our weakness?"

After such words, is it possible to doubt that *Tristan und Isolde* was the fruit of an impossible love forever unattainable from a human standpoint? Much has been said about the nature of the relationship between Richard and Mathilde. In our time, when love has been made commonplace, an affair between a man and a woman cannot be imagined any other way than the sexual. However, on reading Wagner's sentences it seems quite clear that without the renouncement of that kind of love's happiness, there would have been nothing to sublimate, and the will-to-live of the protagonists would never have experienced the "transfiguration" through art; in other words, the opera *Tristan und Isolde* might never have been composed.

Richard launched his boat on the sea of passions somewhere between Ireland and Cornwall. If he had set his course in the direction of Schopenhauer Island, many reefs, whirlpools, and contrary winds would keep him from getting there. The hold of the ship was stocked with the necessary supplies for beginning his new work: German romanticism, the poetic works of Pedro Calderón de la Barca, Hindu and Persian legends, and a complete history of Buddhism by Eugène Burnouf. Before coming to grips with what would shipwreck him on Kareol (Venice), Wagner spent two years, all of 1855 and 1856, preparing himself without knowing it for the love crisis with Mathilde Wesendonck that would hasten the writing of the poem and the beginning of the score of *Tristan*. Richard and Mathilde would do nothing to protect themselves from this storm, thinking perhaps that they were above such factors, or perhaps simply being unconscious of them.

Passion is able to disguise its mystery. Who could have thought that this quiet, bourgeois woman living her well-ordered life, with her conventional behavior and a certain cool reserve, would be capable of standing up to the passionate maelstrom represented in this masterpiece *Tristan and Isolde*? Calm and sober, lacking either cunning or pretense, Mathilde wrote her later fairy tales with a spontaneous naturalness, but she was also driven by a need for perfection. We can discover the medieval Isolde only as a dream figure, an ideal vision.

In January 1855 Mathilde received Wagner at the Baur au Lac, where she still lived. After

Schopenhauer, the conversation rolled on to Goethe and another very romantic theme that inspired so many authors and composers during that nineteenth century: Faust. All sorts of amateurs were trying to write rhymes to imitate the poet of Weimar. In 1855 one of Mathilde's brothers sent her a little collection of poems entitled *Musestunden* (The Hour of the Muse) and dedicated it to his "Dear sister, Mathilde, with brotherly love." He signed it with a "V" in *Fraktur*, intending it to be seen as Valentin, the name of Marguerite's brother in *Faust*. Was the young man thinking of the burdensome character, that magician of sounds, who had invaded his sister's life and always haunted the circle of family and friends at the Wesendoncks'?

As for Wagner, he lived in a world of his own and remained absorbed by the only thing that counted for him—his art. He told Mathilde, among other things, how in 1840 he had also tried to write a symphony on the theme of Faust while he was living in dire straits in Paris. He had composed the first movement, his music inspired by Beethoven. This work was one Mathilde had always loved, and Richard knew it. Liszt, he said, had just finished his three-movement work *A Faust Symphony*, and Berlioz, Liszt announced, had composed a work on the same theme. In *My Life* Wagner noted his own endeavors without mentioning the name of Wesendonck. "By chance, I had spoken to some of my friends," he wrote, "about my *Overture to Faust*, composed fifteen years before in Paris; they wanted to hear it. Their wish gave me the desire to revise the work that had made me change my musical conceptions."

It was then the lively and amorous look of Mathilde that encouraged Wagner to take another look at this youthful composition. He wrote to Liszt in January 1855: "A mad desire has obliged me to modify once more an old overture to *Faust*. I completely rewrote the score and reorchestrated the whole piece, which has changed a lot of things, giving a lot more room to the central part (the second motif). In a few days it will be performed at a concert here. I will call it: *An Overture for Faust*."

Wagner selected an epigraph for his work:

God who remains in my bosom
Can confound my soul;
He who governs within my being,
Can do nothing beyond;
My existence weighs heavily upon me,
I hate life and wish to die![1]

Having become perhaps more lucid—thanks to the characters of the *Ring* cycle, who are more realistic and less cynical than Doctor Faust, Wagner chose to delete this epigraph. "By no means will I publish it," he wrote to Liszt. Mathilde would confirm this in 1896: "Suddenly, he thought it was impossible," she said. "'Impossible,' he cried out, 'to weigh these terrible words down on your heart.' So he just dedicated the score to me and added: *Zum Andenken S.l.F.* [*seiner lieben Freundin*] (In remembrance of his dear friend)."

At the end of November 1854 the new theater director in Zurich, Ernst Walther, persuaded

Wagner to present *Tannhäuser*. He reproached the composer for having allowed his score to be performed in all the theaters of Europe except his. With the encouragement of his friends, Wagner agreed to a performance in Zurich. But they found him only a few mediocre singers, the orchestra was completely inadequate, and the scenery too cheap, almost secondhand. The soprano who was to sing Elisabeth, Maria Jungwirth, had no doubt neglected to read the whole libretto and familiarize herself with the author's intentions, especially concerning the character of Saint Elisabeth of Hungary. She seemed to be totally unaware of the "golden legend" of the medieval saints, for, accustomed to interpreting roles of young maidens, she dressed up in the costumes she had for the stage, with white gloves and a fan on her wrist.

"I was crazy enough," wrote Wagner to Liszt, "to undertake more than I should have: a performance of *Tannhäuser* that is to take place here tomorrow. If you excuse the miserable conditions of the Zurich theater, it will probably go. However, I will not conduct it myself."

The six performances were set for February and March 1855. Wagner watched from a box with his friends Herwegh, the Willes, and the Wesendoncks. Louis Müller, the theater's *Kapellmeister*, conducted. Mathilde reacted vehemently against the mediocrity of the whole thing and pleaded with Richard to take the baton for the orchestra, which he did on February 23. At the end of the opera the artists bowed to an enthusiastic public, and people were astounded to hear the master declare that if the resources placed at his disposal did not improve, he would no longer conduct. Indeed, two days later he left Zurich, before the last three performances, on March 2, 4, and 19. He was going to London for a series of concerts at the Philharmonic Society. On March 3, having stopped off in Paris, he wrote to Hans von Bülow: "In recent times, the public in Zurich called upon me in terrible circumstances; out of friendship for Frau Wesendonck I consented to conduct my *Tannhäuser* once at the divine theater over there!"

≈

But what was the gossip circulating in Zurich's high society about Mathilde and Richard? The latter, en route to London, was not there, so he was not concerned. Slander was spreading nevertheless about the young woman. For what was she to blame? For having received frequent visits from a well-known personality? Not really. But perhaps for being too beautiful, too rich, and too aloof. In the end, what was she thinking of, what did she want, wondered the local gossips. She did not take part in their conversations or go to their teas; she did not come to taste their fine pastries, or if she did, she felt no need to talk about herself or her family. Her pastimes were reading and playing the piano; her receptions were given in honor of writers and artists.

"What does she tell people about herself?"

"Frau Wesendonck?"

"Yes indeed."

"She's a rather common rich woman with nothing to do."

"So what could she possibly say to people a hundred times smarter than herself?"

"These Wesendoncks are in Zurich apparently on business, and in spite of the escapades of brother Hugo in 1848, they have not been banished, not at all."

"The husband is a businessman. She, well that's something else. . . . "

"He is the 'least gifted of our circle,' wrote Emma Herwegh to Caroline zu Sayn-Wittgenstein. Moreover, she considered Mathilde 'a German highbrow.' Concerning the romance between Mathilde and Richard, she maintained: "Between you and me, this love affair resembles what I consider to be love as much as the Wagner's *homunculus* of Goethe resembles a man. They are shadows, and even if they were perfectly beautiful, there is still no reason to sacrifice the last human creature for their sakes."[2]

The only woman in the German colony who stayed away from these wagging tongues was Eliza Wille. She was to become Mathilde's only ally. Many years later she remembered Eliza's role in her life and reminded her of it in a moving speech: "From the beginning of our meetings, we immediately became friends. It was the time of *Sturm und Drang*, the time when I was chased from my paradise of self-satisfaction, from my daily routine . . . when I did not know who to turn to and had only one refuge, one resort: you, my great lady with an unshakable soul."[3]

Eliza's kindness to Mathilde provoked caustic remarks from Emma Herwegh, who described the mistress of Mariafeld as having

> an epileptic nature, . . . one of those women who love spicy situations, as if it were their own tendency, . . . one of those monsters who find themselves to be *interesting* and are capable of ruining whole generations by sacrificing rectitude to feeling, conscience to romantic situations, and who need to *find*, if not *create*, conflicts, which are the necessary element in more than one mediocre novel,[4] . . . one of those women who are capable of treating other people's sorrow with heroic asceticism, especially if the other person is not literate. I admit that one of the four actors in this play is difficult to classify, the one who deserves the deepest compassion; this poor Minna, after having given all that she could . . . is about to be sacrificed to an idol.[5]

Under the guise of decency and "moral indignation," the social world of Zurich was masking its envy, or even the feelings Wagner had aroused in some of the women, such as Emilie Heim and Johanna Spyri. According to Gregor-Dellin, "Frau Herwegh was inconsolable over the fact that she had not been chosen by Wagner as a confidante, rather than Eliza Wille."

However, Princess Caroline, more lucid than her correspondent, replied to her letter in no uncertain terms: "Ah! You are jealous, Emma, beautiful Emma! It is the sacred ailment, the sublime wrong of womankind. . . . But recover, recover fast; be less sacred, less sublime, and more satisfied. Think of it—geniuses belong to everyone; everyone wants a part of them, and considers it a duty to ask for it."

So the left-out spouses, Otto and Minna, were objects of their compassion. When Minna told Wagner about these rumors, she received a reassuring answer from him:

London, May 4, 1855

No doubt Sulzer was not as attentive in his visits as our "honest" Wesendonck, this good fellow who will surely not be affected by slanderous comments from relations and will not agree to such a sad opinion about his wife, as much as, on my side, I cannot accept such a bad one about you; so I agree quite ungrudgingly that you may have any visit you may find agreeable. And this brings me to what you say about the low regard in which Frau Wesendonck has fallen in the eyes of Frau Heim and company. Is it possible that this poor woman has suddenly become so unpleasant that these people can no longer stand her? In that case, I would be all the more sorry that even quite recently she was considered universally to be quite an estimable lady. And if, really, as you tell me in your letter, Wesendonck is very much to be pitied because of his wife's bad reputation, that surely proves a lot of charity toward him, but not toward his wife, who is constantly being degraded, and I admit it is difficult for me to see this compassion as quite sincere and heartfelt. But I hope at least as far as you are concerned, you give these ladies a good example by showing yourself to be more indulgent about tiny peculiarities, which, even if they were real, are excusable and do not have the monstrous characteristics they give them. After that, naturally, I will not force you in the least, if you have a true antipathy for Frau Wesendonck, I assure you that I myself, in spite of the gratitude we owe her husband, will not impose any relationships that would be painful for you; if, on the contrary, your present antipathy be only a certain doubt concerning the honor of this person, I can guarantee you that this mistrust is absolutely undeserved, and that you can even be persuaded that no one better deserves your trust and your friendship than Frau Wesendonck. As for me, with all the differences we have between us, I maintain a firm and cordial confidence in her husband, a trustfulness that he returns to me, and quite rightly.

In the meantime Mathilde had withdrawn from her social life entirely. In the morning she awoke with nausea and dizziness that prevented her from going out, and she pined away in her luxurious surroundings. The doctor prescribed complete rest until the end of her third month of pregnancy. So she took to knitting and embroidery, looking after Myrrha's progress in reading. Otto was satisfied. Some distance from Wagner and the birth of her baby brought his wife and his family life closer to him. On Sundays they often had guests for dinner or would take walks up the hill in Enge, where the new villa was beginning to take shape. The allées of the future park were being drawn up. The types and species of trees were planned, as were the shrubs, bushes, and flowers.

From London, Wagner wrote chatty but carefully worded letters to his dear "uncle and aunt Wesendonck" giving the couple an account of his comical adventures in England, where he was often tripped up by the language and customs of the British. He constantly had problems with the musicians as well as the press, and in spite of the interview granted him by Queen Victoria, who regarded him favorably, his setbacks were numerous. Moreover, British law did not permit fees to be paid for works published in other countries!

The only answers we know of to these abundant missives are in the Burrell Collection.

In one of them, Otto wrote to him on the occasion of his birthday: "I had hoped for further developments over there, and now I can only share your burden. I wish you strength, courage, perseverance, confidence. Say to yourself, *It must be so*, and disregard the vulgarities in front of you. They too will pass, and later you will tell us that what depressed you and what pleased you are only memories. . . . This is really a melancholy letter for a birthday, but our sympathy should comfort you over there, and you will understand of course what is behind of all this. . . . My dear wife sends you a supply of our best wishes." These words seem somewhat enigmatic, but we know that Otto was in part responsible for Wagner's trip to Great Britain. He had given him a letter of introduction to a businessman named Benecke who met him with hostility instead of favor, since he was part of a circle of friends dedicated exclusively to the music of Mendelssohn.

We can easily imagine other reasons Otto suggested, albeit in a friendly manner, that Wagner leave. Wagner, thus prepared by his Zurich friends, let himself be tempted by the promises of a Mr. Anderson of the Philharmonic Society. That the reality was quite different from what he was hoping for can be seen in the long letter he sent to Otto on April 5, 1855: "If I have the courage to persevere in my artistic vocation, the assurance of your friendship will have helped to support my intimate convictions. Be sure of that."

In his sad lodgings in London he tried to work on the orchestration of *Die Walküre*; but, so far from Mathilde, he lost heart. The administrative red tape of the British way of life was crushing him. Exasperated, he wrote again to Otto on May 22: "I was not born to earn money, but to create; and I would be ready to commit myself entirely to this vocation without interruption if the world would assume the responsibility for giving me the means necessary to do so."

In the only letter he addressed directly to Mathilde, on April 30, Wagner tried to encourage the "poor sick woman." Otto answered this missive to reassure Richard about his wife's health in his birthday letter in May: "Thanks to her having had a complete rest, she is quite fine."

During this time, Mathilde was able to peruse the *Hindu Legends*, recommended by Pygmalion. As for Wagner, on reading these same texts he had conceived of a libretto for an opera that he never got around to writing: "The Victors." This subject only plunged Mathilde a little deeper into the world of dreams. At the same time, Wagner was keeping her posted on the progress he was making on *Die Walküre*.

Meanwhile, Wesendonck was overseeing the construction of their villa in Enge. He wrote to Wagner: "We have to be patient." But when Otto mentioned the little Valhalla in Zurich, Wagner answered with his usual epistolary humor: "I see you have given it the name *Hochwyl*, but for me that doesn't count, because I will always call it *Wesenheim*."[6]

Back in Zurich the following summer, Wagner lost his most faithful friend: his dog, Peps. Animals played an important role in the composer's domestic life. In July he had postponed an invitation to dine with the Wesendoncks because the poor dog was ill. But before the summer was over Mathilde bought him another pet, and Wagner named it Fips. "A special bond was created between the Wesendoncks and Minna after they gave them a sweet little dog to replace Peps. The animal was so well-trained and loving that my wife soon cared tenderly for it. I also had affection for it."

Illustration 1. Mathilde Wesendonck. Oil painting by Ernst Benedikt Kietz (detail; see also illustration 17). Courtesy of the Richard Wagner Museum, Tribschen, Lucerne.

Illustration 2. Mathilde Wesendonck in Paris, 1855. Collection of Franz Wesendonk.

Illustration 3. The Wesendoncks' villa in Enge, near Zurich, Switzerland. Stadtarchiv, Zurich.

Illustration 5. Mathilde Wesendonck around 1850. Oil painting by Karl Ferdinand Sohn. Städtisches Kunstmuseum, Bonn.

Illustration 4. Hans Wesendonck, 1862–1882. Collection of Franz Wesendonk.

Illustration 6. Johanna Wesendonck *née* Stein, Mathilde Wesendonck's mother. Collection of Franz Wesendonk.

Illustration 7. Mathilde Wesendonck in Zurich. Collection of Franz Wesendonk.

Illustration 8. Karl Luckemeyer, Mathilde Wesendonck's father. Collection of Franz Wesendonk.

Illustration 9. Otto Wesendonck as a young man. Collection of Franz Wesendonk.

Illustration 10. Karl Wesendonck, 1857–1934. Collection of Franz Wesendonk.

Illustration 11. Richard Wagner in 1853. Watercolor by Clementine Stockar-Escher. Stadtarchiv, Zurich.

Illustration 12. François Wille. Collection of Jürg Wille.

Illustration 14. The Wesendoncks' villa in Zurich. Stadtarchiv, Zurich.

Illustration 13. Eliza Wille. Collection of Jürg Wille.

Illustration 15. The Asyl, situated on the Wesendoncks' property in Zurich. The house was Richard Wagner's home in 1857–58. Drawing, 1857. Collection of Jürg Wille.

Illustration 16. Myrrha Wesendonck, 1851–1888. Collection of Jürg Wille.

Illustration 17. Mathilde Wesendonck and her son Guido. Oil painting by Ernst Benedikt Kietz (see also illustration 1). Courtesy of the Richard Wagner Museum, Tribschen, Lucerne, Switzerland.

Illustration 18. Richard Wagner in 1862. Oil painting by Cesar Willich, commissioned by Otto Wesendonck. Staatliche Kunstmuseum, Leipzig.

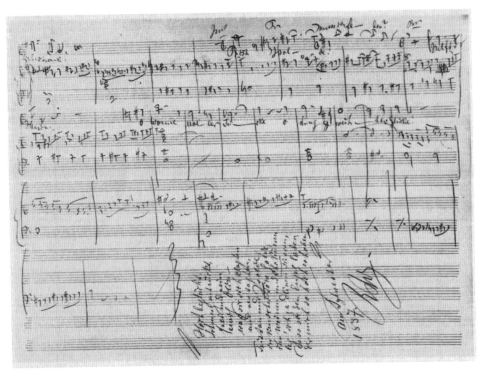

Illustration 19. Last page of the composition draft of *Tristan*, given to Mathilde Wesendonck on December 31, 1857, with the dedication: "Blessed, / Rescued from torment, free and pure, / Yours forever, / The laments and renunciations of Tristan and Isolde,/ in chaste golden language and sound, / Their tears and their kisses/ All that I lay at your feet/ To honor the angel that raised me to such heights." Archive of the Richard Wagner Foundation, Wahnfried, Bayreuth.

Illustration 20. Otto Wesendonck in 1852. Collection of Jürg Wille.

Illustration 21. View of Lake Zurich in 1857. The Wesendoncks' villa is on the left. Collection of Jürg Wille.

Illustration 22. First page of the composition draft for the Prelude of *Die Walküre*, with the inscription "G.s.M." (*Gesegnet sei Mathilde*: blessed be Mathilde) on the top left-hand side. Archive of the Richard Wagner Foundation, Wahnfried, Bayreuth.

Illustration 23. Mathilde Wesendonck at twenty-five. Stadtarchiv, Zürich.

Illustration 24. Mathilde Wesendonck near the end of her life. Portrait by Franz von Lenbach. Collection of Gideon von Redwitz.

On September 13 Mathilde gave birth to a son, Guido Otto. The Wesendoncks proposed that Wagner should be the godfather, but the musician refused on the grounds that it could "bring bad luck." Did he want to emphasize the distance between them? And his dependence on their financial aid—could that have been an obstacle? He would regret it three years later, however, on the child's death. But for the moment, Mathilde was there, superb and satisfied, in her magnificent apartments with a baby in her arms and the lovely little Myrrha at her side. Wagner felt like an emissary of the evil fairy in *Sleeping Beauty*, who brought a curse to the cradle of the young princess. Nevertheless, Otto said, "since you express a certain reserve that seems to come only from your friendship, I came to the conclusion that you would not like to accept the role that I mentioned. On such a subject, there must be no constraint, and your freedom of conscience must remain intact. So you will certainly understand that today I am going to ask an old friend of the family to be Guido's godfather; I am sure he will agree." The christening took place in Saint Paul's Church, where the "old friend of the family," Georg Grüber, from Lindau, as well as the godmother, Emily Loeschigk, a relative of Otto's associates, signed the register.

Otto prudently extended Wagner's absence from his household, by deciding on a trip to Paris for the whole family to visit the Exhibition Universelle before the end of 1855. Meanwhile, the family engaged French decorators and tapestry makers to finish the interior of their villa on the Green Hill.

≈

Settled in Paris with their children and servants, the Wesendoncks spent the winter of 1855–56 visiting first the exhibit in the Palais de l'Industrie near the Champs-Elysées, on which grounds the Grand Palais was later built. It was the first time that the France of the Second Empire had mounted such an impressive show of machinery, inventions, new industrial processes, and technologies of all sorts; twenty-seven categories of activity were represented. People had come from all over to see it, with reactions ranging from mistrust to admiration to surprise (some of the visitors were undoubtedly jealous).

Otto was of course particularly interested in new procedures concerning textiles; a first prize was awarded to Isaac Singer for the invention of his sewing machine. In the domain of artistic endeavors, a gold medal was attributed to a German, Theobald Boehm, the inventor of the modern flute.

As for Mathilde, she investigated trends in furnishing and interior decorating. But this was all simply on the outside. One would like to know what was happening inside her woman's heart. In a photograph taken in Paris at the time, she is seated in a velvet armchair wearing a rather sober dress with lace at the collar and cuffs and holding a fan. In this unaffected portrait, she seems to have forgotten to pose. The brightness of her heyday in Zurich was far in the past: was fatigue or sadness the cause of her blank, melancholy expression?

On January 11, 1856, Mathilde wrote to Minna from Paris about a house near their new villa; she wanted her husband to buy it as the Wagners' future refuge. In the meantime, she complained about her children's health:

> The changing weather makes life difficult for all of us, and the two little ones are ill. I had to keep Myrrha in bed since yesterday because she has a bad cough, and Guido is teething. He's running a fever, which makes him fussy, and he sulks all the time; that depresses me and makes me long for the moment when they will be out of danger. We cannot even dream of leaving before the beginning of next week because the children have to get accustomed again to fresh air. I hope their recovery will go faster than I think and that we will be able to return home with truly joyful anticipation. . . . Shopping in Paris is really exhausting and I would never have the heart to do it all over again.

The Wesendoncks finally returned to Zurich in March to find that Wagner had just finished the complete score of *Die Walküre*. At their reunion with him on the evening of the twentieth, they found him changed; exhausted and irritable, he had brought back from London a severe case of erysipelas. Nevertheless, he had worked on *Die Walküre* to the point of exhaustion—and all while his mind was constantly wandering off in the direction of *Tristan*. His friends brought him their congratulations at a bad time—Siegmund was dead, Wotan resigned to his fate, and Brünnhilde was sleeping on her fire-ringed rock. The well-meaning intentions of these wealthy, upper-class bourgeois triggered a violent reaction from the composer. Art is not to be bought with soft words, he told them—it is the result of suffering. Completely unnerved, "Wagner made a real scene in front of Otto Wesendonck . . . rather than expressing his gratitude, he said Otto would have done more good if he had increased [Wagner's] monthly pension."[7] "I expressed myself with such bitterness on this manner of appreciating my work," wrote Wagner later in *My Life*, "that my poor visitors, wounded and amazed, hurried to leave."

Indeed, how could these people understand that the suffering that Richard was speaking of was nothing more than what he had just described, that of the god separating himself from his beloved daughter in the third act of *Die Walküre*, and that this separation was a prefiguration of the inevitable renunciation of his love for Mathilde Wesendonck? The proof that it was Brünnhilde-Mathilde whom Wotan-Richard was renouncing is heard in the music at the peak of Wotan's "Lebwohl" (Farewell): this love theme between father and daughter, followed by the one in the first act of *Die Walküre*, would be quoted literally in the last measures of *Tristan*.

His "bitterness on this manner of appreciating my work" means, then, that behind the veil of appearances, of current affairs, Wagner was reproaching his visitors for not understanding what he could not say to them. For this to have qualified as a "scene," Richard must have said many more unpleasant things, but thanks to the tact shown by Minna, whose affection had been won by the gift from Mathilde of the little dog, the superficial explanations necessary for the recovery of good relations followed shortly. To excuse himself, Wagner went back to the subject of his "business" with Otto. In July 1856, while being treated by a Dr. Vaillant in Mornex, near Geneva, he wrote to Wesendonck:

You feel hurt when people think of you as a businessman, and it hurts me when you don't want to recognize my business sense. Believe me, I know how to count too, but I have unfortunately never had anything to add up—only so many problems that you shouldn't hold it against me if I make a mistake for once. If you gave me to add together the agreeable things that happen to you from time to time, you would be surprised by my precision. Besides, when you are treated as a businessman and, with a heart full of gratitude and friendliness, only the other part of your self is recognized, you become withdrawn and upset. I'm not talking about the last incident of this kind that took place between us; in that case, you were right to be troubled by an error of mine, an error which became clear to me later on. It is for that reason that in my last letter, I seized the opportunity to make you understand that I had seen it. Also, on how many other occasions did you avoid my friendliness, as if you were in a hurry to get away, as if it frightened you? Isn't it so? And now, it is you who says I do you wrong by my wanting to see in you as a businessman.

This is all that remains of the aforementioned explanatory correspondence between the two men. But we can guess that Otto was on the defensive. He aspired no doubt to be valued by the musician for something beyond his money, at least to reinforce his own image in the eyes of his wife. Richard could not care less about the husband's sense of inferiority when it came to matters of art; rather, he was reacting against Otto's lessons in financial responsibility. The quarrel did not go beyond the phase of simple vexation, however, thanks to Otto's open-mindedness, as well as his fascination with Wagner's genius. Thus the relative serenity of their former relations was restored.

Wagner chose to forget these day-to-day incidents. At home he had to cope with constant bickering with his wife, which Minna's friends only aggravated. Since September he had been working on the composition draft of the first act of *Siegfried*. Besides his health problems, his quarrels, and other exasperations, living in the Zeltweg became unbearable. Mathilde wrote that in their immediate surroundings in the Escher houses, there were no fewer than five pianists and a flutist who practiced daily. Moreover, on the other side of the street, a blacksmith hammered on his anvil so relentlessly that Wagner was forced to make a pact with him: in the morning, while the musician was composing, he would refrain from pounding with his noisy tools. No doubt, added Mathilde, that the circumstances led to the composition of Siegfried's Forging Song.[8]

Wagner opened up to Liszt about his distress: "I'm finished, and I will not be able to continue working unless I find another more appropriate lodging, that is, a little house for me alone, one with a garden, far away from any kind of noise, especially this accursed piano playing, which follows me everywhere, even here;[9] that is what has unnerved me to the extent that, every time I think about it, I don't even feel like working anymore. For the past four years I have tried to make that dream come true. I cannot do it unless I manage to buy the land and build the house myself."

But his publisher, Hermann Härtel, refused to advance him any money for his *Ring* cycle.

Even in Zurich, everybody but the Wesendoncks had turned their backs on him: "My stay here has become very difficult to bear and humiliating because of some intimate social relations that reign in my very own household, without my being capable of giving them *my* own direction. I must admit that here nothing pleases me. Today I could very well abandon Zurich as coldly as I did Dresden earlier."

After Liszt's recent appeal to the Grand Duke, Wagner hoped to settle eventually in Weimar, as he told Otto Wesendonck at the end of August. But this project failed, and to his friends Richard could only give vent to his bitterness: "I create a work of art and the estimated value that the buyer[10] of my work is willing to give me is not even enough to feed the artist during the time of his creation! This is the result of all the glory and success I have achieved up till now!"[11]

However, Otto decided to substitute himself for Härtel: he offered Wagner funds equivalent to the requested advance, to be deducted from the future sale of the *Ring*. Wagner expressed his gratitude in his own way: "You want therefore to replace as much as possible, 'between us,' music publishers and princes? Oh, my God! If I were in your situation . . . I would do the same, for it is more pleasant to give than to receive. . . . I hardly want to thank you for your good proposal, for I am convinced that the feeling you must have in order for you to make such an offer must be a joy that itself encompasses greater compensation than all possible forms of gratitude. . . . If one day I should play a role in the history of art, you would surely not be less famous for it."

On August 11, Wagner asked Mathilde to speak to a Frau Bodmer, owner of a house in Seefeld, near Zurich, since he wished to rent it "for the rest of my life or perhaps for a period of ten years." But this house had long been occupied, and his request bore no fruit.

To these last friends of his, the Wesendoncks, Wagner made a desperate appeal: "From my troublesome, irritating, and tormented hearth, on which everything hurts and imprisons me, I glance at the world around me, and the more I seek to focus on the place where I should find peace and calm, the more it seems to grow strange to me. . . . I see in front of me only a terribly agitated desert with distorted faces sniggering at me, and if I manage to find some people with a trace of sympathy, they are usually accompanied by the shrugging shoulders of powerlessness. Is it possible by some miracle to see in you both power and sympathy?"

Mathilde was deeply touched, and Otto took action. On August 18 they spent the day with Richard in Bern. Otto was thinking of buying the future scores of the *Ring*, and Mathilde was encouraging Wagner to continue composing *Siegfried*.

On October 13 Wagner's friend Franz Liszt arrived for a long-awaited visit with Caroline zu Sayn-Wittgenstein and her daughter Marie. They checked into the Baur au Lac, and social life in Zurich took on a new and unexpected brilliance. For Liszt's forty-fifth birthday Wagner organized a memorable performance of the first act and one scene of the second act of *Die Walküre*. The Wesendoncks, the Willes, Sayn-Wittgenstein, the Herweghs, and others attended. Emilie Heim sang Sieglinde, Wagner sang all the men's roles, and Liszt played the orchestral score on the piano. A banquet followed during which "the conversation turned to Heinrich Heine, on whom Liszt expressed erroneous opinions. Frau Wesendonck having asked Liszt if Heine's name would be one day engraved in the Temple of Immortality, the pianist retorted sharply, 'Yes, but with mud,' an answer that, of course, created a certain sensation."[12]

On November 4 Otto took his whole family and household to Rome for the winter months to enjoy the temperate climate of the Eternal City. It was necessary for Mathilde's health, since she was expecting another child. They settled in the quarter where many foreigners stayed, near the Piazza di Spagna. Wagner, completely absorbed in his creative work, pursued his monologue with his friends through their correspondence to tell them everything he did, thought, and felt. Otto was reassured by the friendly tone in their relations, which apparently hid Richard and Mathilde's amorous interest in each other.

Mathilde was devoted to her children, often telling them stories that she wrote down later in a collection of fairy tales. From her pen, these traditional tales took on a more personal aspect that could seem somewhat strange. In the story of Little Red Riding Hood, for example, the character of the wolf is humorous and original. He seems to borrow the comical language expressed by Wagner in his letters on good days. Mathilde also wrote on the Siegfried of the Nibelung saga with some irony and turned it into a game for her children.

In Rome, the Italian sunshine lightened up the theatrical scenery of monuments and warmed the winter days. The Wesendoncks visited the museums and the churches; they strolled in the streets and enjoyed the *dolce vita*.

However, amidst all the calm and wealth of her situation, Mathilde was certainly thinking of Richard back in Zurich, living in destitution. In the news, an alarming threat was being leveled by the kingdom of Prussia, which wanted to reaffirm its hereditary rights to the Swiss canton of Neuchâtel. The situation presented a terrible dilemma for Wagner: if the Prussians decided to invade the Swiss territory, he would have to run for his life once more from the advancing army of his own compatriots. However, nothing came of it. Mathilde thought of their beautiful, brand-new villa, about to open its doors to her and her family while the genius of her heart was living in poor lodgings.

"He only needs a quiet little house with a garden," she insisted when discussing the matter with Otto.

Wesendonck remembered that a few years earlier, when going through the Sihl Valley on the way back with Wagner from one of their mountain excursions, the musician had shown him a ravishing site in Enge, just across Lake Zurich, with a little house where he would have liked to live. At the time Otto remarked offhandedly that if he bought the land around it, he would give Wagner the plot he wanted. The whole property in Enge indeed later became Otto's, but without the house Wagner wanted, which belonged to a certain Wilhelm Widmann. Now the house was for sale, but Wesendonck hesitated to buy it, preferring to see Wagner a little further away from him and his family. However, in February 1857 he found out that his procrastination had cost him the small property next to his: it had been acquired by a medical doctor, Ludwig Binswanger, a specialist in mental illness who intended to create an asylum for his patients. Otto, dismayed by this prospect, quickly gave an order to buy the land and the house on it, at any price.

Wesendonck, in spite of everything, wanted to please his wife. He decided then that this "asylum" would be Wagner's. So the deal was made. Mathilde had assured Minna for several months that the transaction was in the works—apparently it took her quite a while to obtain her husband's consent. Now it was done, and Mathilde could describe to Minna the inside of the house and its garden. For the name of the new house, they let Richard decide: "We shall celebrate its inauguration together!" And she gave her blessing to the peaceful haven she anticipated for Richard and his wife: "May this little house become a true asylum of peace and friendship, a sanctuary amidst a world of envy, hatred, and jealousy, a sure refuge from worry and distress on this earth! On this house I want to pronounce such words of blessing that only beauty, kindness, and love may live in it, so that the rest and peace of its inhabitants will never be troubled!"

Otto in turn informed Wagner that he would rent him the house and the garden for one thousand francs a year. Two thousand francs had just come into his hands as the manager of Wagner's financial affairs, and Wesendonck considered it two years' rent in advance. Wagner could therefore see himself as completely independent.

Wagner replied to the news with boundless gratitude:

Do you want to know how I received the heaven-sent news today concerning the wonderful solution you decided upon? I felt within myself a deep, deep peace. . . . Very dear friend, up to now I have never had such an impression. Such a profound and benevolent friendship has never before come into my life, and what I felt was not so much for the property acquired as for this heartfelt warmth that your friendship gave me, this certainty of being supported that suddenly delivered me from the worry and the weight of all burdens. Oh, dear and excellent people! What can I say? Like a miracle everything has suddenly changed around me! All my hesitations have come to an end. I now know where to find root; I know where I can create, produce, and find consolation, strength, rest, and satisfaction for my thirst; now, with a lightened heart, I can cope with all the vicissitudes of my artistic career, all my efforts, all my fatigue: for I know where to look for the tranquility and simplicity within the most faithful, the most touching affection. Oh, dear children! In exchange I want you to be proud of me, and certainly you will be! For I belong to you for life, and my success, my serenity, my production will give me happiness: I will cultivate and treasure what I have done so that you also may obtain joy from it!

II

Pygmalion's Kiss

In 1857 the construction of the Wesendoncks' villa was finally complete. To the people of Zurich it was an event no less momentous than the building of Valhalla had been for the giants and dwarves of the Nibelung legend. Everything, even in the style of the house, seemed unusual in the context of the bucolic architecture that bordered the lake. The new palazzo, set atop a hill on the outskirts of the city, gave a vivid impression of domination, not only from a geographic point of view, but also with a suggestion of triumphalism.

The year before the local inhabitants had had reason to be amazed by the creation of the future park and surroundings. Theodor Froebel, a landscape gardener from Seefeld, had been hired by Otto Wesendonck to supervise the transplanting of some sixty-year-old hardwoods and pines near the Paradeplatz in the center of Zurich, in the middle of a building site, to the suburb of Enge. Other coniferous species were planted next to them—*Picea morinda* and *Picea orientalis*—as well as a beautiful variety of red beech, its heavy, twisted branches casting shadows over the lawn. Willow, cedar, and chestnut trees were scattered here and there around the grounds, and an allée lined with elm trees descended the hill to the lake. In front of the windows of the main drawing room, some distance down the path, a circular pond had been put in.

The romantic authors and poets of the eighteenth and nineteenth centuries in Germany had inaugurated the worship of nature. How Mathilde loved to indulge herself in the lush greenery of her walks! She did not have to wait for Wagner to express her admiration for the lovely plants to whom the poets granted a soul. But under the musician's influence, only a few months later she would write one of her most beautiful poems, which was set to music by Wagner:

High-arching leafy crowns,
Canopies of emerald,
You children of distant lands,
Tell me, why do you lament?

Silently you incline your branches,
Tracing signs in the air,

And, mute witness to your sorrows,
A sweet perfume rises.[1]

From 1855 on, before actually even moving into their new home, the Wesendoncks were preoccupied with their park and the care needed to create a paradisiacal space. In August 1856 Wagner reassured them in a letter about the problem of the summer drought: "I have been informed by my wife of your worries regarding the effect of a persistent heat wave on your garden's painstaking plantings; yesterday, on visiting your lovely estate, I was able to ascertain that they had not suffered at all, and I promised your gardener I would reassure you of the fine results of his care. Everything is perfectly kept, and your beautiful flowers and your shrubs were for me a delight."

~

Their new residence was called neither Hochwyl nor Wesenheim; Mathilde named it Wahlheim, "house of my choice." This came naturally from her readings of Goethe, in particular from a description in *Werther*: "Wahlheim is pleasantly situated about one hour from the city, at the top of a hill. When descending the path to the village, in one glance one can take in the whole valley."

In the house, everything was planned for receiving guests. Visitors' carriages drove up under a colonnaded porte cochere. Then, upon exiting the rig, they would enter the first hall through a glass door and find a winter garden with exotic plants and palms under a glass ceiling. Only a few steps up was the grand hall, vast enough to allow the Wesendoncks to organize concerts and recitals for their friends and acquaintances.

Several rooms opened onto this large entrance: a second winter garden; the main drawing room, with its rosewood furniture and armchairs upholstered in dark red silk that gleamed in the evening under the crystal chandeliers; and the library, which was Otto's domain. The predominant overall style was a free interpretation of the nineteenth century influenced by the Italian Renaissance, alternating with what is nowadays called Victorian rococo.

The main hall was a square in the center of the house, as in ancient Roman villas, and onto it opened the dining room, with a half-moon-shaped terrace that provided a splendid view of Lake Zurich and the city. The Wesendoncks had invited Parisian decorators to create red and blue stucco according to a very fashionable technique utilized in France during the Second Empire.

The north wing, on the garden side, had a room for billiards; and on the courtyard side were the kitchen, pantries, and laundry facilities. A heating system blew hot air through a distribution of vents.

After a succession of interconnecting rooms on the main floor, a spacious staircase led to the first landing. "The pride of the house," wrote Wagner in *My Life*, "was a large and elegant hall decorated with Parisian stucco." The musician noted it also for its acoustics—he conducted several concerts there.

Upstairs, in the long room on the garden side, was a gallery with Otto's paintings by Italian and Flemish masters. Mathilde would spend long hours in this room, seated near the grand piano where Richard would play the music he had composed that day. On the balcony in front of the three large windows, just beside the colonnade, Mathilde posed in 1860 for her portrait by Johann Conrad Dorner.

In the middle of the façade overlooking the city, the master bedroom was furnished in a heavy and imposing style. The other rooms in the north wing were those of the children. The servants' accommodations were on the floor above.

Eliza Wille has left us her own vivid description of the Wesendoncks' villa:

In those days, life seemed to be transformed for all those who met in that beautiful villa at the top of the Green Hill, not far from Wagner's little house. Wealth, all the refinements of elegance, and good taste made life into something poetic. The master of the house, with inexhaustible generosity and sympathy, made an effort to succeed in whatever he was interested in, and he admired immensely the extraordinary man that destiny had placed in their path. The young mistress, a woman of refined taste and with a propensity to idealism, was graceful and delicate; for her, the world and life itself were like the smooth surface of calm and majestic waters. . . . A loved and admired wife, a contented mother, she lived in adoration of all that art and the good things life had to offer. . . . The way the house was set up and the great wealth of its master made this beautiful place a hub, where many came together. It has remained a very dear memory to all those who were part of it.

Such was the ideal theatrical setting on which the protagonists of the second act of *Tristan* would soon appear. Several months before Otto Wesendonck had given orders to his architect, Zeugheer, concerning the restoration of the little house on the other side of the garden, formerly called Rosemont and renamed now Asyl.[2]

By the end of April Richard and Minna had moved into the new lodging that Otto had rented to them "for life." "For the past six days," wrote Wagner to Liszt on May 8, 1857,

we have been occupying the little country house that you know of, next to the villa W; it is thanks to the extreme kindness and affection of this family that I owe this happy change. . . . It took us quite some time to move into the little house, which is very nice and just what I wished for. . . . We settled here on a day of terrible weather and ice-cold wind; I stayed in good spirits only by reminding myself that this change was permanent. But now it is over and done; everything is put away and set up according to our needs. My study is arranged in the pedantic, elegant, and comfortable way that you know me for. I have my desk in front of the large window, from which I have a splendid view of the lake and the Alps. All is perfect calm and tranquility. A pretty garden, which is already growing well, gives me enough space for short walks and nice places to rest. At the same time it offers my wife some very pleasant occupations and prevents her from having bad thoughts about me.

Minna established her own domain on the first floor, a few steps up from the garden; the master worked on the second floor, next to a window that opened onto the veranda. There he composed all the poem and the score of the first act of *Tristan*, a few passages in the second act, the first draft in prose for *Parsifal*, and the second act of *Siegfried*, as well as the music for the *Wesendonck Lieder*. Just before he moved from the Zeltweg, on March 31, 1857, he finished the score for the first act of *Siegfried*. In the Asyl he composed standing up in front of his large music sheets, sitting down to rest from time to time on a chaise longue in the middle of the room. "When he was composing, he would sometimes pace back and forth, then go to the piano in the next room to try out a few isolated chords or musical phrases."[3] Then he would jot them down on the score.

In the attic, just under the roof and over Wagner's bedroom, a guest room was reserved for friends, such as the von Bülows. The walls were covered with canvas.[4]

Parsifal: *How fair seem the meadows today!*
Once I came upon magic flowers which twined
Their tainted tendrils about my head;
But never did I see such fresh and charming grass, blossoms, and flowers,
Nor did they smell so sweetly of youth or speak with such tender love to me.
Gurnemanz: *That is . . . the magic of Good Friday, my lord!*

In *My Life*, Wagner related his first days spent at the Asyl and how the idea for *Parsifal* came to him: "On Good Friday I woke up to beautiful sunshine pouring for the first time into our little house; the garden was growing greener, the birds were singing; at last I could sit on our balcony and enjoy the calm I had so yearned for. Filled with joy, I remembered suddenly that it was Good Friday and that once before I had already been struck by a solemn warning in the *Parzifal* of Wolfram. . . . With this idea in mind, I began to quickly outline a drama in three acts, and on the spot I sketched out some of the music."

This text, part and parcel of the Wagner legend, has been examined more objectively through the lens of history. Some of Wagner's biographers brought to light the fact that Good Friday in 1857 was on April 10, eighteen days before the Wagners moved into the Asyl. However, according to the notes the master took in what he called his *Annals*, he could have climbed up the Green Hill during the construction work and spent Good Friday just as he described. Nevertheless, some definitive explanations were given in Cosima's diary entry of April 22, 1879: there she notes that Wagner laughingly admitted that "it was not Good Friday. It was a day like any other, but there was an atmosphere prevailing over nature such that I said to myself, it should have been Good Friday."

In any case, it was here, in the aura of Mathilde Wesendonck, that Richard Wagner conceived of his *Parsifal*, near the one he loved, the one woman who let her spirit be modeled by him so that he could create his work.

∾

Before moving into their new villa, and while the craftsmen were putting on the finishing touches, Mathilde, still in her apartments at the Baur au Lac, gave birth on April 18 to another son, Karl. Six months later, on October 19, the child was baptized at Saint Peter's Church in Zurich. Both families were represented; grandfather Karl Luckemeyer was the godfather. Some friends came to the ceremony to congratulate the parents, but others were there mostly out of curiosity. On every occasion Mathilde's reactions were observed, and tongues were ready to wag at the sight of Wagner in the crowd. One witness, a young man by the name of Robert von Hornstein, seemed more interested in speculating about Richard and Mathilde than in the liturgy of baptism: "I was standing next to Wagner in back of the church. He was in bad spirits. All of a sudden, he murmured in a low voice, 'It's like attending one's own execution!'" This remark sounded strange to Hornstein, who concluded that "it did not suggest any kind of intimate relationship." Should someone have explained to the young man what jealousy could mean to a genius in love?

May brought fine weather as Mathilde recovered from childbirth. Otto tried his best to entertain her. But what better distraction could Zurich offer than a visit to Wagner? The composer invited all his friends to come and see his new house. Even before moving into their new villa, the Wesendoncks would spend evenings at Wagner's Asyl. On July 1 they made the acquaintance of Edward Devrient, Wagner's old friend from Dresden, famous for his acting and playwriting and now director of the theater in Karlsruhe. Devrient would read passages of Shakespeare for the guests one day; the next, extracts from Goethe's *Faust*. Another member of Wagner's circle of friends was Gottfried Semper, who had returned from London one year before to accept his post as a professor at the Zurich Polytechnic Institute. The Swiss writer Gottfried Keller, author of *Der grüne Heinrich* (Green Henry), had also returned from his studies in Berlin. Other guests included Robert Franz, a musician and song composer, and Richard Pohl, an orchestra conductor and musicologist from Weimar. All were admirers of Wagner, who, as usual, would ramble on about whatever came to mind, such as his *Tristan* project, or another idea for the never-completed Buddhist drama "The Victors." He would play passages for them from *Die Walküre* and spoke about the rest of the *Ring* or *Parsifal*.

All these friends who watched the genius before them, comfortably set up in his Asyl, go suddenly from despondency to elation could not help noticing how Mathilde gazed at him and the change in his attitude that her presence seemed to bring about. The two spoke to each other in the musical tones of singers in a love duet, and Richard's eyes sparkled when she was near him.

Richard Pohl noted that if Minna appeared "pale and insignificant, a little homely and prematurely old looking," Mathilde on the other hand embodied "feminine elegance and the idea of poetry." And even before that Liszt had described Mathilde as an "ambassador of the ideal."

Minna, Mathilde . . .

When Hans von Bülow and his wife, Cosima, arrived in August, the group of the three Norns was complete and the catastrophe imminent.

~

On August 22, 1857, the Wesendoncks finally took possession of their sumptuous villa. They continued their social life with their friends, as well as those of Wagner. But among the good bourgeois families of Zurich, as well as in the little group of intellectuals, they were severely criticized. These cliques did not approve of people who changed their social status, defied social distinctions by their independence of mind and spirit, and remained indefinable. Outside of urban centers, where life was cosmopolitan, a sort of caste society maintained its principles—to each his own. That a bourgeois family should so familiarly rub shoulders with writers and artists was unusual. The intelligentsia also had a tendency to remain apart from society. The bourgeois were good for acting as sponsors for artists' basic needs. Wagner and Mathilde seemed a strange pair, and to withdraw, even discreetly, from established norms was a perilous exercise, as we shall soon see.

In Wahlheim, where discretion and show went paradoxically together, life did have a nouveau-riche flavor. Wagner was her master of music and philosophy, but Mathilde's education would have been incomplete without her study of foreign languages.

A highly cultivated professor of Italian came onto the scene: Francesco de Sanctis, age forty, originally from Naples and quite handsome, a refugee in Zurich, like Wagner, from his revolutionary activities in southern Italy. He had participated in uprisings in Calabria in 1848 and was arrested in Cosenza in 1850, where he spent two years in prison. When he was released, he went into exile first in Turin, where he gave courses at the university on Dante and studied the works of Giacomo Leopardi. By 1856 he was teaching at the Zurich Polytechnic Institute. But cultural life in the town was relatively limited. Since October de Sanctis had been in contact with the Herweghs (his wife was a fervent admirer of all things Italian), whom he had met at the home of a colleague, the philologist Hermann Köchly. Emma Herwegh wrote to Caroline zu Sayn-Wittgenstein that she was trying to help the professor get an engagement to give lectures in Berlin.

De Sanctis thus came into contact with the Wesendoncks and of course with Wagner, of whom he did not have a high opinion. In a letter to his friend Camillo Benso di Cavour, he described the composer as a *corrutore della musica* (corrupter of music): "I am now reading the great Schopenhauer, who claims his fame all over the world, and the great Wagner, the genius of the future, as he modestly puts it, despising the present, in which he is not understood. . . . Above all, these people are phonies."[5]

Toward the end of 1857 de Sanctis appeared on the Green Hill to instruct the beautiful Frau Wesendonck in Italian language and literature, to the great annoyance of her irascible and jealous neighbor. Along with the lessons, the *professore* also exerted his Latin charm on his refined and sensitive pupil. Unlike women of the south, a German woman would not confuse bantering flirtation with heartfelt love. But Mathilde did certainly play some subtle word games between Wagner, de Sanctis, and poor Otto. Richard complained about finding her all too often in her Italian books. Was he losing ground in Mathilde's eyes? In any case, he wrote:

"Since Herr and Frau Wesendonck have judged it appropriate to cool their relationship with us to the point that they no longer come to visit us in the evening without a formal invitation, we feel obliged to ask officially whether Herr and Frau Wesendonck might decide to surprise us today, or, if certain professors feel the need to impart their learning to Sir or Madam this very evening, may we await the surprise of their visit tomorrow?" This sarcastic note was accompanied by a musical phrase, a short theme from the first act of *Die Walküre* that Wagner exegetes call the Mitleid (Compassion) motive. Knowing how touchy de Sanctis was, Wagner later nicknamed him Herr von Heiligen (the German translation of de Sanctis). Mathilde was neither winning or losing at this banter. It was just a little calm before the storm. Several years later de Sanctis wrote to Mathilde from Naples, where the wars waged by Napoleon III had contributed to consolidating Italian unity. In response to her asking for a portrait of himself, the charming professor exclaimed: "I see you so high, so high, that it did not even come to my mind to place a portrait of myself before your gracious but slightly ironic smile."[6]

> *Happy lark, if you want to hatch your eggs,*
> *Build your own nest;*
> *As for me, to brood in tranquility,*
> *I cannot make the quiet haven,*
> *The quiet haven in wood and stone—*
> *Ah! Who wants to be my lark!*[7]

Beginning in August 1857 Wagner and Mathilde's neighborly relations took an intimate turn. Wagner would write little notes to Mathilde to tell her whether he had slept well or if he was running a fever, or even simply to ask what the weather would be that day. She would send him little gifts, presents that could also be accepted by Minna, but that Richard would interpret as he wished: "Thank you for the beautiful flowers! The old plant well preserved has kept all its beauty." Another time he wrote: "Here is the lamp shade, may it take on a tint of rose!" Then, finally: "Ah! The beautiful cushion! But too soft! As tired and heavy as my head may be when I am ill—at least at the time of my death, I would like to lay my head on it as comfortably as if I had the right to do so! You will set it up that way for me. Such is my last will and testament!"

Once his comfort was cozily established, Wagner went on to complain about his state of mind before talking about his work. "I have a heavy heart—although it's not the unique thing without which I would possess, as poor as I am, no refuge in this world. That unique thing!"— which, as we know, could be only love. Mathilde gave him material well-being and her heart; Otto gave him money. And yet it was not enough, for Mathilde had to be also the inspiration for his work: "And my dear Muse, does she still remain far away from me? In silence I waited for her visit; I didn't want to trouble her with my supplication. For the Muse, like love, can bring happiness when it desires to. Unfortunate is the man without love who wants to obtain in a violent way what is naturally spontaneous! Force will bring him nothing. How could love continue to be an inspiration if it yields to violence? And my dear Muse still remains far away from me!"

One day, he described to her his progress in composing the second act of *Siegfried*: "At first I found a melody that was impossible to adapt to the score; but I discovered the words in the last scene of *Siegfried*. A good sign! Yesterday the beginning of the second act was revealed to me, in particular the slumber of Fafner, in which I even found a humorous note. You will become acquainted with all that tomorrow when the lark comes to visit its nest."

And the lark flew to him. Every day they exchanged notes, gifts, looks. Wagner shared with Mathilde his daily reading of great authors. Absorbed as he was during this time by the subject of *Tristan*, that is where his diverse readings took him. And he had just discovered a Spanish playwright of the Golden Age, Pedro Calderón de la Barca, whose works had been translated into German by August Wilhelm von Schlegel, brother of Friedrich, the renowned author of *Lucinde*. He spoke about it all that winter of 1857–58: "Work, long walks despite the cold, and in the evening reading Calderón: such were my occupations, during which I hated being bothered."

A glance at the subjects treated by the Castilian poet shows his influence on Wagner: in the first act of *Tristan und Isolde*, a long debate unfolds concerning the princess of Ireland on the question of honor, a virtue dear to Calderón. "I am not far from placing this poet alone on the top," wrote Wagner to Liszt.

> He shows me what Spain is really like, . . . the character of the nation, so refined and passionate, is summed up by the concept of honor—and this honor, along with the most noble and terrible feelings, egotism and sublime abnegation, is, in a way, their second religion. The true nature of the world never appeared as clear, as brilliant, and more absolute, but also with more negative and fatal features. The striking portraits of the poet show the conflict between honor and profound human sympathy. Honor provoked the actions that the world considers and glorifies. Wounded sympathy has its refuge in a generous form of melancholy, almost unspoken, but all the more expressive, by which we distinguish honor and vanity in society. It is this comprehension, which could be called tragic, that Calderón establishes with marvelous precision.

In his *autos sacramentales* the Spanish poet presents one-act plays like those of Felix Lope de Vega, allegories that sparked Wagner's imagination. In *Life Is a Dream*, five characters— Power, Wisdom, Love, Intelligence, and Will—appear on the stage, after which the hero Sigismond exclaims: "You want me to dream once more of greatness that vanishes. . . . Consider me from now on as a man subject to his destiny. . . . I know now that life is but a dream. I know who you are and that you fool any man who falls asleep."

The symbolism in the *Ring* is also reflected in *The Great Theater of the World*, in which the passage from matter to spirit and the sobriety of sensuality are so many signs of Calderón's religious faith: "If life is nothing, it is beyond life we must look for truth."

If circumstances were right, his muse at his side, his head filled with the grandeur of Calderón, and his memory formed by Schopenhauer, romanticism, and the philosophical poetry of the ancient Persian poet Hafiz, it was due nevertheless to material considerations that Wagner decided to undertake his *Tristan*. The publisher Härtel having refused to publish his *Ring*, believing it impossible to represent on the stage, suggested that he write an opera with more reasonable dimensions. On June 28, 1857, Wagner wrote to Liszt: "I won't have to worry anymore because of Härtel, as I have finally renounced this enterprise of finishing my *Nibelungen*, for which I was being obstinate. I led my young Siegfried into the beautiful solitude of the forest; I left him there, under the linden tree, and I bade him farewell with tears of tenderness." On the orchestral draft of the second act, which he had begun in June, he noted: "*Tristan* already decided." And to Liszt again: "I have conceived of a project to compose immediately, in more modest proportions and in a way to facilitate the performance, *Tristan und Isolde*."

Above all, he needed money. He could not live forever on wild hopes. One proposition led him to a decision: "The emperor of Brazil has just invited me to visit him in Rio de Janeiro; I have been promised wonders. So if not in Weimar, I'll see you in Rio!!"

Dom Pedro II, the emperor of Brazil, was a Wagnerian, and Ernesto Ferreira França, an officer of the consulate in Dresden, asked the master if he could compose a work for his sovereign that would be sung in Italian (in Rio they always sang in Italian); he would be repaid in money, glory, celebrity, and perhaps with the construction of a festival theater (why not?). The best part is that Wagner was thinking seriously about the move, at least at the time he wrote to Liszt about it, though not without a certain touch of irony: "I am thinking about having a good Italian translation for this work, and to offer its premiere as an Italian opera at the theater in Rio de Janeiro. The emperor will probably have it preceded by a performance of *Tannhäuser*. I will dedicate it to Dom Pedro, who will soon be receiving copies of my three last operas." And while he recommended discretion on the subject to all his friends and correspondents, he spoke of it to everyone. However, in the end Brazil did not acquire this treasure, and *Tristan* would be born in the throes of the author's suffering and abandonment.

For the moment, there he was, the artist, ready to moor his little boat along the Irish coast, where the princess was waiting for him. Love was that "unique thing" without which his creative work was impossible.

At that moment, in August, the next wave of visitors to Wagner in the Asyl was to leave on the shore the third woman of the *tria fata*: Cosima Liszt, recently wedded to Hans von Bülow. Memorable evenings would unfold with Liszt's young pupil, who played the piano versions arranged by Karl Klindworth, and he sight-read the outlines of the recently drafted *Siegfried*. Wagner sang all the roles and remained oblivious to his audience: Minna the past, Mathilde the present, and Cosima the future were there to listen and be moved, like the three Norns representing the three destinies of man.

Minna had seen the genius's birth, Mathilde sparked his creative life, and Cosima would be at his side at the moment of death. Our mythical Oedipus was still at the time the unwary Wagner, an artist entirely absorbed in his art, surrounded in imagination perhaps by his mother and his sisters over in Leipzig when he was but a child. Experience showed him the futility of pulling too strongly on the cord these women had so diligently woven: after it broke everything went awry, as in *Götterdämmerung.*

We are told that Mathilde was "haughty and proud." That is the way in which Minna saw her: in her palace of marble, surrounded by her beautiful children, whereas she herself, sterile and unloved, was living in a little brick house. In *My Life,* Wagner mentioned only Cosima, "listening with her head bowed to one side, without a word. If she was asked to speak, she began to cry."

Behind them were the two husbands, Bülow the pupil of Liszt and King Marke. And this time it was Mathilde who was overwhelmed by the death of the lovers, so much so that the master had to console her by saying that it could not end any other way. Cosima, who remained stoic, agreed to the tragic ending and enjoyed the triumph of her own reserve. As for Minna, she understood nothing at all; she was drowning little by little in this ocean of passion, her jealousy pulling her to the depths like a millstone around her neck.

Wagner finished the poem of *Tristan* on September 18 and brought the last act as an offering to Mathilde.[8] She would have led him to a chair in front of the sofa and kissed him, saying, "Now I have nothing more to wish for." She wrote a poem herself saying how much she had aspired to this moment: "When the heart has no more desire." When she took him into her arms, the starry night reappeared, and a new star, close to Andromeda, was born. Are not the heavenly constellations the figures of great loves? Wagner wrote: "Your heart, your eyes, your lips were heaven to me. . . . I have the memory of being loved by you with such tenderness, and yet so modestly!"

Tristan: *Heart to heart,*
Lips to lips . . .
Isolde: *The sun is inside our hearts,*
The stars of ecstasy are shining joyfully.

"It was only at this wonderful moment," wrote Wagner one year later, "that I was really alive. You know how much I delighted in it. Not with agitation, anger, intoxication; but solemnly, feeling deeply comforted, liberated and with a gaze that plunged into eternity!" She then dove into an "ocean of suffering" to live this moment of infinity and said "I love you!" Like Tristan and Isolde in ecstasy, they were beyond desire. . . .

"My love for you," continued Wagner, "after this moment could no longer lose any of its fragrance, even an atom of it. . . . I clearly understood that this light would never be extinguished, that your love was my supreme good without which my existence would be a contradiction. Thank you, my beautiful angel, full of love!"

The maiden felt his kiss—
She blushed and trembled: when she raised her eyes
She saw her lover and heaven's light together.[9]

At the close of day Mathilde watched the lake grow dark, engulfing the last rays of twilight. On the balcony of the Wesendonck villa she reread the poem of *Tristan*. A little later, while everyone else was asleep, she came out to listen to the music of the night: the breeze was rustling through the green boughs as crickets sang in the dark.

Pygmalion's kiss was engraved forever on her heart. Remembering Goethe's poem, she murmured:

> *Stay, stay with me, sweet stranger, exquisite love,*
> *sweet and exquisite love,*
> *And abandon not my soul!*
> *Ah! That life I feel,*
> *I feel it for the first time.*[10]

The deafening wind was blowing from the sea of legends; Richard and Mathilde were running hand in hand over a vast spread of land, over the white sand on the beach of love before getting into their little barque. They then drifted slowly on the waves, as in a boat without a rudder, oblivious to the world around them, seeing nothing of the gray clouds piling high on the horizon.

But the storm would soon be upon them, for Isolde was awakening.

The Awakening

A year ago today we spent such a beautiful day together at the Willes'! It was the 'wonderful time'—we were celebrating the eighteenth of September," wrote Wagner from Venice on October 18, 1858. "Coming back from our walk in the hills, your husband offered his arm to Frau Wille; I was thus able to offer you mine. We spoke of Calderón. How well it suited at that moment! At home I immediately sat down at the new piano. I never realized myself how well I could play. . . . It was a magnificent, satisfying day. . . . Did you celebrate it today? Oh! At least that one time, sunny skies had to blossom for us like a flower. That instant has passed away, but the flower has remained; its perfume shall linger on forever in our souls."

This is how Richard Wagner reminded Mathilde Wesendonck of the last peaceful day in their relationship. At Mariafeld the dahlias had withered in the early frost and a few late roses were still shivering with cold on the trellis of the veranda. The vegetation was still dark, dense, and green. Excursions were limited, as afternoons were short. At sunset a thick mist would rise from the lake, enveloping all things as if to tuck them into bed.

On October 19, on the opposite shore of Lake Zurich, on the occasion of the infant Karl Wesendonck's christening, Mathilde was entertaining her family from Düsseldorf. And despite these domestic preoccupations, their troublesome neighbor, the musician living in his red-brick house christened Asyl, would not let himself be forgotten. Wagner kept the young woman informed of every step in the musical composition of *Tristan*, Act I, begun on October 1. On that very day, he wrote a humorous "business" note to Otto, accompanied by his rent:

Dear Friend,

   Here is my first payment for the rent. In a short while, I hope to pay the full sum; perhaps it won't be long. Then you will be able to say:

   Hey! Lord Tristan,
   How well he pays his tribute.
   And to Mathilde:
   The wound inflicted by Morold,
   I am restoring it
   So that he may come back to life.
   I managed this passage well today—I must make you listen to it.

Richard and Mathilde were no doubt playing the main roles in Wagner's new drama, like children imitating grown-ups. In the late afternoon, when he entered the music room at Wahlheim, he would interpret his part as a musician, as a performing artist, but his soul was entirely involved in his hero's plight. Frau Wesendonck, like a conscientious schoolgirl, would be attentive to the master's teaching. But the composer's presence disposed her rather to identify herself with the heroine of the legend. Whenever the musician would start to perform, the triteness of their daily lives would disappear, leaving both of them in a universe of isolated wonder from which material demands vanished. Only a thin veil of appearances separated them from one another, like the hanging tapestry dividing the stage in Act I of *Tristan*, to screen King Marke's nephew from the princess of Ireland.

To underline the double personalities of their heroes, authors of classical literature would create minor characters such as the confidant, who was allowed to express the main protagonist's hidden thoughts—thus Pyrrhus and Phoenix, Andromaque and Céphise, Tristan and Kurwenal, Isolde and Brangäne. In the real world, they are two sides of a single person, but when the doubles are face to face, as in a mirror of action, a crisis may arise.

Besides the fact that they were now near neighbors, outside circumstances such as international events were indirectly responsible for plunging Richard and Mathilde into the passionate phase of their love affair.

Since 1860 the United States of America had been an industrial nation. The California Gold Rush had created a shift of population and investments from east to west. Parallel to this development, a new way of life became evident. And the abolition of slavery was a crucial issue. The industrialized North employed paid hands or indentured servants, while the rural South, with its cotton and tobacco plantations, used black slaves. As western territories became states, the question arose of whether these new members of the union would be slave or free. And conflict between the North and the South jeopardized the stability of the young United States.

In 1857 the question of jurisdiction over emancipated slaves inflamed Congress. Certain states threatened to secede from the union. The prospect of a civil war and a general gloom cast over society reached the world of business, banks suspended their cash payments, prices collapsed, and commercial transactions ceased. In the cities of the North, workers took to the streets crying for "bread or blood!"[1] Panic reached the banks in New York by October. The crisis would extend to the financial hubs of Europe. Unemployment was bound to weigh down on the major industries in France, England, and Germany.

In November the American stock exchange fell into a serious depression. From New York, Hugo Wesendonck, a former revolutionary who had fled the German Confederation in 1848, was sending distress signals to his brother Otto, the chief shareholder of their common business venture in silks. In *My Life* Wagner mentioned this critical period, which almost ruined the Wesendonck family: "I was interested at that time in the crisis of the American money market . . . the consequences of which, during a few fateful weeks, threatened to endanger the whole of my friend Wesendonck's fortune. I remember that the impending catastrophe was borne with great dignity by those who were likely to be its victims; still, the possibility of having to sell their house, their grounds, and their horses cast an unavoidable gloom over our evening meetings; and after a while, Wesendonck went away to make arrangements with various foreign bankers."

Wesendonck, in fact, had to leave in great haste for the United States. He and his brother Hugo managed to save their textile business by reinvesting in a new venture in life insurance, which was to become the Germania Life Insurance Company of America, one of the most important enterprises at the time. As it turned out, Otto emerged from his financial troubles even wealthier than before.

Meanwhile, at the Wesendonck villa in Zurich, as at Wagner's Asyl, the chief protagonists were floating high above the necessities of life. During Otto's absence, Wagner explains in *My Life*, he continued to spend his mornings at home composing *Tristan*, and in the evening they "used to read Calderón." In this way the musical score for Act I was composed and the Prelude outlined.

"The outburst of passion between Tristan and Isolde is a success! I'm absolutely delighted," wrote Richard to Mathilde. King Marke had gone hunting; the ecstasy of Act II could begin. Wagner indicated the scenery: "A garden with tall trees before Isolde's apartments. It is a warm summer night. Hunting horns can be heard in the distance."

True life can easily be transposed into poetic situations through the effect of symbols, a favorite device of the German romantics who greatly inspired Wagner. Lovers have a tendency to see themselves as legendary or historical characters so as to ensure the permanent state of their emotions. Mathilde Wesendonck was at once Isolde and Brangäne, the idealistic mistress and the pragmatic servant. As for Richard Wagner, his split-personality tendencies were well-known. He therefore had no difficulty in assuming the role as the lover Tristan and, at the same time, the practical of Kurwenal.

As in Act II of *Tristan*, Mathilde waited for the night to set in—not necessarily the physical absence of day, but at last the moment when her beloved would rush into her dream world, so to speak, every day, in the morning or the evening, in her own music room. Letters from America brought more or less alarming news, and the distant rumor of financial worries sounded vaguely in her ears like the hunting horns in the forest. Before extinguishing the burning torch that would give Tristan his cue to come to her, a struggle arose from her dual nature; when the scrupulous Mathilde-Brangäne lost, the passionate Mathilde-Isolde ran over to the red-brick house where, on the first floor, the genius of her soul was carving out their love in sound. Minna, fuming with rage and jealousy, watched like Melot from the ground floor as the mock princess mounted the stairway to join her impossible lover, unnoticing and drunk from the philter of the music.

Toward the end of November, while Otto remained far away in every respect, Mathilde began writing poems. The first one, "Der Engel" (The Angel) gives us an idea of the intense passion and high ideals with which the young woman tried to sublimate her love for Richard, whom she presents as another Lohengrin:

In the early days of my childhood,
Often I was told of angels
Who exchange the sublime delights of heaven
For the light of day.
And thus, when anxiously a heart
Languishes in sorrow from the world concealed,
When it longs to bleed to death
And dissolves in floods of tears,
When in prayer it fervently begs for redemption,
Then will the angel come down
And raise it gently toward heaven.
Yes, for me also an angel wafted down
And on its shining wings
Now guides my spirit heavenward
Far away from any grief.[2]

Her passion for Wagner was the reason for that heart languishing in sorrow, concealed from the world and longing "to bleed to death and dissolve in floods of tears," fervently begging for redemption.

This brief description of their states of mind is so true to reality that on November 10, practically by return mail, Wagner composed the music for the first of the five *Wesendonck Lieder*, in one draft. The ascending musical phrase at the end of the piece denotes the conclusion to Mathilde's beautiful poem: "And on shining wings, it now guides my spirit heavenwards, far away from any grief."

Ideas in a well-defined melodic form are constantly repeated more or less unconsciously in Wagner's music, so the leitmotif is thus a natural component of his art. In the song "The Angel," composed in one sitting, the musician repeats a constant motif of his relationship with Mathilde. In the midst of luminous chords in the style of *Lohengrin*, a dark and solemn phrase from *Die Walküre*—in which Brünnhilde announces Siegmund's imminent death—seeps into the musical text, as it did so also in the sonata Wagner wrote for Mathilde in 1853. The composer's mental association between love and death, eros and thanatos, and his passion for Mathilde Wesendonck are thus revealed.

Two versions of this song were written, with two different endings. Less than a week later, at the beginning of December, Mathilde wrote another poem, "Träume" (Dreams):

Tell me what wonderful dreams
Are embracing my senses,
That have not like fleeting foam
Faded away into desolate nothingness.
Dreams which by the hour,

By the day, blossom more beautifully,
And with their heavenly message
Move blissfully through the mind.
Dreams which like sublime rays
Sink into the soul,
To paint there an eternal picture:
All-forgetting remembrance!
Dreams, as when the sun of spring
Kisses the blossoms out of the snow,
That, to never-imagined bliss,
are greeted by the new day,
They grow, they blossom,
In dreaming they give off their scent,
Then softly die away into your breast
And sink into the tomb.

"Life is but a dream," said Calderón, proclaiming his bitterness: "You want me to dream once more of greatness that does not last . . . pomp and glory, ready to disappear in a whisper No! It must not be so . . . Life is but a dream!"

In the evening Wagner read these diatribes on mad illusions that strike human souls blind. But Mathilde preferred her dreams to reality, because her love for Richard was present in them—dreams that "grow" and "blossom," that "in dreaming . . . give off their scent." In the finale of Wagner's lyrical poem known as the "Liebestod," she had read Isolde's vision: "Are they waves of gentle breezes?" These dreams are the food of lovers, short-lived flowers that fade and finally "sink into the tomb."

On December 4 Wagner outlined the music for this song, and the definitive version was composed the next day. In later years, he put all these emotions aside and considered this lied officially as a study for *Tristan und Isolde*. In fact, it introduces, in a simplified rhythmic form, one of the principal themes of the love duet in Act II.

During these winter days of 1857, the music of ecstasy and the poetry of rapture were indeed drowning out the sound of the hunting horns. Was not America far away across the ocean? In Zurich snow laid a white shroud over the countryside, and the beautiful lawn of the Wesendonck mansion was now scattered with a myriad of diamonds when, at night, a moonbeam lingered upon the branches of the barren trees. Like Shakespeare's Juliet, Mathilde could confess to her lover: "Thou knowest the mask of night is on my face." He might swear by the moon that his love was faithful, everlasting. But "O swear not by the moon, th' inconstant moon."

Aloft upon the pulsations of song, the silver waves of music rolled on, delicately enfolding the spirit of those who are doomed to love. *Träume . . .*

She bestowed on him her heart's treasure, her soul—claimed forever. Wearing spiritual gems and flowers like Solomon's beloved, she exclaimed:

My bounty is as boundless as the sea,
My love as deep: the more I give to thee,
The more I have, for both are infinite.

Romeo: *O blessed, blessed night! I am afraid,*
Being in night, all this is but a dream.

But Mathilde's Brangäne was watching, too, and would not let her completely forget her situation; nor would Richard's Kurwenal. So the gold of their "burning desire" was liquefied by the intense heat of the sun and cast into the mold of art. The music and poetry of the *Wesendonck Lieder* express the impossible union in this world between Richard Wagner and Mathilde Wesendonck. Only through the composer's genius was it brought to the highest degree of universality.

Around the middle of December Mathilde brought him a new poem, "Torment":

Sun, you weep every evening
Until your lovely eyes are red,
When, bathing in the sea,
You are o'ertaken by your early death;

But you rise again in your old splendor,
The aureole of the dark world;
Fresh awakened in the morning
Like a proud and conquering hero!

Ah, then why should I complain,
Why should my heart be so heavy,
If the sun itself must despair,
If the sun itself must go down?

And if only death gives birth to life,
If only torment brings bliss,
Then how thankful I am that Nature
Has given me such torment.[3]

The plaintive cry of "Torment" announced the beginning of the real resignation that both of them knew to be inevitable: "death gives birth to life," and "only torment brings bliss." It would be finally the sacrifice of their mutual attraction that would bring their love to attain this fulfillment, as invisible as the sounds of music.

Wagner wrote the music for this lied on December 17, but he was still hesitating about the end, which he redid three times. The first version ended somewhat abruptly with three measures in G major. Because he composed very quickly, it was only in rereading his work that he noticed there were errors that had to be corrected. After a second try, he sent it to Mathilde with a note reading: "It must always become more beautiful! After spending a good, comforting night, my first thought was about this amended conclusion. We shall see if it pleases Frau Calderón when I play it for her in the bass."

Then he rewrote a third and final conclusion resembling the second but with a tighter rhythm. At the bottom of the page, he added: "Here's another ending. It must always be more beautiful."

We do not know whether, during this month of December, it was cold or warm outside, or if it rained or snowed. In the morning, as soon as it was light, Mathilde wrapped herself up in her cape and rushed over the short distance that kept her away from Richard, to be engulfed in "her night." Arriving at the Asyl, she would ask the servant not to bother Frau Wagner and climb up the staircase with a pounding heart and wings on her heels, slipping silently into the room where the master was at work.

In Act II of *Tristan* Isolde feels herself to be a prisoner of the day. From the window at the Asyl Mathilde could see her magnificent villa from afar, like an exotic bird looking at its gilded cage. Tristan says that the day "has torn me away from Isolde, who resembles the sun, swathed in honor and blinding light!" Wagner saw Mathilde in her distinction and also in her social standing, which upheld her with its moralizing principles and conventional codes of marriage. Isolde, for her part, reproaches Tristan for being "the proud slave of day." She wants to take him with her into the night, "there where my heart has promised me the end of my illusions" (for life is but a dream . . .) to "delight with you in eternal love."

> *Love is strong as death . . .*
> *Its flashes are flashes of fire,*
> *The very flame of the Lord.*

> Tristan: *Never to awaken . . .*
> Isolde: *But the day must awaken Tristan.*
> Tristan: *Let the day vanish before death.*

Time flies like the sand dragged away from underfoot when the tide pulls the waves out to the open sea. On December 23, Mathilde's twenty-third birthday, Wagner organized a little concert for her in the hall of the Wesendoncks' villa. Eighteen musicians from the city of Zurich, along with a violin soloist, performed his lied "Träume," which he had just finished and orchestrated for the occasion. Finally, on December 31, for New Year's Eve, he presented Mathilde with the composition outline for the first act of *Tristan* with this dedication:

Blessed,
Torn away from torment,
Free and pure,
Yours forever—
The laments and renouncements of Tristan and Isolde
In the chaste, golden language of sound,
Their tears and their kisses,
I lay all that at your feet
So that they should celebrate the angel
Who carried me so high!

On January 1, 1858, Wagner sent a long letter to Liszt in which he mixed his best wishes and his troubles. He alluded only vaguely to his love for Mathilde: "When I have to tell you about myself in my letters . . . I can think only of things I cannot write."

By New Year's Day Kurwenal and Brangäne had a premonition about the future. *Brangäne*: "He who is in the dream of love should listen to those who foresee misfortune coming to those who sleep. Anguished, I bid them wake up. Beware! The night will soon come to an end."

Indeed, a few days later Otto Wesendonck was back in Zurich. Wagner felt the storm approaching and decided to escape to Paris. His letters to Liszt, quoted by Julius Kapp,[4] show Wagner postponing his final decision: "I am at the end of a conflict which involves the most sacred things for a man! I must absolutely choose. . . . And as I need some silence to discover the way by which I would cause the least trouble, I intend to leave for Paris, where some serious affairs can justify my departure in the eyes of the world, and in particular my excellent wife." A few days later, from Paris, Wagner wrote again to his friend: "At one time it felt necessary to make a decision very quickly. But then I could see how, on the other hand, I am protected from danger by a most wonderful solicitude. Under these conditions, it is impossible to decide on a complete separation. . . . The only thing I have to do is somewhat appease the anguish of the good-hearted man [Otto Wesendonck], and I hope that my absence will have had that effect and that in a few weeks nothing will prevent me from going back."

In fact, on Otto's return, Mathilde told him about the December 23 concert. Her husband was infuriated by the way Wagner had insinuated himself into his household. Richard admitted it himself in *My Life*: "With his honest frankness, Wesendonck expressed some dismay at my having become so familiar in his home. Heating, lighting, and dining hours took me into consideration, which appeared to him to encroach upon his decisions as master of the house. A few explanations were necessary; the result was more or less a gentlemen's agreement."

Mysterious language! Of all human feelings, love is the most difficult to hide. From the silence between Mathilde and her husband at this period of time, these lines must have been written by her.

Oh, ask me not,
Never ask me . . .
I learned to bear many things
Except one—and this single thing
I cannot confess.
Why is my song just a painful cry? [5]

But Otto had had enough and threatened to throw Wagner out. Mathilde burst into tears. She wanted to explain everything to him, but it was impossible to describe the story of *Tristan und Isolde* when it was precisely the drama they were living through. Mathilde offered him two possible explanations: a cynical one and an idealistic one. In the first case, François Wille would have advised his friend Wesendonck to tell his wife that she should not hesitate to jump from the balcony, if she threatened to do so, with an *"Allez hop, Mathilde!"* In the second, Wagner, in a letter to his sister Clara on August 20, 1858, said that "Mathilde had explained to her husband the state of her feelings, bringing him little by little to full resignation."

In reality, Otto Wesendonck had probably understood everything before any explanation was given; he did not need his wife to tell him what was going on. On the other hand, in Wagner's letter to his sister, he mentioned that "she had the strength to reveal herself to her husband so honestly that when she threatened to take her own life, Otto agreed, with all his unshakable love, to keep his distance from her, even to support her in her attentions toward me. In the end he preferred not to banish the mother of his children. . . . He separated us insurmountably and took comfort in his self-sacrifice."

How did Mathilde Wesendonck tell her story to her King Marke? No doubt it was with the help of Mathilde-Brangäne: "I revealed to the king the secret of the love potion" (Act III). I told him how you were taken in by his music, ringing sounds in the whirlwind, submerged, drowned, unconscious—supreme joy!

Did Mathilde tell her husband, "Now I can only die," as Wagner seemed to insinuate? Or could she have murmured, as she had to Richard on September 18, "Now I have nothing more to wish for." Either way, it did not mean that she wanted to commit suicide.

Everything becomes more plausible if one considers more deeply Mathilde's soul; her natural discretion allowed her to speak to her husband in relatively subtle terms. Although she had "no secrets from him," her eloquent reticence must have helped him understand. As for the choice of words, she followed her heart and her generous nature. Not only did she want to spare Otto's feelings, but she loved him. She had always loved him.

Wagner described this period in his autobiography with the mysterious words "unrest in the neighborhood." One can easily imagine how tense the relations between the two houses must have been, especially for the two women. As he had written to Liszt, Richard prudently took off for Paris. He returned to Zurich only on February 6.

So life continued, with Otto present this time. In the morning Wagner would work at home on the orchestration for the first act of *Tristan*. In the afternoon he would take a little walk, visiting Mathilde at twilight; then, in the evening, he would gather some of his friends to read to them aloud his favorite texts of Calderón, Lope de Vega, and Cervantes.

Mathilde continued to write poetry. In her lines for "Stehe still" (Be Still), bathed in resignation in the manner of Schopenhauer, she expressed her aspiration to nirvana in order to forget what made her suffer so much—not to commit suicide. Wagner composed the music for this fourth of the *Wesendonck Lieder* and offered it to her on February 22, 1858.

In town, the neighbors' gossip and reports of servants made for a great deal of material for wagging tongues. People talked about what the supposed lovers might do, and indignation spread regarding this unconventional love story.

"Either he leaves or he stays!"

"It's a melodrama."

"And poor Frau Wagner with her heart trouble!"

"Don't forget Otto. How can he bear it?"

According to the memoirs of the singer Bertha Roner-Lipka, it was said that even Wagner, after these months of uncertainty, had thought of Mathilde as a "silly goose" and had had enough of it."[6]

In March, to make amends for the birthday concert he had offered Mathilde in December that had caused so much commentary, Wagner decided to organize a concert in honor of Otto Wesendonck on his birthday, March 16. But the date was not possible for many of the musicians, so it was postponed to the thirty-first, when it took place in Wahlheim's large hall. "Under my direction," wrote Wagner,

a small but sufficient orchestra for Beethoven performed a selection of symphonic excerpts perfectly, and the rarity of such a house concert created great emotion among the guests, who were sitting in different rooms around the vestibule. At the beginning of the celebration Frau Wesendonck's little girl, Myrrha, offered me a conductor's baton in sculpted ivory, etched with an engraving by Semper (the first and only baton that had ever been given to me). Flowers and plants were placed all around me, and when the concert ended with the Adagio of the Ninth Symphony, in deep tranquility, the audience had the right to think they had been given something quite extraordinary.

But even so, they were criticized. One person was indignant that the concert was scheduled for Holy Week! A whiff of scandal inevitably accompanied everything they did. Frau J. H. Bodmer-Pestalozzi was careful to keep the shades of her carriage drawn as she drove to the Wesendoncks' villa. When she arrived, she was surprised to meet everyone she had tried to avoid, with their disobliging comments; after all, it was in bad taste to indulge in socializing only four days before Easter!

Wagner added that the Wesendoncks "were filled with a strong and solemn emotion. As for me, this occasion produced a melancholy impression, something like a warning of destiny." He had almost called off the concert that morning, sending a telegram announcing he had caught cold during his last excursion to Saint Gotthard and that they would do fine without him: "the musicians can manage on their own." But the date could not be changed, and Wagner finally appeared. At the end of the evening, however, he was physically and morally exhausted. He admitted: "The new affection in my life had attained its epitome and even surpassed it; the cord on the arc was too drawn too far."

Eliza Wille said there were sixty guests mixed with the musicians and the family. During the dinner that followed, she had a feeling of apprehension, which she had already expressed in her last letter to her husband concerning Mathilde's poems: "Frau Wesendonck is writing Wagnerian madness." It could not last. Despite the splendor and decorum, the flowers, the wine, the perfume worn by the women and the rustling sounds of their taffeta skirts, one could hear, like a distant echo, the scene between Tristan and Isolde.

Late that night, after the guests left, Mathilde retired to her apartments. Before closing the curtains, she contemplated the starry sky and watched a star shoot across it. She slept, and in the morning she poured her heart and her soul into a poem:

I dreamed we both were alone in the world,
That I was yours and you were mine.
Your gaze resembled the heavens above
But less cold and nearer to me.
Brilliant stars shone in your eyes;
Suddenly one of them fell upon my heart.
Then the pain of our parting
Made me tremble.
On awakening, I saw we were not alone,
I was not yours and you,
You were not mine.[7]

A poem, an act of an opera, or a work of art relates a precise action and expresses a coherent thought. But real life is far more complex. Richard and Mathilde lived their passion in silence, and their respective personalities had to live double lives in their daily occupations. Wagner had to satisfy both aspects of his existence, so much so that Minna remarked in a letter to one of her friends: "Poor Richard has two hearts. He is pulled to the other side as by a string, and at the same time, habit keeps him attached to me." Moreover, Wagner continued his abundant correspondence to all his relations concerning his travels and his reading.

Mathilde went about her family duties as always, but she had a great need for intellectual endeavors. Conversations with Otto about the stock exchange or politics seemed dull in comparison with what had recently been written on her "blank page." And since Wagner had put a few of her poems into music, she was tempted on certain days to overestimate her own talent. Later on this would make her want to go beyond her actual literary ability.

Meanwhile, since the beginning of the year she had continued to take lessons in Italian with de Sanctis. In February the professor had refused to teach her, giving some polite pretext. Mathilde would not accept his excuse: "I considered these lessons a great favor from you," she wrote, "and I greeted you as a friend, not as a teacher. . . . I would be very sorry to have to abandon these interesting lessons."[8]

She sent him other notes inviting him to tea, to dinner, or for a ride in her carriage. Was this just vanity on her part? We do not know, but it was a way of filling the void Mathilde must have felt during those moments when Wagner was far away from her.

On February 14 de Sanctis finally responded to Herr and Frau Wesendonck's invitation to become better acquainted with Wagner. As soon as they met, however, a furious rivalry began between the two men. De Sanctis considered Wagner a charlatan; Wagner thought of de Sanctis as a pedant. Spurred on by love and jealousy, Wagner argued endlessly with de Sanctis. Finally, on April 6, after a discussion of Goethe's philosophical intentions in *Faust*, a difference of opinion ended in a quarrel. The next day, after a sleepless night over his love for Mathilde and his jealousy over de Sanctis, Wagner wrote the letter that would be fatal to him.

First of all, one should remember Minna's difficult position. If, in Mathilde's eyes, Otto did not have Richard's intellectual and artistic qualities, he nevertheless showed great elegance and discretion in his feelings and open-mindedness—not to mention his immense fortune. Minna, on the other hand, had none of these qualities whatsoever. She was invited to accompany her illustrious husband, but what could she say during these evenings, when they discussed the dramas of Calderón or the philosophy of Schopenhauer? In her opinion, Wagner had been on the decline ever since *Lohengrin*. The *Ring* was an aberration, and *Tristan* was so full of his love for Mathilde that it seemed indecent. She viewed her husband's circle of friends with growing hostility. She could not imagine the relations between Richard and Mathilde as being other than vulgar, reducing them in her mind only to their physical expression. From his point of view, Wagner, in that letter to Clara, depicted his love idealistically, talking of the "purity of his relations" with the young and beautiful Mathilde. In the middle, between these two conceptions, is *Tristan*. But Wagner would always place absolute love somewhere out of this world, like the Grail, in a chalice glowing with the rays of the sun on a high mountain that could be climbed only in winter on the northern slope.

Ideal and real, their love, as in the second act of *Tristan*, was ambiguous—an enigmatic union between eros and agape accompanied by the exchange of looks, kisses, and fond caresses. This physical harmony, which remained mysterious in the operatic work as well as in the relationship between the two lovers, was mentioned by Wagner himself when, eight months later, in Venice, he wrote to his beloved Mathilde:

> No, have no regrets about those caresses with which you enhanced my poor life! I did not know those sweet-smelling flowers emanating from the depth of noble love! The poet's dream had to change into a marvelous reality. That dew of joy that transfigures and fortifies had to fall for once on the arid desert of my life. I had never hoped for so much, but I think I knew it anyway. Now I have been ennobled—I have received my title of knight. On your heart, in your eyes,

by your mouth—I have been delivered from this world. Every part of me is free and noble. The consciousness of being loved by you with that fulfillment of tenderness and yet intimate chastity goes through me in a great thrill! Ah! I can still breathe in the magic perfume of those flowers that you gathered for me in your heart; they were not the seeds of life on earth, but the scent of the supernatural flowers of a divine death, of eternal life. . . . Your loving caresses are the crown of my life, roses of joy that have bloomed on my crown of thorns. I am proud and content. Not a wish, nor a desire! Pleasure, supreme consciousness and strength to withstand everything, strength to face all the storms of life! No! No! Do not repent! Do not repent!

The enigma is resolved in the second act of *Tristan*, but each can find his or her own answer. Undoubtedly, the author of this last letter was aiming at a spiritual as well as an erotic fulfillment, which together compose the two aspects of human nostalgia for the paradise lost.

～

During the night of April 6–7 Richard was unable to sleep. On that evening Mathilde's attention had been monopolized by her Italian professor, and Wagner had quarreled with him over *Faust*. He tried to have a note sent directly to Mathilde, but in vain. At home, a boring friend of his, Hermann Marschall von Bieberstein, was waiting for him downstairs, while his mind was still full of thoughts for his beloved. It was only in the wee hours of the morning that a healing slumber overtook this overgrown upset child. Upon rising, the first thing Wagner did was write his "morning confession," a letter in which, according to *My Life*, he related "calmly and seriously . . . his state of mind." It did not at all reflect Minna's opinion.

"Ah no! It is not de Sanctis that I abhor, but myself for being surprised that my poor heart was in such a state of weakness!" Wagner went on to describe his sleepless night and his jealousy. "Then, in the morning, I became reasonable again, and I could express a prayer to my angel in the deepest part of my heart; and that prayer is love! Love! The deepest joy of the soul in that love, source of my well-being!"

That morning Minna was on the watch, like Melot. She waited for the servant to come out of her husband's bedroom. He was carrying the letter, rolled up in large sheets of paper. Minna intercepted the package, quickly perused the manuscript of the outline—which was none other than the prelude of *Tristan*, with the orchestration noted in pencil—then unsealed the letter and found, in her own words, "the most passionate message of love:"

"When I see your eyes," wrote Richard to Mathilde, "I cannot say anything: anything I could say is inconsistent! Look, everything becomes such an obvious truth, I am so sure of myself when those wonderful, sacred eyes set their gaze upon me, in which I immerse myself. Then there is no object, no subject, all is one and unified in deep harmony. Infinity! Be good for me and excuse my childish behavior of yesterday; by qualifying it in that way, you found the right word. The weather seems mild. Today I will go to the garden; as soon as I see you, I hope to find you for an instant without any disturbance. . . . Take all my soul in this morning greeting!"⁹

Minna was outraged. She had received confirmation of what she had already long suspected. The need to clarify her marital misfortune had been suggested to her by all the local Ortruds—Emilie Heim, Emma Herwegh, the wife of Marschall von Bieberstein, and many others. She would not have done it alone, for in a letter to one of her friends she had admitted she did not care that much if her husband was having an affair. So many other women tolerate that, she said. But this unfathomable love between Richard and Mathilde, flying high above the world, irritated her more than anything.

Quickly she took the letter to Richard, who did not respond to her rage. She then threatened to take it to Wesendonck to inform him, for the worst possible thing would be to outrage a man like that. She said she was even ready to leave him if Wagner made an "honest woman" of Mathilde—at least, that is what she told a friend of hers.

Richard turned around slowly to face Minna and spoke once more; she knew how to understand words only literally, unable to find their real, deeper meaning. He told her he was going out for a walk and that she should promise not to say anything to the Wesendoncks so as to "avoid any tactlessness toward their neighbors, either in his judgments or in his behavior." But as soon as he had turned his back, Minna ran to see Mathilde and threatened to reveal everything to Otto. She had copied the most passionate sentences of the letter that she now held up in her hand.

What could Mathilde do? Call Otto and reveal the details of an affair that she had already explained to him? In any case, she knew the magnanimity of her husband's heart. He would not disown her. And she was right. Whether or not he had been informed of her behavior since his return from America, he would naturally take his wife's side. Wagner would write in August to his sister Clara: "In the evening, on returning home from my walk, I met the Wesendoncks in their carriage about to leave home. I observed the troubled look of the woman and, on the contrary, a most pleased and satisfied smile on the face of her husband." Immediately Richard understood what Minna had done. Their future at the Asyl seemed definitely compromised. According to Wagner, Otto would have reproached him for neglecting to inform Minna about the "purity of his relationship" with his wife. Mathilde reacted with violence. She wanted to break it off with Richard, who then wrote: "When you spurned me and dismissed me from your presence . . . when passionately you gave in to the fear of being betrayed, and when you suspected me of not having seen what was most noble in you, then you appeared to me as an angel abandoned by God."

Was it only Minna's accusations that put her into this state? Minna Wagner was only an incident that revealed Mathilde's soul. She rang the bell that woke her up, putting an end to the sweet slumber in which Richard had rocked her since the beginning of their friendship. Minna was the instrument by which Mathilde finally realized what all this rarefied love looked like from the outside. Gossip suddenly rang deafeningly in her ears. Mathilde-Isolde was suddenly confronted with Mathilde-Brangäne. In an instant, the crystal vase in which Richard and she had laid their utopian love was instantly shattered, as was the idealized image that she had made of it. Their relationship had been reduced to something common and vulgar.

Wagner had to call on Eliza Wille's diplomacy to be forgiven by Mathilde. But the speech of Melot to King Marke had just broken forever the ecstatic duo in the second act between Tristan and Isolde.

Wagner persuaded his wife to go for a rest cure at Brestenberg, on Lake Hallwil, prescribed by the doctor for her heart disease. He tried to erase the past and asked her to forget what had happened, for it "was beyond her understanding."

At the end of April Mathilde wrote the last poem that would be set to music by Richard: "Im Treibhaus" (In the Hothouse), which would also have the subtitle "A Study for *Tristan und Isolde*."

High-arching leafy crowns,
Canopies of emerald,
You children of distant lands,
Tell me, why do you lament?

Silently you incline your branches,
tracing signs in the air,
And, mute witness to your sorrows,
A sweet perfume rises.

Wide, in longing and desire,
You spread your arms
And embrace, in self-deception,
Barren emptiness, a fearful void.

Well I know it, poor plant!
We share the same fate.
Although the light shines brightly round us,
Our home is not here!

And as the sun gladly quits
The empty brightness of the day,
So he who truly suffers,
Wraps round him the dark mantle of silence.

It grows quiet, an anxious rustling
Fills the dark room;
I see heavy drops hanging
From the green edges of the leaves.

In the pale light of day, on the island of Kareol, Tristan lay in agony on his bed of suffering. From the depths of low tonalities, in dark chords, opened the wound from which his pain rose like wisps of fog evaporating on the surface of the sea. The exquisite moments of Dreams (*Träume*) had vanished now in the flow of blood from the lovers' hearts.

> *Thinking of the red blood from my heart,*
> *I drank poison, and in pain,*
> *I collapsed on the way.*[10]

Soon a shepherd would play a plaintive tune on his pipe. Isolde's dream was coming to an end. She had lived with Richard, as in the opera's love duet, until the arrival of King Marke. The music written for "Im Treibhaus" became a springboard for the beautiful Prelude to Act III of *Tristan*. Its painful accents anticipated on the sadness which would come for Richard and Mathilde at the moment of their separation.

On the manuscript it can be seen that Wagner paid great attention to the details of this lied. Corrections were frequent and his handwriting messy. When Mathilde received this royal present from Wagner on May 1, 1858, she wrote at the end of the poem two lines of Isolde's:

> *Chosen for me, lost for me,*
> *Heart beloved for eternity.*

In his despondency, Wagner wrote to Mathilde: "If my death had been predicted as certain this year, I would have relished that thought as being the happiest moment of my existence. Only uncertainty about the time that remains for us to live plunges us into doubt and sin; but it seems to me that the time that remains should exonerate me from all sinfulness. How can I have what I so long for?"

While Wagner was working on his composition draft for the second act of *Tristan*, Otto took his family on a trip to northern Italy. They visited the beautiful lakes area, the Riviera all the way to Marseille, and then the Rhône valley north to Lyon. They returned to Zurich in June only to find Wagner solitary, calm, and hardworking. This solitude was precisely what he needed most for his work. Wrote Herwegh at the time: "Thanks to the absence of his wife, his parrot, and even his dog, I see Wagner more often now. He is perfectly kind, good, and sympathetic. The Wesendoncks have gone to see part of northern Italy."

On Otto and Mathilde's return Wagner was invited to tea at their home. His disposition now calm, he perceived reality more clearly. He informed them of his decision to break off their personal relations and wrote to Mathilde one month later that he had renounced her. However, now that Minna was not watching every move he made, a certain friendship resumed nevertheless between the neighboring houses. Wagner had received a visit from a young pupil of Liszt, Karl Tausig, a Polish Jewish pianist whom he appreciated for his affability and musical gifts. He sent the "little goblin musician" to the Wesendoncks, recommending him to them with great warmth. Tausig remained for a while in Wagner's house while he continued to work on the second act of *Tristan*. Richard kept Mathilde informed of his progress and his score of *Tristan*—the fruit of their love: "What a marvelous birth, this child of ours, so rich in suffering! Is it thus that we must live? Who could abandon their own child? May God help us, poor as we are! Or are we too rich? Do we have to help ourselves alone?"

This time Mathilde answered him, accompanying her letter with lines of poetry that have since disappeared. In a moment of weakness, she expressed her passionate torment to such a degree that Richard replied: "Your letter—how sad it made me! The demon leaves one of our hearts to enter into the other. How can we be victorious? Oh, how we are to be pitied! We no longer own ourselves. Demon, become God. . . . Your letter made me so sad. . . . Demon, Demon, become God!" This note was accompanied by eight measures of music, a start on his outline for *Parsifal*. The theme is not recognizable but some of the chords announce the master's last work. On the autograph score was jotted down: "Where may I find you, Oh, Holy Grail. My heart full of ardent desire is seeking for thee." And to console Mathilde, he added, "'Dear lost child! You see, that is precisely what I wanted to write to you when I found your beautiful and noble lines."

Tristan, wounded on Kareol, was thinking of Parsifal who brought him peace. At the end of his life, twenty-four years later, in Wagner's last work, this terrible demon of unrequited love would have become the God whose redeeming blood cast a red glow on the last chords exhaled by his soul.

In her distress, Mathilde-Isolde, fully awakened by the horror of day's glaring light, was drowning. Only Mathilde-Brangäne could take her by the hand one night, at the beginning of July, to show her the bleeding heart of King Marke and the deep well of innocence in the eyes of her poor children.

Tristan came for the last time and asked her:

Where Tristan now is going,
Will you, Isolde, follow him?

Wagner came to propose the inevitable alternatives: complete separation of the lovers or total union. It was the encounter between day and night. In the world of appearances, it meant abandon, divorce, remarriage.

At that moment, her eyes closed, was Mathilde Wesendonck seeing her life flash before her eyes, like those who are about to die? Did she see her happy childhood again, cozily seated between mother and father, the steamboats on the Rhine, the family reunions in the evening listening to the music of Weber, the man with sad eyes and noble character who had come to ask for her hand in marriage, the children with their gaze as deep as the ocean? Agnes, Mathilde. Night surrendered to day as the stars twinkled out one after the other. She awoke with a terrible start and exclaimed, "It would be sacrilege!"

Like Psyche after her lover's departure, she was condemned to live.

Fifteen years later, now removed from his passion, Wagner wanted to show himself in as idealistic a light as he could. He commented from afar on the events of his life in his autobiography or in the memoirs he dictated to his second wife, Cosima, who took note of his slightest remarks in her diary. Rather than allow an old wound inflicted by the love of another woman to reopen, he protected himself with bitter or sarcastic remarks. On March 14, 1873, on the subject of the word "sacrilege" as uttered by Mathilde, Cosima reported Wagner as saying: "This word, which she did not even understand, suited my proposition very well, because deep down in my heart and unconsciously, I wasn't thinking seriously of what I said." Did she understand the word, and did he know what he was saying? Martin Gregor-Dellin, an authoritative contemporary biographer of Wagner, stated the bottom line: "It is no less true, nevertheless, that he did say it!"

Richard himself gave Mathilde the key to his purgatory when on July 5 he wrote:

I will not come to see you often, for in the future you must meet me only when I am certain to be calm and composed. Before, I would come to you with suffering and desire in my heart; and there, where I was searching for consolation, I brought only trouble and sorrow. That must no longer be so. If therefore you do not see me for a long time . . . pray for me in secret. For you should know how I suffer! But if I come, be sure that I will bring the best of myself. . . . And isn't it you who conferred on me the highest benefit of my existence? Isn't it to you that I owe the only thing that could appear to me worthy of gratitude and interest in this world? And would I not try to reward you for all you have won for me through such sacrifice and suffering? . . . An inner voice calls me insistently to rest, that rest that many years ago I made my Dutchman so desire. It is the intense aspiration toward a land, a home, and not the exhilarating pleasure of a life full of passion. . . . We can be grateful for that good death that envelops and appeases all these aspirations, all that desire! May we die beatified, with a luminous and serene look, with the divine smile of a hard-won victory! And no one must suffer if we are victorious!

With the orchestral draft of the second act of *Tristan* in his ears, Wagner had guests at the Asyl coming and going all summer long against a musical background of chromaticism, people making conversation and gestures like characters in paintings by Brueghel—the tenors Josef Tichatschek and Albert Niemann, along with Niemann's wife, the actress Marie Seebach—then Minna coming home from her cure in Brestenberg on July 15. Upon her arrival the servants erected a small, beflowered arch of triumph at the entrance of the little garden. She kept it up for several days in order to mark a point against her neighbor, and it worked: Mathilde was reputedly vexed by it. On July 21 Hans and Cosima von Bülow arrived, followed by Karl Ritter, Countess Marie d'Agoult, and Karl Klindworth. Despite the presence of these guests, the daily domestic disputes with Minna continued. Wagner went on composing while the piercing sound of Minna's voice grew louder and louder, surpassing even the violins in register.

No wonder the composer of *Tristan* found himself so urgently needing to leave his Asyl, so dearly acquired after such a long time. Throughout his life, Wagner would sacrifice anything for his art. His domestic life had made it impossible for him to work; he thus had to choose once again between his composition (their child) and himself. In this domain, and only in this domain, his self-sacrifice was total. What he could not accomplish in this world with the woman he loved had to be transposed and left to posterity in *Tristan*, that eternal reliquary of love.

And despite her raging passion, why did Mathilde not find the "courage," as we say today, to leave everything and follow Wagner? Real courage—to her mind, was it not to sacrifice her love for the happiness of her husband and children? It is a strange era we live in that considers a heroic action to be weakness. Abandoning everything to follow God is a religious gesture. Later Cosima von Bülow would call on her own brand of courage to create an idol, with Wagner as the center of her religion.

Mathilde Wesendonck has been accused not only of cowardice, but of yielding to the demands of social conformity. However, for years she had faced gossip and slander, unafraid, to the point of appearing to be what she was not. She had lost the esteem of most of the women of high society in Zurich; only one faithful friend remained in the person of Eliza Wille.

She allowed herself to be disapproved of when she tried to persuade her generous husband to help Wagner. And without her husband's huge fortune, she knew she would have been a burden to the beloved genius of her dreams.

But since one looks for commonplace reasons to criticize someone, might they not have said she feared leaving her beautiful home, her comfort, her husband's money and her social rank?

Richard left the Asyl on August 17, 1858. The Wesendoncks did not dismiss him, despite the accusations Cosima later made in letters to her daughter Eva. According to Mathilde's memoirs, "Richard Wagner loved his Asyl. . . . He left with pain and sadness—he left on his own initiative. Why? Idle question. As a mark of this period, we have his great work *Tristan und Isolde*! All the rest is mystery and respectful silence!"

In his journal, Wagner, while in Venice, wrote to Mathilde describing his departure with poignant melancholy:

My last night at the Asyl, I went to bed shortly after eleven, with the idea of leaving early in the morning at dawn. Before closing my eyes, I remembered very clearly the way in which I used to fall asleep in this same bed thinking that one day I would die here. Yes, I would be lying there, and, for the last time, you would come to me in front of everyone, you would take my head in your arms and receive my soul in one last kiss!

Soon a wonderful sound awakened me from my sad dreams, and, very surely coming out of sleep, I felt a kiss on my brow, after which I heard a deep sigh. It was all so vivid and precise that I got up and looked all around me. But no, nothing but rest and silence. . . . And you, at that moment, were you awake, or were you sleeping?

In his letter of July, knowing he would inevitably be leaving, Richard ended his missive, "Farewell, dear beloved angel!" Then in August, he wrote: *"It must be so!"* and finally, "Farewell! Farewell! my beloved. I am going calmly. Wherever I may be, I will always be yours. Please keep the Asyl for me. Good-bye, good-bye, dear soul! Farewell and good-bye!"

On August 17, 1858, at dawn, a short little man with an enormous head above his cape walked swiftly down the path of his Asyl on the Green Hill. He was carrying a briefcase full of music manuscripts, a wound in his heart, and, in his brain, a flood of harmony. His instinct encouraged him to leave that morning all alone for Venice, where, in winter's silence, he would watch on the surface of the dark canals the reflection of empty palaces, arcades, and vaults that spanned man's nostalgia. There, with the premonition of his own death, which would occur twenty-five years later, his impossible love for Mathilde would be the seed fallen to earth that had to die in order to bear fruit; that fruit would survive forever in the masterpiece *Tristan und Isolde*.

PART III

Zurich without Wagner

13

Forsaken Love

———◆———

Say, why this bitter estrangement?
You've carried away my happiness.
Must I bear the burden to spare you?
Give me back to myself once more.

Give me that peace so pure
That your gaze took from my breast:
From her who relinquished love's joy,
Take away the torment of love.

You opened a heaven of joy
With an ecstatic kiss;
Alas! It became the well of tears
That I must forever shed.

Oh! That never in far-off years
My image should afflict you with pain;
May you never doubt
How fervently I loved you.

I pray heaven to pour over your head
All my most abundant blessings;
Pray that I may soon retire
To my solitary and tranquil grave.

—MATHILDE WESENDONCK, "DIE VERLASSENE"
(THE FORSAKEN LOVER), IN *GEDICHTE* (1862)

Settled now in Venice in two large rooms of the Palazzo Giustinian since the last days of
August 1858, Wagner wrote his diary for Mathilde of the "melancholy," the "grandeur,"

the "beauty," and the "decadence" of the city of the doges. "Marvelously beautiful is the Grand Canal at night. Bright stars, moon in the last quarter. A gondola slides quietly in front of the palace. In the distance the gondoliers are calling to each other in song. It is a sensation of such beauty and extraordinary elegance."

They had promised one another to write their diaries, for lovers always need to free themselves through the written word from the fetters of passion and the fantasies of their imagination. Wagner had taken a little notebook with him in which Mathilde had been writing during the spring of that year, probably at the moment when Melot intervened and provoked the famous quarrel. During his voluntary exile in Venice, he read and reread her entries, as well as the last letters she had sent him. Because almost all of Mathilde's writing was later destroyed, only the more or less indirect testimonials remained that Richard commented in his voluminous correspondence and his diary.

On the way to Italy, Wagner first stopped off in Geneva, where he wrote many letters to justify himself. On August 20 he wrote to his sister Clara: "Renouncing all selfish desires, we were resigned to suffer and bear it, but . . . we loved each other!"

Three days later, on August 23, at five o'clock in the morning, he recalled the presence of the woman he loved: "I saw you in a dream, standing on the terrace. You were wearing men's clothing and a traveling hat. Your gaze was fixed in the direction in which I had left. But I was arriving from the other side. Thus you were looking away from me, and I was trying in vain to tell you that I was there until the moment when I called out: Mathilde! Softly first, then louder and louder, only to wake myself up at the sound of my own voice."

He saw her then as the character of Rosaura in Calderón's *Life Is a Dream*. The heroine appears at the beginning of the play at night, wearing men's clothes, standing on a mountain peak. Alone, she has crossed hills and dales looking for her beloved. But at the core of the Spanish drama so well-known to Wagner, Prince Sigismond has been imprisoned by the king, his father, because of the bad omens that astrologers had read in the stars when the young man was born. From Venice, Wagner too was observing the starry night and scanning in its constellations his destiny as a man and an artist.

And here came a comet that appeared in the heavens over Venice in the fall of 1858!

The moon in all its splendor beamed toward me its network of sparkling rays over the sea. I turned my back to it. A little above the Pleiades, grave and clear, with its luminous tail growing larger and larger, the comet stood in my view, wavering in the direction of your home, from which you were contemplating the moon. For me, the comet has nothing terrifying about it because I no longer have any hope or future. Even so, I couldn't help smiling at the turmoil in which it had left people, for with a certain haughty pride I had chosen it as a good omen. Am I myself a meteor? Did I bring evil? Was it my fault? I couldn't stop watching it in the sky.

Next Wagner described the solemnity of the Grand Canal: "To the left and to the right, magnificent palaces; absolute silence, nothing but the soft hush of gondolas sliding gently by.

Large shadows cast by the moonlight." In the night, at his window, he heard music from below. Gondolas full of listeners slid by: voices, instruments, songs. "The last note melts in the light of the moon, which continues to shine brightly, as if the world of sound has become visible." During nocturnal rides, he asked to be taken to the Lido: "All around me I can hear that long, tender vibration of a violin that I like so much and to which I compared you one day: you can now imagine what I feel in the moonlight on the sea!"

All this setting is a stage on which the main actor is torment and where the action is his composition. Wagner needed this calm, this solitude. "My set-up has to be the envelope for my thought process," he wrote to Mathilde. "I hope to heal for you! To keep you for myself means keeping myself for my art! To live with it in order to console you, that is my task. . . . In that way will you be cured through me! Here I will finish *Tristan*, despite the world's turmoil. And with it, if I can, I will come back to see you, to console you, to make you happy. . . . Go, valorous Tristan, courageous Isolde! Help me, come to help my angel!"

So he went back to work. But he did not finish *Tristan* in Venice. On September 15 he plunged into the orchestration of Act II, which he would finish the following spring, just before returning to Switzerland. The entire work was finally completed in Lucerne in August 1859.

That winter in Venice, Wagner, though not naturally inclined to romanticism, felt himself assailed by melancholy. He heard the plaintive strains and ancient ballads that were pervading his music. "A gondolier makes a cry almost like a howling animal, a sound like a deep groan mounting crescendo to an 'Oh!' I felt such a violent commotion from this cry that I could never remember the rest . . . maybe [these notes] suggested to me something of the plaintive and languorous sounds played on the pipe in the third act."

On October 6 his Érard piano finally arrived from Zurich. This extravagant gift had been given to him the previous January by the manufacturer himself in Paris. Wagner reminded Mathilde of all the occasions that this instrument had helped to celebrate at the Asyl. Like his compatriots, he loved birthdays, and Mathilde loved mementos. While the Venetian moving men with their ropes were hoisting the cumbersome crate in the palace's stairwell, Wagner remembered the setting up of that same piano in Zurich on May 2, in the bitter cold of bad weather. That day

I had to give up seeing you on the terrace. The piano was not yet completely moved in when I saw you coming out of the billiard room onto the front balcony. You sat down on a chair and looked in my direction. Then the piano was ready. I opened the window and struck the first chords. You did not know yet that it was the Érard. For a whole month I had not seen you, and during that time it seemed to me more and more clear that we had to remain separated! Now my life would really be over! But this instrument, with its mysterious and melancholy sweetness, attracted me back once more to music. I named it the Swan, which had come to take poor Lohengrin back to his land! It was then that I began to compose the second act of *Tristan*. Life was fading around me like the mist in a dream. . . . You returned. We no longer spoke to each other. The Swan was singing to you.

Now I am completely separated from you. Between us loom the Alps, as high as the sky. . . . I had to wait for a long time. It is here now, at last, the magnificent instrument with the beautiful voice that I acquired at the very moment that I knew I was going to have to lose you. With such symbolic clarity speaks my genie, my demon here! Almost fainting, I fell on the piano. But the insidious will to live knew what it wanted! The piano! Yes, a wing—the wing of the angel of death![1]

The Swan thus formed a link in Wagner's mind between *Lohengrin* and *Tristan* through the theme of impossible love. Throughout her lifetime Mathilde would repeat to herself the passages of Richard's fantastic diary, which she would discover a few months after it was written. To this last, particularly moving passage, she answered, as in a reply to an operatic aria, with a tale: *The Swan*, more easily understood by grown-ups than children. In the absence of her own letters to the beloved, symbols can be detected in it that express what seemed to be her exact relation with Richard. To it he responded simply: "I read the beautiful fairy tale to the Érard; it showed me it had understood by sounding twice as beautiful."

"One day," wrote Mathilde, "The Lord of the world sent a swan to keep His heavenly reflection over the deep water. . . . He created its feathers with the incense of the divine spirit, the perfumes of sunrise and the foam of the sea." Mathilde then told her own story through the heroine of the fable: "Once it saw a child on the shore making sand castles, doing her work with great diligence. . . . The little girl paid no attention to it while she was working. At one moment their eyes met—but she continued to play as if she were all alone. That gaze nevertheless penetrated both their hearts and attached them to each other's look so strongly that they could never be separated."

Mathilde then described the way in which Richard had written on his "blank page:"

The swan would often bring her shells filled with ivory foam or purple corals, sparkling roses from the deep; when he left, sometimes a snow-white feather would remain behind. She put it on and clapped her hands with joy when she saw how pretty it made her look. But when he told her about the marvels he had seen in far-off lands, the manners and customs of strange peoples, proud cities surging from the sea, the flags of all countries hoisted on the masts of swift sailboats, the beauty of heaven and His glorious image reflected in its depths from which it had been chosen—then, as she was suspended on his words, she forgot to play: it seemed to her that all these wonders were emanating from her own childish soul, and that they were wandering together over the shimmering paths on the waves. He then showed her the precious and noble pearl, the symbol of silent grief, and he taught her how to discriminate between truth and lies. And then she trusted him, wrapped her arm around his white neck, caressed the shining feathers, and pressed her head against the soft down of his wings.

Suddenly, he felt the desire to take her with him forever and never be separated from her again.

The swan then defied the "Lord of the world," like Siegmund refusing to go to Valhalla for the love of Sieglinde. "Come down from your golden throne, come down to see and learn from man what love is!" However, like the Dutchman's challenge to God, the swan's impious arrogance rose up to heaven, and he was struck down on the spot:

> The swan's head fell on the little girl's lap and, still singing, he died. Her chest and cheek were spattered with the blood of the beautiful bird; she embraced him tenderly and their souls were united in the flow of his last breath of life.
>
> When the Lord of the Creation saw what he had done, he was seized with pity. He sent his messengers, a legion of angels, to pick up the swan's white feathers so as to adorn the hem of his celestial robe.
>
> The child was never seen again.[2]

~

But all that happened in the lovers' mutual solitude. Each was ignorant of what the other was writing. Three weeks after his departure from Zurich, on September 7, Wagner made a melancholy notation in his diary: "Today, I received a letter from Frau Wille, the first news I have of you." The lovers had asked Eliza Wille to act as an intermediary; she tried hard to keep them calm and counseled them to resignation. In her letter to Wagner she listed their duties: parents, children, order, the conventional world, and respectability. For Wagner, the artist who carried his love to the summits of art with *Siegfried* and *Tristan*, renunciation appeared paradoxically as the result of his amorous passion. The down-to-earth picture described by the "dear spinner" of Mariafeld only embittered him. "Thinking of you," he wrote to Mathilde,

> it never came to my mind, parents, children, duties: I knew only that you loved me and that everything that is superior and noble in this world is bound to suffer. From this height I am afraid to look at the precise circumstances that have made us unhappy. Then I see you suddenly in your magnificent home; I see everything, I hear all the people who will never understand us, who approach us only to separate us with anguish from what is closest to us. And I feel like saying, "It is they who know nothing and understand nothing about you, but who demand everything from you, to whom you would sacrifice all that you are!"

Later, in the same vein, he gave vent to his "old horror for early marriages" and went back to the ideas of Schopenhauer on what he called the "first calls to the reproduction instinct."

But then Eliza Wille told Wagner that Mathilde did not *want* any letters from him, which he found cruel. Eliza must have addressed clever remarks to Mathilde to encourage her to make such a sacrifice. And in conclusion, she would have said: "You must absolutely refuse his letters." Mathilde, no doubt with a heavy heart and a faint voice, would have nodded her head without saying a word.

But Wagner noted again, "I wrote to you—and I keep a firm hope that my letter will not be refused." On September 10 Eliza sent back his unopened missive to Mathilde, dated the second. "You should not have done that! No, not that!" Was it really she who had done this, or was it on the initiative of Eliza, inspired by discreet advice from Otto—whose situation was indeed very delicate?

In September Richard received a short note from his beloved and concluded that their kind intermediary, so full of good intentions, was no doubt clouding the issue: "I understand that Frau Wille cannot bring herself to give you my letters, at least according to her own understanding. From now on, it is impossible to think about their contents, to see how soothing and necessary such communications are—only one thing matters, that they are letters, and she can, she must, hesitate to give them. Otherwise what kind of 'friend' would she be? She can only act according to what her particular situation allows toward all those concerned, and what it permits her, in the best, most noble sense. So then, there is true faith between us!"

But the "friend" finally yielded to Wagner's importunings. On September 3 he wrote:

Today I received your letter—your letter to Frau Wille. That you love me, I knew; as usual, you are always good, profound, and reasonable; I had to smile and almost rejoice in my recent adversity, since you gave me such a great sensation of happiness. . . . I will write to Frau Wille; but also, in the letters I send her, I have decided to exercise restraint. . . . Our love dominates all the obstacles, and each difficulty makes us richer, closer to spirituality, more noble, more concerned with fundamental things, the very substance of this love that fortifies our indifference for whatever is not essential. Yes, good, pure, and beautiful creature, we will win; we are already victorious!

On September 16, the great comfort brought by her missive was still in effect: "Your letter still gives me joy. How sensible, beautiful and charming is everything that comes from you!"

To excuse her silence, Mathilde sent him on the twenty-third a cup and a tea service: "A thousand thanks, inventive and charming creature! By keeping quiet this way, how clear we are expressing what is really unsayable!"

And on October 12, having finished his first notebook in Venice, Wagner sent it to Mathilde. On each page he confided to her his state of mind, his thoughts, his projects. He followed the bent of his own ego, his subconscious, and his genius. He told her everything he had in his head: Schopenhauer, Buddhism, his first drafts for *Parsifal*. Obsessed by the theme of compassion, after many long digressions concerning animals and suffering he concluded: "With you too, my child, I've come to the end of my pity! Your diary that you gave me at the supreme instant, your last letters show you so high, so sincere, so purified through suffering, with so much control over yourself and the world, that you evoke only feelings of joy, veneration, adoration. You no longer see your pain, but the pain of the world; you cannot even imagine suffering in any other way. You have become a poet in every sense of the word."

It was this rare compliment from the pen of Richard Wagner that allows us to measure the literary value of Mathilde's letters. Her pain having become universal in what was no doubt a Wagnerian style, the pupil had imitated the master. Like the little girl with the swan, "It seemed that all these marvels were emanating from her own childish soul."

~

For three days the melodious Érard rang in Wagner's Venetian abode. The voice of that inspired Swan mingled with the singing of the gondoliers, accompanied by the lapping of the wavelets on the canal. On October 9 the master confided again to his disciple: "Now I have begun. With what? I had only the rapid outlines in pencil of our lieder, sometimes too summed up and so unreadable that I was afraid of forgetting them completely someday. I forced myself to play them again; I recalled them completely back into my memory, then took careful note of them. It is no longer necessary to send me yours; I have mine here. It was therefore my first endeavor. I tried out the wings. I never wrote anything better than these lieder, and very few examples in my works are equal to them."

Pages of the diary are missing, as are letters both from him and from her. What is hiding in the ellipses that appear throughout all the editions of this fabulous correspondence are the passages censored years later by Cosima Wagner. They would be reconstituted, however, and published in 1931, thanks to the research of Julius Kapp,[3] but to this day neither the letters nor the Venetian diary have been published in their integral form.

In 1858, however, to work on *Tristan* meant for Wagner that he was united in spirit with his beloved.[4] He admitted as much to Eliza Wille: "Only one thing remains for me: to work." Then, "I am working as if I never wanted to finish [my work], as if I wanted to force death to come and surprise me while I am toiling away. I have never worked in such an intimate way; for me, each line has the meaning of an eternity. . . . *Tristan* is becoming beautiful! But it feeds deeply on me."

Illness, nostalgia, and the silence of Venice in winter sent Wagner constantly back to his work. He ended this first notebook of his diary with repeated farewells to Mathilde:

How will personal relations be . . . between you and me? . . . You will raise your children—may my fervent blessing accompany you in that task! . . . Yes, my child! Let this diary end with that! It will tell you of my suffering, my ascension, my struggles, my judgment of the world, and, especially, my eternal love for you. Accept it kindly and forgive me if it has sometimes reopened a wound. Now I am going back to *Tristan* to let it explain instead of me, for you, the unthinkable art of silence inhabited by sound. . . . Between us, everything is pure and clear; no mistake, no misunderstanding can ever weigh upon us.

Rarely had a genius ever made such passionate vows and entrusted to one woman as many secrets about the mechanism of his thoughts. The Venice diary, destined for Mathilde Wesendonck, belongs to a domain of the most inspired sort of literary creation ever written.

"Farewell then, my angel, my divine liberator, dear and pure woman! Farewell! Be blessed with the deepest devotion from my soul!"

On October 12, 1858, this notebook was sent to its addressee.

What ocean of suffering awakens,
O child, your death in my soul,
And darkens it forever . . . [5]

The next day, on October 13, under the somber gray sky, the cold, dry wind rustled the leaves of the beautiful trees on the Wesendonck estate. In Zurich, the austerity of autumn penetrated Wahlheim and mingled with the laments of a mother and father. The family doctor, a somber expression on his face, had just left little Guido Otto's bedroom, where Mathilde sat in an armchair holding her little boy dead in her arms.

How my heart was full of joy
When, in my arms, you rested, rosy and laughing on my breast;
With every breath I would drink to life in your gaze
With such joyfulness
That I felt myself a woman blessed! [6]

One can face the illness and death of a child only with resignation. Even the nasty gossips in Zurich held their tongues. The wife of Marschall von Bieberstein paid Mathilde a condolence call. She wrote to Minna Wagner in Dresden to describe the event:

Frau Wesendonck received me and frankly, I felt compassion for her when I saw the pale and haggard face of this young woman amid all her wealth. She seemed deeply shaken and broke down in tears in front of me. We spoke only of her present grief, and as she described her pain, she mentioned the "storms" of last summer. She reproached me for not having come to visit her in such a long time and added that recently she had expressly refrained from seeing any of Wagner's friends, so as not to be suspected of wanting to attract them into her own circle. I left with a very sad feeling and with the impression there was no real happiness on this earth. [7]

Emilie Heim also wrote to Minna: "You must already know that the Wesendoncks have suffered an irreparable loss with the death of their oldest son. I saw the poor woman after the unfortunate event and I found her so exhausted and ill-looking that she aroused all my pity." [8]

Minna, however, Mathilde's former rival and self-appointed victim, reacted with an almost puritanical severity. On December 29, 1858, she wrote to one of her friends in Berlin: "The communication concerning the death of little Guido frightened me. May God keep every blow of destiny away from that woman, though she is so cold, and so spoiled by her good fortune; but I believe there is a Providence. I had always thought to myself, if only our Lord would reprimand such impertinence with a child's illness—and now, look! Oh, it makes me tremble."[9]

Before leaving Zurich, Minna had created a scandal by putting a classified ad into the local newspapers concerning the furniture for sale in the Asyl "because of sudden departure." Tongues began to wag again. The good bourgeoisie was only too glad to have such a subject of conversation, to lock the Wesendoncks into their solitude and then criticize them for being distant and reserved.

On September 2, before Minna left, she sent a bitter and damning letter to Mathilde: "Before my departure, I must tell you with a bleeding heart that you have succeeded in separating me from my husband after nearly twenty-two years of marriage. May that noble action contribute to your inner peace and happiness."

During that month of October, no one spoke the word "punishment," though it hovered in everyone's mind.

When the little coffin was lowered into its grave, Mathilde held tight to her husband's arm as if it were a buoy she needed to rescue her. Many words were exchanged between them, but not one was said aloud.

> *The sharp blade penetrated to the marrow,*
> *And the open wound burned me to the depths,*
> *With no promise of healing;*
> *And no medicinal plant can bring the balm of consolation*
> *Or stop the blood from flowing.*

Mathilde was now alone and friendless. Her soul had no other choice than to rise into idealism, in which she was content and could sing her plaintive melody. Her heart's lover had gone south like a migrating bird. Forlorn, she had to cope with the cold winter.

Otto felt his wife was at the end of her rope, her burden too heavy to carry. In a noble gesture, he decided to suspend the tacit interdiction of all communication with Richard. In order to discharge Eliza Wille from her intermediate role, he wrote directly to Venice to inform Wagner about Guido's death. The crisis was over; they would be able to write to one another once more. Wagner answered Otto immediately: "The last words I wrote to your wife contained my blessing for the future of your children! The news you have sent me has deeply overwhelmed me. May the tears of your friend be the tribute of his tenderness! Your children also have become dear to me; when I think of your home, I will see little Guido's empty place. O heavens! How severe it is! How severe! We can only lend a little sweetness and tenderness to this severity; but we must not fight it—it makes us grow, and one day it will be our salvation."

But Wagner did not dare write directly to his beloved. Through Eliza, then, he sent a letter on October 24: "Through you alone did I acquire the beautiful serenity of my soul; I knew you to be so noble and purified that I had to be the same for you. And now, here is grief, that melancholy suffering, knowing you are afflicted by the loss of your son! What a sudden change! All pride, all appeasement so quickly vanished in a tremor of tender anguish; deep sorrow, tears, mourning! The world, so solidly built, is reeling; the gaze sees it only through tears."

Mathilde answered him in a letter and a notebook of her own diary. Richard was impatient to see his beloved again. At the end of his letter to Otto he had written: "How I would like to be at your side to console you!" He therefore asked Eliza Wille to arrange an interview in Mariafeld between him and Mathilde during the Christmas season.

This time, Eliza had to decline. She no longer knew how to remain a sympathetic friend to Wagner the artist and at the same time to defend morals and convention. Having found no other remedy for impossible love than to keep the lovers apart, she asked her husband to answer Richard.

François Wille was anything but sentimental, so he went at it with remarkable frankness. First he reproached the imprudent correspondent for bothering his wife by forcing her to "play a role against which she protests in vain, divided between pain, shame and anger." He claimed that when Mathilde was informed of Wagner's two last letters, she was frightened at the thought he would come to see her again and pleaded that he give up the project. If not, Wille would be obliged to inform Otto: "You, the most accomplished of sophists, you who know how to lie even to yourself, declare solemnly that you forgive, moved by the death of her child"—Wille knew he was speaking to an irresponsible man—"but," he continued, "I know with certainty that up to now, *he* [Otto] is not inclined to forgive, and moreover has decided not to see you again within his family circle."

And since everybody in Zurich knew about Wagner's intimate affairs (ever since Minna Wagner had published her ad in the newspapers), such a visit, even if discreet, would be unthinkable.

"Take your inspiration from Calderón and his principle of honor!" François Wille took the tone of a healthy person speaking to the sick. "It is true that you are also a disciple of Schopenhauer and Buddha, and that at present you are crossing a night of renunciation and purification from selfishness and forgiveness, to follow the orders dictated by desire; it is true also that your artistic imagination wants to settle everything so as to flatter your 'will,' and that to satisfy your whim you want to revive the torment that has just vanished, as well as the destruction, the scandal, and the shame."[10]

Never would King Marke on the Green Hill have expressed himself in this way, even through an intermediary.

> Marke: *Why have you now wounded me so sore?* . . .
> *With your weapon's torturing poison*
> *That scorches and destroys my senses and brain,*
> *That denies me faith in my friend*
> *That fills my trusting heart with suspicion . . . ?*

What Otto did not utter, Wille said for him, and furthermore gave his own advice to the suffering Tristan: "Only one thing matters: let time go by and behave in a dignified manner."

One week later, on November 13, Wagner sent him a reply in the manner of Tristan: "O, King, I cannot say. . . ." Eliza Wille could have dispelled the mistake (like the real Brangäne at the end of Act III); but he understood that she was too kind to attack his real problem. Wille did not know that the motive for his project was of "a very high nature." In his letter to Wille, Wagner asked him to give a message to Mathilde, who had not yet read his diary: "Reassure her that my serenity has been totally recovered, even if it is by other means than the lessons in your letter, which was for me full of knowledge, dear Wille!"

And in the diary for Mathilde, dated November 4, Wagner noted: "The Buddhist beggar had knocked at the wrong door: hunger has become for him a subject of meditation."

∾

After several illnesses and crises of nostalgia, and with work on his composition hardly done, on November 1, "terrible and prolonged torment" made Wagner think of committing suicide. He wrote in his diary: "Now I know it is still possible for me to die in your arms! I'm sure of it. I will soon see you again, certainly in the spring. . . . The last thorn has been pulled out of my soul." And in a passage censored later on by Cosima:[11]

> You tried to find it in the wrong place; it was not my wife but your husband who chased me from your presence. Forgive me for touching once more upon an open wound. For me, it has closed up since this evening. Now I can do anything. . . . Don't place too much importance on my art. . . . For me it is neither a consolation nor a reward; it only accompanies the deep harmony I have with you; it strengthens my desire to die in your arms. . . . With you I can do everything; without you, nothing. . . . My inner self collapses as soon as I notice the slightest disagreement between us. Believe me, my one and only! I am in your hands, it's with you alone that I can reach my destiny.

Then, further on in the uncensored text, he told her about his temptation to commit suicide: "Last night, when I pulled my hand away from the balcony's railing, it was not the thought of my art that held me back! At that terrible instant, I saw in vivid clarity the real pivot of my life, around which my resolution went from death to a new life: it was you! You! I had the impression a smile was hovering over me—wouldn't it be a greater happiness to die in your arms?" At the moment Wagner renounced committing suicide, he felt capable of making a reconciliation: "You see, as I turned around, your husband suddenly became someone else for me. I could shake his hand and ask him humbly for permission to be with you. That's how obstinacy weakens. Your child's death had moved me considerably closer to him. My God, if only I could bring some comfort to him as well! Yes, I want him to keep the mother of his children! She must live—and as a reward, I don't claim anything anymore besides dying in her arms. You must not hold it against me." Strangely, Cosima found it appropriate to cut these lines about Otto.[12]

Meanwhile, back in Zurich, Mathilde shared his delirious dream to die with him, like the little girl in her fairy tale embracing her beautiful white swan. If she could not sail to Kareol, why could she not die too! Besides, what was there left for her in this world from which the child who consoled her was gone? At such a moment as this, she told him of the torment and regret that she continued to experience in spite of everything. "No," answered Richard on December 22, "Have no remorse for your love for me, it is divine!"

"I will see you in the spring," he added.

During the Christmas holidays Mathilde thrust her imagination forward, meeting him in spirit in a new tale she sent him: "On a marvelously mild spring day, the earth looked like a rosebud ready to bloom in the morning dew. At noon the rays of the sun came to attract and delicately caress the buds, for they were still shy and hesitant, like lovers who dare not reveal their sweet secret."

As she did throughout her poetic works, Mathilde would lend a role to the sun, whose multiple attributes appeared in the variety of species of flowers, and whose "strange ideas" became birds. One of these was now hopping around in front of her, and she felt like a "little girl" who wanted to catch it in her apron; the bird flew away, making her romp across fields and prairies, when at last, tired of running, she sat down. The little bird perched on a branch and looked at her. "It was already late in the afternoon; the sun was casting a golden glow on the far-off hills and . . . setting in a sea of dreams while its long shadows, draped in black veils, crossed over the earth."

The little girl thought of what she was supposed to do: her mother was waiting for her to return and was worrying about her being late. But every time she got up to go home, the bird would sing, cry, and weep to keep her with it. She stayed until evening, and the stars began to come out. She picked up the basket of wildflowers she had picked for her mother and got ready to leave. But the bird started singing again, and the child understood its language:

Little child, sweet love,
Don't go away, the fairies are waiting for you
There where the stars are twinkling.
Follow me, follow me!

She ran after it then, even though she knew it was wrong. Such was the subtle mix of emotions in the heart and mind characteristic of Mathilde's soul. "She was already thinking of her mother's joy in greeting such a distinguished guest in their poor abode." It would be splendid indeed, and their inner solitude would vanish. The little girl listened to the song, ran across the wood, and admired the strange bird: "Sometimes its feathers changed colors from pure azure to dark red, like burning coals, or turned green, shining like clear emeralds. Sometimes the bird was all black and dark, iridescent tints glowed on its chest."

Finally, overcome by slumber, she fell asleep on the moss: "Only the river sang in the background, and the wind made the tender leaves tremble on the trees." The bird also slept, dreaming of the stars that fell down from heaven in the form of winged infants with wide-set eyes. One of these pretty babies approached the little girl and held out a toy to her. She would have liked to get up but could not, for her legs were too heavy. She felt as if she were chained to the ground.

"Give me your little wing," she begged the angel, who plucked one off his shoulder. Her two hands were outstretched to take it, her eyes were fixed on the sky—she could see the whole heavens—glory and splendor from a thousand shining suns were streaming down, while hymns in praise of God resounded, singing of eternal and infinite peace. "Ah," she sighed, "How happy I would be up there with all God's saints! But Mother would be sad if I did not come home; and who would take care of her when she is old?" A big tear fell from her eyes. So she returned the little wing. Heaven, angels, and singing—everything disappeared at once, and, sobbing, she woke up.

On the ground lay her basket with her faded flowers strewn around it. In haste, she picked them up and ran off as fast as her legs could carry her. . . . She found the path to her cabin. Suddenly a rustling in the hedge made her heart beat very fast. . . . Alas! It was only a gray sparrow, whose twittering was singing a little morning hymn to the Creator."[13]

In her letters and diary for Wagner, which she would unfortunately destroy a few years later, could Mathilde reveal more clearly than in this tale the main reason for refusing to leave with him—that is, compassion for her family?

By the time Wagner received this present from Mathilde, he too had made some resolutions for the New Year. In his letters from January 1859 on he replaced the familiar form *du* with the formal *Sie*. "Thank you for the lovely fairy tale, friend! It would be easy to explain how in all that comes from you to me, I can find a symbolic meaning." But his letter dwelled on his orchestration of the second act of *Tristan*, his philosophy, and his poetic ideas. "With the thoughtful serenity of the creator, I am now delving into *Tristan*, my work of art that is still in the process of completion. Who could guess what miraculous atmosphere I feel myself pervaded by, torn away from this world to the extent that I can already imagine it defeated? You feel it, you know so! Yes, and none other than you, perhaps!"

In such circumstances, Mathilde was a victim of her own ingenuousness. Duty was calling, and the world was overwhelming her. Carrying the burden of her double mourning—her dead child and her vanished consoling angel—she decked her soul in the grayness of the little sparrow, the monotony of days to come, like a precious gem being buried in the dust of the earth.

Without realizing it, she had passed the romanticism of her youth and her dreams of being in love, to enter fully into the bitter world of the heroines dear to Calderón or Corneille.

14

Voyage to Italy

B y the beginning of 1859 Wagner's situation in Venice had become uncertain. From a financial point of view, his benefactor Julie Ritter's reversal of fortune prevented her from ensuring him his annual pension. As for his friend Liszt, he had been suddenly dismissed from his position as director of the Weimar opera and no longer could have Wagner's works performed.

Moreover, the province of Venice, which had been under the administration of the Austrian Empire since the Congress of Vienna, was sending in troops in what seemed to be preparations for war against France in the very near future, since Napoleon III had sided with the Italian revolutionaries Giuseppe Garibaldi and Camillo Benso di Cavour. As a former revolutionary himself, Wagner was threatened with deportation. However, he was in favor with the local Venetian government, which took legal measures to prolong his stay. But the Austrian police, which, for diplomatic reasons, shared common interests with the kingdom of Saxony, was watching his every move and made the atmosphere around him a stifling one.

In February Wagner wrote to Eliza Wille to ask for a favor. He wished to occupy the second floor in an annex to her house, in the former apartments of her sister, Henriette von Bissing, for three months starting on April 1. After their last exchange of letters, he did not dare write directly to François Wille. But because her husband was out of town, Eliza refused to have the musician in Mariafeld, explaining her reasons to François in March 1859: "The idea of disrupting our life with his presence, his arrogance, his nervous tension, his all and all . . . fills me with despair. I said you were in Mariafeld. *She* must tell her husband that she is against his visit. . . . I don't want Wagner in the annex, not for what people might say, but because it is simply the way I feel. He is not dying; neither is she. We don't have to make this sacrifice. You would be able to handle him; but now the Wesendoncks would think we were bad friends."

Immediately after asking Eliza, and without waiting for an answer, Wagner told Minna in Dresden that he had accepted an "invitation" to Mariafeld. No doubt he wanted to maintain the illusion of good relations with Zurich's high society and at the same time reassure her that he was a "good son." After the Willes turned him down, their relations cooled for several months.

To Mathilde, his alter ego, Richard continued to describe the progress he was making in the composition of *Tristan*: "I am in good spirits because my second act has been completed perfectly." And again, "I have to tell you that I am happy to have received in time a first printed copy of my poem to send you as a present." When Mathilde received this original edition, covered in violet damask,[1] she again wrote Isolde's lines on the title page:

Chosen for me, lost for me,
Heart beloved for eternity.

"At last, yesterday I finished my second act," wrote Wagner on March 10, "and this big musical problem for which the solution seemed so doubtful to everyone, I know I have solved it like no problem ever encountered. It is the summit of my art to date." At the bottom of the original score he wrote, "Endlich! [Finally!] Venedig, 9 märz '59, R. W." A few days before his departure from Venice, on March 18, he sent it to his editor, Härtel, in Leipzig.

On the way back through the Alps, Wagner passed Milan, which was besieged by invading troops. He continued through Como and Lugano, then the Gotthard Pass to Lucerne. "Therefore, for you, my friend, I said farewell to my dreamy Venice. . . . You will hear one day a dream that I put into music over there."

Before settling in for a stay of several months in the annex of the Hotel Schweizerhof in Lucerne, Wagner spent April 2 with the Wesendoncks in Zurich. Otto was there in person to greet him in order to put an end to the wagging tongues of neighbors and relatives. "Uncle" Wagner was a friend of the family with whom they rode through town in a carriage and who smoked cigars on the paths of the grounds surrounding the Green Hill accompanied by the master of the house and a throng of well-behaved children. Nothing could be said about their relations. Mathilde played her role as a kind and discreet wife, completely above suspicion. That theatrical day came to an end without a hitch, Wagner noted in his diary on April 4:

The dream of seeing each other again came true! So we met once more. Was it anything but a dream? What difference was there between what I felt during those hours in your house and that other wonderful dream that haunted my return? It is in fact more real than the other, that serious and melancholy dream. . . . It seems to me I did not see you clearly; we were separated by thick veils of mist through which we hardly heard the sound of each other's voice. In the same way, I do not think you saw me either; it was a ghost, not I, who entered your home. Did you recognize me? Oh heavens! I realize it: this is the road to sanctity! Life and reality assume more and more the substance of a dream. . . . And noticing on your face the marks of so much suffering, raising your thin hand to my lips, I was deeply shaken; a voice cried out that I had an important duty to accomplish. The wonderful strength of our love sufficed until now; it allowed me to attain the possibility of this visit. . . . I could now kiss the doorsill that permitted me to come back to you! So I trust this strength; it will show me how to see you correctly, to see myself with clarity across the veil of expiation that we have thrown over ourselves. Oh blessed saint! Trust me! I will have the strength!

Do not rebuke me for this dream of love
That fills my heart with courage;
Life has become my enemy
Dreams are my friends.[2]

Spring in Lucerne was an enchantment. Blossoming trees and birdsong brought back the will to live and the courage to endeavor. Mathilde, whom Wagner called "Dame Reason," donned her cloak of wisdom when she wrote to him on April 10: "So the child is teaching the master! That noble and divine feeling will make your friend live once more, make her stronger and give her an unshakable serenity for an eternal youth. May she joyfully rest. I also am resting like someone released from death!"

He again began to compose feverishly:

The third act has begun. I clearly realize that I will not invent anything new. This interval of supreme development has given me so much inspiration that I need only bend down to pick up my supply of it in order to nurture the flower. It seems to me that this act, apparently the most painful, will not perturb me as much as could be expected. The second disturbed me deeply. The most intense fire of life gushed out of it with such a flame that it burned and nearly consumed me. When the blaze diminished near the end of the act, when the sweet clarity of a transfiguration in death began to glow across the flame, I found tranquility; I will play this passage for you when you come. I have high hopes for the end!

During the days that followed, he wrote again: "My child, this *Tristan* is becoming more and more terrible! This last act!! I fear this opera may be censored, unless a poor performance turns it into a parody. Only mediocre performances could save me! If they were perfectly done, the audience might become mad. . . . That's what I had to do again. Poor me!"

"Child, child, at this moment, tears are running down my cheeks." He quoted the lines of Kurwenal to his dying master: "It is an unheard-of tragedy! It is overwhelming!"

On April 15 Otto received him again in Zurich, as a confirmation to the world of their good relations, thus restoring his wife's reputation in spite of all the gossip. Wagner stayed for two days and sent a report to Minna:...

Wesendonck invited me here a few days ago; he wanted me to stay in his house, he sent a carriage to the station to fetch me, and he gave me to understand that he wanted to put an end, through our open and friendly relations, to all the exaggerations and distortions of reality. I therefore accepted and came to Zurich on Saturday, I rode in Wesendonck's carriage, I spent the night in his house, and I left on Sunday afternoon, after having taken another ride with the master of the house, and paid one only visit to Heim. That was, we both hope, a very good demonstration, and of course everybody will understand the nature of my relations with the family, which, I may say, already greatly impressed the servants. It was very good and fortunate and removed a heavy burden from my heart. I hope you too will benefit from the result, which was so soothing for Wesendonck. Before leaving Switzerland for good, I think I will accept his invitation once more, but on a day on which there will be a lot of guests.

Immediately Minna wrote to Jakob Sulzer deploring the trickery played on to Otto, for she was well informed of "certain abominations."[3]

For posterity, Wagner in his autobiography left a puzzling remark: "Our meeting again was melancholy, but without any embarrassment. I stayed for a few days in their home and saw some of my former acquaintances. It was like the dream of a dream."

As for Mathilde, she let us guess her reality through her poetry:

What is life?
What is a dream?
What is true, what is false?
Oh, let me dream on,
I have lived enough.[4]

While Wagner pondered his bitterness in Lucerne's foul weather (it rained all the time, he said) and read Goethe, Mathilde occupied herself with her daily life, her children's education, and her Italian lessons. Yet her sorrow remained in her heart, as we can see by the poignant lines she wrote on the death of her son. At times she took his clothing out and looked at it; sometimes she would sing him a lullaby:

Rest, my dear child,
In calm and sweetness, rest,
You, my dear little one, whom early death
Carried to your tomb.

Even if my burning tears
Flow to thee,
I see you happy in my mind
In your cold cradle.

Never would I disturb
Your sweet repose:
So that suffering be far from you,
Sleep, my darling, sleep!

Fly away, my angel!
Fly off to heaven

And weave with the stars
Your bright way.[5]

After Guido's death Wagner wrote a touching letter to the child's sister, Myrrha, who was eight years old. The little girl answered him with her "fine handwriting, which she had learned from her mother." Since relations between them were to be cordial, the children became a subject of conversation. "My greetings to Myrrha," wrote Richard, "and to Karl, who has surprised me so much. I called him Siegfried when he was born and baptized him in my heart, like an uninvited godfather. Truly, that name was lucky for the boy: look what a pretty little fellow he's becoming!"

The bad weather affected Wagner's capacity to work: "I work well for only a short time each day," he wrote Mathilde. "But it doesn't last long, nor do my flashes of inspiration; often I would prefer not to do anything, if I were not afraid of the horrible prospect of an empty day." Mathilde learned everything about Wagner's creative genius, "for," he continued, "I know I am more sincere with you than with myself."

～

The French and Austrian troops that had mobilized in northern Italy were disrupting communications on the borders. In Lucerne, Wagner was still waiting for a trunk he had sent from Venice. Full of sundry papers, there were notes and drafts of his future works, in particular the outlines for *Siegfried*. He was thinking also of traveling—maybe to Paris, or to New York, where Mathilde's brother Edward Luckemeyer, a businessman, had settled. A concert tour of the United States had been proposed to him. But first he had to finish *Tristan*.

Wagner had not managed to obtain an amnesty from the king of Saxony. His letters to Mathilde took on a cynical note when he spoke of the political situation. The conflict would come to a head the following June at the Battles of Magenta and Solferino, in which the French were victorious.

He wrote again to Mathilde about his projects for Paris: "It is quite interesting that I am running toward the enemy capital just when war is breaking out between Germany and France. Mind you, I fear I may lose all notion of patriotism, and I could even rejoice if the Germans were defeated once more. Bonapartism is an acute pain but won't last for long, while the German-Austrian reaction is on the contrary a chronic and long-lasting disease."

Antipatriotism was his answer to the German theaters that had rejected his works. One year later he wrote to Liszt: "Believe me, we have no country. And if I am 'German,' it is certainly within myself that I carry my Germany."

The bad weather persisted, and his nervousness and intestinal problems prevented Wagner from working. On May 8 he mentioned his despair to Liszt and doubted he could manage to finish his opera. He went so far as to say he was finished as a composer! To Mathilde he described his disarray in the face of the work that had yet to be done, sparing her none of the details; at the sentence of the text that began with the words "not to die of desire," the musical transition was lacking, for example. But here in another missive, one full of humor, he sent his enthusiastic praise to Mathilde, the "far-off healer" who had sent him the absolute remedy for his intestinal disorder: zwieback![6] "Now I am completely happy—the transition is accomplished better than one could imagine by the absolutely splendid link between the two themes. What good those zwieback could produce! Zwieback! Zwieback! You are the remedy for composers in distress." Mathilde then sent him such a large supply of these "miraculous" biscuits that he complained about having no place to store them.

Also during this period, Wagner rediscovered the music of J. S. Bach and his contrapuntal technique, in which several themes are interwoven. In the middle of May, during his third visit to the Wesendoncks in Zurich, he played pieces by Bach for Mathilde. He wrote to her on July 9: "What a pleasure it was. Never had Bach given me such a joy: never had I felt as close to him. But that never happens to me when I am alone. . . . As stupid as I may have seemed to you the last time in Lucerne, our meeting produced for me the noblest of fruits. You can verify that now upon seeing my great fervor at work. And I would not be grateful to you?"

On June 10 the Wesendoncks came to visit Wagner in Lucerne. Mathilde gave Richard a recently published copy of Wolfram von Eschenbach's *Parzival*. During the composition of the third act of *Tristan*, Wagner developed an association of ideas between Isolde's lover, in agony on the island of Kareol and the wounded king, Amfortas. Both heroes experienced a similar purgatory in the absence of absolute love. Mathilde Wesendonck remembered all this at the premiere of *Parsifal* in Bayreuth in 1882.

The evening of July 10, the date on which Wagner finished his composition draft, he wrote to Mathilde: "The only thing I sadly miss, my child, is your presence. I know no other person to whom I can confide more fully. . . . When I think of all the goodness and beauty that you have been able to make me express, I am happy that you always managed to stir in me only what was best."

Mathilde thus assisted the genius of her heart and soul to the utmost. She gave him everything—her love, her friendship, and her untiring attention during the difficult birth of his greatest works. And yet, most of Wagner's biographers have minimized her role as inspiration, even sometimes for *Tristan*, in spite of evidence in their correspondence that explicitly contradicts this view.

Throughout this very productive period, Wagner's tone of gaiety and good humor shows us a man satisfied with himself, as in the early days of his relationship with the Wesendoncks in Zurich. More than once he thanked Mathilde for her "beautiful letters," her little gifts, her attention. He praised her talent: "Thanks to the charming lady with her fairy tales! She tells her stories so well and yet does not have the wrinkles of experience, like Grimm!" And another time: "So profoundly and so cleverly have you sought throughout nature for the threads you use to weave your tales that one need only stand once on the parapet of your terrace to know with what you have created this world of fantasy, in which all life is included so charmingly."

In August the Wesendoncks returned to Lucerne, at the very moment when Wagner had finished his rewriting of *Tristan*'s third act, and his hotel bill at the Schweizerhof was—we should not be surprised to learn—paid by Otto. Wagner was trying to fill out the numerous forms he required to obtain his passport for France. During his friends' visit he celebrated from a distance the Dresden premiere of *Lohengrin*, which was taking place on that very day, and he admitted he must have been the only German who had never seen the work onstage! After the Wesendoncks' departure he packed his suitcases and decided on the way to Paris to pay another visit to them on the Green Hill.

> *I would like to come to you like the Spring,*
> *With resounding song, flowers, and voluptuous perfume,*
> *I would like to accompany you through life,*
> *Spread at your feet all the treasures of the earth.*[7]

Once *Tristan* was finally finished, Mathilde felt the painful beginning of their real separation. All she had left of her love for Richard was a kind of maternal affection; she would lavish advice and care on the man she loved. At the end of the century Cosima von Bülow, who had since married Wagner, told her daughter Eva that Richard had complained about the "governess style" of Mathilde's letters. Her remark seems a rather unkind description of Mathilde's final assistance to her friend who was drifting away.

"I want to follow some of your advice," wrote Wagner, "and not worry about anything in the world in the meanwhile." She congratulated him on his attitude, yet the ungrateful genius answered, "But, my child, what makes you see or desire in me a wise man? I am the most frivolous creature one can imagine."

So she played the game and teased him, caressing him with her words, like the little girl with the swan. "Your note today, it is true, was very malicious; but nevertheless, it did please me, since it showed your good humor."

Before leaving Switzerland for Paris, Wagner spent another three days at the Wesendoncks' villa. Otto had managed the situation so well that the whole neighborhood was intrigued by the cordiality of their relations. In *My Life* Wagner mentioned that he was treated with great regard.

At this point he sold his rights to the publication of the *Ring* to Otto. The contract was written up in Zurich and signed on September 8, 1859, between two puffs of a good cigar.

> According to the contract of September 7 of this year, I received for the scores of *Das Rheingold*
> and *Die Walküre*, six thousand francs cash and a letter of exchange for the amount of six thousand francs from the firm Ulrich Zellweger & Co. in Paris.
>
> Signed: Richard Wagner

But two months later, on November 7, having squandered the entire sum of 12,000 francs on his Parisian lodgings and his project for a series of concerts, Wagner wrote to Wesendonck to ask him for another contract of 6,000 francs for his still unfinished opera *Siegfried*.

In December, the editor Franz Schott, in Mainz, offered to publish *Das Rheingold* and proposed to give Wagner 10,000 francs, thus purchasing the rights already sold to Wesendonck, if Wagner obtained his permission. But instead of reimbursing Wesendonck his 6,000 francs immediately, Wagner spent the money on his concerts, stating that he would pay him back later on. This is what he did in June 1860 by "selling" to Otto his rights on *Götterdämmerung*. It had not yet been written, but he proposed to force himself to undertake it and finish within the year.

However, five years later, Wagner requested that Otto hand over the original scores of *Das Rheingold* and *Die Walküre*, which were still in his possession, to King Ludwig II of Bavaria. This meant that Wesendonck, distinguished benefactor that he was, would have given a total of 24,000 francs to Wagner, with nothing in return but the memory of a good deed.

Fearing that the offhand manner in which all this was done might come as a shock to his friend, Wagner wrote Otto on June 17, 1860: "It is quite possible that you may have reproaches for me; but is it possible to postpone them and keep them for another time, so that they may not increase my present bitterness, which is the deepest thing one can feel in life?" Little did Wagner understand this "noble lord," thinking he would bear the composer a grudge! Wesendonck in fact did just the opposite. In 1865 he wrote to Wagner: "I would consider myself more than richly rewarded if, thanks to a marvelous performance, this work became famous."

On September 10, 1859, after spending a friendly evening on the Green Hill in the company of his old friends Herwegh, Gottfried Keller, and Gottfried Semper, Wagner left for Paris, where other events awaited him—not the troops of Napoleon III on their return from Solferino, but rather the members of a certain Jockey Club that, even more dreadful for him, eighteen months later would organize the (bloodless) battle of *Tannhäuser*.

∾

"How lovely to be able to write to you today in Rome!" exclaimed Wagner to Otto on December 12, 1859. "I am especially curious to know how that disagreeable sea voyage went. It is true that my mind need not be put to rest on the subject of your wife, who has already withstood longer crossings; but I hope with all my heart that the children have not suffered too much from it."

In November the Wesendoncks had taken all their household of children and servants to Italy via Geneva, Lyon, and Marseille. There a happier season of joy awaited them, where they could erase some of their sad memories. On November 4 the Willes threw a going-away party for them, where they found their old friends Hermann Köchly, Ludwig Ettmüller, and Keller. According to Eliza Wille, they read Shakespeare's *Merry Wives of Windsor* together. It was done with "a lot of humor" and a "perfect command of the text."[8]

Which role did Mathilde play? We will never know. But certainly the truculent Falstaff could have been played by François Wille!

At the end of the month the Wesendoncks embarked in Marseille on a steamship of the Messageries Impériales. On November 29 Wagner wrote again: "Welcome to France! Now the poet of the *Nibelungen* is coming to you with outstretched hands." The itinerary of the Wesend-onck family on their way to Rome can be established from Wagner's letters. Because Lombardy had been the site of the recent battles between France and Austria, the inland routes were not secure; it was much more prudent to sail south along the coast of Italy.

On the main deck, the children, who had been bundled up in Zurich, were struck by the warm climate of the Mediterranean. Wagner was amused by the way Karl's big hat fell down over his ears—a scene he envisaged in his mind's eye. In the calm of her cabin Mathilde read Richard's last letter, in which he complained about his difficult relations with everyone he encountered: "I cannot be sincere and true with anyone; everywhere there are problems and troubles that I do not know how to deal with. But as soon as you answer, I find myself to be better—everything, including myself, appears noble to me. I feel rescued. My children, that we remain three, it is indeed a great miracle![9] . . . My cordial and joyful greetings accompany you during your voyage to Italy. . . . Enjoy for me the good weather, the poetry of the landscape, the living past, and thus be twice as happy. What ineffable joy it would bring me to be with you!"

At ten in the morning they weighed anchor in the port of Marseille to cross the Gulf of Genoa. The next morning they had to spend several hours in Livorno to obtain visas from the Spanish consulate in charge of the Papal States. Rome at the time was in papal territory, under the protection of Napoleon III. The Catholic nations of Europe had guaranteed its neutrality.

The ship sailed along the Tuscan coast, and in the evening it glided across the peaceful waters between Elba and Piombino. On the third day they disembarked at Civitavecchia, only a few hours by train from the city of Rome.[10] The Roman countryside was tinted blue and green. On approaching the Monte Albino, the brightness of the sun on stone made their eyes water. Then came the majestic city of Rome, spread out on its hills. The travelers' dazzling experience ceased as soon as they got off the train and became part of the jostling crowd.

Mathilde had prepared for her stay in Rome with the Italian lessons she had received from de Sanctis; she now taught a few rudimentary expressions to her children. With Otto she had put together a tour to visit the city's monuments, churches, palaces, and galleries. They made excursions to the countryside, to quaint villages in the shadow of cypresses; to museums, with paintings by Raphael, Murillo, and Pinturicchio, and frescoes by Michelangelo. "You certainly heard with great emotion the religious music played in the Sistine Chapel," wrote Wagner. "And what you said about it brought back to my mind many things that were dormant within me."

All that would have just been a tourist attraction or a lesson in the fine arts if that year in Rome had not made such a deep impression on Mathilde's mind. Until then she had been familiar with the seriousness of Wagner's work, attached as it was to the metaphysical conceptions of German culture. Now she was suddenly confronted by the Italian art of the Renaissance, inspired by the pagans of antiquity. It all produced a temporary calm in her and a new direction in her life. Sculptured stone, polished marble, figures of Venus and Apollo, paintings of sweet madonnas, and sublime nativities together produced an irresistible invitation to forget.

In this artistic nirvana, she turned to mythology and legend as a source of inspiration for her own writing.

From Rome she wrote many long letters to her beloved. None of the passionate vows that we can imagine were in her missives have survived. But in her correspondence with Francesco de Sanctis in Zurich she expressed some of the violent feelings that had shaken her. On April 28, 1860, in mistake-ridden Italian, she confessed to him:

> There are wounds that never heal, but also, what would love be without pain and without memories? It would be like anything else that comes and goes without leaving a mark. I think it is just that those who have loved leave a desert behind them. . . . You speak about the tranquility of the soul; I must say, that doesn't exist for me. That tranquility is a dream. You said many times that you used to dream. I am too familiar with suffering not to respect the suffering of others. The reason for our stay in Rome is precisely to find forgetfulness and give my thoughts, which are too full of the past, another direction. There is no reason for the admiration that you express for me in your letter, because you do not know the pain in my heart; and believe me, if we women have merit somewhere, it is certainly in the heart.

By the time Mathilde returned to Zurich in June 1860, de Sanctis had gone back to southern Italy to join the forces of Garibaldi at the moment of his triumph in Naples. The professor became the governor of Avellino in September 1860, and he continued to write to his former pupil, asking her "not to forget a man who had as much love and esteem for her as he did."

~

From Paris Wagner continued a voluminous correspondence with Mathilde, giving her his impressions of France and the French people, while she did the same from Italy. On January 1 he wrote: "Your letter proves to me that now I can perfectly abandon you to yourself. You have opened your own eyes and looked. . . . Maybe you had neglected to do so before. Look and see for me as well; I need it and I would prefer that no one but you do so in my stead." She had written to him about the "artistic peace" of these pagan stones and the dazzling sunlight on the marble statues, as white as snow. "What you call 'artistic peace,'" said Wagner, "seems to me to act from the outside, like an appeasement of inner disarray. . . . May magnificent peace fall gently on your eyes, child!"

Wagner confided his artistic worries to her. While having the musicians rehearse for his concerts in Paris, he realized suddenly the abyss that separated him from the music of his time. During the first rehearsal of the Prelude to *Tristan*, "It appeared to me that the scales were falling from my eyes. . . . That little Prelude was so inconceivably new for the musicians that I was forced to conduct them from one note to another, as if they were discovering precious gems in a mine." Then, after expressing his anguish, he declared: "Oh! Stay in Rome! How happy I am to know that you are in another world. Look! Contemplate! Meditate well. Do it for me, and it will be a relief to receive from you these intimate and profound images. That will refresh and comfort me as I tremble with fever! You are now my supreme consolation!"

He told her about his concerts in 1860 in the Salle Ventadour. He conducted excerpts of his works: *Der fliegende Holländer, Tannhäuser, Lohengrin,* and that Prelude of *Tristan,* which left the audience deeply perplexed. But in general, the pieces performed, especially the March from *Tannhäuser* and the Prelude to *Lohengrin,* won over to his cause a crowd of admirers and the fervent enthusiasm of Charles Baudelaire, Camille Saint-Saëns, Charles Gounod, and many other Frenchmen. It came as a great surprise to Wagner that, without even knowing the German language, these people expressed a passion for his music. He told Mathilde of his encounter with Edmond Roche, a customs officer, who loved his music as well and took pains to help him through the usual formalities. But, said Wagner, "as he knows no German, I objected and said it was hard for me to understand what pleasure he could have in reading my music, so intimately linked as it was to the poetry and versification. He replied that it was because it was so close to the text that it easily led to the poetry of the music, making the foreign language quite intelligible. What could I say? I have to start believing in miracles . . . and all this at customs!"

His debut in Paris was promising: "People play my *Tannhäuser* and *Lohengrin* impeccably well. They don't seem to be at a loss because of their ignorance of the German language." A bitter remark came nonetheless to his lips: "If in Zurich, out of gratitude for the honest work I did there, you had been capable of building me a half-decent theater, I would have had what I needed for the rest of my life, and I would have nothing to ask of anyone."

Welcomed in Paris at the beginning of his stay, Wagner looked down somewhat on his earlier artistic career. He gave Mathilde the finest analysis of his own mode of thought: "My most subtle and deepest art is what I would call the art of transition, for all my work is composed of these transitions. . . . My masterpiece in the art of building to a climax is no doubt the main scene of the second act of *Tristan und Isolde.* At the start, the first scene shows life overflowing with passion; at the end, the solemn and profound desire for death. Those are the mainstays: see now, child, how I put them together, how we pass from one to the other. That is where the mystery of my musical form lies, and I am audacious enough to declare that never before this day has such a chord, or such a clear ordering in which all details are laid out, been imagined." In the same letter Wagner upheld his ideas with moral considerations: his life experience, his conflicts (lack of "transitions") with his fellow men. He thus spoke of his dispute with Semper on their last evening together in Zurich. In a word, it was necessary to cure once and for all the communication problem between human beings. Was that not the true aim of "transition"?

His stay in Paris left Wagner no time for creating any new works. In January 1860 he gave Mathilde a very detailed report on his concerts, on his quarrels with Berlioz and his meeting with Rossini, on everything he did and everything he thought. What impression did these letters make on the soul of his muse, who had run off to Rome in search of peace and forgetfulness? She could perceive Richard in them through the veil of unreality, while measuring the privilege of being the confidante to such a genius. He wrote: "You know, my child, that I look neither right nor left, nor in front nor in back, that time and the world are indifferent matters for me and that only one thing determines me—the necessity of relieving my soul; therefore you also know the only thing that is important to me."

Finally, after innumerable intrigues, and thanks to the intervention of Pauline de Metternich, the wife of the Austrian ambassador in Paris, Napoleon III personally gave the order to produce *Tannhäuser* at the Opéra. However, the management demanded a ballet in order to satisfy the French audience, notably the members of the Jockey Club, "rich and fashionable young men" of bourgeois extraction or recent nobility who were used to attending only the beginning of the second act of a performance in order to see their mistresses dancing in it. At first, greatly surprised, Wagner refused; he then decided to fulfill the obligation, developing the scene of the Venusberg bacchanal at the beginning of the work. Faithful, however, to his artistic creed, of which the first point was "no effect without a cause," he absolutely dismissed the principle of a ballet in the second act. He showed the minute plans he had made for these modifications, including the dancers' movements, to Mathilde: "I have written to you once more a real *Kapellmeister*'s letter, don't you think? And this time it is also the letter of a ballet director." He worked on it for months, all the while dealing with administrative problems, as in the world of Balzac. By April he was depressed and complained to Mathilde that she did not send long enough answers to his missives. "And why don't you write to me anymore? And Otto? . . . Where can I find the letters now that give me joy? . . . Think of it, dear child: you are all I have in this world; I live for you, by you, and with you; and the game interests me only because I can complain to you about my distress and you, you welcome my complaint so sweetly."

Up until then Mathilde had tried to be strong. She did not want to crush Richard with her own sorrow. Later on, in a poem, she cried out her love that "must never be contrary to anyone!"

I would like to meekly close my lips,
Pronounce not the slightest word,
Even if my heart, with anxious rejoicing,
Threatened to burst in my chest![11]

But after Wagner's insistence, she yielded and described for him the state of her soul during her sojourn in Rome, to which Richard replied: "Your remembrances have made a vivid impression on me. It is incredible to what extent one can bear the devastation of one's life. What is left must be miserably small or sublimely great."

The Wesendoncks left Rome at the end of May; Mathilde's last letter arrived in Paris the day after Richard's birthday. He answered by return post: "This morning in bed, I opened your last letter from Rome and perused its contents. Maurice came to tell me my bath was ready. He found me in tears and quietly shut the door."

For Mathilde, Wagner developed a true chronicle of his time, describing the details of his disagreements first with Berlioz, then with Liszt. A shadow fell on the relations between Wagner and his old friend Franz, who had fallen under the influence of the domineering Caroline zu Sayn-Wittgenstein.

Before their departure from Rome, as was the custom, Otto and Mathilde threw a coin into the Trevi Fountain to ensure their return to the Eternal City. Wagner's letter alluded to it: "Yesterday you drank at the fountain to my health. Oh my child, what did you wish for me? Believe me, the gods could not do any better for me than to let you drink the water of that spring while I was in your thoughts, so that you could learn all the beautiful secrets of Rome."

By June the Wesendoncks were back in Zurich, and in July they took up their social life in the beautiful mansion on the Green Hill. The Italian sunshine had reinvigorated Mathilde, and in the absence of the protagonists who had created such a scandal, much of the gossip that had so entertained Zurich's high society had died down. During the summer Wagner, still in Paris, was ruminating bitterly over how hostile Germany remained in his regard when news came that he had obtained a partial amnesty to the German Confederation—though not to Saxony, his birthplace. Pursuing his correspondence with Mathilde, he developed once more his ideas for *Parsifal* and in September announced the beginning of rehearsals for *Tannhäuser*.

If Mathilde, in Rome, had managed to gain more self-control, Richard was always in the center of her heart. Though set aside in her daily life, he appeared to her in her dreams, where she could see, hear, and embrace him. This is what she buried in such poems as "Mignon," written a few years later. In Italy she had learned to apply some of the Mediterranean influence:

> *Eros plucked a rose*
> *In which a bee was asleep.*
> *He took the rose to his face;*
> *The bee awoke and stung him.*
> *Crying out, Eros ran to Cythera,*
> *Telling her tearfully of his pain:*
> *Mother, Mother, woe to me!*
> *I am dying! A bee has stung me to death!*
> *But Cythera smiled and answered him:*
> *You felt the pain of a bee who stings;*
> *Of the arrows that you send*
> *You never felt the bitter acrimony.*[12]

She sent him presents—three engravings she had brought back from Rome. When she described to him the beauty of Italian painting; Wagner would only shrug his shoulders: "Ah! How passionately delighted the child has become with Raphael! How lovely, delightful, and relaxing it is! I am the only person that all that has never had any effect on. I am still the barbarian who, the whole year I have been living in Paris, has not even visited the Louvre! Doesn't that say it all?" And while the composer had to argue continuously with the mediocre orchestra conductor he was forced to accept for the performance of *Tannhäuser*, as well as with the singers and musicians, the administrators and press, while suffering a long bout of typhoid, Mathilde was living a peaceful and orderly life. "You have paintings and you love them," wrote Richard once more. "You read, you study, you listen; you take from all that whatever you consider to be digni-fied and noble, and you remain insensitive to what you might have neglected. All your letters, even the last ones of this past winter, agree that the happiness of peace and joy has descended upon you." And he ended the year 1860 with a final impulse of theatrical nostalgia by wishing his beloved serenity: "And that rest, it is my present to you! In the happy consciousness of what you are for me, the angel of my rest, the guardian of my life, find also the noble source that irrigates the desert of your existence! Share my rest with me and receive it from me. . . . How I rejoice at this moment being completely immersed in you! Such is my wish, my gift!"

After the dream of love, the dream of rest! What more could one desire?

〜

In February 1861, as the battle of *Tannhäuser* was looming on the horizon, Wagner described to Mathilde in detail the receptions where he mixed with Parisian high society. Reading between the lines, we discover a tangle of intrigues—jealousy, resentment, political ambition. Wagner added an invitation for them to attend the premiere at the end of the month. Mathilde hesi-tated. Would she attend the performance or not? After a moment of uncertainty, she turned him down, seeing in her mind's eye a crowd of hostile socialites looking her over and point-ing their fingers at her, the master's old flame. Besides, she knew that Minna was living with Richard in Paris, and meeting her would reawaken their mutual resentment. In the end, Otto announced he would go alone.

To Wagner's great shock, Liszt did not come either. He was no doubt held back more by the animosity of the Princess Caroline than by his affairs.

The first performance, which had been scheduled for February 22, then postponed to February 25, was finally given on March 13. Otto, who had arrived too soon, attended only the last rehearsals and had to leave before the scandalous public performances took place. On the day of the grand premiere, in the presence of the imperial court and while most of the audience was enthusiastic, the gentlemen of the Jockey Club went wild with rage, whistling, shouting, and making animal sounds in order to prevent the opera from being performed.

The second performance took place on the eighteenth, once again in the presence of the emperor and empress, and the tumult began again in the middle of the second act: "It's the Jockeys, we are lost!" cried out the stagehands in the wings where Wagner was standing. Wag-ner's friends reacted—Malwida von Meysenbug was indignant and von Bülow broke down in tears.

At the third and last performance on March 24, it became clear that without this small group of opponents, *Tannhäuser* would have been a triumph. But the truth was, these frivolous parasites, who knew nothing about art and even less about integrity, were using this occasion to strike indirectly at the regime of Napoleon III, whom they opposed for his complacency toward Austria. Wagner, that half-mad revolutionary—who was he to preach to wealthy young French aristocrats?

The Wesendoncks read the critiques in the Zurich press. Wagner published in German his own account of the event in the *Deutsche allgemeine Zeitung für Musik* on April 7; the article was reprinted in the *Neue Zeitschrift für Musik* on the twelfth.

Mathilde was aghast and did not hide her fury. When de Sanctis, in a letter from Naples, mentioned that a certain Signor Passerini had described her as "only a little angry at Paris," Mathilde answered him immediately in French: "My anger indeed would have existed only in the imagination of this man, or maybe also was it not a humorous little attack against my friend himself? Was he thinking of the failure of *Tannhäuser* in Paris? That did not even make Wagner angry. It was to be expected, even though we did not know the importance of such an infamous and miserable intrigue. The work itself will not suffer from it. The day will come, in a more civilized world, when *Tannhäuser* will be performed in Paris; only patience is necessary. Artistic reforms go so slowly that one can hardly despair of success. In any case, they continue."

The whole Parisian adventure left Wagner with nothing but a "feeling of bitterness and precipitated him again into a new crisis of nostalgia: "My child, where has the happiness of our evenings with Calderón gone? What ominous star made me leave my only worthy Asyl? Believe me, whatever other rumor you may have heard, when I left that little house, my star fell; I cannot fall anymore! Never, never have any other opinion about it! . . . I am not complaining, I am not accusing: it was to be so, but to remain just toward me, you must never forget it!"

In May Wagner consoled himself by going to Venice, where for the first time in his life he heard and saw his opera *Lohengrin*. He wrote immediately to Mathilde: "I have just attended a rehearsal of *Lohengrin*! The incredibly amazing effect of this first hearing of my work in the most beautiful and pleasant circumstances, as much for the artist as for the man, I cannot keep locked up inside me and not tell you of it. . . . Twelve years of my life (and what years!) I was able to relive again!! You were right to have wished me that joy. . . . Ah, if only you could be there tomorrow!"

After Venice, Vienna. He stopped off in Zurich before going back to Paris to settle his business. There, at the Wesendoncks', he celebrated his forty-eighth birthday on May 22, in the presence of his friends Sulzer, Herwegh, Keller, and Semper. A few days later he wrote about this reunion with Mathilde: "A dream came true before dissolving again in the mist of memory!" All these "pretty gifts" and those charming letters comforted him. He had hoped also for more financial aid from Otto, but this time news from America had plunged his friends into consternation. The New York Stock Exchange had fallen brutally following the outburst of the American Civil War. Wesendonck and his brother's American investments were in jeopardy. To a friend in Prague Wagner admitted he was deeply impoverished, that he was preparing to move back to Germany, and that a friend of his (Otto Wesendonck) could not come to his aid. "After all his living expenses were deducted, the Paris *Tannhäuser* brought Wagner the sum of 750 francs."[13]

In June he wrote a letter to Mathilde signed "the Gray One." His good humor came back little by little. In her infinite patience with this enfant terrible, Mathilde answered him in a long, amusing, and poetic letter, one of the fourteen that have remained after Cosima's auto-da-fé:

Maybe it would please our friend if we remind him of the good old days. He knows many things, but he is gray and sad; thank God, he does not know it yet. Ebb and flow, light and shadow, such is the time of youth. Those states of the mind that you indicate in your last letter, the "Gray One" knows them not; besides, we know they will pass, and that is a consolation. While I am here on the balcony, writing to you, the Alps are glowing at twilight in hues of soft red. If only I were able to borrow a rosy reflection to instill it into your soul! . . . Now darkness is closing in, the mountains are pale and dead; silence is so deep! May the calm, calm and holy peace descend in your heart!

During the summer Wagner still complained: the little dog Mathilde had given him had just died. "With this little animal," he wrote, "I have buried many things." "I have not been writing to you because I do not want to give you sorrow. I think only too much about you!"

As for Mathilde, she had asserted herself since her voyage to Italy. In July 1861 she sent news to de Sanctis:

Here, not much has changed. Rome was very enriching for us. The green dining room, where we often had tea together, is now decorated with four beautiful copies of Raphael. That adds something wonderful to the room. Many paintings that we purchased there have followed us, and we continue, as in a great collection of photographs, sculptures, and paintings to live amid beauty, and to renew every day our unforgettable remembrances of Rome. . . . Myrrha has grown a great deal; she likes her studies and still has her sweet, kind temperament. . . . Karl is tall, wild, and mischievous, a real boy who never knows what to do with his strength.

In September Mathilde went to Düsseldorf to visit her sick mother. She died only a few months afterward, and the kind old lady that Wagner used to call "the Queen" would become one of the principal characters in Mathilde's fairy tales.

Wagner was preparing to go to Vienna, but before leaving Paris he came across the big green portfolio sent by his beloved to Venice. On opening it and examining its contents, memories overtook him, and he wrote to Mathilde: "Heavens, what do I see? Two photographs: one of the birthplace of *Tristan*, that is, the Green Hill and the Asyl, and the other of the palace in Venice. Then the original sheets of paper with the outlines, strange embryos, the lines of the dedication too, with which I had sent them one day, . . . the outlines of the first act in pencil, finished; what a pleasure these lines gave me! They are pure and loyal. I also found, written in pencil, the song from which the night scene was taken. God knows, that song pleased me much more than the finished scene, which is superb. Good gracious! It's more beautiful than everything else I have done! When I hear it I tremble to the very ends of my nerves. And to carry in one's heart the omnipresence of such a memory without being blessed, how could it be possible? I then closed the portfolio; but I opened the last letter with the portrait, and a cry burst out from me! Pardon! Pardon! I shall not repeat it!"

Old wounds are so fragile.

~

In August 1861, while traveling between Weimar and Vienna, Richard Wagner spent a day in Nuremberg to visit the town. He remembered a certain outline in three acts and in prose on the subject of the late-medieval *Meistersinger*, which he wrote about in 1845 while on vacation in Marienbad. In September he again faced financial disaster, and he asked his publisher for an advance on *Tristan*, which he hoped to have performed in Vienna during that winter. The money was not forthcoming, so he wrote back to Schott in October promising him a marvelous new opera—*Die Meistersinger von Nürnberg*. He sent the publisher the outline; it was supposed to be a light opera that would be popular and easy to stage. Most important, it would not be as difficult to sing as *Tristan*.

From Vienna Wagner wrote to the Wesendoncks. As usual the musician oscillated between hope and despair. Mathilde invited him to meet them somewhere on his itinerary—why not Venice?

"Next Monday Otto and I are leaving for Italy," she wrote. "We will not stay there very long." Certain allusions show that she was aware Richard was brooding over a new work: "Understanding the pains of giving birth to *Tristan*, I was only thinking for that moment of a short meeting," she continued.

It took place in Venice at the beginning of November. From Vienna Wagner took the train to Trieste, then a boat to the city of the doges. He booked a room at the Hotel Danieli and met his friends the next day. In her letter to Wagner of October 23, 1861, Mathilde had tossed out the idea, in the form of a polite suggestion, that Richard might be able to return to the Asyl: "Will the time ever come again when [our friend] may find rest on the Green Hill? We hope so." On his side, Richard secretly held on to the hope of going back to his little house and living near them. But, he wrote to Mathilde in December, "one hour in Venice was enough to destroy this last and dearest illusion."

What happened?

Wagner had found a Mathilde who was completely assured and calm, as he had always wished for her to become again. But she appeared to him a little too happy for his taste, too lovely, smiling, and elegant, enjoying a new kind of complicity with her husband. Otto, also calm and satisfied, gave an impression of unreality to Wagner, who always saw his rival as a *grand monsieur*, wearing a "monstrous spy-glass" slung across his chest and being the chief obstacle between him and his beloved. In fact Richard had unwittingly discovered in Mathilde that particular glow on the face of a pregnant woman. Indeed, at the beginning of a new pregnancy, her eyes had the radiance of a Titian madonna.

Feeling his presence to be superfluous and his return to Zurich impossible, he explained later to Mathilde: "It was that and only that weighing on me in Venice like lead on my soul." She had noticed his sadness and depression. To cheer him up during their ride in a gondola and their visits to museums, churches, and galleries, she made him talk about his projects and encouraged him to write *Die Meistersinger*. Besides, she continued, his voluminous outline of the subject written in Marienbad was still in her house in Zurich. As soon as she returned, she would send it to him in Vienna.

It was then, going through the painting gallery at the Academy of Fine Arts with his two friends, that Wagner stopped with sudden emotion before Titian's *Assumption of the Virgin* "and . . . resolved to write *Die Meistersinger,*" as he noted in his autobiography. In December, in a letter to Mathilde about his outlines, which were becoming more and more elaborate, he wrote: "Yes, one must have been to Paradise to know finally what there is in such a work!"

And what precisely had he seen in the *Assumption*? A Virgin whose features reminded him of Mathilde Wesendonck, in the attitude of the transfiguration of Isolde singing the "Liebestod," her arms stretched up to heaven. She was showing him Paradise, and for Wagner, that paradise could be won only through his labors. In his mind the trigger was pulled.

As soon as he was back in Vienna, Wagner began a second version, discarding the plan he had already sent to Schott without waiting for news from Mathilde. Wagner's great English biographer Ernest Newman examined these outlines and compared them to the final libretto that Wagner wrote in December and January. In the 1845 version the character of Hans Sachs appeared rather cynical, ironic, and bitter; in the draft of mid-November 1861 Sachs had become gentle and wise. In the first version the relationship between Sachs and Eva was not explicit; in the definitive poem of January 1862 their relation was determined by the resignation of the cobbler, who sees clearly that he is too old for Eva and votes in favor of her love for the young knight Walther von Stolzing. The duo in the second act between Sachs and Eva was absent from the first two versions. It was introduced when the final poem was written. Wagner identified himself fully with the character of Sachs. In a letter to Mathilde he even wrote: "As for Sachs, beware of your heart; you might fall in love with him!" In the cobbler's song, expressing his message to Mathilde, the composer let himself go:

> *O Eva, hear my lamentation,*
> *My trouble and heavy vexation!*
> *The works of art which a cobbler created,*
> *the world treads underfoot!*
> *If an angel did not bring comfort*
> *Who has drawn the lot of similar work*
> *And did not often call me into Paradise,*
> *How gladly would I leave shoes and boots behind!*
> *But when he has me in heaven*
> *The world lies at my feet,*
> *And I am at peace—*
> *Hans Sachs, a shoemaker and a poet too!* [14]

According to the Danish writer Olaf Waage, Sachs's first lines describe an angel kissing him on the forehead. Wagner changed these words, which were too explicitly aimed at Mathilde

Wesendonck, after 1865, at a time when Cosima had decided to do a thorough cleaning of the master's affective memory.

In the third act Eva expresses her gratitude toward Sachs, who now understands everything. The maiden will be able to marry the young knight, who has become a master singer thanks to the cobbler's instruction. The love between Eva and Sachs would materialize in some ideal world, while on earth nature would reign.

> Eva: *Oh Sachs, my friend! Dear man!*
> *How can I reward you, noble man!*
> *What would I be without your love,*
> *Without you?*
> *Wouldn't I have remained always a child*
> *If you had not awoken me?*
> *Through you I have won what people prize,*
> *Through you I learned the workings of the mind;*
> *By you awoken, only through you did I think*
> *Nobly, freely, and boldly.*
> *You made me bloom!*[15]

These words could have been pronounced by Mathilde Wesendonck, the Eva-Galatea, that by the magic of his total art, Wagner linked to the ideal of the eternal feminine: Isolde-Brangäne-Mathilde.

In fact, Eva expressed her gratitude in almost a paraphrase of the passage of the letter of January 16 in which Mathilde wrote: "Our personal relations came back to my memory—I used to see the world as great and rich, in the way you had opened it to the child's mind; my eyes could not be detached from that marvelous edifice, my heart would beat with tender gratitude, and I felt that nothing of that would ever be lost to me. As long as I live, I will always aspire to knowledge; such is your part in my education."

"If I had a choice," says Eva to Sachs, "you would be my husband."

> *But now I am chosen for never-known torment,*
> *And if I am married today, then I had no choice:*
> *That was obligation, compulsion!*[16]

In the middle of Act III the composer dispelled all the equivocations and misunderstandings by introducing, for the only time in all his works, the painful harmony of another opera—*Tristan*—but in a tone of appeasement with this revealing text:

> Sachs: *My child, of Tristan and Isolde*
> *I know a sad tale.*

Hans Sachs was clever and did not want
Anything of King Marke's lot.[17]

What more could he have said?

Wagner once wrote to Mathilde that "for me, art is intimately entwined with life." The issue therefore is not whether Mathilde Wesendonck was his inspiration for *Die Meistersinger*, but that Wagner's works were always the result of his life experience. Seeing Mathilde in Venice on good terms with her husband, perfectly serene, Richard definitely sided with Hans Sachs in regard to Eva. And the Titian Madonna, with her open arms, who reflected the image of Mathilde in the attitude of Isolde's transfiguration in her *Liebestod*, revealed to him a "diatonic" bliss in his musician's soul.

In December Wagner's ideas and feelings were to become reality. On the twenty-first he described to Mathilde his return from Venice to Vienna and how, in the train, he heard an echo "like a overture for *Meistersinger*." He jotted down the musical outline and was surprised at his own aptitude for fantasy and invention.

For Wagner, the end of the year always had a singularly sacred feel—a time to finish with the anguish of the past and make resolutions for the future: "I turned the key and locked the door for this year on *Tristan*." And he ended his letter with a decisive statement: "That I wrote *Tristan* is what I thank you for from the bottom of my soul, for all eternity."

On December 25, upon receiving the new draft for *Die Meistersinger*, Mathilde responded: "I bless you on your new work; I rejoice in its coming celebration. In Venice I would hardly have dared to utter such a hope."

In Paris, at the end of December 1861, Wagner drew up an assessment of the state of his affections. The time had come for a farewell letter to Mathilde Wesendonck: "Thank you with all my heart, dear child! I reply to you with a confession. It will not be necessary to say it out loud: everything in and about you tells me that already you know all. And yet, I feel impelled to give you certainty on my side also. At last, I am fully resigned!" Giving up the idea of returning to the Asyl, he wrote:

I had to recognize at once that the freedom which you need, and to which you must hold fast for your continuance, you can never maintain so long as I am near you. Only the distance between us can confer on you the power to move freely according to your own will. . . . I cannot bear, for the price of my nearness, to see you cramped and oppressed, dependent and ruled. For I cannot require that sacrifice from you, because my presence can offer you nothing more; and the thought that the miserable things I could bring you in such conditions would be bought with your liberty, with human dignity itself, would make me feel that very nearness as a torture. Here soothingness avails no longer. I see that you feel and know it yourself; and how should you not, you, the first one concerned? You have known it for a long time, and earlier than I, who have always remained within my secret heart an incorrigible optimist.

His salvation came through his work and his project for *Die Meistersinger*: "I want to work, nothing more. Then, for you as well, I can be something better. I know it, and you know it too! . . . Of my life you shall hear only what is indispensable, the outermost necessary; inwardly, be assured of that. Nothing whatsoever will occur again, nothing but artistic creation. Consequently, you will be losing nothing at all, but will gain the only worthwhile thing I have—my works. We shall see each other now and then, though, shall we not? Void of all desire, then! Wherefore also, wholly free!"

And yet this farewell was once again only the passing effect of a disappointing meeting in Venice. Eighteen months later Wagner again confessed, this time to Eliza Wille, his undying love for Mathilde beyond all time and space:

"She is and remains my first, my only love! I feel it more and more clearly. It was the summit of my life: the years of anxiety and blessed anguish that I passed under the growing charm of her presence and of her affection contain all the loveliness of my existence."

15

Farewell

ichard and Mathilde's farewell took a very long time. It looked like the circles on a still pond when a stone is thrown in, making the ripples expand, repeat, and finally disappear from the water's surface into some dark, remote infinity. Since the first chromatic chord in the *Tristan* Prelude, composed in December 1857, the notes expressing their sad story of impossible love were like so many heartbeats pulsing throughout the work, unresolved, repeatedly unable to find their harmonic resolution until the "Liebestod."

Their farewell lasted until April 1864, after which there seems to have been a rupture. That is when their correspondence ceased, but a careful study of the letters and documents reveal that the discord was more of a misunderstanding than a rejection. In 1862 King Marke and Brangäne were still watching: Otto Wesendonck and Eliza Wille, with the best of intentions, contributed to the separation of the lovers. And as in the last act of *Tristan*, that alienation had only the appearance of death.

The farewell letter of December 1861 had nothing definite about it. Wagner continued to write to Mathilde from wherever he was. He wandered back and forth between Paris and Germany before settling in Vienna at the end of 1862, during which time his friends and acquaintances, even the von Bülows in Berlin, refused to receive him. Having taken lodgings in a hotel in Paris on the Quai Voltaire, and in a moment of good humor despite his difficult circumstances, he finished the poem of *Die Meistersinger von Nürnberg*, while living far from the idealized medieval Germany described in his opera. On January 25 he packed up the manuscript, still blotched with ink stains and corrections, and sent it to Mathilde Wesendonck. He added a letter in which he could not hide his gaiety, he said, describing how sometimes he could not continue his work because he was laughing or crying. Among the comical effects, he recommended the pedantic buffo-like character of Sixtus Beckmesser and Sachs's apprentice David.

Mathilde had helped him give birth to his work, and as she read the outline of the poem, she reminded Wagner of the little present she had given him—a paperweight in the form of the lion of Saint Mark she had bought for him in Italy: "The winged lion on your work table has awakened," she wrote. "Strength and intellectuality are what it symbolizes. It shakes off the heaviness of its dreams, it tosses its mane to one side." Mathilde thus described Wagner writing his *Meistersinger* poem. She went on: "It makes me happy. I can think of nothing else. For whatever comes from the outside, let us entrust ourselves to Destiny. The enemy is inside of us, in the very abyss of the heart." Having read his last outline, she was the first person in the world to express what so many critics would proclaim one day in all languages on this work of Wagner's: "Almost never, it seems to me, has the source of your poetry flowed as richly and with as much originality as now. Therefore, it is a kind of justice to yourself: it retains that profound and indestructible humor that is part of your character. . . . It appears to me that I have climbed to a certain height and that my gaze has become lost in meditating on the glowing red sunset of a wonderful evening, in a hymn to the Creation! Friendship and farewell!"

∾

"Tomorrow I am going to Mainz to build my nest in Biebrich or Wiesbaden, where I can incubate that egg of *Die Meistersinger* that I have just laid."

At the beginning of February, settled on the Rhine, Wagner made a last attempt to live with his wife, who had left Dresden to join him again. It lasted only ten days, during which Minna, ill and embittered, never ceased her recriminations on the subject of Mathilde. The new crime was that Richard had received a package with little Christmas gifts that had been addressed to Vienna and forwarded to Biebrich. But everything had become an object of discord for Minna, and Wagner, relieved by her departure, wrote to his friend Peter Cornelius that their household in those days looked like a lunatic asylum!

Meanwhile in Zurich, on January 30, Mathilde received notice of her mother's death. With her pregnancy it was impossible for her to make the journey to Düsseldorf. So she traveled in spirit, through her inner life of poetry, to express her mourning:

> *Is it possible that your love,*
> *The strongest of passions,*
> *Has turned away from life*
> *And gone to the grave?*
>
> *No! love has remained,*
> *The strongest of passions.*
> *Your heart alone has given way*
> *When death came to break it.*
>
> *And victorious, above the grave*
> *It is enthroned. The perfect gift,*
> *The strongest of passions,*
> *Oh, Mother, is your love.*[1]

In his solitude in Biebrich, on the Rhine, Wagner was waiting with impatience for Mathilde's reaction to the poem of *Die Meistersinger*: "If only the child on the Green Hill would write to me!" he complained. Then, three days later, he learned the sad news and sent his condolences: "I placed a profound intention in the tears I shed on hearing of your mother's death. . . . Do not pay any attention to *Die Meistersinger*! The manuscript is yours; I only wanted to give you what is yours!"

On March 12 he wrote to her about the reactions of the public during his first reading of the poem in Mainz, then in Karlsruhe at the court of the Grand Duke of Bade. He mentioned his hero Walther's song for the contest in his letter and noted for her the melody he was thinking of using for this purpose:[2] "Far from the golden portals of my youth, one day I went away, lost in contemplation." Wagner summed up: "I wrote the lines according to the melody, you could not imagine. . . . In all that, the people hear only the melody: who will guess my secret?"

According to Ernest Newman, who compared this 1862 version with the definitive form in the work, the young knight, Walther, left his home to look for a new world; while traveling across the land he fell asleep in the forest. His future beloved appeared to him in a dream in the form of a dove. In the final scene of Weber's *Freischütz*, the soul of the heroine, Agatha, also assumes the shape of a dove. The hand of the young maiden was awarded to the winner of the shooting contest, as Eva's was to the winner of the singing contest. Was that the "secret" that Wagner let us guess?

It should be remembered that in Mathilde's youth, *Der Freischütz* was a favorite of hers. She even wrote a play for her children on the theme. The secret could then be, once again, an allusion to Wagner's love for Mathilde, a very Weberian heroine; she alone would be likely to understand all this on reading this first version of *Die Meistersinger*.

After 1865, with the arrival of Cosima to put the master's ideas in order, the dove of this early version completely disappeared from the text. All these winged creatures—the angel coming down to kiss the cobbler on his brow, the dove symbolizing the ideal woman in the eyes of young Stolzing—flew away with the past. "Who will guess my secret?" And since "the people hear only the melody," look for the solution to the enigma in this text, where the ideal, the supreme reward for his art, was associated with the love of a woman whose delicate features resembled the heroine of *Der Freischütz*: Mathilde Wesendonck.

In spite of the distance, Richard continued, as in the past, to entrust her with many of the secrets of his art; for example, how he had got the idea for the music in the Prelude of Act III and the climax, in which the people pay solemn homage to Hans Sachs with the first eight lines of Martin Luther's hymn "Wacht auf!"

Wake up! The day has come:
I can hear singing in the green hedge
A wonderful nightingale.

This is how Wagner, in 1866, described the third act of *Die Meistersinger* to King Ludwig II of Bavaria. But in all his writings, whether to Mathilde or to the king, it never occurred to him to express the narrow-minded patriotism that he is reproached for even now.

In Wagner's work, for example, in the final chorus of the last act, when Sachs defends "the people of the German empire" from a "false *velche* majesty,"[3] he added that one should understand the eternity of German *art*, not of the German state.

> *And even should the Holy Roman Empire*
> *Dissolve into mist,*
> *For us there would yet remain*
> *Holy German Art!*

For Thomas Mann, "at that time, the idea of the nation meant everything that was good, lively, authentic—it was poetry and spirituality. . . . These lines of Hans Sachs, first set down by Wagner in definitive form in 1845 in Marienbad, prove how much his idea of nationalism was completely spiritual and devoid of politics. They show an almost anarchic indifference to the state, providing that what survives is German in spirit, that is, 'German art.'"[4]

In his letter to Mathilde on his birthday, May 22, 1862, Richard congratulated himself on his own genius: "It has become obvious to me now that this work will be my most accomplished masterpiece, and that I will finish it."

In Zurich Mathilde was paid a visit by Wagner's friend Peter Cornelius. "He is a nephew of the famous painter," commented Richard. "He likes me very much, and you have seen what I say about him. Write to him, my child; he likes you too!"

Wagner was touched by the young man's devotion. Indeed, the good Cornelius had made the trip from Vienna to Mainz in February just to hear the first reading of *Die Meistersinger* at Schott's, despite his poverty and the flooding that had made the roads almost impassable. That spring, greeted warmly by the Wesendoncks on the Green Hill, he looked around with adoration on everything he knew to be dear to the master. To one of his friends in Vienna, Josef Standhartner, another enthusiastic Wagnerian, he wrote: "At the Wesendoncks' I was in ecstasy when, at dusk, the last rays of the sun illuminated the objects in the study . . . when the poplars and linden trees in the park trembled in the wind."[5]

In a long, awkward poem, Cornelius described the villa as "an enchanted castle" in which "the only secret is the mistress, whose husband knows her sorrow. He consoles her."

In Mathilde the poor fellow found everything admirable: "I look at this woman, [who is] a profound and unforgettable image, a beautiful form with a beautiful soul; she has sanctified her home with her angelic hand."

Wagner's description of his solemn, naive young friend Cornelius brings to mind the character of David, the apprentice to Hans Sachs. When Cornelius returned to Vienna, he no doubt recited his lines like the boy in *Die Meistersinger*:

> *On Jordan's bank, Saint John did stand*
> *To baptize all the peoples of the world.*
> *A woman came from a distant land;*

From Nuremberg she had hastened.
Her little son she carried on the river's bank,
Received there baptism and name.
But when they wended their way homeward
And got back to Nuremberg,
In the land of Germany it soon transpired
That the person who on Jordan's bank was named John,
Was called Hans on the River Pegnitz.
Hans? . . . Hans![6]

In June, while old master Sachs smiled for his feast day, Mathilde on the sixteenth gave birth to a child: Hans. Like the apprentice, Peter Cornelius expressed his wonder at Mathilde's work, as he usually did at Wagner's. Lost in his own imaginary world during his stay at the Wesendoncks' villa, he saw Mathilde's child as a bond between Sachs and Eva, as a reconciliation for everything that seemed irreconcilable! In his own poem, Cornelius puts these words into Wagner's mouth:

Here joy enlightened me;
Here, for the first time, my heart loved,
Before this marvelous and magical Psyche.

When the young man saw the painting of Mathilde by Dorner in 1860, he imagined the master, also before an easel, painting with sounds: "Each brushstroke was full of harmony."

In a letter to Otto Richard expressed his concern: "The last news I received from you took a weight off my heart. May Hans and his mother thrive!"

Wagner's composition of *Die Meistersinger* had reached a stalemate. His muse, weakened by childbirth, was unwell. His passing adventures did not suffice to ignite the inner flame of his genius. Hounded by his constant need for money, on July 21 he turned once again toward his "usual source of capital".[7] "You can easily guess that I must be at the end of my rope to commit the indelicate action of calling on you to help me." Nevertheless, Otto gave his consent, and on July 26 Richard was able to thank him for the salutary influence it had on his situation and his state of mind. At the time the musician had been posing for a portrait ordered by Wesendonck from the painter Caesar Willich. He had thought of asking Otto to suspend the painting and give him the money he needed instead. But the portraitist went on painting, and Wagner, impatient and ironic, frequently alluded to it in his letters.

On September 24, he asked again with a touch of humor: "Today, it is in the quality of chief crook that I address you—-if possible, lend me again some money." Having obtained what he wanted, on the twenty-ninth Wagner exclaimed: "Wesendonck, you are unique!"

The promises he made to Schott did not persuade the publisher to advance him any sum whatsoever on the unfinished score of *Meistersinger*. So Richard sold him the manuscript of the five *Wesendonck Lieder*: "I offered my publisher the five poems written by my lady-friend, Frau

Wesendonck," he wrote in *My Life*; "I set them to music at the same time I was working on *Tristan*." Because an original manuscript had remained the Wesendoncks' possession, at which point Mathilde donated them to the Wahnfried archives in Bayreuth, the second version of this score, the one written in Venice from the penciled outlines, was utilized for the engraving of 1862. Wagner had entitled them *Fünf dilettanten Gedichte für Frauenstimme in Musik gesetzt* (Five Dilettante Poems set to Music for Woman's Voice). The Wagner buff Henri Perrier explained delicately: "In the first title, it appeared that Wagner, who was no dilettante, was not the author of the poems; but the second version is utterly ambiguous."[8]

According to Baron von Bissing, Mathilde had been flattered by this anonymous publication. That anyone could think that *her* poems might possibly have been written by Wagner filled her with pride.

The *Wesendonck Lieder* were performed for the first time on July 30, 1862, at the villa of the Schott family in Laubenheim, near Mainz, in company of an intimate circle of friends. The event was recorded by Wendelin Weissheimer, a young musician and enthusiastic admirer of Wagner: "Before a small group of selected listeners, Miss Emilie Genast sang the *Five Poems*, accompanied at the piano by Hans von Bülow. The effect was fascinating. Everyone was seized with emotion, and Cosima von Bülow broke into tears. Franz Schott rubbed his hands with satisfaction and carefully locked the manuscript up in a drawer."[9]

Ludwig Schnorr von Carolsfeld, the tenor who would later create the title role of *Tristan* in Munich, commented: "The publication of these five Wagner songs had a great effect here. They were very popular but not well understood."[10]

As for Mathilde, interviewed in the last years of her life about her participation in Wagner's work, she confided to the journalist Albert Heintz the reason the text of the *Wesendonck Lieder* had never been included in a collection of her own poetry: "These songs received the consecration and illumination of the great master and I would never be so presumptuous as to consider them mine."[11]

~

"Frau Wesendonck is ill," wrote Eliza Wille on July 10, 1862, to her family. On August 4 she repeated: "She is still very ill." Her illness was indeed serious. Her physical and moral trials had exhausted her. However, the pretty infant by her side did fill her with the desire to recuperate and to live. And the vital force within her, like a tree's sap, would again cause her soul to blossom with poetic expression.

In the autumn Mathilde published her poems for the first time: *Gedichte, Volkslieder, Legenden, Sagen* (Poems, Popular Songs, Legends, Sagas), signed "M. W," with no other explanation. But the letter of thanks dated December 1 sent to her by Ettmüller, the German philologist in Zurich, permits us to date this edition with certainty. To one of these poems, entitled "Der Neck" (The Water Sprite), Wagner reacted enthusiastically: "The poem you sent me today was very beautiful, I think even a masterpiece."

It resounds uniquely, so sweet and free,
From the shore of Maelar,
The ancient melody of the man of the sea
On the tranquil beach.

And all are alive, attentive, waiting
While the sun sets slowly on the horizon,
And the little fish raises its head from the waves,
And looks around sagely, sparkling.

A man heard it nearby.
Surprised, he remained silent,
And felt so happy that it hurt,
Knowing not why.

Two children were playing in the sand
In the golden dusk.
The naive children taunted the man of the sea:
"Fiddler, leave your fiddle in peace!"

Their mother spoke, and spoke with prescience,
The pious little mother:
"Though the water sprite plays for thousands of years,
happy he will never be."

The old man cried in wildest grief;
Discouraged was he in his tears.
Sobbing over the foamy sea,
He shut his singer's mouth.

But at night, the children gaily told
The story to their mother,
How they made the old man silent,
The old, gray, sorrowful man.

Gravely the mother reflected, and was sad;
She made them return again
To the open sea
To find the musician.

And when they arrived before the roaring sea
The waves rose menacingly,
And, heavy with thunder, grumbling gloomily
They roiled and rumbled in the wind.

Fearful, they begged the fiddler softly:
"Come out of the damp mist,
We are poor and blamed you wrongly;
Play your little song again."

The mother spoke and said truly,
The pious little mother:
"You must play on for a thousand years;
You could again be joyful."

They begged him so fervently,
"Play on, dear musician!"
The old man could not resist.
He began to play loudly and cheerfully.

It echoed all so sweet and free,
And the wavelets rolled one upon the other.
From the water sprite's tune, the ancient melody
Lulled them all to sleep.

"The spirit of the legend appears quite differently to me now," commented Wagner. He saw himself, no doubt, in the skin of the old man of the sea, but in the situation described by Mathilde—the isolation of the artist almost unrecognized by the world: "For the water sprite, there is some hope; as far as I am concerned, I no longer know what hope is, and I cannot even hear an encouraging promise."

In this first publication, Mathilde revealed clearly the themes of her inspiration: maternal love in the lines to her dead child, Guido, and filial love to her beloved mother, who had recently died. And love, great love, would shine through her verse in "Die Verlassene" (The Forsaken Lover), "Erinnerung" (Remembrance), and "Beharrliche Liebe" (Faithful Love), which, one may be sure, dealt with Wagner.

"REMEMBRANCE"

Many years have passed
Since I saw you leave;

And yet, 'tis strange
It is as if you were at my side.

I still hear your eager step
Echoing along the way.
I still hear the sound of your voice:
I have forgotten only my pain.

Your gaze still shines with the brightness of stars
In the depths of my happy soul,
And, surprised, here am I,
Wonderfully healed and comforted.

Like balm, your dear hand
Lay on my heart
When sleep plunged it into oblivion
And led it to the land of dreams.

When sleep closes my eyes
At the end of mortal torment,
What shyly formed in the depths of my soul
Will be true delight.[12]

"FAITHFUL LOVE"

Already the evening nears,
The sun is setting.
It is time to ride
To our last abode.

My love, from above,
Do not look at me;
On the path, go astride
Your horse, go home.

Look around me;
How deceitful people can be!
Enviously they look at us,
Envious of our love, of our constancy!

Leave them their resentment,
Their aggressive and vile spirits.
Mine you will be,
Yes! Mine!

If it cannot be today
Then 'twill be in a year
We shall belong to each other,
We shall belong!

If it cannot be here
Then 'twill be in the tomb
We shall belong to each other,
We shall. [13]

In another type of poetry, that of legends and sagas, Mathilde took her subjects from Germanic and Scandinavian folklore: *Olaf, Eckhard the Blond, Melusin, Maria*. In an underlying Wagnerian atmosphere, she read, guided by Ettmüller, the original version of the *Niebelungenlied* and took inspiration from such German authors as Walther von der Vogelweide, whose verses she translated into modern German.

In a second collection of poems, published in 1874, Mathilde deleted everything that could lend itself to a personal interpretation and replaced the love poems for Richard with the tribulations of the mysterious and ambivalent character of Goethe's Mignon.

In the novel entitled *Wilhelm Meisters Lehrjahre* (Wilhelm Meister's Apprentice Years), Mignon, who is at the same time woman and child, falls in love with the hero, who returns her feelings only in friendship. The girl, part of a troupe of circus performers, sings her desperate love for Wilhelm, to whom she remains faithful until death:

Only those who know nostalgia
Have lived what I suffer.

In an echo of the pain of Goethe's chaste Mignon, Mathilde, called "child" by Wagner, repeats the same theme of melancholy regret:

Profound nostalgia gnaws at my youth
Like the worm inside the flower.
All my hopes and desires,
My very growth, have been thwarted
Before the tempest of life. [14]

In this period, apart from Eliza Wille, her faithful friend, no one could guess the love Mathilde had kept in her heart for Richard. A handwriting analysis of Mathilde revealed a naturally introverted personality. She wore a mask, even for those who were close to her, hiding from all her inner life, constantly bathing in memories. The poem "Mignon" seems to express her innermost soul. But around her family and friends her self-control remained constant. Many years after Wagner's departure, Mathilde would still sing to relieve her heart: "Only a painful renouncement remains; such is the lot of Mignon on this earth."

In the twenty-five stanzas of the five-part poem, the poet resumed her story with Richard: the dream, the awakening, the renunciation, the resignation. In the guise of Goethe's character, Mathilde slips quietly to the door of her beloved, suffers intensely from his indifference (in the years after 1864), and finds no remedy for her ailment: "My poor heart loves only you, you alone."

One time I wished to follow my desire:
To be happy, just once!
Just once, to taste the fulfillment
Of the world's supreme joy.
One night I was resolved
To glide quietly to your door.
I knew it was unlocked;
I wanted to be there.

At the foot of the staircase
A sound stopped me dead:
I saw approaching in the hall
A woman's form.
Soundlessly she opened the door
And slipped inside.
Suddenly footsteps behind her
Locked the door shut.

Incredible pains
Plowed through me,
My heart stopped beating,
My blood stood still.
I could hear death coming.
No salvation for me,
I lay prostrate on the floor
In torturous pain.[15]

Her children remained Mathilde's only reason for living, and for them she would bear anything. In 1887 Eliza Wille wrote to her: "You are lucky! You have lived for your children, you have suffered for them, and, thank God, you did not sacrifice them to what was not meant to be." Indeed, Mathilde's tender affection tended to create a nest of perpetual love. In March 1864 she published a collection of fairy tales and playlets, *Märchen und Märchenspiele*, with the dedication "For my children, Myrrha, Karl, and Hans, a three-leaf clover, so that they may say in the future how much a mother loved them, whether in pain or joy."

She included in this volume all the stories she had written since Wagner's departure: *The Strange Bird* and *The Swan*, then *The House of Sugar, Christmas Eve*, and *The Lady of the Forest*, as well as her playlets of the same period, *Siegfried, Cinderella, Little Red Riding Hood*, and *Perseus*.

In all of these texts reality is represented by poetic symbols that undergo multiple transformations. Characters of her own invention live in this dream world and evolve from a larval stage to the butterfly reaching for the sky.

The following year, in 1865, Mathilde finished another work, *Naturmythen* (Myths on Nature) and dedicated it to Eliza Wille, "the dear spinner of Mariafeld." But the poet did not fear to rewrite with real ingenuousness texts already written and rewritten by great authors. She had already said as much to Wagner in *The Swan*: it seemed to her that "all these marvels were emanating from her own childish soul." On many occasions she repeated it—writing a *Wacht auf!* without the genius of Wagner. In fact, over time the quality of her works diminished. Galatea, in her spiritual isolation, was losing her luster. Only the contemplation of her beloved could perhaps have restored her brilliance.

When, from Vienna, Wagner remembered Mathilde's birthday in December 1862, he sent her a few words that caressed her soul: "I dreamed delightfully of you last night, as soon as I fell asleep. May this dream signify all the good I can wish you, dear lady-friend! It was pleasant to see that amid all the distress and misery of the present, the dream reminded me just in time of your birthday. It was beautiful, and I can see that dreams at least still care about me."

To this Mathilde briefly replied: "I knew it! Dreams are faithful! The more reality moves away from us, the more dreams are present. May heaven send us many of these dreams!"

◇

Settled in Vienna, Wagner produced a new series of concerts featuring excerpts from his works. By January 1863 he was in debt again. Although his fame was growing in Europe, his financial situation improved only slightly on a trip to Russia, where his concerts in March and April in Saint Petersburg and in Moscow had notable success and brought in a good sum of money. Back in Vienna in May, he moved to a new apartment belonging to the Baron von Rackowitz in Penzing, where he spent freely money on creating luxurious surroundings. As usual, he was living far above his means, so that by September everything he had earned was gone and his debts again began to accumulate.

In his solitude, however, "the only thing" was again missing. In January he wrote to the young Mathilde Meier: "I'm missing a country, not the one on this earth, but the one of the heart." And in June he confided to Eliza Wille: "One of these days I will have to write again to the Wesendoncks. But I can do so only to the husband; the wife, I love too much. My heart is too sensitive, too full when I think of her." He could not write to her, he said, without being guilty of deceit toward Otto, whom he greatly esteemed and respected. But nor could he keep his feelings to himself. What should he do? What can he say? He cried out to Eliza from the bottom of his heart: "She is and remains my first, my only love!"

In June, however, he could enjoy his new lodgings in Penzing, which had a garden. While working on the score of the first scene of *Die Meistersinger* he found himself in need of his muse. Thinking constantly of Mathilde, he continued in his letter to Eliza Wille: "She will always remain admirable and my love will never fail; but to see her is no longer possible without this terrible constraint that . . . would bring an end to our love. . . . Would I let my beloved believe wrongly that she leaves me indifferent? It is very hard."

Although by now Wagner had obtained an amnesty for all of Germany, he still suffered from a moral imprisonment:

Ever since I left Zurich I live as if I were still in exile. . . . My only desire is to have rest in my own home so as to be able to devote myself entirely to my work. . . . I opened the green portfolio she had sent me in Venice—so much suffering since then! And now all of a sudden, bathed in the charm of those days, it was so ineffably beautiful! There, in that portfolio, the outlines for *Tristan*, and the music for her poems! Ah! Dear! One loves only once, whatever exhilaration and joys that may pass before our eyes in our lifetime! Yes, I am fully assured that I will never stop loving her, only her, in this world!

Indeed, Wagner was not trying to burden Mathilde with another confession of his love. The day after writing this letter to Eliza Wille, he wrote to his beloved's husband, dwelling mainly on "outside events," as he had promised Mathilde beforehand. But the descriptions of the trip to Russia and the new lodgings in Vienna were pervaded by the scent of growing bitterness. An echo of his nostalgia was nevertheless obvious: "You are the only people on this earth to whom I belong, in a manner of speaking—things are that way, we cannot go back and begin again. That I belong to you is the result of all kinds of suffering and sacrifices that you have made."

Mathilde knew how to read between the lines. She saw Richard's distress, and she no doubt had the opportunity to read his letter to Eliza Wille. She always chose symbolic gifts to embody her feelings, thus the new portfolio to encourage Wagner to work on his *Meistersinger*. "Until now, the green portfolio was quite enough," he declared. "What is completely finished must be included in the new one, with all the vestiges of wonderful old times."

In response to the expression "wonderful old times," Mathilde sent him, on July 3, the sheets to be contained in the green portfolio, with her handwritten lines of poetry, preceded by the quotation from *Tristan*, epigraph of their love:

Chosen for me, lost for me,
Heart beloved for eternity.

This was followed by stanzas written during the blissful days and evenings of discussions on Schopenhauer and Calderón; then, to be placed among the "vestiges," one new poem dated May 22, 1863, Wagner's fiftieth birthday, in which Mathilde expressed all her humility and generosity to Richard:

A great and pure soul
Inside the little flower
That with all its being
Lives in the sun's light
With only one thought:
The desire to be beautiful.
Although the golden ray
Kisses a thousand sisters,
It knows not envy
And greets the ray with joy
And turns fore'er to him
And breeds perfume for him.
If he forgets,
Its loving eye closes in silence,
Bows down its little head,
And, after a light sigh, expires.
Oh my heart, how great would be your sorrow
If you were pure like the flower?

I dug a grave,
I put in it my love,
And all my hopes and desires,
All my tears
And my happiness and my grief.
And after depositing it all,
I lay down in it myself. [16]

Richard's response to this poem is missing from his correspondence, like so many others that disappeared, and we shall soon see why. With these poetic lines, Mathilde had added, "I will write you soon," with no other comment. But Wagner, on August 3, referred to her "last good letter," which is missing.

The Wesendoncks were on vacation in the Rhineland when Richard sent his salutation to her as a poet with the words "Dear Master!" He complained of not receiving any missive more "explicit" than the one she sent. But he generalized about his dissatisfaction: *"Maitre*, I am not happy! And I am quite tired of living." Despite the luxurious furnishing of his apartment in Vienna, he could not work. He blamed the Germans for barring his way to the theaters, whereas the Czechs, the Hungarians, and the Russians were acclaiming him in their countries. No man is a prophet in his own land, and the situation left Wagner acutely disgusted. "No one wants to hear my works," he complained. Finally, however, at the end of this long letter, he confessed his real problem: "I see I must put a stop to my correspondence—your husband would rightly accuse me of bothering you. Really, dear lady-friend, it is difficult for me to write to you. All the sweetness that is rekindled in me from time to time is a memory of the past: but I cannot and dare not say so in my letters!"

Mathilde had explained to him that she had to take care of her fragile health, as well as of Otto, who suffered from rheumatism. When it came to Otto's illness, there seemed to be a secret code between them regarding his attitude toward Wagner, because Richard understood it in a literal as well as a figurative sense: "It seems that all sorts of calamities have beset [Otto], who is still bothered by his pains in his neck. . . . I think Otto must have had enough of me, as he already tried to help me! . . . Nothing happens; all was spent in vain!"

From Schwalbach, where she was staying with her family, Mathilde answered:

Your long letter has come to crush my heart with all its weight today. . . . But I am not bothered by the problems that you have brought me, for I have compassion for your suffering. It ennobles all my being to be able to suffer with you. However sad your letters may be, when I think of their meaning, they become dear and friendly to me, especially when I think they were written *by him* and *for me*. My friend, I am afraid you could say many terrible things and I would not hold it against you! . . . Whoever could help you should be very happy! I get dizzy thinking of all the discouraging things around you. . . . I don't have to tell you how much I suffer on seeing you run around the world to give concerts. And even if heaven were full of the crowd's applause, it would not be a sufficient reward for your sacrifice. I follow your so-called triumphs with a bleeding heart, and they make me almost bitter when I am told they are happy events. I feel how little you are known, that is, how little you are understood, and as for me, I know you and love you.

A series of invitations addressed to Richard contradicts Wagner's biographers concerning the attitude of Mathilde Wesendonck during this period of 1863–64. The first was issued on August 9:

My heart always calls you back to Switzerland; but this heart is selfish and must not be listened to. Would a refuge in Switzerland outside the first Asyl be impossible? Until now my tears have defended the Asyl against the intrusion of other tenants; but I have little hope of obtaining any more than that for the future. . . . If you really intend to give us the pleasure of a musical hearing under your own direction, I propose that you come back to the Green Hill for a little while, to be taken care of by the Child, and then talk about the rest. You tell me nothing about your work besides the fact that the portfolio is getting filled up. And I would let you have tea with someone unknown to us? Cruel, miser, to take away from me the pleasure of sending you someone. Don't you know that fulfilling your smallest desires is my only consolation for your painful letters, and you could well allow me to do so!

The answer came from Richard, who was still depressed but repentant: "To write such things to you! I should not have sent them to you; but you did the same thing, one day, with the remark that "what is written, is written!""

Then, on September 23 as Otto was suffering from rheumatic fever and muscular inflammation (Mathilde cared for him night and day), she spoke of a "painful illness apt to either improve or get worse" that would be in either case of long duration. Nevertheless, for the second time she invited Wagner to visit them: "How happy I would be to offer you a really peaceful and comfortable stay! Autumn in Switzerland is often very beautiful; even in winter we are very well at home here. Hopefully it will not, but if Otto's illness were to last longer than expected, would it be possible for you to spend Christmas with us? . . . I hope with all my heart, for you and for us, that it could be even sooner."

On October 20 she wrote again, "I hope to see you soon in Zurich, before or after the performances in Karlsruhe." Otto's health was improving.

Mathilde's fourth invitation was dated October 27:

The thought of seeing you here soon is more and more on my mind; it will be a joy for my heart to see you settled here in the best possible way. . . . Life is a science . . . we have to learn. As on the waves of the ocean, the water can be still; in the same way, the sky can be blue, without clouds. There are moments in life when Destiny has to hold its breath. May God grant us one of those moments!

What I wish so fervently for is also so small that you may smile; it is to see you at least once a year in our home, in a familiar manner so that you may know every corner in the house and the children should not be strangers to you. I have always tried to have them keep a vivid memory of our life as neighbors, and even today they know the Asyl under the name of "Uncle Wagner's garden."

Mathilde described for him how the little house had become an annex to their villa: "The rooms on the ground floor have been arranged for Karl's studies, with lodgings for his private tutor. Thus the little house has come under my special care, and I can keep it from ruin or neglect. Needless to say, even that gives me a certain melancholy joy. . . . For the heart, everything is important here; it remains forever ideal, and the world has little hold on it. It opens with a golden key, and it escapes when the world thinks it has it well in hand."

Wagner answered her immediately: "You can imagine, dear lady-friend, what importance your letter had for me! . . . If you want to welcome me, my wish would be to stay a little while in your home, maybe around Christmas."

Mathilde's last invitation was sent from Prague, on a November evening in 1863: "Many things in life are destined to be forgotten; very few are unforgettable. But of the latter can be measured the value of our existence on earth. *To be or not to be*, such is the question here too. Existence is afflicted by the Cross. I would like to go to Karlsruhe, but Otto has not yet recovered all his strength. He is still weak and has to be spared the slightest emotion. Would it be possible for you to come around the fourteenth? He has himself expressed the desire. . . . I hope the Green Hill will become dear to you again one day."

Wagner's visit to the Wesendoncks took place not on November 14, but on the twenty-first. He had asked Mathilde in advance to have his meals brought to his room so as not to upset the household: "Meals with the family are reserved for special occasions, and for that I need an express invitation from you."

It was a worn-out man who appeared in the hall of the Wesendoncks' villa that evening. He had been traveling all over Germany looking for a benefactor who would meet his needs. But the concerts in Prague and in Karlsruhe, as well as the ceremonies of the court of the Grand Duke of Bade, brought him only kind words and half-promises. Arriving in Zurich, he thought of reviving his relationship with good old Wesendonck: "I spoke freely of my situation with these friends," wrote Wagner in *My Life*, "but I saw no hint that they might help me."

This time Otto seemed determined. He had had enough of the prodigal son's conduct. In convalescence after eight weeks of rheumatic fever, he was again rebuilding the fortress surrounding his domestic happiness, even if it was hard to imagine Otto Wesendonck exerting absolute authority over his household. Was it not perhaps the soft tyranny of a sick man who might have a relapse, whose psychosomatic symptoms could be a permanent threat to his family's happiness? In any case, he needed the undivided attention and compassion of his wife, who devoted herself to whoever was weaker than her. What else could she do but yield to her tenderness as a mother and nurse? To Richard she said nothing; she walled herself off in silent grief. Wagner too was enclosed within himself and his position in the world of the artist. He saw her as if she were on the other side of a window: he did not understand, thinking that she let herself float on an ocean of conventional behavior.

In his diary, where Richard daily noted everything he did, he wrote that evening: "Short visit to Zurich—of no effect."

Taking up his pilgrim's staff once more, he left. On writing to Mathilde on December 15, he explained he could not go on: he expressed his great physical, psychological, and moral fatigue. It was no longer possible to deny that he had run up his debts again, and he had no strength to undertake another series of concerts. On the twenty-first he congratulated her in advance on her birthday and assured her that he would be with her "in thought."

But she felt him retreating little by little from her life, despite her efforts to keep him near her. When she turned to Otto to try and awaken his generosity toward the musician, she came up against insurmountable fortifications. A devoted and dependent wife, a mother chained to her children, she could have cried out like the Brünnhilde of *Götterdämmerung*: "Was könntest du wehren, elendes Weib?" (How could you prevent it, wretched woman?).

~

On December 21 she wrote to her beloved for the last time, as in an answer to the Oedipus of 1853: "The slightest news from you, dear Friend, is a thought from you to me and, as such, the dearest greeting that my heart could desire! I am grateful to you for any communication, short as it may be. We need nothing else, for it is as if there is an invisible thread leading us through life before the immensity of the world of emotions to which we belong. The knot of the mysterious Spinner who joins the threads of our destinies is undeniable. We can only break it. *Do you know how it happened?*"[17] And since Otto remained insensitive to her supplications, Mathilde warned Richard: "Nowhere can I find any financial resources for you; I've been racking my brain, but it is impossible to obtain anything. So now I keep quiet, rather than give you any illusions and vain hopes in which I myself do not believe." She recommended him to Henriette von Bissing, Eliza Wille's sister, who could possibly lend him some money: "It did me good to know you have Frau von Bissing in Löwenberg and Breslau. Blessed are those who can do good on this earth! They alone know what happiness is!"

Their destinies were linked now only for eternity, like those of Tristan and Isolde. In preparation for Christmas, Mathilde sent the Child-God to Richard to console him: "The Child-Jesus said he wanted to go to Vienna. . . . I would have liked to go with him; but Child-Jesus has certain privileges in this world."

Wishing to end the year 1863 well, Richard made a brief appearance at the Hofburg in Vienna to conduct the Overture to *Der Freschütz*. Perhaps an invisible dove was floating over his head that evening. Was it the soul of Agatha, or Eva, the muse of the knight von Stolzing? Or did she have her wings spread to fly away or her gaze fixed on heaven like Titian's madonna?

Bathed in the memory of these imaginary creatures created by geniuses from the familiar land of her dreams, Mathilde contemplated the heavens, lost in the music emanating from her soul:

An angel came down to me also
And, on shining wings,
Bears my spirit away from all torment
To heaven.[18]

16

The Rupture

———————

Wagner's extravagant and reckless spending in Vienna could only lead to utter financial ruin. He would sign short-term drafts "in order to pay the preceding ones which had arrived just as short at a due date."[1] He sought the generosity of other friends—not the Wesendoncks, for after Mathilde's last letter of December 1863 he realized that Otto no longer wanted to support him. In desperation, he solicited Harriet von Bissing, Eliza Wille's sister, but she too refused. Because she was a rich widow, he had even thought of marrying her for her money; but the lady understood him perfectly and wrote to Eliza: "If I saved Wagner, he would still prefer only Frau Wesendonck."

Nor did the projected performance of *Tristan* in Vienna come off. The work was declared "impossible to play." Hounded by his creditors, Richard decided to run off to Switzerland, but, not daring to appeal directly to Otto, he wrote on March 14 to Eliza Wille, begging her to intercede with her friends from the Green Hill to assure him a "tranquil refuge" where he could finally finish the score of *Die Meistersinger*: "As former invitations that had been addressed to me in the past by my friends have not yet been taken up, I thus enclose this last attempt, decisive for me, which is of the most important nature, since the saving of my work depends on it. Frau W. is perfectly free to set up my study in the main part of the little house I occupied before. . . . I beg you to communicate, as fast as possible, what I am writing, and if I have addressed myself first to you, it is to learn first whether my wish might possibly be granted."

But Wagner was unable to wait for a reply. He was forced to leave Vienna in a hurry on March 23, pursued by creditors, bill collectors, and the police, who were hot on his heels. From Munich, where he spent a sad day wandering the streets, he sent word to François Wille announcing his arrival. He justified himself by saying he was "using his rights of hospitality as an old friend," adding that he would be at the station in Zurich on Saturday, March 26, at four o'clock in the afternoon. He hoped there would be a carriage waiting for him to drive him to Mariafeld. . . .

Receiving his letter on the very day he was to arrive, Eliza Wille was very disturbed. Her husband was traveling in Constantinople and, wishing not to receive this difficult guest in his absence, she called immediately on Otto Wesendonck, who did not respond until the next day, Easter Sunday. "I have just received your lines sent yesterday morning, dear lady. I am also surprised. I hope you can give shelter to Wagner. *I cannot do so.*[2] You can judge perfectly for yourself. I still have much to say, but I will be brief. I will say nothing to my wife today, for she needs some peace and quiet. My poor brother-in-law died peacefully on the seventeenth of this month in Menton. My father-in-law and my sister-in-law, now a widow, have gone home alone. We have had enough mourning. I do not know if I notified you about it. We did not make an official death announcement."

On March 27, then, Mathilde knew nothing of Richard's arrival at Mariafeld. She was informed sometime later on, for she sent some furniture and a piano. She was a little angry with her husband for having hidden Wagner's presence, but she ignored the terms in which Otto had clearly refused the friend she had invited so many times. She may even have been a little vexed that Richard had first addressed Eliza Wille instead of writing to her. But this was only the beginning of the final misunderstanding.

So began Wagner's sojourn at Mariafeld, the details of which Eliza Wille related with all her writerly gifts. Disappointed by the missed invitation and informed of Otto's attitude, the master was in a dreadful mood and refused to see anyone. His apartment in the annex house, which had been closed up for a very long time during the winter months, was practically impossible to heat. He ate alone, walked alone, and visited no one. "I can still see him pacing to and fro on our terrace," wrote Eliza, "wearing his long brown velvet tunic and his black cap, making him look like some patrician in the engravings of Albrecht Dürer."

Good, kind Eliza understood him, calmed him, comforted him, and confessed: "His state of mind was that of a son who needed his mother." He told her things about his daily life that he would have normally written to Mathilde, if he had not thought that she had refused to see him. Eliza tried to stimulate in Wagner some hope for the future. "How can you talk to me about my future when my manuscripts are at the bottom of a cupboard?" he replied. He also wrote: "The world owes me a living. . . . Is it so unheard-of to demand that the little bit of luxury I feel like having should come my way? I who am preparing pleasure for thousands and thousands of people!"

"There came a time when I was counting the days until my husband's return," confided Eliza. The hours she spent in his gloomy company were difficult to bear, and she wrote to François: "I find Wagner dreadful. It is terrible to have him here. You will have to send him away."

The artist was not well and complained of insomnia; he read Schopenhauer and drank Vichy water. He was completely absorbed in himself, blamed everything on his poor state of health, which prevented him from composing, and looked at Eliza as if she were a mirror. He talked about himself endlessly, seeing himself as King Lear wandering on the moor. Occasionally he would calm down enough to emerge from his obliviousness. Eliza would then speak timidly to him about the beauty and elevation of music in general, at which the genius exclaimed: "Oh, poor woman, why did I not play some music for you during all this time?" He sat down and played immediately for her a scene from *Tristan*.

In the telegraphic notes he jotted down in his diary called *The Brown Book*, Wagner mentioned the visits between Wesendonck and himself. In *My Life*, to round out the rough edges, he wrote: "To forestall any misunderstanding, Frau Wille wanted me to see my old friends from Zurich, but my state of health, which was worsened by the cold temperature in my difficult-to-heat apartment, made it impossible; in the end it was Otto and Mathilde Wesendonck who came to see me in Mariafeld. It seemed to be a time of trouble and crisis for the couple, the reasons for which I could guess; but my attitude toward them was the same as usual."

Moreover, Wagner learned that the Wesendoncks, in agreement with the Willes, had decided to establish for the distressed musician a pension of one hundred francs a month. But during Otto and Mathilde's visit Richard threw the money back in his friends' faces as an insult to his genius, reproaching them in his most caustic, even coarse manner for not receiving him at the Asyl and for not really understanding anything about himself and his art. On April 25 he noted in *The Brown Book* only one word on the subject: "Scene."

It was not the first time that Wagner, who was a nervous wreck, had thrown such a fit of anger against his friends. But this time Mathilde was flabbergasted—she still did not know the way in which Richard had been flatly refused by Otto. She did not dare say anything in her husband's presence because she thought Richard was referring to her last letter on December 21, in which she said she could not do anything more for him. She thought his violent and undeserved reproaches were blown way out of proportion. What! Did he not know the struggle she had endured for him, between mourning for her child, her mother, and her brother? Not to mention Otto's long illness, hanging over their heads like the sword of Damocles? What she had suffered and what she was still suffering for him? But she did not say all this.

The queen of silence bids me be silent;
I grasped what she concealed,
I conceal what she cannot grasp.[3]

Finally François Wille returned home. He gave Wagner to understand that he wanted to be master of his own house and that their guest had exceeded the limits of hospitality. Richard thus left Mariafeld on April 30, 1864, entrusting Eliza Wille with a last sealed letter for Mathilde in which, according to *My Life*, he announced his immediate departure from Switzerland and begged her "in the name of friendship" not to take care of his affairs, everything having been arranged the way he wanted it. He also probably apologized for the stormy interview of a few days before. But Mathilde, still deeply wounded, no doubt on impulse sent the missive back to Eliza unopened, who sent it back to Richard with a note in which Mathilde had explained her reasons to Eliza.

And Richard still did not know that she did not know.

Under the influence of his passion, Wagner replied that his unopened missive was "a last letter, a holy letter. . . . Let her then try to find me again; she had me near her at a certain time and she knew me; that she could have lost me and badly judged me, I can understand it, but I cannot excuse it. Let her repent!"

Eighteen months later, in October 1865, Mathilde finally accepted this last letter from Eliza's hands and returned her impressions. Eliza sent in turn another letter, joining Mathilde's answer, to Richard, who was living at that moment in Munich with the wife of Hans von

Bülow. Wagner read Mathilde's letter, showed it to Cosima, and decided to send it back to Eliza on October 22 with a comment in which he blamed the whole misunderstanding of April 1864 on Mathilde's "weakness." Should she not have been strong, as in 1858, and obtain for him everything he wanted—a refuge, love, and inspiration for his work? Like an *enfant terrible* he pushed away his real happiness, burned what he adored, and, in a rage and on the rebound, punished poor Mathilde for her crime of lèse-majesté. Richard's answer to Eliza Wille on October 22, 1865, along with Mathilde's explanatory letter, was discovered by Cosima before it was posted. From it she formed an idea of the contents of Wagner's "last letter" to Mathilde and took offense. One can see from the entries in Wagner's *Brown Book* that he regretted having shown her Mathilde's answer, for Cosima would not easily be appeased. "I should have asked [Eliza] to send it back to me," he explained to her. He even claimed to have forgotten what he had written, not to mention the bitterness of the moment. Apparently, he was walking on egg-shells in order to restore harmony in his new household: "I did not demand that Frau Wille give the letter to Mathilde at all costs, but simply mentioned in passing that if she had not yet asked to read it, Frau Wesendonck should know from her, Frau Wille, that she would have nothing more to learn about me—this in order to explain why I have not sent her any other greeting since then. Secretly, I was malicious enough to wish upon her the humiliation that reading that letter could have caused her." At this time it is quite certain that we are dealing with a new Wagner, living under the influence of another woman.

The proof that Wagner was still in love with Mathilde in 1864 when he left Mariafeld is that he accepted from the Willes everything he refused from Mathilde: François almost pushed him out the door, and Wagner thanked him on the first evening of his trip; Eliza sent him moralizing letters, and Wagner answered her with praise. Only blind passion could dictate his choice to completely break it off with his "one and only love." Many years later poor Eliza reproached herself for her conduct; writing to Mathilde in 1887, she exclaimed: "My God, why did I not destroy and burn Wagner's last letter?"

Yet, on her threshold, on that last day of April 1864, Eliza Wille gave her blessing, like a good fairy, to the artist as he left Mariafeld: "Something will happen!" she prophesied. "What? I have no idea! But it will be something good. . . . Be patient. It will lead you to happiness!"

Before saying farewell, while brooding on the adversity he had suffered and Mathilde's last words—"Friend, what will all that come to?"—a despairing Wagner had written to his friend Cornelius: "What I need now is a miracle; if not, I am done for!" In a twist of fate, only two days after Wagner left Zurich the private secretary of King Ludwig II of Bavaria, Franz Seraph von Pfistermeister, rang at the Willes' doorbell on behalf of the young sovereign, whose first action in mounting the throne was to call to stay with him forever, so as to express his eternal gratitude, the god of his youth: Richard Wagner.

～

"I would be the most ungrateful of men if I did not tell you immediately of my immense happiness!" wrote Richard to Eliza Wille a few days later. With a trembling hand, she showed the letter to a reeling Mathilde. "You know that the young king of Bavaria sent for me," continued Wagner; "I was introduced to him today at court. He loves me with fervor, the fervor of first love; he knows everything about me. He wants me to stay forever near him, that I may work, rest, and have my operas performed. . . . He would like me to finish the *Nibelungen* and will have it performed as I wish. . . . All financial worries will be laid to rest; I will get whatever I need, and the only condition will be that I stay near him."

That summer Ludwig set Richard up in the Villa Pellet, on Lake Starnberg. From there the musician, now on the outs with the Wesendoncks, wrote to Eliza Wille everything he would have written to Mathilde. Knowing that Eliza would inevitably show his letters to Mathilde, did he not secretly wish for that "humiliation" they could cause her? He described the passionate love of the young sovereign for his music, and after retracing the events that had led him to this point, as in a long monologue from the *Ring*, he was full of wonder for the new king and sighed: "Ah, at last a love that brings neither pain nor torment!"

But his soul at bottom was still cruelly wounded. A few days later he let loose with a number of nasty sentences intended for the Wesendoncks' eyes:

It's the impertinence in the soul of the Philistines concerning their "practical wisdom" and their complacent presumption toward those rare minds that are deep and misunderstood to believe themselves the only ones who are sensible and wise. Their abominable shrewdness, their ridiculous incapacity to correctly understand and appreciate the matters of life . . . is simply one of the attributions of *instinct*, which drive animals to hunt for their daily necessities. . . . We are therefore forced to put up with the fact that the world may never understand us and allows itself to lament our impracticality. But when this state of mind is felt in the domain of morality, . . . when a feminine soul forgets the instincts of love, when from the high position of philistine morality she begins to judge, to lament, and . . . to exhort the object of her love, then the situation is no longer bearable.

Mathilde did certainly not deserve such explosive harshness, but Wagner was shaking off the fetters of his passion by heaping scorn upon his idol. He smashed his poor ivory statue into a thousand pieces, walling his Galatea up in deep silence.

He continued writing to Eliza Wille until July, at which point Cosima von Bülow officially entered his intimate life. At Starnberg Wagner complained once more of his fatigue and his solitude and admitted to Eliza that he could not live without the eternal feminine. Cosima arrived just in time to solve his problem.

The daughter of Franz Liszt was very unhappily married to Hans von Bülow, the young orchestra conductor who had been so devoted to Wagner. She fell into Richard's arms and sealed their liaison with the greatest gift he had ever received from a woman: paternity. In September Richard mentioned something discreetly to Eliza about his new acquaintance: the Bülows had a "tragic marriage."

After Starnberg, Richard and Cosima would become the subjects of gossip in Munich, where a caricature appeared in the press showing the couple walking arm in arm in the streets of the Bavarian capital, followed by the unfortunate husband carrying the score of *Tristan* under his arm. The influence that the impetuous musician seemed to have in the royal court of Ludwig II, the unconditional favors granted by the sovereign, the immoderate taste for luxury in his new lodgings—despite Bavaria's extremely critical political position, situated as it was between Austria and Prussia—made Wagner very unpopular among Munich's citizenry.

King Ludwig remained unruffled. He manifested his impatience only when it came to hearing *Tristan*. All during the winter of 1864–65 Wagner worked on the details of his project, and in February rehearsals began with two exceptional singers, Ludwig and Malvina (Garrigues) Schnorr von Carolsfeld. To Eliza Wille Wagner wrote feverishly: "Yes, come! The performances will be *marvelous*, there has never been anything like it. It is to live this experience that I had to suffer so much!"

In January Cosima wrote to Mathilde to ask her to send some of the literary manuscripts of Wagner that she still had in her possession. Mathilde replied directly to Richard, telling him she could not separate herself from anything of his without a "specific desire" coming from him. She put together a table of contents of the portfolio, which began with the title of one of Richard's Paris articles on *Der Freischütz*.

Although he had promised not to write to her anymore, in January 1865 he sent her a letter asking her to send back to him the contents of the large portfolio "of the Green Hill" so as to satisfy the pressing demands of His Majesty: "impossible to do otherwise," he wrote, and then, a little further on, "*He* really loves me!" Then, in a mixture of bitterness and irony: "In the old days, one could get me much more cheaply. Now my powers of observation have become much more acute, and the delusion of inconceivable weaknesses that made people back away from me, as if I were a madman, is now almost impossible to maintain." But at the end of the letter he softened a bit, despite his declarations to Cosima: "Will you still accept my thanks for your Christmas presents? . . . There remains an old letter to read; will I find it in the portfolio? Farewell! Affectionate memory!"

In 1896 Cosima told her daughter Eva that in July 1864 in Starnberg, Wagner said to her: "She [Mathilde] will never get a letter from me again!" She added, "For Christmas 1864, Frau Wesendonck sent him presents without receiving a word of thanks." That is why Richard expressed himself with such hesitation in writing: "Will you still accept my thanks. . . ." Cosima also pointed out that Mathilde sent them as a gift a device for cooking eggs, with the note "the egg of immortality"—a funny and ironic riposte to Wagner's remark: "Tomorrow I am going to Mainz to build my nest in Biebrich or Wiesbaden, where I can incubate that egg of *Die Meistersinger* that I have just laid." But in order to dispel any clouds marring the blue sky of his new and fertile relationship with Cosima, so inclined to jealousy, Wagner confided to her laughingly: "*Schumann macht dumm!*" (Schumann's music makes the people who listen to it stupid!). This was Richard's petty vengeance against the new interests of his friends on the Green Hill, who would be visited for a while by Johannes Brahms and the anti-Wagnerians.

"As the performance of *Tristan* drew near," explained Cosima to her daughter, "Wagner did not even mention her." She wrote to the Wesendoncks, but Mathilde replied that only an invitation from the master could concern her. When Cosima showed this to Richard, he himself sent a word to her: "Lady-friend, *Tristan* is turning out to be marvelous. Are you coming?"

In fact, on June 10, 1865, in the presence of King Ludwig II, Hans von Bülow conducted the world premiere of *Tristan und Isolde*, the story of an impossible love, smothered but still alive. Mathilde-Isolde was conspicuous by her absence—not from the stage, but from the audience. The Willes did not attend either, although they were traveling in the vicinity of Munich. In September Wagner expressed to them his disappointment. But on the subject of the performance, with which he was completely satisfied, he wrote: "The feeling of a dream did not leave me for one moment; I was surprised, and still am, that one can have such an experience. It was a highlight in my existence, and yet, it was made *bitter* by certain *absences*![4] Yes, made bitter! How petty-minded you all seem to me, you who ran away from such emotions!"

Richard judged the pettiness of his absent friends in comparison with the height of his artistic inspiration. It was not meant to deride the memory of their hospitality when he was penniless. And given his current situation and success, Eliza was intoxicated by the way her prophesies had come true. Had she not said "Something will happen" only two days before the king's emissary came to see Wagner, and "That will lead you to happiness" hardly two months before he began his liaison with Cosima? No doubt she also remembered something Hans von Bülow had said in 1857, when the newlyweds visited the Willes at Mariafeld: witnessing the relationship between Richard and Mathilde, Hans declared that, for his part, unlike Otto Wesendonck, he would not hesitate to give up his wife if that could contribute to inspiring the great Wagner!

In Greek tragedy, the words pronounced by the oracle of Delphi were not immediately or fully understood, and thus, as he was destined to do, Oedipus unwittingly killed his father and married Jocasta, his mother. Perhaps it was the sound of his own music that prevented Richard from hearing the chant of the mysterious "spinner,"[5] prophesying from the world's peaks. He must have known in some confused way that he would only be able to achieve his goals by loving a woman who was already married, a maternal wife who would replace the one he had left in growing out of his childhood. All his love affairs were thus ruined; only the daughter of Liszt dared to go the distance.

Cosima had many reasons to do what Mathilde had refused. Unlike Mathilde, the illegitimate child of the great Hungarian piano virtuoso and Countess Marie d'Agoult grew up in a rather sad atmosphere: her education was mediocre, and she and her brother and sister saw little of their illustrious father, who was constantly criss-crossing Europe on concert tours. Cosima met Wagner for the first time in Paris when she was still an adolescent. Immediately and passionately taken in by his music, she consented to marry a supporter of his, Hans von Bülow, one of Liszt's best students. He had offered to marry her, he said, to give a great aristocratic name to his master's illegitimate child. Cosima saw in him an apostle of Wagner, whom she adored. As for Bülow, his admiration for the composer made him accept everything afterward, including his wife's infidelity.

Did Cosima wait for the moment when Richard would finally be relieved of his passion for Mathilde Wesendonck? The circumstances seem to support this idea. But for many years, as can be seen in her diary, Cosima kept in her heart feelings of fear and jealousy regarding the muse of *Tristan*.

In October 1865, when Wagner showed Cosima Mathilde's letter to Eliza Wille that revealed some of the contents of her famous "last letter" to him, he tried to justify himself in his lover's tormented eyes. On October 28, hardly a week after his first excuses on the subject of Mathilde, his reproaches to Cosima, recorded in his *Brown Book*, sounded like those he had made to Minna: "What is your love if you have so little faith in me? . . . Why do you so often wrongly interpret what I say?" This leitmotif pervaded Cosima's writings after 1866.

In her memoirs written for her daughter Eva, she mentioned the edition of tales Mathilde sent to Richard in 1864. Cosima must have begun to read *The Strange Bird*, then *The Swan*. We can imagine Wagner's embarrassment, trying to pass off his discomfort with an ironic remark, recorded immediately by Cosima: "That's what she tells her children!"

From then on Wagner accommodatingly emphasized Mathilde's shortcomings in order to please the woman who had at last given him the home he had so long desired, a mental refuge, and progeny. In the first days of November 1865, wishing to offer Cosima a new pledge of his love, he gathered together all of Mathilde's letters, written over a twelve-year period, and sent them to Eliza Wille, who was staying with her family in Hamburg at the time. On November 16 she warned her husband: "I received Wagner's letter; the package he speaks of contains the letters of Frau Wesendonck, which he wants her to destroy herself. He says he wants to put his papers in order by getting rid of the past."

∾

Toward the end of her life Eliza Wille was still writing to Mathilde:

> You are fortunate to have been for one of the greatest geniuses of our time what Frau von Stein was for Goethe. You have been and will continue to be honored by all. The time will come . . . when everything will fall into place, thanks to Wagner's first letters, which you have in your possession. Nothing will diminish your role. Charlotte von Stein did not have to partake in the life of Christiane Vulpius,[6] because the latter was the mother of his children. . . . Think also that the loving and courageous help of Elisabeth could not take Tannhäuser away from his demon. You possess something very beautiful, very magnificent, very sublime, something you shall never forget or lose.

It has been said that Mathilde Wesendonck tried to fashion her image by selecting only what she wished to keep of her huge correspondence with Wagner. However, recent discoveries have shown not only that this is far from the truth, but that the manipulation of the master's letters to Mathilde is entirely attributable to Cosima. According to her, the musician had expressed the wish that the missives be destroyed, while Mathilde, for her part and out of sheer respect for his genius, had never been capable of modifying even the slightest comma. On the contrary, having copied them faithfully by hand, she kept the originals until her death.

Two years following her death in 1902, in a first edition of these letters published in 1904, Wolfgang Golther, the editor, wrote in the foreword: "Frau Wesendonck did not consider herself to be the sole possessor of the letters addressed to her. She protected them carefully, keeping them for posterity, copying them so as to make them suitable for publication, accompanying them with illustrations and facsimiles. The Wagner family, in a move that was unusual for them, yielded their royalties to [Mathilde's] son and descendants. Furthermore, she specified that all proceeds should go to the Bayreuth scholarship fund."

In 1987 I discovered some unpublished correspondence between the Wesendonck and Wagner families that shed a harsh and clear new light on the matter. In the autumn of 1903 Golther received from Karl Wesendonck and the Baron von Bissing, Mathilde's son and grandson, respectively, copies of the master's letters for publication. Golther then wrote to Wagner's widow, Cosima, to obtain her consent. On October 6, 1903, she replied: "I am surprised to learn that there are still letters that should have been destroyed long ago."

Obviously Cosima wanted to prevent the publication of these materials. So she borrowed the original letters from the Wesendonck family in order to censor them. First, on December 12, 1903, she thanked Karl for the package containing the collection of copies executed by Mathilde. She wanted to read them all, she said, before sending her approval to Golther. On December 22 she wrote again to Karl in a rather sarcastic tone: "I am glad to see your mother get the glorification she was expecting." (The word "glorification" [*verherrlich*] was a deliberate exaggeration.)

On December 28, to Fritz von Bissing, Mathilde's grandson, she went a step further in her perfidious diplomacy: "The trouble is," she wrote, "that all these letters, according to the will of the master, my famous husband, should have been destroyed, and quite often he would tell me how much he loathed the idea of seeing his intimate thoughts displayed in print. Your dear grandmother's letters were all returned to her. . . . The royalties from these letters [from Wagner] are mine. Can you imagine what a dilemma this is for me? I am ready to give up my rights to your uncle [Karl], but for that I must ask you to send me in exchange the original manuscripts and the diary."[7]

Three days later, on December 31, having received an affirmative answer, Cosima expressed her satisfaction that they had consented so promptly to her desires. Thus not only the copies but the original letters of Richard Wagner to Mathilde Wesendonck fell into her hands. The very next day, on January 1, 1904, seeing a delay in the mail, she could not help reiterating her demand with great impatience: "*I am expecting* the *original letters* and the *diary*."[8]

This is when she must have censored the letters: many of them disappeared, and some had passages deleted, as is shown in the first edition by ellipses; entire passages from the Venice diary addressed to Mathilde were cut out. Cosima then sent a copy of this expunged correspondence to Golther, who finally published them in a volume with a long preface.

Six months later, when Karl Wesendonck asked Cosima to send back the original letters of Richard to his mother, Cosima answered him at length. On June 2, 1904, she made an astonishing declaration: "I can hardly tell you how much I had to fight against the tears in my heart. . . . I had the impression that a long and painful story had reached a consoling and luminous ending, thanks to your gesture of kindness toward me, which unites us all, as well as the past with the present. . . . I destroyed the letters to your mother. I could not consider them my property, and I had to make the sacrifice that your mother could not."

Mathilde would have liked to publish all of Wagner's letters *in extenso*. After her death, they were to belong to the world. But it seems that Cosima wished to suppress a few passages in which she felt she was involved. Some of them were pieced together, however, by Julius Kapp in 1931.[9] Indeed, in the Venice diary Wagner told Mathilde about the curious incident in 1858 between Cosima von Bülow and Karl Ritter in which, confessing to each other their respective matrimonial disasters, they decided to die, though they did not take any action toward that end. Other episodes concerning Wagner's relations with Liszt were also suppressed. But that was not enough to appease Cosima's rage: later on all of Wagner's documents, letters, and manuscripts were systematically purged of anything that did not fit with the image of the genius that his widow wanted to create for posterity.[10]

Thus, in November 1865, Mathilde Wesendonck received the package containing her own letters, "to be destroyed." On opening it, did she hear the first chords of the Prelude of *Tristan* resounding in the silence of her room? There, spread out before her, lying on the floor, like the autumn leaves on the ground of the park, were the pages of the old days, filled up with her fine handwriting, which revealed all her inner life to the man she had loved so passionately.

In the black marble chimney, on the hearth, the flames enveloped the logs; as the bark was consumed, it fell away into ashes, like a mask peeling off a face. She heard the music sung in her heart invading her soul, like the fire penetrating each piece of wood. She could see the most poignant scenes of her life again, and nostalgia plunged her into the dream world of love, Isolde's dream:

> *My God, 'tis a very sad kiss,*
> *The kiss one receives in a dream;*
> *For 'tis a painful absence that sighs within us*
> *To the bottom of the heart.*

> *My God, 'tis a very sad love*
> *The love one lives only in a dream.*
> *Joy and happiness wash away like foam*
> *When comes the glow of dawn.*

She could remember the hour of choice, of duty, of sacrifice, and the renunciation that followed. Ah! If he only knew . . .

If you knew how I suffered,
You would say comforting words.
And my heart would find at last in your arms
The rest it aspires to.

But when in praying I spread my arms
To greet that joy I yearn for,
The goal fades away
Inaccessible forever.

Her letters fell from her hands, one after the other, to join the music and the flames. She opened them without rereading what she had written, presented them to the embers, and watched their slow destruction before the cinders.

I could bear very well only to see you,
A prey to my torment, so near to you.
And even if I were far away,
With you before me, I was happy.

You, everyone loves you,
You love many others,
You are like the brilliant sun that gives joy and blessing.
My poor heart loves only you, you alone.

"Chosen for me, lost for me," she murmured to the sound of her soul's music.

Before tossing it into the flames, she took the diary she had written for him, contemplating the notebook and turning the pages without reading them. Outside night had come and autumn was advancing, treading furtively toward winter, toward death.

So many memories had assailed her that evening, and the pathetic little face of Mignon, sick with love, was vivid in her mind. Only Eliza, the healer of her soul, knew how she suffered.

And yet, when you said to the Friend[11]
The word so short of eternal faith,
You broke my heart;
A start, a cry, it was all over.[12]

17

The Antidote

———◆———

Here I am alone, and my gaze
Looks down into the far-off valley.
My eye stares at the blue,
Incapable of seeing anything.

Dark clouds appear
So bleak and heavy.
As if they would cry
Even before night falls.

How enviable seems to me
Their fugitive fate!
Their torment they pour
Into the bosom of the earth!
. . .
But me, sadly I return
To the silent house.
Outside, the air makes me tremble
So bleak and heavy, 'tis dark in the air.

—Mathilde Wesendonck, "Ich steh'allein" (Alone),
in *Gedichte, Volkslieder, Legenden, Sagen* (1862)

Mathilde Wesendonck had known Clara Schumann since 1857. One year after the death of her husband, Robert, the virtuoso pianist, devoted to the memory and music of her brilliant husband, went on a concert tour to enable the world to hear his last compositions. In Zurich that December she gave two recitals in the hall of the former Casino, playing, among other things, the *Symphonic Etudes*. Wagner came to applaud, and Mathilde, who attended regularly these musical evenings, did not go unnoticed by witnesses. In her memoirs Bertha Roner-Lipka drew a disparaging picture of Mathilde, whom she described as a "small, undeveloped creature with a face like a rodent," and an unlikely picture of Wagner throwing himself at the feet of Schumann's widow to express to her his devotion: "Today a new era in music begins for me," he was supposed to have said; "I thank you for giving me this opportunity."[1] These words were no doubt exaggerated, and the lady was probably imputing to Wagner her own reactions. But despite Richard's praise, Clara Schumann noted in her diary on December 7, 1857: "I haven't much to say about Wagner. He is extremely kind toward me, and I am so much the less fortunate that I cannot show him in return the least bit of sympathy."

If this incident was of little importance in itself, it was nevertheless a symptom of a growing uneasiness in the world of music. A contemporary of Wagner, Schumann had met him in Leipzig during his youth; in Dresden they became friends. In addition to being held in high esteem as a composer, Schumann was a music critic who sometimes wrote negative articles on Wagner's work in his newspaper, the *Neue Zeitschrift für Musik*. Although he greatly admired the young *Kapellmeister*'s conducting, he had expressed doubts about his *Fliegende Holländer*. He said he had found traces in it of Meyerbeer! As for *Tannhäuser*, which he criticized severely after only reading the score, he had the honesty to admit that he had changed his mind after having seen it performed on stage.

Wagner admired Schumann's music, but he did not accept the critic's analyses. However, the two men enjoyed meeting, taking walks together, and spending evenings at the Schumanns'. This did not prevent them from arguing bitterly about opera and the music of the future. Concerning Mendelssohn and Meyerbeer, their opposing opinions separated them forever. Each considered himself to be the true heir of Beethoven, and they quarreled about his succession like heirs to the throne. Politics in 1848 had developed into an irreconcilable division of radicals on one side and conservatives on the other, and these two tendencies divided the musical world as well.

Clara was not very appreciative of Wagner's presence: she considered him a fanatic. She worried about the mental health of her husband, who would collapse a few years later into dementia and death. She also mistrusted the people who gravitated to Wagner, especially Liszt, and thought of them all as a circle of exalted minds.

After 1853 a very young musician came into the life of the Schumanns who would soon become the figurehead of the traditional conception of German music: Johannes Brahms. On discovering this young talent, Schumann immediately considered him his "artistic heir." After Robert's death, Clara kept up a long correspondence with him, and a relationship which has been described as an "impassioned friendship."[2]

Brahms, born in Hamburg in 1833, was of humble origins. An introvert, he nonetheless had many loyal friendships. All his life he enjoyed living well, going to cafés, and corresponding prolifically, yet he remained a bachelor. Awkward yet kind, he was shy, seeming to fear putting his deep feelings into words—a difficulty he would nevertheless overcome very well in his music. Recruited into the standing "Quarrel between the Ancients and the Moderns" of his time, he rapidly became the symbol of the opponents to the "music of the future" without having written a word himself on the subject.

In 1857 the publication of Liszt's symphonic poems with a preface that was equivalent to a true manifesto ignited the gunpowder. Joseph Joachim, the great violinist, disowned the composer of *Les préludes*, writing to Liszt: "[Your music] is contrary to the genius of the great masters who have nurtured my soul since I was young." And Bülow, who was a fervent advocate of the moderns—that is, of Wagner—but who would pass into the opposing camp years later, declared in 1858: "We are working in two completely opposite directions." The traditionalists then had the idea of making their own declaration of principles defining their aesthetic positions. And in 1860, following an indiscreet remark, the "protest," which was still only a draft, against the new German school of Liszt and Wagner was published in the *Berliner Musik-Zeitung Echo*, even though the four authors—Julius Otto Grimm, Joseph Joachim, Bernhard Scholz, and Johannes Brahms—had not given their permission. Brahms regretted the incident, for he thought that the term "leaders" used in the text was far too general, and that it was necessary not to lump Liszt, whose compositions he abhorred, in with Wagner and Berlioz, whom he esteemed as musicians.

In this climate of tension between the clans constituted by the artists and their disciples, Clara Schumann's mistrust was comprehensible. At the time she met Wagner in Zurich next to his muse for *Tristan*, she was an irreproachable widow. But when Wagner fled from the Asyl, Mathilde, who had kept her distance from their aesthetic quarrels, had no reason to deprive herself of the music of Brahms, Schumann, or anyone else. In Zurich concerts were still organized regularly by the Friends of Music Society; Wesendonck helped finance their expenses, and Mathilde would meet the musicians and encourage them. We know that long ago she had been anointed a "Faithful Protector of the Arts."

Invited to the Wesendoncks' villa, Clara Schumann gave a recital there in 1862 on which she played Beethoven's Piano Concerto in G major. But she stood aloof from certain members of Zurich's bourgeoisie that she suspected of having ties with the Wagner clan.

Brahms had been living in Vienna since 1862 but often spent his vacations in Switzerland. During the winter of 1863–64 he gave a series of concerts organized by the association to which the Wesendoncks belonged. On November 10, 1863, Mathilde heard for the first time an orchestral work by the young composer from Hamburg, the Serenade in D major. She also met two of the musician's friends, Theodor Billroth and Wilhelm Lübke—fierce anti-Wagnerians both. Billroth, originally from northern Germany, was an eminent surgeon and, since 1860, a professor at the University of Zurich. A real force of nature, he went mountain climbing, wrote scientific and medical reports, and played violin, viola, or piano at an almost professional level in chamber-music evenings with his friends. In the quarrel concerning the music of the future, he passionately took sides against Liszt: "[Theodor] Kirchner and [Brahms] played on two pianos a few symphonic poems of Liszt. What horrible music! *Dante, Mazeppa, Prometheus*. In the *Dante*, we did not go past the "Purgatory"; I vetoed it from a medical point of view, and we purged ourselves with the new sextet just published by Brahms. Brahms and Kirchner played it four-hands."[3] Billroth would also write long letters to Mathilde until 1871.

These Zurich friends of Brahms did everything they could to worsen the relations between the masters of the day, but in Vienna Wagner's friends tried to reconcile them. On February 6, 1864, Cornelius and Tausig organized a meeting between Brahms and Wagner in the house of the physician and Wagnerian Josef Standhartner. Brahms played his Variations on a Theme of Haydn, to which Wagner responded with admiration: "We see what can still be taken from old models when we meet someone who knows how to use them."[4]

On November 19, 1865, Otto and Mathilde attended a concert of the young musician, whose reputation was growing. It was in Basel his Piano Quartet in A major and the Gesänge für Frauenchor, Hörner, und Harfe (Songs for Women's Chorus with Horns and Harp) were first performed, along with works by Schumann, Schubert, and Bach. Two days later, at the Association's concert in Zurich, Brahms himself played Bach's Chromatic Fantasy and Schumann's Piano Concerto and conducted his own Serenade in D major. Not since Wagner's departure seven years earlier had Mathilde felt so impressed by the manifestation of a genius. But contrary to her experience with Richard, in which the man and his work were inseparable, Brahms's music left her with complete peace of mind, and she was able to meet the composer without the slightest anxiety. At the end of the evening Brahms wrote to Clara Schumann to tell her how pleased he was that his friends Billroth, Lübke, and Wesendonck had asked him to give them a private hearing of his Serenade. "All the expenses were paid by them," he added.

It was no doubt in the first weeks after the auto-da-fé of her letters to Richard, in November 1865, that Mathilde invited Brahms to the Green Hill. The end of her correspondence with Wagner and the presence of another woman in the life of the man who had vowed to her eternal love left an emptiness in her heart and anguish in her soul. With Richard gone, Mathilde wanted to replant the desert that her existence had become with new blossoms. But if she never became an anti-Wagnerian like Nietzsche, burning what he adored, she nevertheless allowed herself to be taken up by the circle of Brahms and his friends, without, however, fully gaining their confidence: her long relationship with Wagner made her suspect in the eyes of the conservatives. And no less so for the musicians of the future, as can be seen in Eliza Wille's letter of 1867, written after she attended a concert with Hans von Bülow in Munich: "I did not see Bülow, or rather I did not speak to him, but I attended his two evenings of quartets, which were performed perfectly. I went with my family; they say he had the tactlessness to answer those who asked him if he would pay a visit to the Wesendoncks, 'No, because they are not true friends of Wagner.'"[5]

Rejecting both sides, Mathilde received Brahms in her home and, with her usual innocence, spread out on the table before him all the Wagnerian outlines and documents she still had in her possession: the Wesendonck Lieder, Tristan, Das Rheingold, Die Walküre, and Acts I and II of Siegfried, as well as the Album Sonata. Brahms leafed respectfully through these fascinating composition drafts in silent admiration. Later on, he would say of himself that he was "the best of all the Wagnerians."

Mathilde never ceased to admire Richard's work. Like another friend and benefactor of Wagner, Maria Kalergis-Muchanow, she could have described Brahms as being "of a different type from Wagner, the first composer of that period."[6]

~

On the Green Hill, from the terrace, Mathilde would contemplate from time to time the still-unoccupied Asyl, the nest of her love for Richard. "Do what is necessary to keep the Asyl for me," he had written, but she knew now that he would never come back. The "silent refuge in wood and stone" loomed before her like a silent reproach.

"Ah! Who then would be my swallow?" She would peruse the letters from the old days. She knew every sentence of them. The spring of 1867 broke out in a harmony of tender green and birdsong. The wind made the young leaves of the magnificent trees rustle. Between nostalgia and the will to live existed subtle ties to which her memories were linked. With her poetic soul, Mathilde wrote to Brahms:

> For a long time I had hoped the spring would bring you back to see us, like a swallow. . . . But the spring has advanced toward the coming summer, leaving back its youth and its dreams. What do you think? If only we were not obliged, poor children that we are on this earth, to endlessly advance and on tiptoe! But alas, even if we felt the desire to stay back, we would see everything changed all around us and would feel like strangers in our own lives. . . . In a few days, it will be summer. . . . During the musical festivities our house will greet the Stockhausen family, but unfortunately I will not be there. The little green nest, quite close by, will remain unoccupied, however, and I will give orders before my departure for Saint Moritz; I will watch over it with a light heart, so that a swallow might at any moment find a refuge."[7]

Every summer now, Mathilde felt the need to go for a cure in Saint Moritz, in the Swiss canton of Grisons, where the altitude and iron-rich water helped her to overcome her fatigue and arthritis. But a few weeks before the summer season, she had musicians perform Brahms's Piano Quintet in her hall. The audience was taken aback by this new music and its thick, dense sonorities. Mathilde wrote to the composer about some of the public's unfavorable reactions: "This grown child needs time, much more time! Give it to him then. But we felt an immense pleasure listening to your extraordinary and original work."

Brahms, of course, could not care less about Mathilde's impressions and allusions, for he could see Wagner lurking in the background. The story of Richard and Mathilde was common knowledge, and his friends in Zurich had told him every detail about Wagner's stay at the Asyl. Billroth, a man of the world with a rather cynical attitude toward women, received Brahms regularly in his elegant apartment in the Plattenstrasse, where there was much laughter, drinking, and gossiping about local personalities, punctuated by the playing of chamber music with his friends.

Clara Schumann approved of Brahms for declining the invitation to stay at the Asyl: "You are right to refuse their invitation; it would have weighed heavily on you and created obligations for you toward them."[8]

∾

In July 1865, gathering together the manuscripts of his works so as to offer them as a gift to his new benefactor, King Ludwig II, Wagner remembered that the original score of *Das Rheingold* was still on the Green Hill. He wrote to Otto Wesendonck asking that it be sent to him but could not help revisiting the past:

> Although I hardly manage to find the necessary peace of mind to consciously imagine my past life, I have only to hear your name to clearly remember one of the most important periods of my life. . . . No friendship, no love succeeded in bringing me either true peace nor real rest. . . . Let me dream of rest in reminding myself of the time when I was living and producing under your protection. It was a time of powerful creation; and now, despite tremendous effort, *we are very far from being able to give to the world creations comparable to those of that era.* The troubles that caused me to break with you six years ago should have been avoided.

Wagner then alluded to the events of 1864: "They estranged me so much from my own life that you yourself, you did not really acknowledge me when once again, recently, I turned to you [for help]. This sad impression should have spared me too. I thought it was possible, it would have been beautiful, very beautiful, sublime even, if it could have been like that; but one does not have the right to demand the sublime, and I was wrong."[9]

Something of a prisoner of his own destiny, Wagner saw how much everything had changed for him: a woman brought him the warmth of a home and a king, the solution to his material problems. The evidence was there: from then on, his work belonged to Ludwig II of Bavaria: "Try to understand me, and do not harbor any bad feelings when I ask you to give up in the name of friendship and with kindness, for the king of Bavaria, the score of *Das Rheingold* that is in your hands. The king must and will know your rights to these works. I am sure he will not leave you without compensation."[10]

In August Otto responded. His pride was apparently hurt by the idea that Wagner could doubt his generosity: "Have I not long since renounced, expressly and in writing, all the rights to the publication and performances of the *Nibelung*? It cannot be in question now, nor do I look to receive any compensation for it from either the king or you. I would rejoice that the young sovereign might learn that long ago another mortal warmed to your work. . . . I cannot deny that it was hard for me to separate myself from *Die Walküre*, and now you want me to also give up the score of *Das Rheingold* to your royal protector. I often contemplate it, I admire it, and it is dear to me. Nevertheless, my answer was not in doubt when you wrote to me. I offer it, then, to your art-loving king, and I would consider myself more than richly compensated if, by a wonderful performance, this national work were recognized. Then, I hope, you will invite us; we would certainly not miss the occasion for anything in the world."[11]

Wagner was moved. He tried to thank Otto in writing, and in this way to exorcise the past.

But he ended by admitting that only intensive artistic labor could cure him from the "deep wounds" from which he still suffered.

In the end it was the king of Bavaria himself who paid homage to Otto's noble gesture when he wrote to confer (though unofficially) the "von" on Otto Wesendonck so as to honor his patronage to Wagner—something he viewed as comparable to a feat of arms in the service of the kingdom:

> Dear Herr von Wesendonck,
>
> I hurry to express to you my most cordial thanks for your kind relinquishing of Wagner's *Rheingold* score. . . . I know that in the past you gave an affectionate refuge to the struggling artist, who bore unthinkable suffering; I wish to tell to you, dear sir, of my deep gratitude, for it is to your sympathetic interest that we owe the immortal works Wagner created in Switzerland.[12]

But the intrigues at the royal court of Munich, the scandal provoked by the Richard-Cosima-Bülow triangle, the birth of two children whose paternity was justifiably attributed to Wagner, and the political pressure of Austria and Prussia over the kingdom of Bavaria led the composer to flee once again to Switzerland, where he found, at His Majesty's expense, another house in Tribschen, near Lucerne. There he would finish the score of *Die Meistersinger* at Cosima's side. He returned to Munich only to direct the first rehearsals of its world premiere on Sunday, June 21, 1868, under the baton of Hans von Bülow. He had sworn not to attend the performances, but that day, called to the royal box by the monarch himself when the curtain rose, he remained at Ludwig's side throughout the whole opera, and on the king's order, recognized the public's applause by saluting from his box. This enormous breach of etiquette was added to the already long list of scandals being kept by Wagner's enemies.

Otto Wesendonck and the Willes were in the audience, and Eliza assures us that "the performance was splendid." Richard thanked Otto for attending the two performances; yet, it seems Mathilde did not accompany her husband. Where was Mathilde, the Titian madonna who in Venice inspired Wagner to compose *Die Meistersinger*? On June 1 she had received from her friend the brand-new edition of the piano score of the work with the dedication: "To my dear friends of the Green Hill with my gratitude." We do not know the real reason she did not go to Munich. Was it the same one that had prevented her from being present at the premiere of *Tristan*?

It is true she dreaded confrontations with her past, and on such occasions she would make sure to be absorbed by other things. The children were growing up, and Mathilde was very attentive to their education. Seventeen-year-old Myrrha was shy and pretty; eleven-year-old Karl was succeeding brilliantly in his studies; and six-year-old Hans had a romantic streak like his mother. A few years later a private tutor who entered into the service of the Wesendonck family when they were living in Dresden left several notes about the youngest son, describing him as "cheerful, clever and natural." Mathilde seemed to particularly have affinities and similarities of character with him, whereas Karl, more distant, was endowed with a seriousness beyond his years.

Wanting to introduce her children to the joys of the dramatic arts, Mathilde adapted *Der Freischütz* for their puppet theater. Her other project was to publish an illustrated volume, *Deutsches Kinderbuch in Wort und Bild* (A Children's Book in Words and Pictures), which consisted of charming children's verses and delightful illustrations done by a talented artist, Ernst Schweinfurth, whom she had met in Rome. The world evoked in the book was populated with characters from romantic literature or legend that formed a link between past and present. In a short poem entitled "Nero," for example, she described a dog that was her children's companion; but an attentive reader of Weber's libretto for *Der Freischütz* would meet, near the end of the opera, Agatha's pet dog, also named Nero.

Nero was a Roman emperor
Who, to light the houses of Rome,
Set fire to the whole town.
The Christians, covered with tar,
Burned there like torches.
But the Nero I mean is not a nasty king
But a good and faithful dog
Who eats, snores, and grunts with pleasure.

Deliberately or not, Mathilde's life was changing little by little. As a mother she was immensely tender, simple, direct, spontaneous, and warm; but as a woman she was hesitant and reserved. Her passion gone, she searched for an antidote to her loneliness, her jealousy of Cosima, and her bitter disappointment in Richard. In her isolation she felt her way along, writing poems in which her dreamy romanticism would yield to a certain didactic formalism.

Brahms's friends also contributed greatly to this conversion, as did the pedantic ways of Ettmüller. Billroth, Lübke, and the musicians Kirchner and Friedrich Hegar, who constituted the local "Parnassus." They would all gather at the concerts where everyone was following, step by step, the progress of the remarkable composer from Hamburg. It was at this time that Brahms composed his *Deutsches Requiem*, performed in Zurich on February 27, 1869.

During the same period Mathilde kept up a correspondence with Brahms.[13] Their letters turned constantly around invitations that were accepted or missed, in the tone reminiscent of that seen in her exchanges with Francesco de Sanctis. "You cannot imagine how much joy and pleasure I had in reading your letter in your beautiful and refined handwriting!" wrote Brahms to Mathilde. Then, one time, when he was spending half a day in Zurich, he wrote: "I had the firm intention of paying you a visit, but Hegar told me you were not at home. I cannot hope to catch up on what I missed." Brahms nevertheless remained distant. It was likely that he was mistrustful because of Mathilde's former attachment to Wagner. And if, more than once, she expressed to him her desire to receive him in her home, he could not find one unkind word from her pen about Wagner.

Concerning the reactions of Richard's enemies at the premiere of *Die Meistersinger*, which Mathilde either could not or did not want to attend, Billroth wrote to her: "I did not send you Lübke's critique of *Meistersinger*. I cannot imagine that you would take him too seriously. As I thought the article might upset you, I did everything in my power not to let it fall into your hands rather than send it to you. Until now I have not had time to peruse the score of *Meistersinger*, but I doubt that either the subject matter or the music would be to my liking."

Mathilde did not intervene in this new quarrel between the "ancients" and the "moderns." Her admiration for Richard's works remained intact, yet she considered Brahms to be the other great heir of Beethoven. "I would regret having lived in this century if I had not kindly but insistently asked you to come and visit us," she wrote Brahms.

In spite of the attempts of his friends who were overtly hostile to Richard Wagner, Brahms was interested in the Wagner events in Munich. In 1869, on the order of King Ludwig and against the composer's will, a performance of *Das Rheingold* was given, followed the next year by one of *Die Walküre*. "I very much feel like going to Munich to see *Rheingold*; perhaps I will see you there," wrote Brahms. Mathilde replied immediately by quoting a paragraph of Richard's, sent to Otto, in which he expressed his reservations. It was not what he had hoped for his *Ring des Nibelungen*, but he was resigned to letting it go on with whatever means were available. The dress rehearsal took place in the king's presence on August 27, under the direction of Hans Richter. But it was only on the following September 22 that the world premiere was given. This almost one-month delay prevented the Wesendoncks from attending.

Wagner had remained in Tribschen; he was afraid of going to Munich, where fierce debates were ringing out against him. And of the many characters who were reunited on the Green Hill, Mathilde was not the only one to undergo life changes. Wagner too, the eternal Dr. Jeykll and Mr. Hyde, who felt himself to be the target of Munich society and "philistine" vengeance from the royal court of Bavaria, let himself be carried away by his old tendency to write pamphlets. He thus dusted off one of his old diatribes, written in 1850 against Jewish musicians: *Jewishness in Music*.[14]

It was re-edited in March 1869 despite a general uproar of protest from his friends, many of whom were Jewish. This old libel, written during his years of famine and disillusion, issued from a pen dipped in vitriol. Cosima, who would prove to be even more anti-Semitic than her husband, was also perplexed about the publication of this document. In exhuming *Jewishness in Music*, explained Ernest Newman, Wagner was said to be trying to answer a question asked by his former benefactor, Maria Kalergis-Muchanow: why was the press so constantly hostile to him? The only answer that he could find was that "most of the press belonged to the Jews." It did not cross Wagner's mind that a great many people would be insulted by this abusive generalization, and that by publishing it he would be hurting himself. Otto Wesendonck also sharply disapproved the brochure. That is why, one year later, Wagner sent him another leaflet, this time on Beethoven, adding: "Here is something quite new coming out of my retreat. I did not send you *On Conducting*, because you disliked the one on Jewishness, and I feared that this new essay would not meet with your full approval either."[15]

Why did Wagner put out such an offensive text as *Jewishness*, at a time when he no longer had much reason to complain? He also took out his spleen on the French, although more humorously, following the Franco-Prussian war of 1870, in *Une capitulation* (A Surrender). The apparent impetus for this pamphlet no doubt lay in the nationalism sweeping over Germany, provoked by the coming war between Prussia and France. On the other hand, one cannot deny the growing influence of Cosima in the life of the master, illustrated by a letter of Peter Cornelius in 1865: "Impossible nowadays to see Wagner alone, to have a conversation with him; and never does a letter get to him without Cosima opening it the first and reading it to him."[16]

Indeed, Cosima had liberated Wagner from the strenuous effort of answering his mail, from all pecuniary negotiation, and from all direct communication with his friends, supposedly in order to allow him to dedicate himself entirely to his music. However, Martin Gregor-Dellin treats as "pure slander" any possible influence of Cosima on Richard's ideas about anti-Semitism and Francophobia. On the other hand, Ernest Newman shows much greater evidence to the contrary: on the subject of a Jewish author inspired by the *Faust* of Goethe, Cosima claimed that no Jew could possibly understand such a great German author, that the "race" most likely to develop culture was the Germans, and that the only hope for the French was to assimilate to Germanic culture; she found the French "repugnant," believing that in France "honorable feelings between a man and a woman were impossible." Finally, upon the death of the great Jewish orchestra conductor Hermann Levi, who conducted *Parsifal* in Bayreuth in 1882 and was a dear friend of Richard's, she praised his services and faith in Wagner, "in spite of his race."[17]

In 1868–69 there is no doubt that Wagner himself expressed these ideas, at least in theory, which would be a scandal in these disastrous writings of his, for the first edition of *Jewishness* went back to 1850, when he was in France taking revenge on the Jewish composer Meyerbeer. Nevertheless, without wanting to absolve Wagner for his literary anti-Semitism, past or present, we are forced to admit that the proximity of Cosima favored the reappearance of these tendencies, which had lain dormant during his years of creativity in the aura of Mathilde Wesendonck. As for the latter, if she tolerated among her correspondents any of the anti-Semitism that was in fashion during the years of the *Kulturkampf*, she never translated any of it into word or act.

~

Mathilde's poetic gift had been revealed under Wagner's influence; but it was during these years of inner transformation, and under the influence of Brahms, that she turned to playwriting. She dreamed of continuing her role as a muse for a great musician and collaborating in his work, as she had done in old days with Richard. This time, she had a precise idea: to give the genius nothing less than the libretto for an opera! But before talking about it to Brahms, she made a few attempts on her own. The first try was in 1866. Attracted by a romantic subject, she looked into the popular medieval legend on Genevieve of Brabant. A *Genovefa* libretto had been written in 1841 by Friedrich Hebbel that inspired Robert Schumann to compose an opera at the same time Wagner was working on *Lohengrin*.

Henceforth, from the beginning to the end of her dramatic works, Mathilde Wesendonck would invariably stage a noble and courageous woman, forever misunderstood by the people around her. If Mathilde burned her own letters and her diary, she left us her autobiography in her plays. Genovefa was the first: the wife of Siegfried, count of Trier, the heroine was unjustly accused of adultery by the seneschal Golo, who was secretly in love with her. At her trial she was sentenced to death. Lacking the good luck of Elsa, who was saved by Lohengrin, Genovefa was spared nonetheless by the servants whose task it was to kill her. Siegfried finally recognized his wife's innocence, but Genovefa had suffered too much to go on living.

Mathilde composed her melodrama *Genovefa* in three acts, with lines in iambic pentameters, and changed the nasty Golo into a brother of Siegfried. The personality of the protagonist developed through motherhood in tender scenes with her child; then she died in the arms of her husband, to whom she had remained faithful despite all temptations.

Mathilde wrote to Eliza Wille: "As soon as you return, you will find on your table my *Genovefa*, printed and nicely bound. It does not give me too much satisfaction." Indeed, budding playwright that she was, Mathilde felt her heroine was not credible, this paradoxical woman who was hiding while she revealed herself, like all the heroines she would create later on. "I am hard-working and nothing else," she added. Self-published in sixty copies, *Genovefa* was reserved for her immediate family. She received encouragement from Ettmüller, but it is unlikely that she showed this first dramatic attempt to Brahms. At the time, however, the musician seemed to be searching for a subject for an opera: "I took a text of Goethe, *Rinaldo*, and tried to set it to music. But the work ended up as a sequence of airs, recitatives, and choruses, becoming in that way more of a cantata."

The themes she utilized were almost always taken from old Germanic legends. In 1868 Mathilde published a new drama entitled *Gudrun*; this time she hurried to send it to Brahms. In this five-act play, inspired by one of the oldest epic poems in German literature, the author dwelled on her obsession of a woman faithful unto death. The character of Gudrun reminds one of Mathilde in 1857–58—the courageous, suffering, misunderstood wife. When he received her libretto in Hamburg, Brahms sent her his first reactions: "The scenery around me these last eight days, the sea, only the sea, reminded me often of the time of Gudrun—the sky continually gray, a typically Nordic atmosphere, which can contain poetry."

The story is set in the time of the Viking and Norman expeditions. Gudrun-Isolde-Mathilde, the daughter of the king of Frisia, was engaged to be married to Herwig, who has been vanquished by the king of Normandy and his son, Hartmut. In Act II there is a conflict resembling the one in *Tristan*. The Normans being victorious, Gudrun was taken prisoner and put in a boat with Hartmut, who wanted to seduce her; but the young woman remained faithful to her roots and to her fiancé, Herwig. The plot is complicated by numerous secondary characters—a tyrannical future mother-in-law, an unfortunate sister—and the whole thing is bathed in theatrical impressionism inspired by both Schiller and Wagner. On the first page of the libretto Mathilde put a quote by Gotthold Lessing: "Der Mensch muss nicht müssen" (man must not be obliged). According to her grandson Fritz von Bissing, Mathilde expressed here her taste for the evolution of the free will of personality and human dignity. The notion of duty was for her an inner obligation that must harmonize with the world. She sought to reconcile the contradictions of her era's restrictions on women by honoring faithfulness above all, accepting all the suffering required to attain this goal. She remembered the lessons of Calderón but did not forget those of Schopenhauer.

But the confusion of literary styles and many incoherencies in the text made *Gudrun* poorly adapted to the stage, although certain monologues were touching and poetic. Numerous allusions to *Tristan*, the *Ring*, and the dramas of Schiller and even Shakespeare were a mark of naivety.

"So, ambitious and hard-working women put lazy men to shame," wrote Gottfried Keller to his friend Ludmilla Assing. "Frau Wesendonck has had books printed for children and a drama, *Gudrun*."

"It's a masterpiece," exclaimed one of Mathilde's admirers, the writer Alfred Meissner, still charmed by the play. Brahms also declared he was delighted but had some reserve as to the libretto's ability to be staged as an opera.

In August 1869 an impatient Mathilde finally wrote to Brahms asking him why he did not compose for the stage. "And the opera libretto? It would be up to the musician to settle upon the exact lines the poet is to follow. The experience could be attempted once the subject is agreed upon. It is only in the water that one learns to swim!"

But Brahms's concept of opera was the exact opposite of Wagner's. For the latter, the lyrical drama could only be a complete union of two elements: the text and the music, in continuous symbiosis, without arias or numbers, the music developing not in established forms, but in accordance with the literary ideas. Brahms, on the contrary, defined opera as a "compact musical form" containing "isolated numbers, linked by spoken dialogue."[18] According to Claude Rostand, "[Brahms] believed that only certain important episodes should be underscored by the music, allowing the librettist the space and the freedom to develop the subject dramatically; for his part, this gives the composer an advantage, for instead of dissipating his efforts on the entire thing—which means those efforts would necessarily be diluted—he can, on the contrary, concentrate on these chosen episodes to give them all their dramatic force."[19]

But because Brahms also admired the Wagnerian type of opera, the conflict seemed to him unresolvable, and he abandoned all his stage projects. This great composer told his friends the real reason he would not write an opera: "Next to Wagner, it's impossible."[20]

From that time there took place on the Green Hill, in the true French tradition of literary salons, a nineteenth-century version of the court of Philaminte.[21] Galatea had become a feminist activist and intellectual surrounded by her admirers—Ettmüller, Gottfried Kinkel,

Conrad Ferdinand Meyer, Otto Benndorf, and others—who would gather together to praise or respectfully criticize Mathilde's exploits in the realm of literature. On many an evening opinions were expressed on art, literature, religion, politics, and philosophy. But the scholars she entertained on these occasions were only a pale reflection of the greats of the old days—the Wagners and the Liszts. Each came to recite verse or read prose and offer praise or present critiques, whispering in the wings a few snatches of the great debate of the gods on Olympus. For it was there that Wagner and Brahms were considered to be, and their quarrel took place only through the polemics created by their followers.

The defender of the music of the future, Hans von Bülow, who had long been an enemy of the Brahms circle, would soon change his mind. As for Hermann Levi, the orchestra conductor devoted to the music of Brahms, he would take Wagner's side. And if Brahms defined himself as "the best of all Wagnerians," Wagner confided to Cosima on one of his good days, "Brahms composes as Bach would have liked to do."[22]

Notwithstanding their mutual respect as composers, these two paragons of nineteenth-century music would nevertheless have a few disagreeable exchanges. While Wagner was living in Vienna, his friend Tausig gave Brahms the original manuscript of the Paris version of *Tannhäuser*. When Wagner tried to get it back, Brahms refused, telling Wagner in a polite but sarcastic letter he could buy back his own score by sending Brahms a luxury edition of *Das Rheingold*.

Brahms's friends would throw out anti-Wagnerian jibes at their opponents, and the great symphonist would never go to Bayreuth. At the same time, Wagner, in pedantic form in an article published in the *Bayreuther Blätter*, called his rival a "player of *csárdás*" and a "street singer."[23]

$\sim$

In 1870 the storm clouds that were gathering over Europe presaged the great international conflicts that were to ensue. Alliances had become uncertain since Prussia had defeated Austria at Sadowa and Bismarck had achieved German unity in his own way. In Rome the Vatican Council had revealed divisions, particularly in Germany. In Berlin and in Paris antagonistic concepts of nationalism were to end in armed confrontation. In July, while Wagner was staying in Tribschen, near Lucerne, the king had commanded that *Die Walküre* be staged in Munich on June 26. Brahms attended the performance, as did the Wesendoncks. A good number of Wagner's French friends also came: Camille Saint-Saëns, Judith Gautier, Catulle Mendès, and Philippe-Auguste Villiers de l'Isle-Adam.

And in August, just as Mathilde was about to leave for her cure in Saint Moritz, a more famous personage, King Wilhelm I of Prussia, was taking a cure at Bad Ems, near Koblenz. A controversy regarding the succession to the Spanish throne was the object of a meeting between the Prussian sovereign and the French ambassador. Wilhelm assured Napoleon III's emissary that his cousin Leopold, prince of Hohenzollern, had renounced his claim to the Spanish crown, but when the French official asked for a guarantee on the matter, he was politely turned down. On July 13 Wilhelm had a missive sent to Berlin to explain the situation. Bismarck in turn published a summary of the events. In France the incident was interpreted as a diplomatic slap in the face, while the Germans considered it a humiliation of their sovereign.

On July 15, as the French audience members in the Munich premiere of *Die Walküre* in Munich were about to travel to Tribschen to meet the great composer, Cosima wrote: "The newspapers have announced the proclamation of the dogma of papal infallibility and war!" Franco-Prussian antagonism had reached its height. In Paris, at the National Assembly, the moderation of Adolphe Thiers was drowned out by the clamor of the majority, and there were demonstrations in the streets. Brünnhilde's love would not suffice to appease the god's anger, and the thundering sound of cannons would soon be louder than the powerful voices of the Valkyries.

On July 19, in an outburst of bellicose delirium, France declared war on Germany.

18

The Departure

"I have been here for two weeks already with Myrrha," wrote Mathilde to François Wille from Saint Moritz. "I feel how invigorating the air is in Engadine. All our strength is flowing back, and before the majesty of nature the soul expands."[1] This is how Mathilde passed her summertime cures, in the silent and idyllic setting of the Grison Alps. A forest road ran through the high valley of the Inn River, and the hikers on the path would find, only a few kilometers southwest of their resort, the superb lakes of Sils and Silvaplana. There Mathilde would stop to contemplate their mirrorlike reflection on the bank near Sils-Maria, a village designed for poets. Indeed, eleven years later, in 1881, Friedrich Nietzsche would also sojourn there, where he was struck by the beauty of the site; it is said he even had a mystical experience there, his vision of "eternal recurrence."

If Mathilde is far from having the genius of these great men, her infallible intuition made her feel the intensity of poetry that overwhelmed the imagination of other writers. In this otherworldly spot she picked up bits and pieces of inspiration like a bouquet of alpine flowers, making her painful metaphors of the past an abstraction and enjoying the delights of Parnassus:

> *Limpid, calm, and so green,*
> *As if you hid in your depths*
> *A verdant prairie, covered with flowers*
> *Exhaling precious fragrances.*
> *Above you float in the colors of*
> *Sapphire and purple,*
> *The souls of the dead, like butterflies . . .*[2]

She went on to describe the little village, the hilltop chapel, and the unchanging peacefulness of the scenery.

Yet, every evening in August 1870, as soon as she returned to her hotel in Saint Moritz, Mathilde would run in to see the latest bulletin displayed on the walls of the lobby giving news of the war. She was annoyed that Switzerland remained Francophile, and that instead of posting the "German victories" of Froeschwiller and Saint-Privat, the local newspapers lamented the "French defeats." It hurt her pride, and when the German dispatches finally arrived, Mathilde, in her patriotic audacity, would hurry to post them herself.

In Berlin Chancellor Otto von Bismarck took advantage of the opportunity, which Napoleon III offered him on a silver platter, to invade France and enlarge Germany's borders, thus realizing his personal political ambitions. With the diplomatic incidents of the summer of 1870, anti-French feelings, long simmering in Germany, came to a boil. As soon as Bismarck pointed out to the Germans that France was "their secular aggressor," the war seemed inevitable. In the chancellor's memoirs, he added: "I did not doubt that a Franco-Prussian war would be necessary before the general organization of the German states could be achieved." Besides, the German people were persuaded that the fault lay uniquely and exclusively with France, which had no allies, England and Austria having withdrawn their support.

In Tribschen, comfortably settled with Cosima and their three children, Richard Wagner composed the music for the third act of *Siegfried* and wrote an essay on Beethoven. The premiere of *Die Walküre* in Munich was an extraordinary success. Brahms, Joseph Joachim, Liszt, and Wagner's French friends were enthusiastic. The latter, despite the explosive political climate, flocked to Switzerland to congratulate the composer. They arrived on the evening of July 19, the very day the government declared war on Prussia. In her diary Cosima noted: "The impression is very painful, even if these little gentlemen are charming. We are playing music." Very animated discussions followed, of which Cosima added the details; she finally stated, "R. demands of our friends to realize how much we hate the French." However, Judith Gautier, who had insisted on their coming to Tribschen, said nothing of such a strange attitude on Wagner's part, and in her autobiography she described a scene in which the master came to wake up his guests by knocking on each one's door and singing *La Marseillaise*. Cosima's conclusion, then, could only be her own, for the French friends in question never broke off their relations with Wagner.

It was also during the summer of 1870 that the von Bülows' divorce was granted, and on August 25 Richard and Cosima were married. Judith Gautier and Catulle Mendès sent their regrets at being unable to attend the wedding at the Protestant church of Lucerne, and the next day Mathilde Wesendonck sent a bouquet of edelweiss to the new couple, Mr. and Mrs. Richard Wagner . . .

≈

The excess of patriotism of 1870–71 in Germany grew all the stronger as German intellectuals began to become conscious of their cultural and artistic identity. Ever since the Renaissance, a culture based on the civilizations of ancient Rome and Greece had dominated Europe. But the political strength of Prussia in this period advanced the German view of the world, which had already blossomed in the literature and music of romanticism.

And everyone took part in the war's delirium! During the winter Wagner composed a *Kaisermarsch* (Imperial March), which he sent to Berlin; in March Brahms, in Vienna, observed the occasion by composing a *Triumphlied* for solo baritone, eight-voice chorus, and orchestra, in order to celebrate Germany's victory. According to Cosima's diary, Wagner had a low opinion of this work: "We are frightened by the intellectual poverty in this composition that even our friend Nietzsche thinks highly of—'it is Handel, Mendelssohn, and Schumann all bound in leather.'" As for Brahms, who was generally reserved about his personal feelings, he dedicated his cantata to the King Wilhelm I, who had been proclaimed Kaiser, and admitted to Hermann Levi: "I must come to Germany, I must have a part in the joyfulness. I cannot wait in Vienna. Long live Bismarck! It is the only way for me to express the feelings that have overwhelmed us all so profoundly."[3]

If everywhere else the idea of pan-Germanism had the wind in its sails, on the Green Hill a calmer sort of patriotism ruled. Unlike Cosima, Mathilde did not vituperate against the French, but she felt the stirrings within herself for her native land. Her first impulse was to impose a few sacrifices on her family: "For want of fuel, we have postponed the feast for Christmas to New Year's Eve. We will light up only one little tree for the boys. In our family, patriotism has become contagious. Little Hans declared he did not want any presents for Christmas—our troops needed so much more than he did."[4]

Society gatherings were reduced, and Mathilde contented herself with calling together her court admirers for readings (as in the old days) that took place generally around seven in the evening, followed by a supper at ten. In January 1871 she took on charity work, collecting food and clothes for the German soldiers on the front, and she thanked François Wille for encouraging her young son Karl to become a "courageous German." It awakened nostalgia for her homeland in her, and in no time she was writing verse again, no less exalted than that of her contemporaries, as well as patriotic songs, no less childish:

> *Arise, my German people,*
> *Arise from the Rhine to the Baltic.*
> *Body to body, heart to heart,*
> *You, my people, with the souls of heroes.*
> . . .
> *You did not want the war.*
> *With noble fervor*
> *you'll fight for liberty.*

What people would have wanted war? The "courageous Germans" had given their trust to Bismarck, whereas he was taking the last measures to integrate the southern *Länder* into the Confederation of Northern Germany and then, to top it all off, on January 18, 1871, to declare Germany an empire.

In her own world, Mathilde, who understood little about political events, saw them through the eyes of a poet and let her thoughts ramble on in so many litanies:

German heart
Heart of grandeur
Grandeur in misfortune and in pain.
In the joy of your victories
You are so good, so great, so pure.
You are the heart of Europe.[5]

Meanwhile, more prosaically, the chancellor signed the peace treaty with France and annexed Alsace and Lorraine. After the Napoleonic Wars and the French invasions of the early 1800s, it appeared justified. Bismarck thus achieved his own masterpiece in the victory of Germany, its dominance in Europe, and the right to conquer its neighbors.

Artists wrote epic poems and Mathilde dreamed of the great battles of the past on reading Franz Kugler's life of Frederick the Great. She even began to rewrite this book in the form of "dramatic images," which she dedicated to the youth of Germany. It was like an impetuous flood, and some serious people tried to tell her so. Alfred Meissner put on kid gloves to criticize her: "Your domain is in the sensation, the feeling, the conflicts of the heart and all that emanates from feminine intuition. The incursion you have made on the battlefields of the Seven Years' War is a patriotic sacrifice on your part, but not a work worthy of your genius."[6] Ulrich Wille, François and Eliza's son, in military service at that time, said that some of the scenes written in dialect made him laugh till he cried, and that the whole thing gave a warm image of Frederick. When her edition arrived in Tribschen on Wagner's work table, where the music sheets of his pompous *Kaisermarsch* were spread out, Cosima noted: "He [Wagner] disapproves of women thus putting themselves on the market; he found it to be distasteful"— a reflection that one could more easily imagine coming from a conventional bourgeoise than from the daughter of one genius and the wife of another. But in her diary Cosima never missed an occasion to abase her heart's rival to posterity. As for her husband's judgment of Mathilde's work, he was adamant, she said—Richard pushed it aside like "rubbish."

≈

The troubled times notwithstanding, Mathilde had not given up her project of writing an opera libretto for Brahms. This time she rediscovered a famous page of history that described the Battle of Hastings. In her dramatic narration, Harald and William of Normandy ("the conqueror") were contending for the throne of England. Mathilde introduced a female character, Edith, referred to as Schwanenhals (Swan's-Neck), who was in love with Harald. The latter had to renounce this love for the hand of Leonora, the King Edward's sister, whom Harald was to marry in order to reign in England. Edith retired to a convent, whence, after the battle, she was asked to come and identify the body of her beloved. When she found his body, she exclaimed "Harald!" and, like Genovefa, fell dead on the ground.

In this drama, which stretched the limits of coherence, Mathilde imitated in free style the theater of Schiller, Goethe, and Shakespeare. It was not the literary quality that prevailed as much as the account, between the lines, of another tragedy: that of love in the life of the author. The examples are numerous and often sound like an echo of Wagner's operas. In Act I, Scene 1, for example, Edith exchanged with her confidante, Ellen, her views on love, which could as easily have been heard in a conversation between Waltraute and Brünnhilde: in Ellen's words, "To love humanity is great and noble; but to love one man more than anything, more than oneself, more than God, is a sin!" Or between Tristan and Isolde: in Edith's words, "God is love; can love rebel against love? Bad counselor, you offend God if you ignore His nature!" Further on Edith praised again the nature of love, which some call "blind": "Love does not make one blind, but clear-sighted!"

In Scene 2, set in a garden like that of the Wesendoncks' villa, the protagonists were surrounded by magnificent trees, and the encounter between Harald and Edith, a dialogue on a breathless rhythm, reminds us of the one in the Act II of *Tristan*. We see the waiting for the beloved, then the lovers engaging heart to heart in a high-minded conversation worthy of one between Richard and Mathilde:

Harald: *You helped me to find myself and gave me what is the most precious*
   thing in the world; I feel myself to be a better person since you have loved me.
Edith: *If you saw yourself as I see you, you would not speak that way.*
Harald: *It would be wonderful, too wonderful perhaps for me. In your*
   loving eyes I am another Harald, different from the one you see.

Wagner had written in his Venice diary on January 1, 1858: "Right now I have been ennobled; I have received the investiture of the highest knighthood. Your heart, your eyes, your lips have taken me out of this world. Every morsel of my self is free and noble now."

Then Edith defines herself as a "blank page": "Who am I for you? An ignorant woman."

Despite its incoherencies, its lengthy paragraphs describing the Norman court, its alternating sequences, as are found in Shakespeare, of comedy and seriousness, in the background are the ever present autobiographical elements: in Act IV, when Edith, accompanied by Ellen and hidden under the balcony, attends Harald and Leonora's wedding, she cannot help crying out: "Oh no, no, no! He cannot love her, he cannot love her!" And Ellen hastens to reply: "But even so, he can marry her!" What was Mathilde thinking of when she sent the bouquet of edelweiss the previous August, for Richard and Cosima's wedding?

Toward the end, alone in her convent, Edith has fatal premonitions concerning the outcome of the Battle of Hastings. The mother superior of the order comes to console her, but through her tears, Edith, purified by her suffering, reassures the nun that she is well as long as her heart can beat with compassion and intense love for mankind: "What I am, I am through love."

The last scene shows Edith standing in front of Harald's corpse. She gives a heart-rending cry, then falls dead at his side. It was William the Conqueror, like Fortinbras at the end of

Hamlet, who provided the conclusion of the drama: redemption is obtained through human love, and Edith redeemed Harald's sin. Finally, William declares to his dead enemy:

> *There you are conquered, you the brave,*
> *And yet you are the conqueror.*
> *Here is William, who envies you,*
> *You who lie in the dust at his feet,*
> *Envies you the pure love of this noble woman.*

Without knowing the context—the affair between Richard and Mathilde—it was difficult for Mathilde's contemporaries to appreciate the author's noble feelings, and the work's numerous structural and stylistic flaws rendered her intentions opaque. Her usual, better-informed, public reacted with timid criticism: Alfred Meissner observed that her heroine remained "passive, almost vegetative," throughout the play. Conrad Ferdinand Meyer recognized Mathilde in the role of Edith, but he found the heroine to be far less a woman than the real one. Gottfried Keller formulated a detailed critique, not without a touch of sarcasm. Mathilde answered him, "Do accept my thanks for all your critical remarks; however, I find your analysis ridiculous." Keller was one of those writers who are "a little too robust," and, Mathilde confided that he "discouraged her confidence." In defending her work, she complained that he was more preoccupied with secondary matters than with the essentials, which he had not deemed "worthy of interest." But the author of *Der grüne Heinrich* did not hesitate to underline her weaknesses and her imitation of the styles of the great authors, almost to the point of copying them. Then, too, he was sarcastic about William's last declamation, since it "did not relate to the feudal system of the Kingdom of Normandy, but rather to a modern peace conference."

Mathilde was not accustomed to receiving real criticism, having been generally spared it out of admiration for her charm and deference to her fortune. As Meyer, a fervent admirer, wrote, "She is a kind of queen in the local literary circle, and one must pay respect to majesties."

From Brahms, for whom she destined her drama in the form of an opera libretto, there was apparently no reaction.

~

Another member of the literary salon of our Philaminte was Gottfried Kinkel, a former revolutionary of the 1849 insurrections in Bade. A scholar, writer, and politician, he had first fled to London, then to Zurich, where he occupied a position as a professor of archaeology and art history. From the beginning of his sojourn in Switzerland, he was fascinated by Mathilde, to the point of keeping up an ample correspondence with her. However, he became disenchanted with her at the start of the war in 1870 because of an event related by Fritz von Bissing. After the disaster of Sedan, Napoleon III was replaced by the republic in France, and Kinkel, faithful revolutionary that he was, thought that Germany should thus put an end to Franco-Prussian hostilities. On a visit to the Wesendoncks, he complained that his son had left to be a nurse in the German army and fight against the French. His declaration was very badly understood by Mathilde, who remained attached to the love of her country, whatever the political regime might be, whereas Kinkel adhered fully to the republican principles founded on the revolution. This incompatibility of ideas led to a breach in relations that became official in a farewell poem, *To a Lady of Society*. Kinkel published it for the "queen" of the Green Hill,[7] without naming her, and he abandoned himself to metaphor-stuffed insults:

> *All our ties were empty and false.*
> *A real woman is like a green field,*
> *But you are like a desert of sand,*
> *Burned by the heat of vanity.*
> *Even if at times your gold buys for you*
> *An imbecile who plants many flowers in it.*

Mathilde copied it and sent it to Otto Benndorf with a handwritten commentary in the margins: "incomprehensible verse."

> *You wear the perfumes of this world*
> *Who are born in other people's earth;*
> *No flower of yours has roots,*
> *None carries seeds.*
> *You are sand, and sand you remain, always.*

This brutal bitterness, so passionately expressed, was that of an admirer disappointed in his amorous hopes. But Mathilde answered Kinkel rather ironically instead, comparing him to a skinny Pegasus who lacked the pasture of imagination. She closed this little tournament by declaring that the lines written against her were even worse than her own. No doubt she thought she could pay her faithful followers with a witty remark or a gracious smile.

The archaeologist Otto Benndorf, a professor at the University of Zurich from 1869 to 1871, was more of a diplomat and less of a poet. His friendship with Mathilde lasted for many years in a correspondence containing critiques of her works that were far more subtle, in which he tried to be gentle with her, yet advising her tactfully.

As for Meyer, the novelist and renowned poet tended to remain a partly obsequious admirer. He deemed Mathilde's patriotic songs "noble and pure"; but about Edith he expressed some reservations, for that drama filled him with both "happiness and concern." He advised her to set aside the first outline, which was a bit "agitated" and "too subjective," for a while and take it up a little later when she could muster the necessary dispassion. His letter, a model of gallant criticism, ended: "A woman has discovered a treasure; will she have the strength and the patience to bring it into the light?"

Patriotism and poetry would not be the only subjects discussed in those scholarly gatherings on the Green Hill. All the currents of thought were examined: naturalist and pantheist philosophy, the policy of Bismarck (who had led the *Kulturkampf* movement of the 1870s), religion, scientism, and the First Vatican Council. Mathilde followed the trends of the time and changed with them, donning with little personal judgment the emperor's new clothes. But this headlong rush was only temporary. Despite the evangelical behavior of her heroines—Genevieve, Gudrun, Edith—Mathilde prided herself on having a "liberal mind" and clung to the ideas of the progressive theologian David Friedrich Strauss, the German version of Ernest Renan, who saw in science the promise of humanity's inexorable progress.

All this empty effervescence, this pseudo-intellectualism, was a sad substitute for the rich evenings of olden days in the company of Calderón, Shakespeare, and Schopenhauer. And a music full of brass and dense harmony like that of Brahms was necessary to supplant the insidious chromaticisms hastily buried in the secrets of a woman's heart, bereaved of its vanished love.

~

At the end of October 1870, the Wagners were on a visit at Mariafeld. Cosima went alone to the Villa Wesendonck to see Mathilde and in her diary commented: "I found in this woman a charming brunette," she noted, "whereas I had seen her blonde four years ago in Munich; that disconcerted me. I was pleased by the very friendly way she received me. I looked at her paintings and thought how strange a dream was life. Eleven years ago, when I tried to stir up in her a softer feeling toward R., who would have thought then that I myself would have become part of his great destiny?"

Further on in her diary she criticized Mathilde's patriotic writings, which greatly displeased her. It is true that these songs, sometimes a bit sentimental, exalted the German heart but never disparaged the French, as the letters and diary of Cosima do abundantly. As for the "blonde" having become a brunette, Mathilde at forty-two might have wanted to mask her first gray hairs, and the hair dyes at the time must have been far less subtle than those of today. Besides, Cosima, ten years younger than Mathilde, was known to have particularly beautiful and abundant hair. A small victory for the daughter of Liszt—and a bit unworthy of her!

Back in Zurich in February, Cosima returned to see Mathilde, but this time in the company of Richard. In her diary she described the visit to the Green Hill, dipping her pen in a mixture of honey and acid on the subject of her former rival: "We paid a visit to the Wesendoncks; I'm glad to have succeeded in bringing R. after a seven-year absence. Frau Wesendonck was happy to see R.—and to see him happy. The fact that her hair was dyed black bothered R. a little bit, but he got used to it and found her kind. The children behaved magnificently . . . and are going to play with the Wesendonck children." And the next day, she noted again that her daughters had found the villa "too beautiful for them" and that the children as well as their toys were too perfect—Everything is so free and joyful here." As for Wagner's attitude, Cosima insisted: "He said that 'Frau Wesendonck's black hair has completely dispelled his memories.'"

After the fall of Napoleon III, proclaimed in September 1870, and the establishment of the republic in France, the Government of National Defense, presided over by General Louis-Jules Trochu, called up a new army to "maintain the integrity of the national territory." Léon Gambetta, a strong man but "an unscrupulous statesman," wrote George Sand, could not control the situation, and on October 27 the troops of François Achille Bazaine surrendered at Metz. The other army corps were defeated, and at the beginning of February the troops in the east, under the command of General Charles-Denis Bourbaki, retreated to the territory of Switzerland in order to avoid being taken prisoner by the Prussian troops of General Edwin Freiherr von Manteuffel.

The Swiss, especially in the canton of Zurich, came to help the fugitive soldiers. After the armistice, twelve thousand French soldiers were to be repatriated on March 8, 1871, but the process did not in fact begin until after the thirteenth. This delay played a role in the events that led to the departure of the Wesendonck family.

On January 31, 1871, the *Tagblatt* of Zurich published an announcement that a "German evening" would be held to celebrate the proclamation of the German Empire and commemorate the king of Prussia's birthday: "We cordially invite all the Germans who wish to salute the resurrection of the Reich, as well as the Swiss, friends of the German cause, to the main hall of the Tonhalle on Thursday, February 2." The invitation was signed by Professor Gottfried Semper, Adolf Gusserow, Adolph Exner, and Otto Wesendonck.

In Switzerland public opinion was divided, but a majority of the citizens maintained their sympathy for France. Letters of protest arrived in the office of the newspaper for having published this invitation. One Zurich resident wrote: "We have had enough of the provocative and cowardly people among us who found refuge on our territory when they were fleeing the German princes, and who now agree with the most bloody prince among them."

The local authorities postponed the evening to Thursday, March 9, a day after the fugitive French soldiers were to be evacuated. But this departure having also been postponed, for practical reasons, the evening was placed under the protection of the Zurich police force, and the French soldiers were consigned to their barracks.

Commander Emil Pestalozzi informed Otto that disturbances were likely to occur. He enjoined the German guests not to leave the area and told them that in case of any provocation, he would defend the Tonhalle with his troops.

Meanwhile, the friends and families of the German colony were arriving in the hall, which was draped in the imperial colors—black, white and red. Behind the podium hung a large canvas representing "Germania" protecting the German Rhine. On the tables were spread platters of cold cuts, sausages, and "German" candies, along with beer mugs and little flags of the victorious land. The Association for song and music set the tone, and the speeches turned into satisfied harangues on the successful unification of the German states, though they were still waiting for Austria to join them.

Outside a crowd of Zurichers of all social classes had gathered. Many people were out taking a walk, and a small group of young instigators started to yell out insults and jibes at the participants, followed by rocks and cobblestones thrown at the windows of the building. A struggle took place between the police force and the demonstrators, who outnumbered the others. The official report put the number of rioters at "a few thousand," although the journalists reported that there were only a thousand.

To make the situation worse, about twenty French officers who were drinking wine and beer in the nearby restaurant Der Schlauch poured into the street to help the Zurich police, and they threw themselves into the fighting with cries of "Vive la France!" and "Vive la Suisse!" The Germans rushed out to fight the intruders with bottles and bludgeons. When the police returned with reinforcements, a few wounded lay on the ground. A French sergeant was captured by the Germans and surrendered to the authorities; the soldiers were ordered to calm down. But a few rioters continued to throw cobblestones at the guests inside the hall. The military band had stopped playing music, the lights were extinguished, and the women and children were grouped together in the middle of the room. The crowd outside grew, attracted by a sight that was rare in Switzerland: a revolution around a beer mug. At nearly two o'clock in the morning, the Germans, dazed and furious, were finally evacuated under the protection of the Swiss army. At dawn the Tonhalle was vandalized by the rioters, the "Germania" and her Rhine were torn to shreds, and the banners and flags bearing the Prussian colors were trampled.

In the evening, threats were made to set fire to the Wesendoncks' villa. Otto did not dare take the road, but rather put his wife and children on a boat and directed his family toward the little private harbor of the Baur au Lac hotel. The next day, Friday, March 10, Otto and the other organizers lodged a complaint. Their little celebration in honor of the German victory was not meant to be provocative, and they did not understand what had happened. Finally a protest was sent to the canton council: "Although we were acting in self-defense, the police and the troops scarcely supported us. We hope and believe that in the future the authorities will take to heart to need to protect the life and possessions of peaceful German residents. We cannot help considering them to be responsible for the damages now and those to come. We expect the people and civil servants who failed to do their duty to be punished as required."

The Prussian government was informed of the incident and sent a warning to Bern, which in turn asked the Zurich authorities to explain. The canton council replied asking for help, describing a critical situation that was "uncertain and unclear." Law enforcement was indeed the prerogative of the local Swiss troops, who took the part of the French soldiers. For several days, then, there was a "putsch" in Zurich.[8] The end result was four dead and several wounded at the hands of the Tonhalle rioters; the agitators were sent to prison.

The official motive given for these events was "hatred of the Germans." The powerful conqueror of the French inspired a deep-rooted reaction of fear from the Swiss, and from fear to hatred the distance is short.

In Germany indignant comments against Switzerland were published in the press. Because of the atmosphere this created in Zurich, most of its German-born professors, such as Otto Benndorf and Adolf Gusserow, decided to leave the country. Billroth had already resigned in 1867 to go to Vienna. He wrote to Mathilde on March 21, 1871: "The Swiss and the inhabitants of Zurich fear greatly for their existence. Yet nothing will happen to them. The idea of nationality is deeply ingrained in human nature, and Greater Germany, so powerful now, remains a magnet that attracts still more powerfully."[9]

Since 1869 the Wesendoncks had shifted their gaze back to their mother country. A trip to Dresden and Berlin convinced them that their children should have the benefit of a more German education than they were receiving in Zurich. Besides, Myrrha, who was now twenty, was engaged to an aristocrat from Saxony, Moritz von Bissing, a relative of Eliza Wille.

In the face of the political conflict with the new German Empire, Keller shrugged his shoulders: "As soon as Imperial Germany agrees to incorporate the republics, Switzerland will be able to enter the Reich." Writing to his friend Ludmilla Assing, he described what followed: "Frau Wesendonck has left with her husband and children because of our Francophile opinions. I have fallen into disgrace because I did not praise her poetry, which I advised her not to publish."

As for Meyer, the day after the riots he wrote a note to Mathilde saying how revolted he was by such a "brutish explosion" and declared himself in sympathy with the Germans.

So the long Zurich episode in the lives of Otto and Mathilde Wesendonck came to an end. Wahlheim was immediately put up for sale, and the choice of its former occupants was then fixed on going to Dresden, where they settled in 1872. Mathilde left, certainly full of indignation, but she seemed more like a tired queen, sweeping the ground with the royal hem of her ermine cape and leaving in the dust the scattered fragments of her former jewels—her youth, her love, and her artistic illusions. Parting from this lofty abode and the city where she had reigned for over twenty years, she returned to her homeland, thinking that perhaps there she might once and for all heal her longing for the past, which was like "the worm that eats away the flower." But in reality, neither the antidote represented by Brahms nor the return to her mother country could have released her from her intimate drama and her love for Richard Wagner.

PART IV

Return to Germany

Dresden

O n April 1, 1874, the Wesendoncks' elegant carriage approached the train station. Twelve-year-old Hans, Otto and Mathilde's youngest son, made the coachman stop and jumped down into the crowd of travelers. He threaded his way through the busy throng, looking for Hugo Göring, his future tutor. Years later, after Hans's death, this man would leave moving memories about the young boy he met that spring day. His appearance was striking, he said: tall and slender, with a Nordic face and laughing blue eyes "radiant with joy," topped by a head of wavy blond hair.[1]

Seated next to his young professor in the landau, Hans pointed out the city's principal monuments along the way; after the bridge over the Elbe, he showed him the Royal Theater, where, twenty-one years earlier, Richard Wagner had served as *Kapellmeister*. But the original concert hall in which the harmonies of *Rienzi, Der fliegende Holländer,* and *Tannhäuser* had first resounded no longer existed. Destroyed by a fire in 1869, an ordinary wooden structure had replaced it temporarily, while the new building designed by Gottfried Semper was under construction.

Leaving the labyrinth of the old city, they rode alongside the walls of the vast palace of King Johann of Saxony; the horses ran swiftly along the Pragerstrasse, passing in front of the royal ministries, superb art galleries that boasted 2,400 paintings by the great masters, and fine bookstores. Then they turned left on the Sidonienstrasse. Shortly afterward the carriage stopped at the corner of Wienerstrasse and Goethestrasse, not far from the royal gardens, in the neighborhood called the "English quarter."

Hans invited his passenger to get out in front of an elegant Renaissance-style building in which the Wesendoncks had settled since their arrival from Zurich two years before. They entered by the garden portal under the façade, designed by Manfred Semper, the son of the great architect, before which stood a replica in antique bronze of a child in prayer. Göring noted that the spring sunshine lit up the house and the superb garden that was kept with great care.

An old servant opened the door for them, and the new tutor was then greeted by the master of the house. Otto was now fifty-nine and sported an imposing beard. His almost legendary friendliness was always straightforward. According to one witness who used to visit the family during the 1870s, "Herr Wesendonck was one of the most intelligent, the kindest, and the most warmhearted of men that I ever happened to meet."[2]

Hans led his tutor to his room, showing him on the way his own space for work and play; then he introduced him to his brother, Karl, with his "stiff and pedantic look." The older brother was irritated when Hans teasingly called him "this respectable old man." Göring noticed that it was not easy to communicate with this seventeen-year-old boy, whose exceptional intellectualism and erudition proved a barrier to enjoyable conversation. "We did not have mutual interests," wrote the young professor. "He was lacking in that which is attractive in a person, that is, enthusiasm and the desire to share one's joy with others."

"Hans, always laughing, clever, and natural, introduced me then to the servants, who consisted of two men and six women, joyfully adding the characteristics of each of the 'dignitaries' of this wealthy, aristocratic household."

The child then presented him to his mother. Mathilde received him in her room, which was decorated in blue silk. The professor was dazzled by her charm and beauty. Göring was surprised by the radiance of her face, even though she was forty-six years old. He knew nothing about the stories of Mathilde and Wagner and added that no one in Dresden knew anything about her past relations with the great musician: "It was only said that she was an elegant lady who, in her beautiful mansion, which she called the 'house of joy,' gave magnificent receptions of unforgettable beauty, and that she liked to gather the intellectual elite there for animated conversation." He claimed that her tactfulness enabled her to effect reconciliation between many of the artistic or scientific world who had been enemies.

But two years before, prior to leaving Zurich, Mathilde had felt some sharp disappointment. Soon after the events of the Tonhalle in March 1871, she and Otto went to Germany, and in April they had bought a new home. "Dresden is charming," she wrote to Otto Benndorf, "despite the presence of a few philistines."

On arriving in the Saxon capital Mathilde was a little unsure at first, having lost the comfort of her court of admirers. They had booked rooms at the Hotel Bellevue while negotiating the purchase of their new house and had called upon the son of the great architect Gottfried Semper, to make the necessary modifications to its interior, thus taking their first steps toward their new life.

Returning to Zurich for the last time, Mathilde lived the months that remained as if she were already gone: "I have renounced once and for all the social life of Zurich—neither theater nor concert," she confided to Benndorf.[3] "For the people here, we've already moved away, even though we are staying to celebrate Christmas and will leave for Munich around the fifteenth or twentieth of January." Indeed, at the end of 1871, in the Wesendoncks' villa on the shores of Lake Zurich, Mathilde was happy to announce an addition to the family: "I rarely awaited Christmas with as much impatience as this year for the present of an adorable fiancé for Myrrha. My heart swells with pleasure at the idea of seeing happy faces lighted by the glow of Christmas candles."

Myrrha and Baron Moritz von Bissing were to marry in August 1872. Mathilde was very busy helping to set up their future home in Breslau, where the young man was a captain in the royal cavalry. In her letters to Benndorf she idealized the young couple and projected on them her own feelings: "The two fiancés see paradise in their new lodgings, where they will belong to one another without being disturbed. Let's leave them to their illusions."

The entire year was therefore devoted to Myrrha's happiness. Mathilde spoke endlessly about the linens, the furniture, and the china she had chosen with her daughter at Meissen. She flung herself into the details of the ceremony and their future apartment. But to Benndorf she admitted secretly her sorrow:

> The wedding will leave a void for me—a house without Myrrha! But on contemplating their two happy faces, I chase away my selfish ideas and try to quench the selfish desires and pain that distress me so. Our children are not born for us. They do not belong to their parents; the contrary is true—the parents remain at the disposal of their children and the latter must exist for themselves. It has become impossible for me to think of the two fiancés separately. They found each other in love and since then, they love each other more and more. . . . Their destiny is dear to me, and I do not know, outside of death, how they could be separated.[4]

In early 1872, in the midst of the wedding preparations, the Wesendoncks moved from Zurich to Dresden. "All this chaos has fatigued me," wrote Mathilde, "and I tend to avoid any other traveling." From the Hotel Bellevue near the old bridge over the Elbe, Mathilde described her new "palace" in her letters to Benndorf: "The renovation of our house in the Goethestrasse is slowly progressing. Manfred Semper informed me that I could not begin furnishing it before May. However, I am quite satisfied with the improvements made, and the house is becoming quite habitable."[5]

Her greatest desire was to start a new social life, but after twenty years in Switzerland, a land of exile for so many revolutionaries, Mathilde discovered a very different mentality in this old kingdom of Saxony, which was attached to its traditions and etiquette. To Benndorf she mentioned her disconcerting beginnings in Dresden society: "If you ask me my impressions of social life in this city, dear friend, I will answer you that my acquaintances are limited to my family and the circle of the Bissings and their friends. I feel somewhat out of place. Try to imagine my mood in the middle of a society full of Excellencies with heavily decorated uniforms and starred hats." She depicted with humor the reactionary type: "Herr von Seidlitz, for example, a good-looking man, aristocratic from head to foot, condescends to tell me about his preoccupations: 'Think of it, dear Lady, how regrettable and dangerous it is to live with all the new things that Bismarck is trying to introduce into our society.' In this case, to avoid answering, I prefer to sit down on the bench behind the stove." She told her friend on another occasion about her distrust with regard to conformity and etiquette when she attended a concert from a stall where the following notice was put up: "Reserved only for ladies having been presented to the royal court." She said she had entered with such a haughty look that the ushers did not dare stop her, and she sat there comfortably to listen to the music. Advising Benndorf's wife to do as much, Mathilde concluded: "She only has to walk in with dignity and full of *grandezza*. . . . There is no other way to have a good seat."[6]

~

During this period of transition, Mathilde found herself divided between her family life and her love of nature. In Dresden the spring arrived in great beauty: "White cherry blossoms, innocent and bright, peach trees in tender pink on a blue and yellow background," decorated the banks of the Elbe. To Eliza Wille she had written a few words: "No one can help anyone else; each one must overcome their own problems. That absolutely corresponds to my innermost character."[7] And she felt impelled to entrust her "secret" to nature.

Sunday afternoon excursions by steamboat on the Elbe and promenades in the picturesque area east of Dresden known as Lusatia inspired Mathilde to write poetry based on Sorbian folklore.[8] In it she found sympathy with all living creatures and compassion for other people's misfortunes. "While the sparrows are chirping on the roofs," she wrote to Benndorf, "an afflicted human heart is often in torment and seems to ignore the beauty of the flowers that are blooming outside."

Mathilde thus perceived a conflict between the exterior world—her comprehension of social and political phenomena—and her inner life, which was trying to grow in the realms of art and poetry. At first she set herself against the fatalism that she found in a novel by Eliza Wille. Complaining to her friend at Mariafeld about the cruel destiny that Eliza had reserved for her characters, Mathilde protested: "Tell me that it is only a caricature of life! Must we really be so despondent? Do you not think that in the end poetry, truth, and beauty will triumph?" Eliza's heroes had lost their gamble with life, whereas Mathilde strove courageously to succeed:

But what! Our mother Earth, does she know only poverty and barrenness? Is she only rich in suffering, even for us, her favorite children? Does she know only vain efforts, misery, destitution, combat, shattered hopes, and unsatisfied nostalgia? Is there only suffering and death, renunciation, and nowhere, really nowhere, a little consolation? Among so many people who crawl like vermin on the earth, are there not some who have wings to spread and who rise above this misery toward the sun? Is there no architect capable of building an edifice that reaches the sky, and who can see with delight his work achieved? . . . Will he not have the reward of banishing the tatters of misery and rejecting all traces of inconsolable poverty? When work is done, the trace of the rugged hand that cut the stone is erased, and in a completed masterpiece one never knows who set the first stone. Yes, life is not just suffering. Life is work . . . continuous work that leads to a preestablished objective. When it is attained, the desert turns into an oasis. . . . Triumph will not be refused to the sons of this earth, who struggle valiantly to build their destiny with their own hands.[9]

Such was Mathilde's idealism at the start of the 1870s. Following in the steps of the humanists, she pursued, with compassion for the poor, the destitute, and orphans, a kind of utopian vision of humanity and society. Closely related to the principles of Saint Simon, Mathilde also believed in human beings' continuous progress, thanks to the discoveries of science, the new god of Renan and David Friedrich Strauss. Scientism was in fashion, and these idealists could not imagine how the sorcerer's apprentices of the twentieth century would affect their ideal. During this period, knowledge and technology were for Mathilde a true source of hope.

On the other hand, for Richard Wagner, scientific determinism, like the materialist revolution of 1848, could not undermine his deeper, infinitely more complex, and evolving philosophical ideas.

After having laid the first stone of his future festival theater in Bayreuth on May 22, 1872, his fifty-ninth birthday, Richard, accompanied by Cosima, began a concert tour in Germany in order to call upon the indispensable subscribers to finance his enormous project. Since February, in hotels or on the road, he had been working on the composition draft for *Götterdämmerung*, the fourth opera of his cycle, which he would finish two years later.

He began his "campaign" by asking his old friends and acquaintances to set up committees of patrons (the *Patronatverein*) who would be responsible for contributing and collecting the necessary funds. Some have claimed that Wesendonck had refused his financial aid during the construction of the theater,[10] but Otto's letter to Wagner of September 17, 1873 proves the contrary: "As a 'patron,' I would like to be able to relieve you of your worries in this great enterprise, while feeling my own shortcomings. . . . I will come to Bayreuth for the meeting [of the *Patronatverein*]. In any case, it is my firm intention to do so."[11]

On January 12 the Wagners were in Dresden, where they met the Wesendoncks. The next day Richard attended a performance of *Rienzi* given at the Royal Opera. But he found it so distorted by the numerous cuts in the score that he said it looked like a "hen without feathers." Disgusted, he left after the fourth act and finished the evening in the company of Otto and Mathilde.

On the evening of the fourteenth Wagner invited his Dresden friends to a banquet at the Belvedere restaurant, on the terrace of Brühl overlooking the Elbe, where concerts were often given. The Wesendoncks were seated facing the Wagners, and Richard found other old acquaintances such as the painter Ernst Benedikt Kietz, the musician Anton Fürstenau, the cellist Friedrich August Kummer, the singer Josef Tichatschek, and the physician Anton Pusinelli and his wife. "The evening was very lovely," commented Cosima in her diary; "R. went over his old memories of Dresden, of *Rienzi*, of the people who had protected him, and ended with an emphatic speech to the musicians who were present to whom he can only say 'au revoir,' for their dismissal would be refused; they are therefore separated despite their love for each other, but united together by eternal art."[12]

On February 6, passing once more through Dresden, the Wagners attended a performance of *Lohengrin* and met the Wesendoncks there. Dining together the next day, Cosima reported their dispute on the subject of David Friedrich Strauss's book *Der alte und der neue Glaube* (Old and New Faith). A few months earlier, when the book was published, Mathilde had upheld the theses of this precursor of Renan in a letter to Benndorf: "Faith and the conception of the world have been totally overturned by the progress of natural science. Strauss remained faithful to himself, but public opinion has come to bear his way of thinking . . . Even today, this book is an act of courage that honors this great man. As for me, I follow Strauss on the difficult road to the future."[13]

However, Wagner did not only have grievances against the Protestant theologian and historian: Strauss had had the bad judgment to side with the anti-Wagnerians, even criticizing the music of Beethoven. In the "Pastoral" Symphony, for example, Strauss claimed to be bored because the powerful storm that was described in it did not fit with the joyful peasant feast that preceded.[14]

At this point in his life Wagner had put aside his revolutionary illusions and could no longer acknowledge the temporal messianism of these fashionable prophets of progress. At that very moment, this spiritual reaction, which was presaging the composition of *Parsifal*, also created a distance in his relations with Nietzsche. As Cosima said: "[Strauss's book freed us] from redemption, from prayer, and from Beethoven's music."[15]

Mathilde was still at the stage of mythologizing man's place in society. She saw religion as an obstacle to her ideal of perpetual progress, and she fully subscribed to the ideas of Bismarck, whose ministers had come out in 1872 with a word defining his antireligious policy: *Kulturkampf*, the spirit of which was to "fight for the development of progress and civilization." In fact, the nationalist frenzy that had seized Germany after the war against France was manifested in an exaltation of all things German. This new identity for the German soul was to be expressed through art and language, which rejected the *barbaros*, the non-Germanic element, according to Martin Luther, and thus everything that was cosmopolitan and "international." The diverging forces of this cultural revolution were thus named: Judaism and Catholicism.

If the anti-Semitic undercurrent of the 1870s was mostly of a cultural order, the antireligious laws passed by the minister of education, Adalbert Falk, affected principally the Catholics, who were suspected of treating with the political enemies of Prussia, namely Austria, France, and the Vatican.

Although a poet, Mathilde was assailed by the spirit of rationalism. In expressing herself on every subject, did she think she could overcome her own contradictions? She confided to Otto Benndorf her religious skepticism and her faith in an ideal future: "Soon theologians will be exhibited like mummies in museums. In the nineteenth century they play the same role as the astrologers of the Middle Ages. Astrology has been replaced by astronomy; theologians will be replaced by men of science. . . . The key for the future of humanity is progress."[16]

Wagner, who was moving toward the completion of his *Ring* and who was already pondering the composition of *Parsifal*, a metaphysical subject par excellence, saw in religion something more than a social and political phenomenon. Later on, taking the Greeks as models, Mathilde would think that by closing her eyes to the supernatural, it would be possible to find beauty as an end in itself: "All beauty leads to humanism," she wrote in 1874.

What most discredited Mathilde in the opinion of her contemporaries was not the content of her statements, whether in letters or conversations, but the fact that they were expressed by a woman, and a bourgeoise to boot. She would be blamed by Cosima, who considered it bad taste for "a woman [to] thus put herself on the market." And later Mathilde would answer Benndorf's literary criticisms with the boldness of an early feminist, setting herself in opposition to a society that wanted to enclose womankind into the limits of masculine domination: "You are an opponent of the emancipation of women. You do not approve of a woman who communicates her feelings to others. . . . When I put myself forward and 'dare' to say something, I am very conscious of the reason for which I am daring to do so. . . . Twenty years from now, I can foresee it—no one will understand any longer that the field of action for women had been reduced in such a way. I am patient. I can wait."

∽

In 1872 in Vienna, Johannes Brahms was named director of the Gesellschaft der Musikfreunde (the Friends of Music Association). While his private life was peaceful and orderly, his musical genius provoked endless discussions. In 1873 he finished his Variations on a Theme of Haydn and his first two quartets. It seemed as though he had given up his project of composing an opera.

Preparing to publish a new collection of poems and still haunted by the memory of the wonderful times when she would bring her lines to Master Richard, Mathilde thought of reminding the great Brahms to set her verse to music:

Of course, you have never encouraged me in the least to send you my poems. Because I know you, I suppose you have your reasons for that—I have not aroused in you any interest in my poetry. That is your business, my dear! I am not going to quarrel with you on that subject. But my role is to observe your continuous evolution, even at a distance, although with my sincere interest and true admiration. I now have a little collection of songs that I think, I know not why, could attract your attention. If I am mistaken, the wastepaper basket is not so far from your desk that it will be impossible to quickly get rid of the intruders.[17]

In June Brahms answered: "Thank you for what you have sent me. Your writing has indeed awakened in me an interest. . . . From a musical point of view, I manage only with difficulty to select a subject. . . . If I were of the opposite sex, I suppose I would immediately set your new poems to music." The musician suggested that she instead develop the cycle on *Mignon*, then awkwardly excused himself in order to get out of his predicament. It seems obvious that Brahms could not miss the Wagnerian influence with which Mathilde's poetry was imbued. Having already heard the *Wesendonck Lieder*, he was not mistaken in guessing the amorous relationship in which they had originated. Moreover, he had been informed by his friends in Zurich of the affair, and being himself rather misogynous, Brahms would systematically reject all of Mathilde's poetic propositions.

But Mathilde would not give up. The following year she composed lines to be set to music in the form of a cantata. On November 24, 1874, she treated Brahms to her pan-Germanist whims three days after finishing her poem "For a Cremation Ceremony":

I wish to draw your attention this time to this old and beautiful custom of cremation, which, from all points of view, corresponds more to the ideas of the nineteenth century, rather than this deplorable and ugly Semitic custom of burial and inhumation. The point is to first give this act an artistic and ideal consecration to raise it to the rank of an action worthy of our people, the greatest of civilized peoples. What could be better than to invite the muses to the funeral ceremony? You understand me; I am thinking of a kind of oratorio or requiem, but without any biblical text, of course! I am sending you a short poem, the content of which corresponds to the goal to be achieved. I am convinced that all enlightened people and scientific scholars will declare themselves to be partisans of the principle of cremation as soon as we have found for it a noble and beautiful form.

In her subconscious, scenes and impressions of her past and present life unfolded in an invisible film reel. The subject of cremation that Mathilde was trying to justify was in reality a distant memory of her relations with Richard Wagner. She remembered first the reading of the *Hindu Legends*, sent by Richard, or rather his letter from Venice of January 1, 1858: "Thus embalm the supernatural flowers of divine death, of eternal life. In olden days, these flowers adorned the hero's body before the flames transformed it into divine ashes; in this tomb of flames and perfumes the lover would thrust herself forth to mix her ashes with those of her beloved. They were then one and the same element. No longer two living beings, but a divine and primordial substance for Eternity! . . . These flames would burn luminous and pure! The flame clear and innocent would be for no other being before you and me."

And how can one not think of the final blaze of Götterdämmerung, where Mathilde must have found a lyrical expression of her pantheistic spirituality when Brünnhilde joins Siegfried in the flames that would save the world:

> *Bright fire has seized my heart,*
> *Longing to enfold him,*
> *And be embraced by him in monumental love,*
> *To be united with him.*[18]

Undoubtedly the inspiration for her poem on cremation came from that source; Mathilde may not have been conscious of it herself, but time and again, the fact is that her writings revealed, little by little, the images embedded in her inner life.

Naturally, Brahms was appalled by the six pages in manuscript of the very naive Mathilde. He immediately sent her poem to his friend Billroth with a note: "Do you not find that extremely interesting? Do you not want to express your gratitude to this genius of a woman? I would join my greetings with so much pleasure! Unless you, the famous surgeon, you know a way to kill an author's high opinion of herself? In any case, the adjoining leaflet will amuse you, you and your wife, for at least a quarter of an hour!"

On November 27 Billroth answered pitilessly: "Yes, yes! If one wants to know what should be done, one must ask noble women! Oh, Mathilde! What has happened to you? She does not seem to have anyone to warn her against the consequences of such a lack of good taste. My wife and I had a good laugh. Thank you for sending it! The flames sputter out of the smoke! We must escape! The fumes are smothering us!"[19]

Rumors spread in the circle of Brahms's Viennese friends. Lübke wrote to the Stockhausens in Berlin: "Frau Wesendonck wrote to Brahms a cantata on cremation, asking him very seriously to set the text to music. It represents for her the most important factor in humanity's progress, an idea in favor of which Art should entreat the world. I suggest that she take for her poem the string quartet recently published by Kirchner; for listening to such sounds gives one the desire to be burned to death, and one does not regret leaving a world in which dear friends compose and publish such things!"

The rumor then spread to Berlin, and Mathilde must have been informed of it, because at that point her correspondence with Brahms ceased. However, if the great musician on the moment had greeted Mathilde's project with derision, the subject nevertheless preoccupied him years later. In May 1891 he wrote to his publisher, Fritz Simrock: "As for me, I would like my body to be cremated. If such is the case, you will naturally pay for the expenses on my account."

∾

During that same year, 1874, Mathilde also published a new collection of poems under the same title as that used for her 1862 collection: *Poems, Popular Songs, Legends, and Sagas*. If she was already the laughingstock of the Brahms clique, she would also meet with failure on the part of those she considered faithful friends. Through her doctor in Dresden, who knew Otto Benndorf's sister, she learned what was being said about her, and on December 11 she complained to a friend who she had believed was devoted to her: "It seems that I was criticized in an unpleasant way for my person and my work. . . . What hurt me so deeply, if it is true, is that your parents claim to have repeated your own judgment of my poetry. You have misjudged, and if I am well-informed, *condemned* my work." She reproached him for his indirect criticism and defended herself by underlining her words: "'*My poems and I are one.*' I believe in them as I do in myself. To understand a poem or an individual, it is necessary to recreate the atmosphere around one's lines, like the feelings around an individual. If you expect the poems to create this indispensable environment by themselves, I could forgive you for rejecting them." She then mentioned a few positive critiques of her poetry in the *Wiener Presse* and the *Neue freie Presse*. But Paul Lindau, who would express mixed feelings about the Bayreuth Festival in 1876, was hostile to Mathilde, as was the journalist in the *Dichterhalle*, whom she suspected of being none other than the "traitor" Kinkel.

"Your words cannot hurt me more than your disdainful silence," continued the poet. At the end of her letter she added: "I swear from now on that I will never disturb you again with my writing."

When Mathilde sent her little volume to Wagner, the self-righteous Cosima did not miss the chance to join the chorus of detractors. In her diary she wrote: "There is one thing I do not understand: that some women want to be spoken of, deliberately and officially, for their pleasure. I have the impression that their life experience should make them more silent, bringing them back to their essential task of raising young men to be courageous and young women to be good wives." Of course, Cosima's diary was not intended for the public, but for her children. It was thus necessary, she thought, to forge the highest and most moral image not only of their famous father, but also of their mother, the worthy daughter of Liszt.

In mid-December 1874 Benndorf answered Mathilde with kindness, but he maintained his reserve concerning her poems. Mathilde answered: "I can see you were not my opponent. Thank you for your precision. I abhor intrigues. . . . My enthusiastic nature gives me sometimes the naive impression that everyone loves me and finds me charming. That's why, that evening, I felt myself soaked with ice water, and my disillusion was truly profound. All that was good for my behavior in the future. That disillusion has remained, and I still suffer when you say you approve of my poems only halfway or reluctantly." With her poetry misunderstood, Mathilde saw everything collapse around her. If she still tried to justify her patriotic songs, she put her nationalism in the past: "You quoted the poems that I wrote when I was patriotic."

"You do not like poetry," she declared to Benndorf, who found that her lines were "not very sincere" or "far-fetched." "Did you not guess all their honesty?" cried Mathilde, underlining her words:

They were written with the blood of my heart. How is it possible that words that are warm and true, surging forth from the human heart, may not find an echo in another human heart? That makes me skeptical about what you call the "mystical sympathy" that relates us. In truth, that sympathy is an illusion if we must fight against the essential divergence of our opinions. It is true, I always felt it, and the blow does not come as a surprise. You must have guessed it when I questioned you with my eyes. But tell me, at what level do you have pleasure in seeing me? Why are we so willingly together? In the presence of a woman, men take "pleasure" in many things, even on seeing the way they are dressed. The abyss that separates us now is between us. Past, finished, the blow hurts me much more than the wounds life has inflicted on me, wounds that no one has cared to heal. It is difficult to argue about the value of a poem. It does not exist for someone who does not feel it. Your criticism of the fact that I published these poems deals not only with their form, but with their content.

Here is an indication of the relationship between Mathilde and Benndorf. If all these men who surrounded her—writers, professors or artists—were only interested in her charm and beauty, she, on the other hand, valued them for their minds and their intellectual strength. It was in this manner that she thought her feminine soul would find the fulfillment to which she so avidly aspired.

Despite this cold phase in their friendship, Mathilde sent her holiday wishes for the new year to the Benndorf family, whose youngest son, Hans, was her godchild. But even then she could not help pursuing her justification:

> My husband has made every effort for the truth not to be hidden from me, and thanks to that I remain down-to-earth. For years I have heard no flattery. I live retired and alone, for my children, my books, my interests, and also a little for my sense of beauty. If by chance—and it is very rare—I mingle with society, I always find a little group in a corner. These are the people with whom it is possible to exchange reasonable words. We chat then about everything concerning the world. Nothing personal. I *was* always proud and I still am. . . . No flattery can affect me. On the other hand, I cannot find anything that joins me to a soul resembling mine. . . . I hope that these few words may suffice to throw the right light on the behavior of the "sovereign." . . . One can only live in peace with one's conscience if one has always tried to attain the heights, far from praise or criticism.[20]

However, her idea of a "retired life" in the Wesendoncks' Dresden palace was an unusual one. Contemporary witnesses spoke of sumptuous receptions, of dinners preceded by lectures or recitals on the occasion of which local scientists and artists, singers from the Royal Opera, and famous musicians would rub shoulders.

In Saxony's high society, Mathilde received among many other people of quality the Baroness Clementine von Wedel, who left a few written reminiscences about the Wesendoncks. She found them to be "very sociable," and with her father, a general, she attended many of these grand receptions, "which were always very congenial." But as a young lady of twenty at the time, the baroness remembered Mathilde as something of an enigma, describing her as "unique in her way." She saw her as being aloof and claimed that she had never heard her say anything particularly "intelligent" or "witty." Was it this reserve that Mathilde meant by being "retired"? But the baroness also described Mathilde with a touch of nastiness, saying that she had nothing of the "great lady" nor even the quality of being a good mistress of the house, contradicting all the witnesses that Mathilde had received since her Zurich days. The baroness dwelled on the errors in etiquette committed during Mathilde's receptions; according to her, the hostess did not seem to have "the least interest in these domestic details." Fascinated nonetheless by her "remarkably clear eyes," the baroness expressed some idle reflections on Mathilde's amorous life, claiming to have even asked her indiscreetly if, since her marriage, she had ever happened to love a man other than her husband, and if that love had been reciprocated. To that, she asserted in a 1913 article, Mathilde gave an "enthusiastic affirmation," reinforced, as she stated confidently, remembering the exact terms, by a provocative "Thank God!"

This portrait of Mathilde Wesendonck in Dresden shows her to have been a bit wary of her social circle, not least by that comical "Thank God!" Nor did she repress her irony and wit. That she may have been somewhat aloof from others is no surprise to anyone when one remembers how and by whom that former "blank page" had been filled up. In fact, all that signifies merely that Mathilde was alone, even when her drawing room was full of people. She continued to plan literary projects, to study classical authors, and to look for inspiring subjects in Germanic legends, such as *The Myth of Baldur*, which she published in 1875. But no other soul had ever come to truly share her inner solitude, neither Otto Benndorf nor Johannes Brahms. And if she dreamed of building a better world for humanity, she would remember that in human love a solitary heart could not suffice for itself. All of that would come back to her in 1876, at the first Bayreuth Festival, like an overflowing river from which would gush out, in a clear, living way, the image of her "one and only love" for Richard Wagner.

> *A peaceful joy resounds within my soul,*
> *Like the chiming of bells in the tepid night,*
> *A sound graciously muffled that develops and grows*
> *That plays in my breast like a lyre!*
> *Is it a greeting to me from your heart?*
> *A thought of you that makes me so happy?*
> *Is it the joy of your love, so long contained?*
> *Is it the melancholy sigh of having been abandoned?*
> *Is it the flutter of a blessed new hope?*
> *Is it a glimpse of your heart, open like my sky?* [21]

All of Wagner's enemies would have liked to see his Bayreuth project fail. Even the king of Bavaria had to put a limit on his financial contribution to the building of the theater, as well as to the composer's oversized ambition to organize a festival during which *Der Ring des Nibelungen* would be performed according to all the master's precise instructions. After the numerous intrigues stirred up against him at the Munich court, Wagner no longer wished to appeal for support to any government whatsoever, including Bismarck's: "The expenses incurred by my venture should be encumbered only to individual patrons." The Baroness Marie von Schleinitz presided over the committee of subscribers for the Bayreuth Theater of Festivals, and among the first patrons to sign up were, of course, Otto and Mathilde Wesendonck.

One week before opening night, in August 1876, King Ludwig II arrived in secret to attend the dress rehearsals, which were, in fact, special performances in honor of His Majesty.

Wagner had originally wanted his festival to be an artistic and almost religious event, open to all social classes. However, kings, princes, and emperors from all over Europe were greeted instead, including the colorful Dom Pedro II of Brazil. At the railway station, Wagner was congratulated by Kaiser Wilhelm I for having managed to set up a festival that he declared to be a "national affair." Wagner later commented ironically on this remark, asking plainly: What did the "nation" have to do with his work and achievement?

The Wesendoncks stayed at the Reichsadler Hotel, situated at that time on the Maximilianstrasse, not far from Wahnfried, the Wagner family's new abode. The whole town was decorated for the occasion, displaying long banners in the colors of the German Empire, from second-floor balconies, along with Bavarian pennants in blue and white. Shop windows along the main street and in the marketplace were stuffed with photographs, engravings, statuettes, and medallions bearing images of the composer wearing a crown of laurels. In the Opernstrasse a shoemaker even topped a bust of Wagner with a halo made up of ankle boots.[22]

On August 13, 1876, an extremely hot day, the prologue of the cycle, *Das Rheingold*, was performed. The spectators, bearded aristocrats in evening attire and elegant ladies equipped with lacy fans, were assembled in front of the rustic red-brick theater. It looked like a temporary building, like a ship moored there for the occasion, still bobbing on the wavelets made by the wind in the surrounding wheat fields. On a hillock of groves and greenery, its situation was somewhat reminiscent of the Wesendonck villa in Zurich; it too had been nicknamed the Green Hill.

The crowd standing outside the Festspielhaus before the performance was quite cosmopolitan. Besides meeting the crowned heads of Europe, Mathilde saw some of her old friends from Switzerland again: Ignaz and Emilie Heim, Ludwig Ettmüller, and Fritz Hegar. Among the French, she especially noted the presence of Camille Saint-Saëns, Judith Gauthier, and Catulle Mendès. Anton Bruckner came from Vienna, and Tchaikovsky made the long trip from Moscow. All the arts were represented: the painters Franz von Lenbach and Hans Makart; the actress Marie Seebach, an acquaintance of Mathilde's; and the journalists and critics, among them the terrible Eduard Hanslick from Vienna and Paul Lindau, who had been so severe on Mathilde's last publication. The missing included Hans von Bülow, as well as Brahms and his faithful circle: Joachim Raff, Joseph Joachim, Ferdinand Hiller, and Max Bruch.

During the festival the Wesendoncks were often seen chatting with Wagner's intimates: Liszt, Malwida von Meysenbug, Edouard Schuré, Gottfried Semper, and Mathilde Maier. Nietzsche was also present, but he remained aloof. Suffering more and more from severe headaches, he could no longer bear the effects Wagner's music had on him.

When the spectators entered the theater, everyone was surprised. As in an amphitheater on the model of that at Ephesus, the seats were placed on curved rows rising up to the gallery, which was simply a continuation and was called the *Fürstenloge* (the box reserved for royalty). There was nothing on the sides, no one sitting opposite one another, no *vis à vis*, no chandelier in the middle of the ceiling, as in every other theater; only gas lamps to the left and to the right illuminated the house. A murmur of astonishment echoed through the room. You could not even see the orchestra in the pit—no stands, no musicians—they were told they would not see any of them at all!

Mathilde smiled with understanding, remembering Richard's words when he was making plans for a theater of the future: "Music will rise out of the pit like celestial voices," and the scenery onstage "will appear as in a dream." As for the spectator, "the state of his soul will be favorably disposed toward ideal things."

The lights then went out; you could not even see your own hand in front of your face. The only important thing now was the sound: "Imperceptibly, you start to hear, and the surprise is that you do not even know when the sound you are hearing actually began."[23]

E-flat major.

"Little by little, the sonority rolls in like a wave, the brass instruments unfold their resounding metal language, powerful and lovely, and carry you along with them."[24]

The next day, on August 14, *Die Walküre* was performed. In the darkened opera house, Mathilde watched the unfortunate Wälsungs, Siegmund and Sieglinde, appear on the stage, both tragically destined to death through love. And she remembered those magic moments with Richard near Fluntern, where he was composing Act I and writing in the margin of his score "G.s.M."—*Gesegnet sei Mathilde* (blessed be Mathilde)—enigmatic hieroglyphics whereby Richard displayed his love for her. In the forest after the spring rain, the moonlight flooded the countryside: *Der Lenz lacht in den Saal*!

She had come to him that day like Sieglinde; then, one night, she dreamed she was poor Mignon, Goethe's child-wife heroine. That evening in the Festspielhaus, her soul walked forth in the shadow. She wrote six new poems at that moment, poems that have gone unpublished to this day:

> *I would like to come like the spring,*
> *With song and echo, flowers, fragrance*
> *And exquisite pleasure;*
> *I would like to accompany you through life,*
> *And to spread before you all the treasures of the earth.*[25]

Siegfried was performed on the sixteenth and *Götterdämmerung* on the seventeenth. Two other *Ring* cycles were given before the end of August. Wagner greeted his patrons with as much obsequiousness as possible, but, exhausted, from the difficulties his enterprise had occasioned, he could mumble but a few words to each benefactor. However, according to witnesses, he stopped in front of Otto Wesendonck, tapped him jovially on the shoulder, and assured his old friend that he was still in the same financial straits as he had always been! Mathilde received only a sad smile. Did she perceive in his eyes a glimmer of the old days? The sole document left by Mathilde concerning the first Bayreuth Festival in 1876 is the manuscript of her six unpublished lieder revealing what she would probably have liked to sing to Richard Wagner. They could have been put into music only in an afterlife where impossible love stories are finally resolved.

> *Just once more, an hour,*
> *I would like to sit at your feet,*
> *To receive from your lovely mouth*
> *The holy declaration of your love*
> *And enclose it in my reeling heart!*

> *Once more to press your hand in mine,*
> *To bask in the sun of your gaze!*

I would be childishly content
To bury in the abyss of my pain
All my peaceful happiness.

That must never harm another!
I would like to seal my lips docilely,
Never to pronounce a word,
Even if my love with anxious joy
Threatened to burst in my chest! [26]

"That must never harm anyone else." After the summer of 1876, Mathilde's vision of the world began to enlarge. The epic poem of the *Ring* awoke in her an intense interest for the Greek authors of antiquity. She plunged into the study of Homer, then into fragments written by Goethe: *Ulysses in Pheacie.* She conceived a drama, *Odysseus*, in three parts, of which *Calypso* would be the prologue. The second was to be *Nausicaa*, and a third, according to Fritz von Bissing, was to be *Penelope*. By projection, we find once more the character of Mathilde in the traits of the daughter of King Alcinous, loved by the noble Ulysses in an impossible love which had to end in abandonment. At the moment of their parting, Nausicaa pronounced a speech worthy of Mathilde to Richard:

Nausicaa: *I matured in this painful hour when I was taken by*
your love. . . .
I saw great happiness vanish before me.
An instant of my love for you is better than an eternity of human
happiness.
Ulysses: *Chaos, night, and shadow lie before me!*
May there be no night in my heart.
I carry with me your divine image,
Let it be my guiding light.

When Mathilde sent this dramatic poem to the master of Bayreuth, she wrote a dedication that was like the scent of flowers, exhaling the perfume of love around the funeral pyre of Siegfried and Brünnhilde in the flames of *Götterdämmerung*:

Take to flight, my song,
And bring the greetings of a faithful heart;
Set them down at the feet of the man who like Ulysses
Knew how to suffer and endure.

The Black Sail

The house on the corner of Goethestrasse and Wienerstrasse resounded with voices, laughter, music, and applause. On the evening of May 14, 1880, Otto and Mathilde Wesendonck greeted Dresden's high society with their usual amiability. A select public had been invited to a comic version of their own *Siegfried*, imagined by the house poet, with the subtitle "A Comedy for Everyone and No One." She noted on the leaflet that this was indeed a "world premiere" given by the "brothers of the German-Saxon Parnassus," expressly "by the young for the young."

Since that morning she had been busy with the details of the costumes as well as the preparations for the reception that was to follow. Her friend Marie Seebach was there to direct the actors, and Reinhold Becker (on the poster she wrote "Rheingold" Becker) accompanied them on the piano with music made up of eight leitmotifs by "Master Richard."

Hans Wesendonck had the leading role of Siegfried. Perfect casting—at age eighteen Hans was ideal: his blond hair and bright eyes, his athletic adolescent body, and his elegant gestures made him a credible protagonist. At that time it was a little boy, Myrrha's child, Fritz, born in 1873, who took most of his grandmother's attention. The question was serious: how could she make the wings of his costume as the Forest Bird stay on his shoulders? "And you must speak louder," she added to the seven-year-old. "Or else you may not be heard in the last row."

Ah, if Siegfried knew
Where Brünnhilde was,
He would hunt no more
The fox or the bear!

Bravo! Well done! His bright little voice was moving. At the end of the show, Mathilde embraced him and congratulated him. Talking about this grandson to Eliza Wille, she wrote: "Fritz von Bissing is a charming and lovely child. When he talks about his grandmother, he says: 'We two, we love each other very much.' He is an adorable little boy."[1]

The evening unfolded with good humor. Besides the "well-rhymed little lines by Frau Wesendonck," the mistress of the house had informed the audience, "We do not know what time it will be over, for there will be many a surprise." The performance took place in the garden, where a temporary shelter had been set up for the audience. After a scene with the dwarves,

Siegfried, still asleep, spoke aloud about Brünnhilde. Stretching out his arms to embrace the woman of his dreams, he found himself holding a bear. The legend mixed the fairy tale of *Sleeping Beauty* with the story of *Wieland the Blacksmith*. The result was a delightful parody that made everyone laugh.

This social event of May 1880 was to be among the last happy moments that Mathilde patiently created during the years she lived in Dresden. But as each time she tried to build a new edifice to shelter her wounded soul, life would cruelly remind her of the ephemeral character of all earthly happiness: Hans, this darling son, the hero of the evening, would hardly have better luck than the Siegfried of the legend, and like him, he would soon meet a tragic fate.

In Dresden, Otto and Mathilde were known as connoisseurs of the arts. Second-rank musicians who played at the royal court and in the concert halls and who knew of Mathilde Wesendonck came to venerate the muse of *Tristan*. A few foolhardy people, such as Reinhold Becker and Wilhelm Seifhardt, tried to set the "queen's" poems to music, but one could see that her heart was no longer in it. In fact, each day the gap between her inner life and daily reality widened.

On attending a performance of *Tristan* in Munich, a musician friend from Dresden reported Mathilde's disappointment concerning the scenery, as well as the orchestra, which she found too dark and melancholy. She no longer perceived the velvety sweetness of the Érard that Richard knew how to play for her alone while she would drift along with him on the shining wings of the "swan." Soon she would attend performances of Wagner's operas only in Bayreuth; it was there, in the room's unique and complete darkness, that she would relive almost each year after 1882, the moments of mystical union with the beloved; but this would not prevent her from continuing to go to the concert hall, for the love of music and to meet the musicians. Moreover, although she was no longer interested in Brahms as a person, she enthused about his symphonic works. In 1878, at the Hofkapelle of Dresden, Franz Wüllner conducted the Second Symphony in D major. Mathilde's love for music knew no obstacles, no cliques, and she praised the talent of Hans von Bülow, who had "gone over to Brahms," as much as that of Hermann Levi, the orchestra conductor "chosen by Wagner" for *Parsifal*.

During her last year in Dresden she wrote to Benndorf on the subject of music: "In my solitude, I imagined a princely consolation: I am having all the quartets of Beethoven played for me—every Sunday at twelve-thirty. The audience and the musicians are delighted, and everyone finds exceptional joy in it. These scores resound magnificently in my music room, . . . seventeen quartets, two at each meeting—the first one composed during his youth, the second from his artistic maturity."[2]

~

At the beginning of the winter of 1881–82 the Wesendoncks gave one of their last musical evenings in Dresden. They received the professor and composer Hermann Scholz-Beuthen, considered by Liszt at the time to be the best interpreter of Chopin. Already old, Scholz was accompanied by one of his young students, Otto Richter, who later wrote about this visit.[3]

Greeted kindly by the boys of the house, Hans and Karl, the guests were first assembled in the "art gallery," where Otto and Mathilde were accustomed to meeting their friends. At the age of fifty-four, Mathilde still gave the young Richter an impression of youth. After the dinner, which he described as "brilliant," readings and recitations of poems took place, with Scholz playing some of his own compositions as well as those of Chopin. Franz Ries, a virtuoso violinist, accompanied at the piano by Scholz, played Brahms's Sonata in G major, and the grandson, Fritz, turned pages. "Then," said Richter,

> we were favored by a special number—a lady of the Royal Opera, Frau Clementine von Schuch-Proska, sang the *Wesendonck Lieder* with the music of Wagner, which were almost unknown at the time. A deep emotion ran through the audience.... During the performance Frau Mathilde, to whom these five songs had been presented as 'the most intimate homage of the great master,' was sitting in the shadows in a corner of the room, escaping the guests' gaze. No one could guess the reason for this solemn piety, which, in the deepest part of a silent soul, was protecting her sanctuary from any profanation.... This behavior seemed somewhat strange.

Mathilde's last theatrical endeavor, dated this same year of 1881, was a drama in four acts, *Alceste*, based on Euripides' tragedy. This story, already artificially dramatic in the original form, was a good vehicle for the poet to express her own obsession with fidelity and her tendency toward self-sacrifice. Alceste, the wife of Admete, the king of Thessaly, consented to die in order to save her husband, but Heracles, touched by the spouse's generosity and the king's hospitality, snatches Alceste from the jaws of death and brings her back to earth.

Once again Mathilde had created a woman who assumed her destiny, suffered in secret, and discreetly accomplished a great act. This was the last depiction onstage of the dual personality of the author, torn between the obligation to keep her love for Richard to herself and the need to confess it out loud to the whole world. In the words of Admete, Mathilde expressed the feelings she had been hiding from everyone since Richard Wagner disappeared from her life:

> *At that moment I understood*
> *What had given pleasure and value to my life,*
> *And I looked down at the abyss that had opened on misfortune.*
> *What we possess, we understand it not*
> *Until we have lost it.*[4]

Regret, solitude . . .

Alceste was first published in 1881 and reprinted in 1898. Moreover, it was the only drama of Mathilde to be performed onstage at a charity benefit. It was also one of her last works in which she revealed her own inner struggle between being silent or speaking out. In 1878 Cosima had guessed the nature of this dilemma when, in a letter to Mathilde, she alluded to the *vita vecchia* (old days): "Many troubles cannot be expressed when one is silent. Maybe I understand you more than you may think. . . . I know the truth about your silence. I know that as soon as one speaks, there are always misunderstandings that can slip into what one says. . . . Those who prefer words to silence are mistaken, because everything that is said can easily be distorted."[5]

Eliza Wille, Wagner's other confidante, also looked back on her past so as to unburden her soul, for the Victorian era had walled women up in their "discretion." The mistress of Mariafeld had written novels in which only Mathilde could understand the meaning of their allusions: "I admire your capacity to plunge again into the situation that we have all known," wrote Mathilde. "We stood before life as if it were an enigma. Even the most gifted among us did not have the key to understand the signals destiny had sent us."

~

In 1875 Karl Luckemeyer died in Düsseldorf. Uncharacteristically, Mathilde left no written word about her feelings regarding her bereavement. According to what we know through her letters—and it is little—Mathilde had got on well with her father. But the old man with thin lips and a severe look in his eyes was apparently not often informed of his daughter's state of mind. We know that she inherited a fortune, which in 1878 allowed her to buy a house in Austria in the region called the Salzkammergut, on the Traunsee. From then on that was where Mathilde spent the summer months, up until the end of October. In 1881, when the improvements and accommodations were finished in her new villa, she wrote: "In my solitude, I have become acquainted with the profound beauty of the landscape in Traunblick. Personally, I find this countryside and house almost more beautiful than our 'princely' estate on Lake Zurich."

And strangely, this new summer home of the Wesendoncks was situated in relation to the lake on a site resembling that of Wahlheim on the Green Hill. On the shores of Traunsee, southwest of the city of Gmunden, Traunblick occupied in the village of Altmünster the same situation, with the same exposure, on a green elevation, and on the same side of the lake, as the beautiful palace they had had in Enge. Only the style of the villa had changed: this time it was well integrated into its surroundings.

Mathilde would cultivate her family solitude. She was fond of saying, "We were all together in our refuge," even though the theme of solitude returned time and again in her writings.

Regret, solitude, escape . . .

May my wings spread open
To flee to unexplored land,
To dissolve in boundless space
That my daring eye has seen

. . .

To flee until the end of days
There where no heart is in pain,
To flee where no complaint
And where no suspicion of desire may be;
Ah! in that pure, far-off place
I shall feel no more my own pain
And jubilantly embrace in my heart
The fairest of all the stars![6]

"I am alone with Hans in Dresden," wrote Mathilde to Otto Benndorf on January 15, 1881. "My husband, Myrrha, Fritz, the governess, and the servants are sailing up the Nile in a *dahabeah* (an Egyptian sailboat). Myrrha has caused us a lot of worry ever since she contracted pneumonia at the last cavalry festivity she attended in Hannover. The doctors say that the tip of a lobe of the left lung is still in danger of infection. This condition could be cured only by the force of heat and sunshine in countries of the south."

The European passengers coming on ships from Marseille and Trieste disembarked in the port of Alexandria. "I have just received the first letter of the fourth and fifth of January, mailed in Alexandria on the sixth," continued Mathilde. "Except for being seasick, the voyage went well." They then took a train to Cairo, from which they embarked on either a steamboat or a sailboat for the excursion up the Nile. It was at that time the most expensive and also the most pleasant treatment for tuberculosis. The Wesendoncks spent two winters discovering the beauty of the Nile valley. The first year Mathilde had remained in Germany: "I took the risk of letting my husband accompany Myrrha because someone had to remain at home for Hans, who is in his last year before beginning his baccalaureate education." But the following winter, in December 1881, Hans having left for his studies in Bonn, Mathilde went with Otto to take care of Myrrha in Egypt. Fritz was eight years old. He had such an indelible memory of these trips that he later devoted himself to the study of Egyptology.[7] In his writings on his grandmother he mentioned a short sojourn in Pau, in the Pyrenees, where treatments for tuberculosis were offered. He remembered that in the Basque country Mathilde had had a beret made in velvet that she sent to the master of Bayreuth.

In January 1882, after a stay in Cairo, they all embarked on the picturesque sailboat to travel up the Nile valley to Aswan. This excursion would last about two months, and the boat's slow pace allowed them to observe the country and its ancient monuments. From the Pyramids of Giza and Memphis to Karnak, Luxor, and Thebes, the sun-flooded countryside reminded Mathilde of her poetic dialogues with nature:

Sun, you weep every evening
Until your lovely eyes are red.
When bathing in the sea
You are o'ertaken by your early death.

But you rise again in your old splendor,
The aureole of the dark world;
Freshly awakened in the morning
Like a proud and conquering hero![8]

In the land of Ra, the sun god, son of Isis and Osiris, who dies each evening in the Nile, then is reborn each morning in the east . . .

The white sail of the *dahabeah* swelled in the desert breeze. The stone merged on the horizon with the yellow sand; blues and grays in the sky stretched endlessly on a long, bright canvas. After many weeks, the city of Aswan loomed, green, rich, and colorful. At the port of Nubia, under the date palms, vendors from Sudan and Abyssinia sold their wares, set out on blankets on the white streets—animal skins, ostrich feathers, silver rings and bracelets, and pottery of all sorts. On the river, they stayed on the island of Elephantine, where blocks of inscription-covered stone and fragments of sculpture had not yet yielded their secrets. From the highest point of the island, one can see the brown and black rock formations of the Nile's waterfalls.

January 1882, then February.

Myrrha's cure was doing her good. They traveled back down the river and finally reached Cairo once again.

Meanwhile in Germany, severe cold weather had set in. The students in Bonn were on holiday, and the new students were initiated by their older schoolmates. It was a classical ragging in joyful company: they drank, they ate, they ran through the town in disguise—and those who resisted were plunged into the Rhine. In the freezing cold, Hans Wesendonck contracted a raging case of pneumonia while Myrrha was recovering in the Egyptian sun.

When they returned to Cairo Otto and Mathilde were given the news of their son's death. Impossible but true! Young Siegfried on his first voyage on the Rhine, like an implacable ransom for his initiation to the world, had been slain by fate. Sailing down the Nile, Mathilde had not seen, hoisted onto the mast of their little boat, a black sail.

In the blooming May of your life
You received the most insidious blow,
As from Hagen's ancient spear,
Which struck young Siegfried, near the source.
Thus winter, envious, with poisoned arrow
Pierced your adolescent chest!
And the flower fell, broken in the winter tomb
And covered with snow in the horrible grave.[9]

Over the next three years Mathilde would write twenty-two poems devoted to Hans, whom she constantly referred to as her sun, who had vanished in the springtime of his youth. She would no longer write any poems about nature, nor any incoherent dramas. She would close herself into a wall of silence and confess her grief in a few lines and tales that resembled Buddhist-inspired meditations. She would publish only works that had been written before the young man's death.

Hans Wesendonck was buried in the old cemetery in Bonn, where Moritz von Bissing was garrisoned. The family had a monument erected on which was placed a bronze statue by Gustav Kietz of Antinoüs, the beautiful favorite of Emperor Hadrian. On his head he wore not the laurels that crowned the heads of poets, but a garland of poppies, as a reminder that sleep was close to death and, perhaps, that life was but a dream.

It is there that they would all be one day, reunited with Hans under the heavy baroque tombstone of their family grave.

> *You were the joy of my heart;*
> *Gaiety reigned wherever you were.*
> *Woe to the house you have left,*
> *Woe to the heart you have fled,*
> *Forever abandoned it will be now,*
> *Forever abandoned, forever alone!*
>
> . . .
>
> *Alas, what else have I to bring*
> *To the boy so young and so gay*
> *But flowers on his premature tomb,*
> *Nothing but his mother's pain.*
>
> . . .
>
> *The roses of my love,*
> *Wet with the dew of my tears,*
> *I strew them in my songs.*

In Dresden, the house in the Goethestrasse would no longer be a place of joy: "I would like to be named 'Cheerful' / But 'Woeful' is my name" (*Die Walküre*, Act I, Scene 2).

Too many memories were attached to this home where the family had spent the last ten years. At the end of 1882 the Wesendoncks moved away to settle in Berlin, in the Tiergartenstrasse. In the months following Hans's death, Mathilde's only consolation would be the Bayreuth Festival, which would stage the world premiere of Wagner's last work, *Parsifal*.

Mathilde never dared to send her love poems of 1877 to Richard. They had met during the summer of that year at Bad Ems, where Richard was taking the cure at the same time as Mathilde and Myrrha. On July 3 Cosima noted in her diary: "Frau Wesendonck and her daughter. This sort of company weighs a bit on R. It is a kind of intimacy, but with no deep agreement." If one can believe the master's wife, Wagner and Mathilde had nothing to say to each other and could share only a kind of dull familiarity. If Wagner let only boredom show in Mathilde's presence at a time when he was writing passionate letters to Judith Gautier, the inspiration for *Parsifal*'s Kundry, that was not the case for Mathilde, for the last of her six songs, written that same year, revealed that her secret love was still fervent:

> *My bosom is a seashell,*
> *Your love is the pearl,*
> *Shut tight within*
> *Until the day it will burst.*
>
> *Someone will then find the pearl.*
> *Inestimable, true, and pure,*
> *It will not manage in the least*
> *To weigh the value of your love.*
>
> *The pearl, is it an illness?*
> *Well, I believe so! And that is why*
> *I wish to die of it,*
> *And in that bliss, celebrate my loss!* [10]

"Many pains cannot be expressed when one is silent." Mathilde's heart could no longer be contained. For Richard's birthday on May 22, 1879, she sent him this last greeting, inspired by *Die Meistersinger*:

> *After a long night of silence,*
> *I salute you, Master,*
> *In the splendor of a May morning!*
> *May the suffering you have endured on this earth*
> *Drown in this snow of flowers!*
> *When the sun sends us its beams in May,*
> *Think only of the delight*
> *That your coming brought us.*

In 1882 the Wesendoncks took the train to Bayreuth. The long trip was regularly interrupted by stopovers, refreshments, rest, and meditation. Mathilde, dressed all in black, viewed the trees and hills along the way with nostalgia; villages flew by as in a dream. And her inner landscape was strewn with memories and the familiar faces of her dear departed or of friends who had become unrecognizable with age. At the festival she would emerge from her shell, joining the crowd to see Richard in his glory.

That year the Bayreuth Festival opened on July 26 with the world premiere of *Parsifal*. There would be sixteen performances before it closed on August 29. The Wesendoncks stayed in the city for two weeks, and Mathilde wrote to Jakob Sulzer that she had attended the new opera five times.

During an intermission she was introduced to a French writer and friend of Wagner, Edward Schuré. Very moved on meeting Mathilde, he described her in her mourning clothes: "Under her veil of dark lace, I could see a refined face with a sad and gentle look, the sparkle of which gave me a sudden piercing glance, revealing an extraordinary concentration of feeling and will. A small, nervous, black-gloved hand shook mine. . . . I will never forget the impression of her face and her gaze. They were those of a beautiful soul, long silenced and with a heart like a tomb."

Love is not love
which alters when it alteration finds . . .
it is an ever-fixed mark
That looks on tempests, and is never shaken. (Shakespeare, sonnet 116)

Among all the letters Richard sent her, Mathilde preserved like a real treasure his precious comments on *Parsifal*. When Cosima wrote to her in 1878 to explain to her the dates of the work's outlines, upon reading "May I rectify . . . ," Mathilde must have shrugged her shoulders and smiled. As if she did not know! And before anyone else: she had been informed in 1857, from the very beginning of this supreme masterpiece through its subsequent evolution and almost to its definitive completion. All his revelations to his beloved muse show that the initial germ for *Parsifal* came as a direct result of the suffering caused by their impossible love, transposed to a metaphysical level. First of all, during the terrible summer of 1858 Richard had sent Mathilde a musical phrase with these words: "Where will I discover you, O Holy Grail? Full of fervent desire, my heart aches for you." Then his long letters on human compassion as the source of the world's liberation had led him to develop, for Mathilde, the entire plan for his future work.

In 1859 in Lucerne, while composing the third act of *Tristan*, Wagner identified himself with his dying protagonist and universalized his suffering. About *Parsifal*, he wrote to Mathilde:

Quite recently, the conviction came back to me again that this would become a most difficult labor. All things considered, Amfortas is the center of it, the main character. . . . Suddenly it appeared terribly clear to me: he is my Tristan of the third act, but with a progression of unthinkable intensity. The wound created by the spear and another wound in the heart—the unfortunate king has no other hope than for death; to obtain this supreme remedy, he aspires more and more to the vision of the Grail, to know if it could heal his wounds, for everything else has failed. But nothing, nothing can allay his suffering. However, the Grail gives him in return this unique thing—that he cannot die and the Grail increases his suffering because it grants him immortality. According to my conception of the Grail, it is the chalice of the Last Supper, in which Joseph of Arimathea received the blood of the Savior on the cross. What terrible significance Amfortas's situation thus takes on before this miraculous chalice; he who suffers from the same wound made by the spear of a rival in an amorous adventure shall find his only salvation in the consecration of the blood that once flowed from the Savior's side as He was dying on the cross, renouncing the world, saving the world, suffering for the world! Blood for blood, wound for wound—but here and there, what an abyss between that blood and that wound! In ecstasy, in adoration before the marvelous chalice, which glows with supreme brightness—through it Amfortas feels life renewed in him, and death cannot approach him! He lives, he lives again, and, worse than ever, the fatal wound burns him, his own wound! Even adoration becomes painful! Where is the end? Where is redemption? All the suffering of humanity for all eternity! . . . He had been named to keep the Grail, not because he was worthy of it, but because no one had recognized as deeply as he the miraculous force of the Grail. . . . It devastates him and gives him divine salvation and at the same time eternal malediction!

And I should execute that and also write the music for such a subject? No thanks! Whoever wants to do it can! I will not burden myself with such an effort.[11]

∼

The rehearsals took place during the whole month of July, with Hermann Levi as conductor. Wagner was visibly fatigued by the enterprise, even though this second Bayreuth Festival in 1882 presented far fewer scenic problems than had the *Ring* in 1876. But the master was ailing—he had had several minor heart attacks.

The public was as cosmopolitan as at the first festival. Few French composers were missing, and the spectators greeted them with respect: Ernest Chausson, Léo Delibes, Vincent d'Indy, Gabriel Fauré, André Messager, and the ever-faithful Saint-Saëns. Anton Bruckner came from Vienna, as did the young Richard Strauss. Mathilde, in her mourning clothes, tried to steer clear of the crowds. Remaining in her box in the theater, she struck up an acquaintance with a young Englishwoman, Mary Burrell. The two became friends and wrote to each other for several years, until Mary's death. Her letters covered many touching and delicate matters, especially concerning the relationship between Richard and Mathilde. Mary Burrell traveled all across Europe in order to collect unpublished documents on Wagner's life, intending to write an immense biography of him. During her short lifetime, however, Mary was unfortunately unable to go further than the first volume, which covered only the musician's childhood, but left it in a form that took the place of a full-fledged classical biography.[12]

Before meeting Mathilde, Mary had studied singing with Johanna Wagner, a niece of Richard. Someone, she said, had brought her the *Wesendonck Lieder* when she was still but a child. Mary explained to Mathilde: "I will always consider that moment to be my first introduction to you. Of course, when I read those poems, you were speaking to me very distinctly through them, even if I was not yet totally conscious of it."[13]

This was why Mary was so moved to meet the muse for *Tristan* that summer of 1882. Thanks to Wagner's music and her friendship with Mathilde, she could easily guess the intense passion that had existed between them, and she would refer to it frequently in her letters.

Mary often asked Mathilde to reserve one of the royal boxes, the *Fürstenloge*, in the Bayreuth theater so that the two ladies could attend the festival seated side by side. "I have a great desire to share the box with you, because I am always afraid of being seen by other people in case, during the opera, I should burst into tears."[14]

The Honorable Willoughby Burrell, her husband, was happy to converse with Otto Wesendonck, especially because the latter spoke perfect English. Mary said that although she herself felt perfectly at home in the German language, such was not the case for her dear husband!

The lights went down. The distinctive sound coming from the invisible orchestra rose from the depths of the pit. The thread of Mathilde's memories came to life again in the darkness, and time would vanish, as Richard said in his text:

Parsifal: *I scarcely move,*
Yet seem indeed to have come far.
Gurnemanz: *You see, my son, time here becomes space.*

"All the dreadful tragedy of life," Wagner had written to Mathilde, "can be narrowed down to the fact that we are all separated from one another in time and in space; but since time and space are only a way of seeing and have no reality in the eyes of a perceptive person, the most tragic suffering should be explained only as an error of the individual. . . . Only with you do I wish to talk about such things! Then time and space, which contain really nothing more than torment and distress, disappear!"[15]

And then, one year after putting aside his project on the Grail, he exclaimed: "Let Geibel do it and Liszt compose the music." But he confided again to Mathilde Wesendonck: "*Parsifal* has awakened in me vividly; I see it more and more clearly; when the moment comes, the writing of this poem will be an unheard-of pleasure for me. But that could take many years! That's why I would like to keep to the poem. I stay away as long as I can and will only do it when it becomes irresistible. Then the marvelous progress of 'giving birth' makes me forget all my misery." Years before he began his last opera, Wagner described to Mathilde in detail the double character of Kundry and the profound motivation of the heroes. Attracted and repelled in turn by the subject of *Parsifal*, Wagner was making his own way toward the Grail, which was an answer to his suffering. "If I ever finish this poem," he wrote to Mathilde, "I will have done something very original. But I cannot imagine how long I should have to live in order to be able to complete all these projects."[16]

At the 1882 festival a brand-new, revolutionary piece of technology was inaugurated for the gradual transformation of the forest in Act I into the temple of the Holy Grail: large rolls of scenery showing the countryside were unscrolled as the characters walked, as in a film. Then, from the back of the stage, at the sound of the bells, the knights of the Grail appeared in the shadows. They all assembled around a table for Communion in a setting inspired by the interior of the Siena Cathedral. In their midst the tortured Amfortas groaned, and the voice of Titurel could be heard from afar: "Uncover the Grail!"

"It is of an incomparable beauty!" continued Richard. "And the double meaning of this vessel, as the chalice of the Last Supper—certainly the most magnificent sacrament of Christianity!"[17]

How will Amfortas heal? Who will solve the enigma of suffering?

Enlightened through compassion, the innocent fool,[18]
Wait for him, the appointed one.

In September 1882 Mathilde described for Jakob Sulzer the "divine musical language" of a work that seemed to her a pure marvel. But in the same letter, returning to her progressive ideas of the 1870s, she wondered about the apparently "irrational" text of Wagner in *Parsifal*: "Humanity, full of sin, eaten up by the need for redemption through faith, celebrates in this work its supreme transfiguration. But then, the thinkers, the scientific researchers of the nineteenth century? Would we have not learned or forgotten anything?" Mathilde seemed to think that *Parsifal* was the negation of rational reality, of judgment and reason. Unlike Wagner in this work, she refused to see sin as the source of all suffering. And she discovered, through this interpretation of the Grail legend, a Wagner who had become deeply Christian: "The tendency to religious reverie and the belief in miracles," she confided to Sulzer, "are common to all the poor in spirit. We are living at a time of clerical reaction . . . and enlightened men can contemplate the future only with anguish. . . . When I listen now to *Parsifal*, I fear that the world may return to Catholicism!"

Later on, Paul Claudel would confirm Mathilde's suspicion, but unlike her, he rejoiced in this return to Christianity. On the subject of the premiere of *Parsifal* in Bayreuth, he wrote:

That year the triumph of materialism was at its peak. The glory of Taine and Renan reigned. Not a book, not a newspaper was published without there being an attack on religion. . . . It was the moment when, alone on top of the hill in Bayreuth, over a debased Europe, over a Germany wallowing in gold and pleasure, Richard Wagner confessed his faith in Christ and the sacraments. . . . He had passed through materialism and Buddhism, and Protestantism, and nationalism and Schopenhauer and Kundry, and his enemies and his admirers; he went beyond his dream and found the Real Presence![19]

Ecce homo . . .

Mathilde joined Nietzsche in thinking that all religion was an illusion: "My eyes search for man redeemed and find him not!" she wrote. "If the father's love, the heavenly banquet symbolized by the Last Supper, has any meaning for the conscience of men of today, the divine love it represents should be in relation to nature."

Sacred Nature. But man does not live by bread alone, or on the plants of a purely rational world. Upon reflection, Mathilde would come to understand that her choice between what she considered to be an "illusion" and the "truth" was childish. And when it came to dealing with her own suffering, in the end it was in Buddhism that she would seek the nirvana of forgetfulness and find the human wisdom to help her to live.

As for Wagner, in 1868 he had confided to the French poet Villiers de l'Isle-Adam, on the subject of his relationship with art and religion, these words, full of an unquestionable religious dimension: "The work of an individual without faith will never be the work of an artist, since it will always lack the flame that gives enthusiasm, raises the soul and makes it grow, warms and fortifies the person. . . . A true artist must be one who creates, unifies, and transforms these two inseparable gifts—science and faith. As for me, since you are asking, you should know that above all, I am a Christian and that any ring of truth you may be impressed by in my work is inspired and created by that fact alone."

Sulzer, the recipient of Mathilde's biting words, those of a *mater dolorosa* and a forsaken lover, at the end of his long article on the festival of 1882 summed up the principal reason for the annual pilgrimage to Bayreuth for generations to come, beyond all philosophical or religious divergences: "We are leaving the solitary temple of the *Fichtegebirge*, with overwhelmed hearts full of deep emotion," wrote Sulzer. "But we also feel we are better now than we were before entering it."

~

After the exhausting summer of 1882, the Wagners left Bayreuth in September to spend the winter in Italy. It was in Venice, on the mezzanine of the Palazzo Vendramin Calergi, that the household—wife, children, and servants—moved into fifteen beautiful rooms. The five months preceding the death of Richard Wagner resembled a patchwork, in which all the elements that had crossed the master's tormented existence came together to find at last their proper place. Friends came and went like actors on a stage, and Wagner delightedly indulged himself in his reminiscences, overjoyed to recall episodes of his past. The monologues, the fleeting images, and the events of this long road of "tragicomedy in happiness and misfortune" that his destiny seemed to have followed were faithfully written down by Cosima, the iron sybil, who held the key to the future. Every day she noted his comments, his walks, his visits, and his dreams. Wagner, who was suffering from frequent mild heart attacks, dispensed bittersweet humor, discussing with Liszt, who was staying with them for a while, the project for a symphony in one movement, and revealing on the canvas being painted of him by Auguste Renoir a "painful smile, bitter and disillusioned."[20]

He was still dreaming of Mathilde Wesendonck, but Cosima would assure the reader of her diary that these fantasies were always negative: he once confessed to her that he was between Minna and Mathilde, but he pushed both women away, saying, "Neither of the two."[21]

A perfect spouse, Cosima was also his psychoanalyst. Lying on the couch, Wagner talked about himself, ready to free himself of his anguish, to his wife, who kept a notebook within reach. "We talk about his dreams," she said. "Frau Wesendonck appears rather often in them recently." But so as to reassure us, or to reassure herself, she added: "Unfortunately always mad and disagreeable. . . . He said to himself: 'Good, that also is over.'"

Until Christmas 1882 the house was full of guests. Liszt and Wagner played cards together, quarreling over nonsense and making up right away. Afterward, in January, only a few intimate friends were left: Hermann Levi, Paul von Joukowsky, and the children.

He would take slow-paced walks through the streets of Venice, crossing the Rialto Bridge, sitting on the Piazza San Marco, contemplating the extended blue ribbon of the Lido on the horizon, where the waves seemed to call down the sky to meet them. In his room, which he had done over in blue silk, Wagner created instinctively the scenery for his death, which he felt to be close, perhaps even dreaming of his own birth. Some time beforehand Cosima had reported another dream in which Richard was looking at Mathilde Wesendonck as she nursed a baby. "The child had a strange head of hair with a prematurely old face; R. thought it even had gray hair; 'Everything is so instinctive here,' said R. Then a powerful vulture swooped down on the mother and child. R. started to chase it away but it dashed back down again on them."[22] We know that one of the Muses of antiquity was also depicted giving her milk to the poet. Was Wagner not dreaming of the time when he received his inspiration from Mathilde's presence?

In the evenings, on the Grand Canal, he heard the gondolas gliding by, breaking the wavelets, which reflected the rays of the moon into a thousand shining lights. From his deepest memory reappeared the image of the Palazzo Giustinian, the chromatic sounds of *Tristan* associated now with the suffering in *Parsifal*. But now it was real and present. In the street, everywhere, he would stop from time to time, clutching his vest, his hand on his heart, waiting for the pain in his chest to subside.

A last musical phrase, the theme called "Porazzi," came back to him repeatedly during those days. Its ascending chromatic scale recalls the nostalgia in the *Tristan* Prelude, and Wagner constantly played it on the piano.

In November he dreamed of a beautiful garden that belonged to the Wesendoncks. Was it the one of the Flower Maidens in *Parsifal*, or in the second act of *Tristan*? This metaphor of the garden of Eden, for Richard as for Mathilde, was always present in their past love. Now Richard teased Cosima, reminding her of a letter she had sent him in Venice in which she referred to Mathilde as his "poetic friend"; and Cosima answered: "I could say no more, since he had introduced her to me as a saint, a fact that he does not want to recognize." But to close any further discussion on the matter, she added: "I asked him in the end if he loved me, and he replied: 'You are for me the only Isolde.'" It was obvious that for Richard Wagner at that time, Mathilde was only the memory of a great love.

In his room of the Palazzo Vendramin, which he called his "blue grotto," Wagner was thinking of writing an apologia in defense of womankind. He had begun an essay, entitled "On Feminine Nature in Humankind," in which he intended to treat marriage, monogamy, and polygamy, as well as the problem of fidelity, describing his subjects as "the power of the human being on nature, woman 'raised far above it, even higher than the natural law of sex.'"

On Sunday, February 11, "R. saw, in a dream, Frau Schröder-Devrient; telling me about his dreams," wrote Cosima. "He said: 'All the women I knew are now parading before me.'" After Wagner's death Daniela picked up her mother's pen to continue the diary and note some of his last remarks: "In one of his dreams in the last two days he was getting letters from women; one from Frau Wesendonck, the other from a forgotten lady. . . . He did not open either of the two letters, putting them on two opposing sides of the table and saying, 'Cosima would be jealous.'"

Born of a woman, raised and inspired by a woman, he dreamed, swathed in blue silk, of his return to the womb. The symbolic and invisible feminine figure had then hoisted onto the mast of his destiny, a black sail under the Venetian sky.

On February 13, sitting at his worktable, violent chest pains pierced him through. He collapsed and died a few minutes later in the arms of Cosima. On his sheet of paper he had just noted these words: "The process of emancipation for women will occur only in ecstatic convulsions. Love. Tragedy."

The Sleeping Maiden

On the green hillside, surrounded by woods,
Stands a house, precious and calm
With a long view over the countryside. . . .
At the foot of the slope
A lake reflects the heavens
Where golden stars bathe in clear ripples.
And there, on the shore, a great mountain looms:
By name, the Traunstein, with its ancient lore:
'Twas in ancient times a giant.
A woman slept at his side
In sleep as deep as death.
Her sweet body was healed
From the pain and sorrow of life.
The Traunstein stands wakeful before the tomb;
He waits and guards, night after night,
And shuns the goodness of sleep.
Each morning, when the light of day softly kisses the sleeping maiden,
Tears roll into his eyes. Would she awaken to him?
But she remains asleep, immobile and cold,
And ignores the passion of love.
Of her divinity only her appearance remains.
I can see her from my window; nothing disturbs her peace.
Hush, my heart, you too one day
Will know its rest in death.

—MATHILDE WESENDONCK, "DIE SCHLAFENDE GRIECHEN"
(THE SLEEPING MAIDEN), 1884

From her window overlooking the Traunsee, Mathilde would contemplate the mountain-
ous country bordering Salzburg. The summit of the Traunstein, capped in fluffy clouds,

overshadowed the dark-green waters of the lake at Altmünster and recalled the legend of the giant and the beautiful maiden, sleeping in a stony death; some said she awakened at night to kiss the hero of her dreams and at sunrise fell back into her tomb. The inhabitants of the village called the mountain, with its Grecian profile, the Erlakogel.

> *Her body, with its graceful bearing,*
> *Made its bed in hard stone;*
> *In the mist of death's sleep*
> *She rests, the royal maiden. . . .*
> *When everything sleeps,*
> *When the world sinks into a dream,*
> *When the wavelet stands still,*
> *When the sea almost breathes no more,*
>
> *With the timid step of the doe*
> *She stands over Traunstein*
> *And plants a kiss on his noble brow,*
> *A kiss that love inflames.*
>
> *At this, the ancient hero trembles*
> *With the remembrance of love's pain;*
> *He shakes with terror*
> *From head to foot.*
> *And yet, as day climbs once more*
> *To the summit and the bed of stone,*
> *The maiden rests and sleeps*
> *As if all were forgotten.*[1]

In front of the Wesendoncks' Villa Traunblick the lawns ran down to the water's edge and the landscape was dotted with clusters of trees: red ash, pine, and spruce, as on the Green Hill in Zurich.

Mathilde had received the news of Wagner's death a few months earlier, in Berlin. She wrote a few formal lines that she felt obliged to compose:

> *The pain swells like the waves of the sea;*
> *Before the genius's coffin, all humanity bows.*

She wrote of "deliverance," of "nostalgia," and of the "torment of Amfortas," but it was impossible to find Isolde's burning heart in this cold eulogy.

Did the heroine possess a dual personality? Once more, it was in her dream world that

Mathilde would think on Wagner's death, in a completely different way, far from the official pomp and circumstance of his national burial in Bayreuth. She reread his letters and the diary of Venice . . . that same Venice where he dreamed for the last time of all the women of his life. The night before leaving the Asyl in August 1858, Wagner had told her how he imagined his death: "Before closing my eyes, I was strongly impressed by the memory of the time when I used to fall asleep, saying to myself that one day I would die here—I would be thus lying on my couch and you would come to me for the last time, taking me into your arms, in front of everyone and receiving my soul in a supreme kiss! . . . Where can I die now?"

It was the death of Tristan in Isolde's arms, "in front of everyone." Had the ancient legend finally triumphed? Two Isoldes—one, Isolde-the-blonde, the real one, far off; the other, Isolde-with-the-white-hands, who received his last kiss in her stead.

But Mathilde had written something else for Richard Wagner's death, and she hid the sheet of paper on which she had written in secret in the manuscript containing her melancholy poems about Traunblick. In her fine handwriting, hesitantly, on a page full of ink blots, deletions, and alterations, she expressed her true feelings, one year after the master's death. Once more she projected Richard's and Mathilde's destinies onto a legendary love story, this time the one about the giant of the Traunstein and the maiden of the Erlakogel:

Once upon a time there were two brave hearts
That were ready to share joy and pain.
No one knows how it happened,
But their peace vanished.
Their love was still fervent,
But the more they loved,
The more they were separated.
One hid from the other
The deepest wound of their heart,
And each one knew that the other
Was far from being healed.
A great and powerful fate separated the lovers
But desired their union in their death.
In the deep peace of death, she lies at his feet,
And he cannot take his gaze away from hers,
Which is so gentle.[2]

In her everyday life she was still carrying a heavy burden, mourning her son Hans. Myrrha, who was also very ill, visited her, along with young Fritz. In 1883 Karl married Eveline von Hessenstein. From their union would be born Otto-Gunther in 1885 and Inga in 1887. Mathilde would republish her *Deutsches Kinderbuch* for them in 1898.[3]

Other friends and acquaintances came to visit her: Emil Hess, a local musician from Gmunden, and the Hungarian pianist and composer Ödön Mihalovich, director of the music school in Budapest, who complained of the "Hungarian arrogance" that was snubbing the young and brilliant Gustav Mahler, in spite of his tremendous talent, "just because he was Jewish."

Mary Burrell, tirelessly criss-crossing Europe, wrote Mathilde letters full of musical and literary allusions. Although she was discreet when it came to Mathilde and Wagner's relationship, she referred constantly to the master by capitalizing "Him," as if he were a god, and she revered every sentence Mathilde sent her about him. She praised Mathilde's personality with unbridled enthusiasm: "Your mind is made of a very different fabric than ordinary minds, and you are not easily intimidated or influenced."[4]

During her years of research Mary would meet all the witnesses still capable of speaking to her about Wagner. However, in all her letters she placed Mathilde on a pedestal near the author of *Tristan*: "You are the only true Wagnerian that I know, generous and disinterested. . . . What a joy it is for me to have met you."[5] Her eyesight failing and suffering constant headaches, Mary would express to Mathilde her gratitude for all her letters, naming her the *Freudenbringerin*, her "messenger of joy"; and Mathilde in turn would assure Mary of her affectionate friendship: "You are having problems with your eyesight?" she wrote. "But you must protect and take care of those eyes like precious jewels. They should be like your mind and spirit, always as clairvoyant."

During the 1880s, at the end of each October, the Wesendoncks would go back to Berlin to spend the winter. Otto would be occupied by his painting collection, and Mathilde would have Beethoven quartets played in her house on Sundays.

Summer after summer she would immerse herself with delight in the darkness of the Bayreuth theater to celebrate, with the Tristan of her soul, their mystical marriage. In 1886, after the tragic death of Ludwig II of Bavaria and just as Liszt was dying in Bayreuth, she attended, alongside Mary Burrell, the first performance of this work, the "child" of Richard and Mathilde, in the festival theater. Conducted by Felix Mottl and directed by Cosima Wagner in person, for an entire month the festival theater mounted performances of *Tristan* alternating with those of *Parsifal*, that tragedy of Amfortas that Wagner designated as his "Tristan of the third act."

The compatibility between these two works was perfect. On rereading Richard's letters, Mathilde, remembering their love, was seeking a solution to the riddle of the world and of suffering. For, in his musical testament, Wagner had forever abandoned Schopenhauer's thesis that suffering was rooted in desire and had embraced the Christian view, according to which suffering originated in sin. Mathilde remembered that Schopenhauer wanted to take Christian doctrine toward Buddhism, in which suffering ceased to exist in Nirvana—in renunciation and forgetting.

Back in 1856 Wagner had shown Mathilde his outline and musical sketches for a Buddhist drama, "Die Sieger," in which the heroine suffers from the torment of an impossible love. She would attain full redemption only by renouncing to her passion and entering a Buddhist community. In 1858 Richard wrote to Mathilde:

As soon as Savitri declares herself ready for all the commitments, having understood the immense connection between the suffering in the world and her own, he [Buddha] will accept her into the community of saints, and thus she attains the highest degree of purification. He [Ananda, her unrequited lover and the hero of the work] thus considers his existence to be freeing, vowed to all beings, perfect, since he can also obtain salvation for the woman. . . . Blessed Savitri! You can follow your beloved everywhere now! You can remain at his side forever! Blessed Ananda! She is next to you now, the beloved; you have won her forever![6]

Blessed Mathilde, who possessed these letters and remembrances of Richard! However, Buddhist sublimation made only a brief appearance in Wagner's work. For, after hesitating between this subject for an opera and *Tristan*, it was the latter that was the victor, and *Parsifal* its metaphysical echo. Mathilde had not followed Wagner's intellectual evolution to its end, for hers changed direction when the beloved left. Richard realized this when he wrote to his Galatea: "The more I exclaim—'Help me, stay with me!,' the more distant you become; and a voice answers me: 'In this world, in which you take on this distress in order to achieve your visions, in this world she will belong to you not! But all the insults, all the torment, all the lack of understanding that make you suffer—this atmosphere envelops her also; she belongs to it, and it has rights over her. Why then does she find happiness in your art? Your art belongs to the world; and she too belongs to the world!'" Buddha, great and loving, shows that art "is the most invincible obstacle to happiness. . . . Blessed Ananda, blessed Savitri!"

∽

In 1888 the Germans experienced the national mourning of "the year of three emperors" (*Dreikaiserjahr*). Wilhelm I died in March, and his son, crowned Friedrich III, followed him to the grave in June, leaving the imperial throne to Wilhelm II.

That summer, on July 20, while Bayreuth was preparing the first performance of *Die Meistersinger*, Myrrha, who had been very ill for a long time, was traveling with her son, Fritz. She died suddenly in a hotel room in Munich, carried off by tuberculosis. Alone and distressed, the child called on his grandparents, who came immediately.

This new and unexpected shock would be the last blow to Mathilde's public life. She shut herself off from the rest of the world. The only remedy for her sorrow, coming from her meditations on oriental wisdom, was to write tales inspired by Buddhism: first, a charming story of a mouse transformed into a young girl who could not find a husband to her liking, if not in another mouse; then a sort of parable of the sower, but whose harvest was nirvana. . . .

In reality, it was to the figure of Buddha, as described by Wagner in his letters, that she turned to: the "saint," the one who knows because he is enlightened by compassion. In five manuscript pages, preceded by a list of Buddha's attributes, Mathilde reconstituted a scene in the first act of *Parsifal*—in the shade of a forest, overlooking a lake. The knights of the Grail had disappeared with King Amfortas; Mathilde replaced Gurnemanz with Gautama Buddha, the "perfect one" sitting under a bodhi tree. Lotus flowers floated on the water, and a magnificent swan traced arabesques in the azure. Coming out of the woods, a young boy, Siddhartha, seeing the bird approaching the shore, took an arrow from his quiver and shot it. The bird fell to the ground. Buddha knelt in front of the dying victim and reprimanded the child.

"Alas! What have you done?"

"It was my prey and I shot it down!"

"Have you no remorse? Do you have the arrogance to be proud of what you did? Look at this poor animal in agony, dying at your feet. . . . Look in its eyes and see the world of sadness and suffering. . . . It did not do you any harm; you should be ashamed."

Buddha then went to the fountain, scooped up some water, and washed the swan's wound. He embraced it, caressed it, and spoke to it, putting the bird's neck around his own like a shawl. Echoes of a little girl caressing the bright feathers of her white swan. In fact, there is a strong resemblance between Wagner's sacred swan, struck by the arrow of young Parsifal, and the one of Mathilde's tale *The Swan*, struck down by the anger of the divinity. Both victims aroused profound pity: Parsifal laid down his arms and the "Lord of the world" regretted his gesture, picking up its white feathers so as to "adorn the hem of his celestial robe." Furthermore, Wagner's musical expression of the dying swan's gaze in the first act of *Parsifal* joined, at the same interval of an augmented fifth, the description of the tears on the exotic flowers in the hothouse of the deeply compassionate Mathilde.[7] But at a distance of thirty years, compassion had become resignation, and Mathilde's swan now healed under the beneficent influence of Buddha.

Young Siddhartha-Parsifal, contrite, wanted to flee; Buddha showed him a refuge in his heart. In his example, he who has compassion and love will dispense health, protect those who suffer, and thus save the world.

For Mathilde, human wisdom therefore replaced the Grail. Like Nietzsche, she wanted to flee the metaphysical transcendence implicit in the master's last work, for the will to live, even in a world transformed by Wagner, seemed irremediably marred by suffering and misery. And she mixed supernatural "hope" with Schopenhauer's "desire." But who would not understand that a mother who had lost four of her five children during her lifetime might have some philosophical weaknesses?

Concerning Buddhism, Richard had taught her and then abandoned the principles that he had adopted for himself. Mathilde reread his words: "You know how I unwittingly became a Buddhist. Without realizing it, I also have an affinity with the Buddhist maxim of begging. . . . The religious man walks through cities and men's streets, shows himself unclothed, possessing nothing, and thus obtains, by appearing to believers, the precious occasion for them to perform the most noble and deserving of works . . . in giving alms." What good Buddhists Otto and Mathilde Wesendonck showed themselves to be by their undying generosity toward him!

~

On November 21, 1884, Mary Burrell, the noble and distinguished collector of Wagner documents and biographer of the master, wrote to Mathilde: "I fear that I am wicked enough to understand the Album Sonata affair." This original piece by Wagner had been composed and dedicated to his muse, Mathilde, in 1853. It was published after the musician's death under this new title and became an object of controversy. "It is not a 'sonata for an album' by any means," noted Mathilde in her reply to Mary. "Wagner deeply loathed that fad of albums, which he found ridiculous. Why publish it under that title if not simply to degrade it?" But to avoid any confrontation with Cosima, Mathilde concluded laconically:"I don't understand." However, Mary Burrell insisted: "You were not to be allowed to possess any unpublished music after his death. It was to be published with his authority and without your name, as a bagatelle in his life. It makes me boil and fume and rage to see how everything you did is kept in the background. And yet, I sympathize with you in taking it so calmly! Some day it all must and shall come right."[8]

This was also, in fact, what Eliza Wille said when the mistress of Mariafeld protested Cosima's methods of trying to enclose Wagner into a myth. "I confirm," wrote Eliza to Mathilde, "that at one time, *you* thought well of Cosima. . . . The proof of it is the letter you sent me at that time."[9] It is true that Mathilde had proven to be benevolent toward Cosima despite Cosima's jealousy and dislike of her husband's onetime muse. In December 1874 Mathilde had written to Cosima, lending her an open mind and a compliment on her role as the "faithful protector" of Wagner's *Götterdämmerung*.

Eliza went on to describe to Mathilde how she only just managed to avoid a lawsuit with the Wagner family on the subject of the master's letters to Eliza Wille, which in February and March 1887 were published in Berlin's *Deutsche Rundschau* as *Fifteen Letters of Richard Wagner, Accompanied by Memories and Explanations*. Eliza must have directly contacted Cosima, who had answered her vaguely even as her lawyers were preparing the lawsuit.

Cosima, jealous of her husband's long-ago love affair with Mathilde Wesendonck, tried everything in her power to forge a definitive version of the musician's life experience. The lawsuit was settled, but Eliza Wille warned Mathilde to keep his letters safe: "The letters which unmask her must humiliate her and be an expression of justice." Further on, in a postscript, she added: "Keep the letters you have, which are valuable; reveal them only if the time is ripe. See to it that the law is on your side."[10]

In fact, Mathilde had secretly prepared the publication of Richard Wagner's letters to herself, which eventually appeared in 1904, two years after her death. Did she inform her heirs of Eliza Wille's warnings? Either they had no idea of the legal aspects of the Wagner family's rights or they simply did not want to wait.

In the last years of her life, Mathilde did not particularly dwell on these thoughts. She spent her time alternating between her Berlin mansion at In den Zelten 21, the Bayreuth Festival in July, and the late-summer sojourns at Villa Traunblick in Austria. Only a noteworthy event such as the publication in 1896 of Houston Stewart Chamberlain's biography *Richard Wagner* could have made her react publicly to rectify the blatant injustice with which she was treated in this work. As she perused the luxurious first edition, bound in fine leather and abundantly illustrated with engravings, facsimiles, and musical examples, she must have been surprised indeed to discover that Wagner's critical period in Zurich was spoken of so lightly and slightingly, as if it were of little or no importance: "In 1856 the wealthy merchant Wesendonck and his wife played the roles of benefactors in Wagner's life, comparable to that of Frau Ritter." Chamberlain did go on to mention their hospitality and their sympathy, the Asyl and the *Five Songs*, the poems of which had been written by Mathilde, whom he described as "not an ordinary person." But the compliment was entirely negated by the way he commented on Richard's relationship to his friends: "And yet, all these friendships contained a common flaw: all those who helped this man did not fully realize who and what he really was. They could hardly suspect his true greatness. Although their generosity was quite voluntary, it did not appear to them as it was—as, in a certain sense, an obligation. They were unaware of performing a duty, such as we have seen with Liszt. In that way, their generosity always gave [the master] the feeling of its being a handout."[11]

The author, also known for other fallacious works, obviously wanted to flatter the Wagner family—so much so that, in 1908, he eventually married Eva, a daughter of Richard and Cosima. His bibliographic sources were apparently limited, and it is surprising to see that he was actually shocked by the reaction of Otto and Mathilde Wesendonck. On the Zurich episode—"Such was the life of Wagner from 1849 to 1859"—he shamelessly concluded in 1896, "Next to and beside these manifestations of his genius, what is called 'the events in Zurich' are of no real importance."

Mathilde closed the beautiful gilt-edged book and in her mind saw all those years go by, the peak of their existence, now described as being "of no real importance." On January 13, 1896, she decided to break her silence and protest, at first by writing to Chamberlain himself, who defended his own "goodwill" or at least his "ignorance" regarding her personal relationship to Wagner. He declared he was even ready to correct any errors he might have made and develop, if necessary, Wagner's life at the Asyl. But on consulting a later edition, the French translation of 1908, besides applying the epithet "a couple of the elite" to the Wesendoncks and adding a few terms that changed nothing, such as "kind attention," "constant hospitality," and "enthusiasm for his art," Chamberlain did not modify any of the above-quoted passages that hurt the Wesendoncks. Was he scrupulously following the directives he had received from Wahnfried? His assiduous correspondence with Cosima between 1888 and 1908 may give us reason to think so. And he did not consult Karl Friedrich Glasenapp's *Life of Richard Wagner*, the first of six volumes of which was published in 1894. It was this writer who had been chosen by Wagner himself in Bayreuth as his official biographer. But Chamberlain, who had also neglected the private edition of *My Life*, thought it preferable to place all his trust in what Cosima, his future mother-in-law, had to say about it.

On January 17, 1896, the journalist Albert Heintz, in the *Allgemeine Musik-Zeitung*, raised his voice to defend Otto and Mathilde Wesendonck against Chamberlain's offensive remarks. In his article he described how the Asyl was placed at Wagner's disposal and the pleasant life that Otto Wesendonck's generosity had offered him, which allowed the musician to compose, in 1857, the first act of *Tristan* and the first half of *Siegfried*. He mentioned the episode of the performance of the lied "Träume" for Mathilde's birthday, as well as the concert on the following March 31 in honor of her husband. He underscored Mathilde's influence on Wagner's creative spirit and how she gave him, besides the *Five Songs*, the "impulse in Venice to compose *Die Meistersinger*." And, Mathilde hastened to add, "We remained friends until death."

On the following February 14 Heintz allowed Mathilde herself to speak in her own words when he published her only "official memoirs". "Houston Stewart Chamberlain claims we did not understand Wagner's genius," she wrote.

> His genius is only comprehensible if one really knows the man himself. The pure and simple character of Otto Wesendonck does not correspond in any way to Mr. Chamberlain's description. On the contrary, Otto was happy to be his sponsor. He helped Wagner without any regrets whatsoever. . . . What hurts me the most is that Chamberlain does not want to believe that Wagner's friends in Zurich were able to give him funds without his being aware of it. This is how one puts the true value on what is given. One does not need to be a Liszt or a Wittelsbach to know what the word "to give" signifies. True nobility is where noble hearts live. He who likes to give always finds the best way to do it. My husband does not remember all the details (Otto is eighty years old), but he remembers well his profound love for the master and his work. He never misses an occasion to listen to an opera or a concert of Wagner's music. The way in which he aided the master was devoid of any hypocrisy.

Despite his advanced age, Otto responded to Mathilde with a twinkle in his eye when she read to him the published articles on Richard Wagner. Ill and disabled, Otto scarcely left their residence in Berlin. Mathilde devoted herself to his welfare: she would read the newspaper to him every day and talk about current events; she would also remind him of the marvelous old days. The name of Wagner, with its infinite resonance, seemed far away to him, like the roar of the waves breaking on the shore—ebb and flow. On November 18, 1896, Otto Wesendonck, a great-hearted man who, "having crossed the ocean so many times, could not possibly have a narrow mind," died at the age of eighty-one, leaving Mathilde alone on the water's edge, in her world of memory.

> *Give me a heart of bronze*
> *In a chest of steel,*
> *That I may travel calmly*
> *Through this vale of tears.*[12]

"My son Karl gives me his faithful support," wrote Mathilde in thanking Otto Benndorf for his letter of condolence. "We are working together with courage. Fritz is in Cairo, where he is preparing to sail up the Nile in a *dahabeah* to Luxor. He hopes to decipher an inscription on the temple."

Eliza Wille had died in 1894, and Mary Burrell, whose eyesight was deteriorating, would die in 1898. In one of the last letters that Mathilde wrote to her from Berlin, she mentioned Siegfried Wagner, who was a student at the Technische Hochschule Charlottenburg, in a suburb of the city: "He visits me regularly. His judgment is quite advanced for his young age. He is quite affable, and we understand each other."

> *Give me a heart of bronze*
> *In a chest of steel,*
> *That those who I most loved*
> *Gave me the most mortal of pains,*
> *I bleed from a thousand wounds,*
> *Never will I heal.*

In the summer of 1897 the *Ring* and *Parsifal* were on the Bayreuth Festival program, and in 1899 *Die Meistersinger* was added as well. At the end of August Mathilde retreated to her villa in Austria. In a charming poem, she said that she was still living as a woman of the world, receiving "many visits from noble ladies"—the roses in her garden. Observing and conversing daily with them, as she did in the old days with the exotic plants of her hothouse, she would lend them a soul: "In the silence of night, the red rose and the white rose swore mutual fidelity until their death."[13]

More and more, her garden had enlarged: from the closed space in her heart where rare and marvelous plants grew, where flowers with supernatural fragrances thrived, it had extended far down to the edge of the lake in which the stars of past nights were bathing. Beyond the limits of the forest and the mountains, her garden also embraced the giant of the summit, who was still waiting for the dawn to awaken the royal woman of his heart: the sleeping maiden.

> *She remains asleep,*
> *In the deep slumber of death;*
> *And her sweet body is healed*
> *From the pain and sorrow of life. . . .*
> *Hush, my heart,*
> *I promise that one day*
> *You too will to repose in death.*

Epilogue:
Isolde's Love-Death — "Liebestod"

At the end of July 1902, on a suffocatingly hot day, a jolting train left the smoke-filled railroad station in Berlin with a distinguished elderly woman traveling in a first-class carriage, performing once again a ritual that over the years had become immutable. Mathilde Wesendonck was on her way to the Bayreuth Festival, where she would see performances of *Der fliegende Holländer*, the *Ring*, and *Parsifal*. In her seventy-fourth year, she still had that beautiful dreamy look in her eyes, as well as her enigmatic smile, so striking in Franz Lenbach's portrait.

Sitting in the dark opera house, she would share her beloved's art in a reverential, almost religious contemplation. Outside, she did not recognize any of the men and women of this new century that she had so often thought of in the past. They crossed her field of vision like phantoms. All alone since Otto's death in 1896, she seemed to be above these modern times, floating dreamlike until late summer, when she would arrive at her harbor—the peaceful and splendid Villa Traunblick, where, on the other side of the lake, the silhouettes of a giant and a sleeping maiden, sculpted by nature in the mountain, would be waiting for her.

At the end of those long August days, while she waited for the usual visits from her grandson, Fritz, and her son Karl with his children, she was greatly fatigued. She even gave up her habit of walking down to the lakeside at nightfall. Instead, she had her meals brought to her room where from the balcony she would gaze meditatively at the countryside, watching the giant Traunstein light up in the flames of the setting sun and darken sadly before the maiden at dawn.

The day before August's last evening, Mathilde sat in her room. Sometimes she got up to look out of the window, as if expecting someone. She sent her servant to bed and fell asleep late that night. Around four o'clock in the morning, she felt restless and unable to sleep. She preferred not to disturb the servants, but her restlessness grew into agitation, and she finally rang for help.

From that time on she saw shadows hovering over her and bustling about the room with small bottles of elixirs and medicines. The tinkling of glasses gradually gave way to a silence in which she could hear only the sound of her own voice. Then she began calling softly to someone who was approaching from afar, on a road that seemed to open into a cone of light. She spoke the names of all her beloved children.

As the visitor's appearance grew more and more distinct, a crowd observing the scene gathered on both sides. Everything was lit up by a glow that did not come from the sun. Then she was alone in the midst of the luminous circle. She heard voices around her, almost like a chorus. The figure now standing before her on the wings of a white swan resembled one of his legendary heroes.

In the assembled crowd Mathilde heard someone ask, "Who is it?," followed by whispers: "It's him! It's him!" Finally, suddenly, she recognized the glorious apparition. She had been waiting for him for so long, the lover of her soul. He said:

There where Tristan is departing
Will you, Isolde, follow him?
In the land that Tristan means,
The sunlight never gleams.

She arose, walked toward him, and said:

How shall I flee from the land
That encompasses the whole world?
Where Tristan's house and home is,
There will Isolde stay.

Outdoors, above the Traunsee, in the hot summer day, the maiden with silent lips and closed eyes was dreaming again, in her stone death, among the ash and the pine trees.

Early in the afternoon, when the sun had passed its zenith, Mathilde Wesendonck opened her eyes for the last time to fade into the night of transfiguration.

How softly and gently he smiles;
How fondly he opens his eyes . . .

NOTES

CHAPTER 1

1. Mathilde Wesendonck, "An die Mutter" (To Mother), excerpt, in *Gedichte, Volkslieder, Legenden, Sagen* (Zurich: Kiesling, 1862).
2. Paul Luchtenberg, *Wolfgang Müller von Königswinter* (Cologne: Verlag der Löwe, 1959).
3. Geneviève Blanquis, *La vie quotidienne en Allemagne à l'époque romantique, 1795–1830* (Paris: Hachette, 1959).
4. Friedrich Wilhelm Freiherr von Bissing, *Mathilde Wesendonck: Die Frau und die Dichterin* (Vienna: Verlag Anton Schroll, 1942).
5. Victor Hugo, *Le Rhin: Lettres à un ami* (Paris: Ollendorff, 1906), 1:180.

CHAPTER 2

1. In Mathilde Wesendonck, *Gedichte, Volksweisen, Legenden, Sagen* (Zurich: Kiesling, 1874).
2. Marie-Luise Baum. This person claimed that Mathilde ignored the existence of Otto's first wife. This hypothesis is hardly plausible given the close relationship between Mathilde's and Otto's families even before the couple's marriage. Besides, in his letter to Sophie, Otto refers to his future wife as "Mathilde" Luckemeyer.

CHAPTER 3

1. The *Vormärz* is the period that immediately preceeded the Revolution of 1848.
2. According to Franz Wesendonck, the German fleet was mobilized for several months.
3. Eliza Wille, *Quinze lettres de Richard Wagner, accompagnées par souvenirs et éclaircissements*, trans. August Staps. Brussels: Veuve Monnom, 1894.
4. Hugo Wesendonck, *Erinnerungen aus dem Jahr 1848* (New York: The author, 1898).
5. Louis Benedictus, "De Paris à Bayreuth," *La vie moderne*, September 2, 1882.
6. R. W., *Ma vie*, 3:14.

CHAPTER 4

1. M. W., excerpt, in *Gedichte* (1874).
2. Melvin Maddocks, *Les premiers transatlantiques* (N.p.: Time-Life, 1982).
3. Ibid.
4. Goethe, *Seefahrt*.
5. Ibid.

CHAPTER 5

1. Richard Wagner, *Une communication à mes amis* (Paris: Éditions Gallimard, 1976).
2. R. W., letter to Ernst Benedikt Kietz, December 30, 1851, in Martin Gregor-Dellin, *Wagner au jour le jour* (Paris: Gallimard, 1976).
3. Richard Wagner, *Opéra et drame*, trans. Jacques-Gabriel Prod'homme (Paris: Plon, 1913), pp. 192–97.

4. Here Wagner is referring to the state of lyric opera before Carl Maria von Weber.

5. Richard Wagner, *Ma vie*, trans. Noémi Valentin and Albert Schenk, 3 vols. (Paris: Plon, 1911–12), 3:14.

6. The phrase *Sturm und Drang* (literally, "storm and stress") comes from the title of a play written in 1776 by Friedrich Maximilian Klinger. This term designates the German school of preromanticism.

7. Charles Baudelaire, *Oeuvres complètes* (Paris: La Pléiade, 1954).

8. Ibid.

9. Ibid.

10. *Die Walküre*, Act I, Scene 3.

CHAPTER 6

1. R. W., *Ma vie*, 3:51–52. Wagner began dictating this text to his wife, Cosima, in 1865.

2. Albert Heinz, article, *Allgemeine Musik Zeitung*, November 14, 1896.

3. Wagner never used the term *Leitmotiv*. It was coined later by Hans von Wolzogen.

4. R. W., *Une communication à mes amis*, 136–37.

5. R. W., letter to Theodore Uhlig, April 4, 1852.

6. Thomas Mann, letters of R. W., in *Wagner et notre temps* (Paris: Livre de Poche, 1978).

CHAPTER 7

1. Ernest Newman, *The Life of Richard Wagner* (New York: Alfred A. Knopf, 1937), vol. 2.

2. Eliza Wille, *Quinze lettres de Richard Wagner*.

3. *Die Walküre*, Act I, Scene 3.

4. R. W., letter to Franz Liszt, June 16, 1852.

5. R. W., letter to Karl Gaillard, January 30, 1844; cited in Mann, *Wagner et notre temps*.

6. Martin Gregor-Dellin, *Richard Wagner: Sa vie, son oeuvre, son siècle* (Paris: Fayard, 1981), 360.

7. R. W., letter to O. W., June 11, 1853.

CHAPTER 8

1. Marc Gaillard, *Paris au XIXe siècle* (Paris: Nathan, 1981).

2. Albert Heintz, article, *Allgemeine Musik-Zeitung*, November 1896.

3. Otto Strobel, in Newman, *The Life of Richard Wagner* (New York: Alfred A. Knopf, 1937), vol. 3, page 211.

4. Poem sent by M. W. to R. W., July 3, 1863.

CHAPTER 9

1. M. W., "Am Giessbach" (The Cataract), in *Gedichte* (1874).

2. Paul Guiton, *La Suisse* (Grenoble: Librairie Arthaud, 1930).

3. Ovid, *Metamorphoses X*, in *Latin Poetry* (Boston: Houghton Mifflin).

4. Ibid., lines 452–56.

5. *Die Walküre*, Act II, Scene 2.

6. *Tristan und Isolde*, Act III, "Liebestod" (Love-Death).

7. In ancient Greece, *érōs* referred to human love (both carnal and spiritual), while *agápē* was the word used for divine love.

8. Ovid, *Metamorphoses X*, lines 473–76 and 492–94.

9. In the legend of Tristan and Isolde, the black sail signified that Isolde was not arriving on the vessel in view.

CHAPTER 10

1. Goethe, *Faust*, Part I, Scene 3.
2. Emma Herwegh to Caroline zu Sayn-Wittgenstein, in Marcel Herwegh, *Au soir des dieux* (Paris: Peyronnet, 1933).
3. M. W., letter to Eliza Wille, August 28, 1872, Mariafeld archives.
4. An allusion to novels written by Eliza Wille.
5. M. W., letter to Eliza Wille, August 28, 1872, Mariafeld archives.
6. "Wesenheim" is a punning allusion to Nibelheim (home of the dwarfs) and Reisenheim (home of the giants) in *Das Rheingold*.
7. See Gregor-Dellin, *Richard Wagner: Sa vie, son oeuvre, son siècle*.
8. According to a chronicle in Zurich, Mathilde paid the blacksmith for his hours of enforced idleness.
9. Wagner wrote this letter from Mornex, near Geneva.
10. His publisher, Härtel.
11. R. W., letter to Otto Wesendonck, September 1, 1856.
12. Wagner, *Ma vie*.

CHAPTER 11

1. M. W., "Im Treibhaus" (In the Hothouse), texts of the Wesendonck Lieder first published with the music in Mainz by Schott in 1862.
2. The German *Asyl*, French *asile*, and English *asylum* all connote a haven of peace.
3. Jürg Wille and Werner Zimmermann, *Richard Wagner in Zurich: Eine Chronik der Villa Wesendonck*, ed. Präsidialabteilung der Stadt Zürich (Zurich: The Präsidialabteilung, 1983).
4. The rustic house where Wagner once lived has now been remodeled by the new owner, who has renamed it Villa Schönberg.
5. Francesco de Sanctis, *Lettere dall'esilio, 1853–1860* (Bari: B. Croce, 1938).
6. Originally in French.
7. R. W., note to M. W.
8. According to a local legend, Wagner would have read it to her sitting on a bench under a wild cherry tree. He probably read her passages in this way, and brought the complete text to her home on September 18. As for the "kiss," Wagner ambiguously uses the word *umarmen*, which means "to take in one's arms." However, from a symbolic point of view, the kiss that Pygmalion gives Galatea is an expression of timeless love, introducing the promise of a new life, as in the "Liebestod."
9. Ovid, *Metamorphoses X*, lines 492–94.
10. Goethe, *Bleibe, bleibe bei mir*.

CHAPTER 12

1. T. Harry Williams, *Histoire des États-Unis*, vol. 2 (Lausanne: Rencontre, 1968).
2. M. W., "Der Engel" (The Angel), unpublished.
3. M. W., "Schmerzen" (Torment), unpublished.
4. Letters to Liszt reprinted in Julius Kapp, *Richard Wagner et les femmes, d'après des documents inédits* (Paris: Perrin, 1914).

5. M. W., "O frage nicht, du sollst mich nimmer fragen . . . ," in *Gedichte* (1874).

6. Recollections of Bertha Roner-Lipke in Wille and Zimmermann, *Richard Wagner in Zurich*.

7. M. W., "Mir träumte es wären wir Beide / Auf diese Welt allein . . . ," in *Gedichte* (1874).

8. M. W., letters to Francesco de Sanctis.

9. R. W., letter called "The Morning Confession," in letters of R. W. to M. W., *Letters of Richard Wagner: The Burrell Collection*, ed. John N. Burk (London: Gollancz, 1951).

10. M. W., "Für rothes Herzblut hab'ich Gift getrunken," in *Gedichte* (1874).

CHAPTER 13

1. Wagner uses a play on words here: the feminine *die Flügel* means "wing"; the masculine *der Flügel* means "grand piano."

2. M. W., "Der Schwan" (The Swan), in *Gedichte* (1862).

3. Julius Kapp, "Unterdrückte Dokumente aus den Briefen Richard Wagners an Mathilde Wesendonck," *Die Musik* 23, no. 12 (September 1931): 877–883.

4. Max Fehr, *Richard Wagners Schweizerzeit*, vol. 2 (Aarau: Verlag Sauerländer, 1953).

5. M. W., "Klage der Mutter" (The Mother's Lament), excerpt, in *Gedichte* (1862).

6. Ibid.

7. Frau Marschall von Bieberstein, letter to Minna Wagner, November 3, 1858, in Richard Wagner, *Letters of Richard Wagner: The Burrell Collection*, ed. John N. Burk (London: Gollancz, 1951).

8. Emilie Heim, letter to Minna Wagner, ibid.

9. Minna Wagner, letter to a friend in Berlin, in Richard Wagner, *Richard Wagner to Mathilde Wesendonck*, trans. and with a preface by William Ashton Ellis (London: H. Grevel, 1905).

10. François Wille, letter to R. W., in Fehr, *Richard Wagners Schweizerzeit*.

11. See Kapp, *Richard Wagner et les femmes*.

12. Ibid.

13. M. W., "Der fremde Vogel" (The Strange Bird), in *Gedichte* (1862).

CHAPTER 14

1. The author had the privilege of holding this edition, which belonged to the collection of Baron von Bissing, in her hands and perusing it.

2. M. W., "Mignon," excerpt, in *Gedichte* (1874).

3. Fehr, *Richard Wagners Schweizerzeit*.

4. M. W., "Mignon," excerpt, in *Gedichte* (1874).

5. M. W., "An Guido" (To Guido), in *Gedichte* (1862).

6. Zwieback is a type of biscuit or cookie that used to be given for upset stomach.

7. M. W., *Lieder* (1877).

8. Mariafeld archives, courtesy of Jürg Wille.

9. A reference to the good relationship between Otto, Mathilde, and Richard.

10. The details of this trip by steamship are noted in the Baedecker guide *Central Italy* (1869), Franz Wesendonk Collection.

11. M. W., *Lieder* (1877).

12. M. W., "Eros and das Beinchen" (Eros and the Bee), in *Gedichte* (1874).

13. Gregor-Dellin, *Richard Wagner*.

14. *Die Meistersinger von Nürnberg*, Act II, Scene 6.

15. Ibid., Act III, Scene 4.

16. Ibid.
17. Ibid.

CHAPTER 15

1. M. W., "An die Mutter" (To Mother), in *Gedichte* (1862).
2. This notation has no resemblance to Wagner's final version.
3. *Velche* is a derogatory term applied to anything foreign.
4. Thomas Mann, *Souffrances et grandeur de Richard Wagner* (Paris: Poche, 1933).
5. Peter Cornelius, quoted in Marie-Luise Baum, ed., "Mathilde und Otto Wesendonck," in *Wuppertaler Biographien*, ser. 3, *Beiträge zur Geschichte und Heimatkunde des Wuppertals* (Wuppertal: Born Verlag), 6:135–38.
6. *Die Meistersinger von Nürnberg*, Act III, Scene 1.
7. Henri Perrier, *Les rendez-vous wagnériens* (Lausanne: La Tramontane, n.d.).
8. Ibid., manuscript. Perrier is the retired president of the Cercle Richard Wagner in Lyon, France.
9. Preface, in *Richard Wagner: Sämtliche Werke*, Bd. 17, *Klavierlieder*, ed. Egon Voss (Mainz: Schott, 1976).
10. Ludwig Schnorr von Carolsfeld, letter to Joachim Raff, reprinted in Richard Wagner, *Sämtliche Werke*, Bd. 17, *Klavierlieder*, ed. Egon Voss (Mainz: Schott, 1976).
11. *Allgemeine Musik-Zeitung*, January 17, 1896.
12. M. W., "Erinnerung" (Remembrance), in *Gedichte* (1862).
13. M. W., "Beharrliche Liebe" (Faithful Love), in ibid.
14. M. W., "Mignon," excerpt, in ibid.
15. M. W., "Mignon," part 4, in ibid.
16. M. W., letter to R. W., May 22, 1863.
17. A reference to R. W.'s dedication to M. W. in 1853 in the sonata: "Do you know what is happening?"
18. M. W., "Der Engel" (The Angel), unpublished.

CHAPTER 16

1. Perrier, *Les rendez-vous wagnériens*.
2. Emphasis in original.
3. *Tristan und Isolde*, Act I, Scene 5.
4. Emphasis in original.
5. One of the Norns of Scandinavian mythology.
6. Charlotte von Stein (1742–1827), the wife of Baron Gottlob Ernst von Stein, inspired Goethe with a great passion. Christiane Vulpius (1765–1816) became Goethe's mistress and bore him five children. He eventually married her.
7. All these letters from Cosima Wagner are unpublished. They are in the possession of the descendants of Myrrha von Aretin, Mathilde's great-granddaughter.
8. Emphasis in original.
9. Julius Kapp did not reveal the source that allowed him to reconstruct the letters. He gave us to understand that an original edition would have been published, before Cosima censored the letters, by Duncker of Berlin.
10. After the correspondence between Wagner and Mathilde was published in 1904, Golther expressed his surprise at Cosima's attitude. In his opinion, "the Wesendonck family had 'satisfied all of Wahnfried's desires.' Frau Wagner could have forbidden the edition. . . . The attitude of Wahnfried is wrong and hostile." Concerning the contradiction between appearance and historical reality, Golther concluded: "Frau Wesendonck reacted objectively." And if she was idealized by the

master in these letters, "it means she was more for him than Frau von Stein was for Goethe. That is quite something!" (Richard Wagner Foundation Archives, Wahnfried, Bayreuth).

11. Cosima.

12. M. W., "Mignon," excerpts, in *Gedichte* (1874).

CHAPTER 17

1. Bertha Roner-Lipka, *Erinnerungen*, quoted in Zimmermann, *Richard Wagner in Zurich*.

2. Claude Rostand, *Brahms* (Paris: Fayard, 1978).

3. Letter quoted in ibid. Theodor Kirchner (1823–1903) was an organist, pianist, and composer. From 1862 to 1872 he conducted the concerts and chorus of the Association in Zurich.

4. Ibid.

5. Eliza Wille, letter to M. W., February 10, 1867 (Mariafeld archives).

6. Rostand, *Brahms*.

7. Erich H. Müller von Asow, *Johannes Brahms und Mathilde Wesendonck: Ein Briefwechsel* (Vienna: Luckmann, 1943).

8. Clara Schumann, letter to Brahms, on July 8.

9. R.W., letter to O. W., July 31, 1865.

10. Ibid.

11. O. W., letter to R. W., reprinted in *Bayreuther Blätter* (archives of Myrrha von Aretin).

12. Ludwig II, letter to O. W., August 28, 1865.

13. Müller von Asow, *Johannes Brahms und Mathilde Wesendonck*.

14. Wagner's attitude toward Jews, like that of many at the time, was a kind of cultural anti-Semitism connected to nationalist sentiments that arose in reaction to the rigid monarchies established after the French Revolution. It was not personal, as shown by the way he ran after Hermann Levi to convince him to conduct *Parsifal* and by his invitation to Karl Tausig to play transcriptions and sight-read his scores at his Asyl home. He disliked Meyerbeer for professional reasons: his frivolous (as they seemed to Wagner) operas and his refusal to go to bat for Wagner when the Paris Opéra refused his *Fliegender Holländer*.

15. R. W., letter to O. W., December 4, 1870.

16. Peter Cornelius, letter to his fiancée, quoted in Kapp, *Richard Wagner et les femmes*.

17. Newman, *The Life of Richard Wagner*.

18. Karl Geiringer, *Brahms: Sa vie, son oeuvre* (Paris: Buchet-Chastel, 1982).

19. Rostand, *Brahms*.

20. Ibid.

21. Philaminte is a character in Molière's *Les femmes savantes*, a bluestocking who presides over a literary salon.

22. Cosima Wagner, *Journal,* 4 vols., trans. Michel François Demet (Paris: Gallimard, 1979).

23. Letter, quoted in Rostand, *Brahms*.

CHAPTER 18

1. M. W., letter to François Wille, August 14, 1868.

2. M. W., "Maria-Sils-See" (Lake Sils Maria), excerpt, in *Gedichte* (1874).

3. Rostand, *Brahms*.

4. M. W., letter to François Wille, December 24, 1870.

5. M. W., "Das deutsche Herz" (The German Heart), in *Gedichte* (1874).

6. Friedrich Wilhelm Freiherr von Bissing, *Mathilde Wesendonck: Die Frau und die Dichterin*

(Vienna: Verlag Anton Schroll, 1942).

7. M. W., letter, quoted in ibid.

8. The "putsch" of Zurich has been described in J. Weber, *Die Zürcher Vorfälle, vom 9 bis 11 März 1871* (Zurich: Schmidt, 1871); Hans Schmid, *Zürcher Taschenbuch* (Zurich: Verlag A. Bopp, 1926); and Rudolf von Albertini, *Zürcher Taschenbuch* (Zurich: Verlag Buchdrückerei, 1951), 118–34.

9. Theodor Billroth, letter to M. W., March 21, 1871.

CHAPTER 19

1. Hugo Göring, "Erinnerungen an Mathilde Wesendonck," fragment (Bonn Archives).

2. Baroness Clementine von Wedel, *Personliches von Mathilde Wesendonck*, May 18, 1913, no. 573 (Bonn Nationalbibliothek).

3. They did spend one intimate evening on November 29 for a reading of *Edith*, in the company of the Willes.

4. M. W., letter to Otto Benndorf, December 1871.

5. M. W., letter to Otto Benndorf, March 21, 1872.

6. M. W., letter to Otto Benndorf, February 28, 1872.

7. M. W., letter to Eliza Wille, October 17, 1871.

8. The Sorbs are Slavs living in the region of Lusatia, southeast of Dresden. Their language is related to Polish.

9. M. W., letter to Eliza Wille, April 28, 1872.

10. See Geoffrey Skelton, *Richard et Cosima Wagner* (Paris: Buchet-Chastel, 1986).

11. O. W., letter to R. W., September 17, 1873 (National Archive of the Richard Wagner Foundation, Wahnfried, Bayreuth).

12. Cosima Wagner, *Journal*, January 14, 1873.

13. M. W., letter to Otto Benndorf, September 15, 1872.

14. Wagner, *The Brown Book*, April 1873.

15. Cosima Wagner, quoted in ibid.

16. M. W., letter to Otto Benndorf, December 1871.

17. M. W., letter to Brahms, May 1873; quoted in Müller von Asow, *Johannes Brahms und Mathilde Wesendonck*.

18. *Götterdämmerung*, Act III, Scene 3.

19. Letters, in Müller von Asow, *Johannes Brahms und Mathilde Wesendonck*.

20. M. W., letter to Otto Benndorf, December 29, 1874.

21. M. W., "Lieder I," manuscript (1877).

22. All details relating to the first performance of the *Ring* in Bayreuth are accounts from contemporary newspaper articles (see bibliography).

23. Maurice Lefèvre, review, *Revue d'art dramatique*, September 1, 1892.

24. Ibid.

25. M. W., "Lieder II," manuscript (1877).

26. M. W., "Lieder IV," manuscript (1877).

CHAPTER 20

1. M. W., letter to Eliza Wille, May 26, 1876.

2. M. W., letter to Otto Benndorf, January 15, 1881.

3. Otto Richter, "Eine Erinnerung an Mathilde Wesendonck," *Zeitschrift für Musik*, May 1934.

4. M. W., *Alceste*, Act III, Scene 4.

5. Cosima Wagner, letter to M. W., January 17, 1878.

6. M. W., "Neue Lieder" (New Songs), unpublished (1876–77).

7. Fritz von Bissing was an assistant to François Maspero in Cairo from 1896 to 1904. He went on to become an associate professor at the University of Munich.

8. M. W., "Schmerzen" (Torment), excerpt, unpublished.

9. M. W., "An Hans" (To Hans), unpublished (1882).

10. M. W., "Lieder VI," unpublished (1877).

11. R. W., letter to M. W., May 30, 1859.

12. The exceptionally large size of Mary Burrell's book must be noted: 55 × 71 cm (22 × 28 inches)!

13. Mary Burrell, letter to M. W., August 9, 1883.

14. Mary Burrell, letter to M. W., March 13, 1884.

15. R. W., letter to M. W., August 1860.

16. R. W., letter to M. W., March 2, 1859.

17. R.W., letter to M. W. May 30, 1859.

18. *Parsifal*, Act I, Scene 1.

19. Paul Claudel, *Rêverie d'un poète français* (Paris: Les Belles Lettres, 1927); author's translation.

20. Gregor-Dellin, *Wagner au jour le jour*.

21. Cosima Wagner, *Journal*, January 16, 1879.

22. Ibid., January 17, 1874. The word for vulture in German is *Geier* and the surname of Wagner's stepfather was Geyer, so some authors have advanced psychoanalytical interpretations of these dreams.

CHAPTER 21

1. M. W., "Die Jungfrau am Traunsee" (The Maiden of Traunsee, 1884).

2. According to their marriage certificate, Karl registered his name as "Wesendonk," without the "c." In the margin of the document it is noted that the name should be written with -*ck* at the end, by decision of the court in Berlin, November 4, 1883. The title *von* was recognized by the registry in the same way, with -*ck*. But following the spelling reforms of 1900, the family name became Wesendonk.

3. Mary Burrell, letter to M. W., February 24, 1885.

4. Ibid.

5. Ibid.

6. R. W., Venice Diary, October 5, 1858.

7. Several allusions converge here: Mathilde's Buddhist drama, her tale "The Swan," and Wagner's *Parsifal*.

8. Mary Burrell, letter to M. W., Burrell Collection.

9. This letter is missing. Eliza Wille wanted to destroy Mathilde's letters from her time in Zurich if she did not want them.

10. Eliza Wille, letter to M. W., March 9, 1887. Courtesy of Jürg Wille.

11. Houston Stewart Chamberlain, *Richard Wagner* (Munich: Verlanganstalt für Kunst und Wissenschaft, 1896).

12. This poem of Mathilde's was set to music by Reinhold Becker (unpublished manuscript, dedicated to M. W.) Another version was composed by Ödön Mihalovich.

13. M. W., "Traunblicks Besuch" (The Visit to Traunblick, 1887).

SELECTED BIBLIOGRAPHY

BOOKS

Ayçoberry, Pierre. 1968. *L'unité allemande*. Paris: Presses Universitaires de France.

Baedeker (Guides). 1873. *Allemagne et Autriche*.

————. 1902. *Berlin*.

————. 1869. *Italie centrale*.

————. 1898. *Égypte*.

Barthou, Louis. 1935. *La vie amoureuse de Richard Wagner*. Paris: Flammarion.

Baudelaire, Charles. 1954. *Complete Works*. Paris: La Pléiade.

Benvenga, Nancy. 1983. *Kingdom on the Rhine*. Essex: Anton Press.

Bergfeld, Joachim. 1968. *Otto und Mathilde Wesendonck: Bedeutung für das Leben und Schaffen Richard Wagners*. Bayreuth: Mühl.

Bertaux, Pierre. 1962. *La vie quotidienne en Allemagne en 1900 au temps de Guillaume II*. Paris: Hachette.

Bissing, Friedrich Wilhelm Freiherr von. 1942. *Mathilde Wesendonck: Die Frau und die Dichterin*. Vienna: Verlag Anton Schroll.

Blanquis, Geneviève. 1959. *La vie quotidienne en Allemagne à l'époque romantique, 1795–1830*. Paris: Hachette.

Boyer, Philippe. 1985. *Le romantisme allemand*. Paris: Éditions MA.

Chamberlain, Houston Stewart. 1896. *Richard Wagner*. Munich: Verlagsanstalt für Kunst und Wissenschaft.

Claudel, Paul. 1927. *Rêverie d'un poète français*. Paris: Les Belles Lettres.

de Sanctis, Francesco. 1938. *Lettere dall'esilio, 1853–1860*. Bari: B. Croce.

d'Indy, Vincent. 1937. *Introduction à l'étude de "Parsifal" de Wagner*. Paris: Mellotée.

Erismann, Hans. 1987. *Richard Wagner in Zürich*. Zurich: Neue Zürcher Zeitung.

Escher, Conrad. 1913. *Die Villa Rieter in der Enge*. Zurich: Neue Zürcher Zeitung.

Fehr, Max. 1953. *Richard Wagners Schweizerzeit*. Vol. 2. Aarau: Verlag Sauerländer.

Fierz, Jürg, and Hanny Fries. N.d. *Zürcher Spaziergänge*. Zürich: Orell Füssli.

Fink-Töbisch, Grete. 1963. *Mir erkoren, mir verloren*. Graz: Stocker Verlag.

Fourcaud, Louis de. 1923. *Richard Wagner: Les étapes de sa vie, de sa pensée et de son art*. Paris: Hachette.

Gaillard, Marc. 1981. *Paris au XIXe siècle*. Paris: Nathan.

Gautier, Judith. 1909. *Le troisième rang du collier*. Paris: Juven.

Gaxotte, Pierre. 1963. *Histoire de l'Allemagne*. Paris: Flammarion.

Geiringer, Karl. 1982. *Brahms: Sa vie, son oeuvre*. Paris: Buchet-Chastel.

Girard, Louis. 1981. *Nouvelle histoire de Paris: La Deuxième République et le Second Empire, 1848–1870*. Paris: Hachette.

Glasenapp, Carl Friedrich. 1904–11. *Das Leben Richard Wagners*. 6 vols. Wiesbaden: Breitkopf & Härtel.

Gregor-Dellin, Martin. 1981. *Richard Wagner: Sa vie, son oeuvre, son siècle*. Paris: Fayard.

———. 1976. *Wagner au jour le jour*. Paris: Gallimard.

Guide bleu. 1935. *Suisse*. Paris: Hachette.

Guiton, Paul. 1930. *La Suisse*. Grenoble: Librairie Arthaud.

Herwegh, Marcel. 1932. *Au banquet des dieux*. Paris: Peyronnet.

———. 1933. *Au soir des dieux*. Paris: Peyronnet.

Herzberg, Marthe. 1948. *Richard Wagner: Artiste illustre, homme méconnu*. Brussels: Wellens & Godenne.

Hugo, Victor. 1906. *Le Rhin: Lettres à un ami*. Paris: Ollendorff.

Kapp, Julius. 1914. *Richard Wagner et les femmes, d'après des documents inédits*. Paris: Perrin.

Luchtenberg, Paul. 1959. *Wolfgang Müller von Königswinter*. Cologne: Löwe.

Maddocks, Melvin. 1982. *Les premiers transatlantiques*. N.p.: Time-Life.

Mann, Thomas. 1978. *Wagner et notre temps*. Paris: Livre de Poche.

———. 1933. *Souffrances et grandeur de Richard Wagner*. Paris: Poche.

———. 1978. *Richard Wagner et "L'anneau du Nibelung."* Paris: Poche.

Müller von Asow, Erich H. 1943. *Johannes Brahms und Mathilde Wesendonck: Ein Briefwechsel*. Vienna: Luckmann.

Newman, Ernest. 1937–60. *The Life of Richard Wagner*. 4 vols. New York: Alfred A. Knopf.

Ovid. 1957. *Latin Poetry*. Boston: Houghton Mifflin.

Perrier, Henri. N.d. *Les rendez-vous wagnériens*. Lausanne: La Tramontane.

Pourtalès, Guy de. 1932. *Wagner: Histoire d'un artiste*. Paris: Gallimard.

Rebatet, Lucien. 1969. *Une histoire de la musique*. Paris: Laffont et Bourgine.

Ribot, Th. 1895. *La philosophie de Schopenhauer*. Paris: Alcan.

Rostand, Claude. 1978. *Brahms*. Paris: Fayard.

Roz, Firmin. 1956. *Histoire des États-Unis*. Paris: Fayard.

Schneider, Marcel. 1960. *Wagner: Collection solfèges*. Paris: Seuil.

Schuré, Edward. 1922. *Femmes inspiratrices et poètes annonciateurs*. Paris: Perrin.

Skelton, Geoffrey. 1986. *Richard et Cosima Wagner*. Paris: Buchet-Chastel.

Waage, Olaf. 1935. *Richard Wagner og Mathilde Wesendonck: En oversigt*. Copenhagen: Brenner.

Watson, Derek. 1979. *Richard Wagner: A Biography*. New York: Schirmer.

Wesendonck, Hugo. 1898. *Erinnerungen aus dem Jahr 1848*. New York: The author.

Wesendonck, Mathilde. 1862. *Gedichte, Volkslieder, Legenden, Sagen*. Zurich: Kiesling.

———. 1874. *Gedichte, Volksweisen, Legenden, Sagen*. Zurich: Kiesling.

Westernhagen, Curt von. 1978. *Richard Wagner*. Cambridge: Cambridge University Press.

Williams, T. Harry. 1968. *Histoire des États-Unis*. Vol. 2. Lausanne: Rencontre.

Winslow, R. P. 1949. *Mathilde Wesendonck: The Secret behind Wagner's "Tristan and Isolde."* 2nd ed. New York: William-Frederick Press.

BROCHURES AND ARTICLES

Albertini, Rudolf von. 1951. *Zürcher Taschenbuch*. Zurich: Verlag Buchdrückerei.

Baum, Marie-Luise. 1960–61. *Die Wesendoncks aus Elberfeld*. Wuppertal: Romerike Berge.

———, ed. 1961. "Mathilde und Otto Wesendonck." In *Wuppertaler Biographien*, ser. 3, *Beiträge zur Geschichte und Heimatkunde des Wuppertals*, 6:135–38. Wuppertal: Born Verlag.

Benedictus, Louis. 1882. "De Paris à Bayreuth." *La vie moderne*, September 2. Collection of Jean Cabaud.

Bunsen, Marie von. 1903. "Eine edle Frau." *Deutsche Revue*, February. Staatsarchiv Zürich.

Diefendorff, Jeffrey. N.d. *The German Background*. N.p.: Germania Life Insurance Company. Collection of Franz Wesendonk.

Fuchs, Reinhard. 1965. "Weg und Schicksal der Sammlung Wesendonk." *Bonn General-Anzeiger*, February 13. Stadtbibliothek Bonn.

Göring, Hugo. N.d. "Erinnerungen an Mathilde Wesendonck." Stadtbibliothek Bonn.

Heintz, Albert. 1896. Articles. *Allgemeine Musik-Zeitung*, January 17 and February 14.

Kapp, Julius. 1931. "Unterdrückte Dokumente aus den Briefen Richard Wagners an Mathilde Wesendonck." *Die Musik* 23, no. 12 (September): 877–883.

Lefèvre, Maurice. 1892. *Revue d'art dramatique*, September 1. Collection of Jean Cabaud.

Osten, A. von. 1912. "Ein Erinnerungsblatt an Mathilde Wesendonck." *Zürcher Wochen-Chronik*.

Richter, Otto. 1934. "Eine Erinnerung an Mathilde Wesendonck." *Zeitschrift für Musik*, May 1934.

Schmid, Hans. 1926. *Zürcher Taschenbuch*. Zurich: Verlag A. Bopp.

Schubring, Paul. 1904. "Richard Wagner und Mathilde Wesendonk." *Frankfurter Zeitung* 144, May 25.

Schulze-Reimpell, Werner. 1979. "Ein Meer der Leiden und Qualen." February 10–11, *Bonn General-Anzeiger*, February 10–11.

Stucker, Hans. 1967. *Luckemeyers Schiffe führen bis nach Mainz*. Düsseldorf, January 24.

Villiers de l'Isle, Adam. 1887. *La revue wagnérienne*, June. Collection of Jean Cabaud.

Weber, J. 1871. *Die Zürcher Vorfälle, vom 9 bis 11 März 1871*. Zurich: Schmidt.

Wedel, Clementine von. 1913. "Persönliches von Mathilde Wesendonck." May 18. Stadtbibliothek Bonn.

Wille, Jürg, and Werner G. Zimmermann. 1987. *Richard Wagner in Zurich: Eine Chronik der Villa Wesendonck*. Edited by the Präsidialabteilung der Stadt Zürich. 2nd ed. Zurich: The Präsidialabteilung.

Wolff, Irmgard von. 1977. "Niemand wusste von ihrer Beziehung zu Wagner." *Bonn General-Anzeiger*, October 29.

Zimmermann, Werner G. 1986. *Richard Wagner in Zurich: Erinnerungen von Berthe Roner-Lipka*. Zurich: Hug.

Correspondence and Diaries

Letters to Mathilde Wesendonck from Mary Burrell. Courtesy of Baroness Myrrha von Aretin.

Wagner, Cosima. 1979. *Journal*. 4 vols. Translated by Michel François Demet. Paris: Gallimard.

———. 1980. *Das zweite Leben: Briefe und Aufzeichnungen, 1883–1930*. Munich: Piper Verlag.

Wagner, Richard. 1904. *Tagebuchblätter und Briefe, 1853–1871*. With a preface by Wolfgang Golther. Berlin: Duncker.

———. 1905. *Richard Wagner to Mathilde Wesendonck*. Translated into English and with a preface by William Ashton Ellis. London: H. Grevel.

———. 1905. *Richard Wagner à Mathilde Wesendonk: Journal et lettres, 1853–1871*. Translated by Georges Khnopff. With a preface by Henri Lichtenberger. Berlin: Alexandre Duncker.

———. 1911–12. *Ma vie*. Translated by Noémi Valentin and Albert Schenk. 3 vols. Paris: Plon.

———. 1913. *Opéra et drame*. Translated by Jacques-Gabriel Prod'homme. Paris: Plon, 1913.

———. 1924. *Lettres à Otto Wesendonk, 1852–1870*. Paris: Calmann-Levy.

———. 1935. *Lettres françaises de Richard Wagner*. Collected and edited by Julien Tiersot. Paris: B. Grasset.

———. 1943. *Lettres de Richard Wagner à Minna Wagner.* Translated by Maurice Remon. With a preface by G. Samazeuilh. Paris: Gallimard.

———. 1951. *Letters of Richard Wagner: The Burrell Collection.* Edited by John N. Burk. London: Gollancz.

———. 1975. *Das braune Buch: Tagebuchaufzeichnungen 1865 bis 1882.* Edited by Joachim Bergfeld. Zurich: Atlantis.

———. 1976. *Sämtliche Werke.* Bd. 17. *Klavierlieder.* Edited by Egon Voss. Mainz: Schott.

———. 1976. *Une communication à mes amis.* Paris: Éditions Gallimard, 1976.

———. 1980. *The Diary of Richard Wagner: The Brown Book, 1865–1882.* Presented and annotated by Joachim Bergfeld. Translated by George Bird. Cambridge: Cambridge University Press.

———. 1986. *Richard Wagner à Mathilde Wesendonk: Journal et lettres, 1853–1871.* Translated by Georges Khnopff and Stanislas Mazur. With a preface by Henry-Louis de la Grange. Paris: Parution.

———. N.d. *Lettres de Richard Wagner à Théodore Uhlig, Guillaume Fischer, Ferdinand Heine.* Translated by Georges Khnopff. Paris: Juven.

Wagner, Richard, and Franz Liszt. 1900. *Correspondance de Wagner et de Liszt.* Translated by L. Schmitt. 2 vols. Leipzig: Breitkopf & Härtel; Paris: Fischbacher.

Wagner, Richard, and Cosima Wagner. 1964. *Lettres à Judith Gautier.* Paris: Gallimard.

Wesendonck, Mathilde. Letters and manuscripts. National library of Zurich.

———. Letters and manuscripts. Mariafeld archives.

———. Letters to Otto Benndorf. Courtesy of Baroness Myrrha von Aretin.

Wille, Eliza. 1894. *Quinze lettres de Richard Wagner, accompagnées par souvenirs et éclaircissements.* Translated by Augusta Staps. Brussels: Veuve Monnom.

INDEX

CREDITS

All quotations in English from *Der Ring des Nibelungen* (*Rheingold*, *Die Walküre*, *Siegfried*, and *Götterdämmerung*) come from the four libretti published in 1964 by the Friends of Covent Garden, translated by William Mann, slightly modified. London: The Shenvall Press.

The quotations from *Tristan und Isolde* are from the libretto accompanying the Deutsche Grammophon CD conducted by Carlos Kleiber, English translation of text by Lionel Salter (Hamburg: Polydor International GmbH, 1982), slightly modified.

The quotations from *Die Meistersinger von Nürnberg* are from the libretto accompanying the Philips CD conducted by Silvio Varviso and recorded live at the 1974 Bayreuth Festival, English translation of text by Peter Branscombe (Philips Classics, 1974), slightly modified.

The quotations from *Parsifal* come from the libretto accompanying the Deutsche Grammophon CD conducted by Herbert von Karajan, English translation of text by Lionel Salter © 1970 (Hamburg: Polydor International GmbH, 1981), slightly modified.

Translations of the poems of the *Wesendonck Lieder* are by Thomas Quinn, slightly modified, from the libretto accompanying the Decca CD of a 1957/1960 recording featuring Kirsten Flagstad and the Vienna Philharmonic, conducted by Hans Knappertsbusch (London: Decca, 1986).